Ernest Dichter and Motivation Research

Also by Stefan Schwarzkopf

DIE ANATOMIE DES MACHTWECHSELS: DIE SOZIALDEMOKRATISCHEN REGIERUNGSÜBERNAHMEN VON 1969 UND 1998

Also by Rainer Gries

PROPAGANDA IN DEUTSCHLAND

PRODUKTE ALS MEDIEN

UNSERE FEINDE: KONSTRUKTIONEN DES ANDEREN IM SOZIALISMUS

KULTUR DER PROPAGANDA

PRODUKTE UND POLITIK: ZUR KULTUR- UND POLITIKGESCHICHTE DER PRODUKTKOMMUNIKATION

ERNEST DICHTER: DOYEN DER VERFÜHRER (with Stefan Schwarzkopf)

PRODUKTKOMMUNIKATION: GESCHICHTE UND THEORIE

Ernest Dichter and Motivation Research

New Perspectives on the Making of Post-War Consumer Culture

Edited by

Stefan Schwarzkopf

Associate Professor in Business History and Marketing, Copenhagen Business School, Denmark

Rainer Gries

Professor of Communications, University of Vienna, Austria

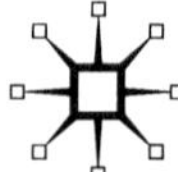

First published 2010 by
PALGRAVE MACMILLAN

Palgrave Macmillan in the UK is an imprint of Macmillan Publishers Limited, registered in England, company number 785998, of Houndmills, Basingstoke, Hampshire RG21 6XS.

Palgrave Macmillan in the US is a division of St Martin's Press LLC, 175 Fifth Avenue, New York, NY 10010.

Palgrave Macmillan is the global academic imprint of the above companies and has companies and representatives throughout the world.

Palgrave® and Macmillan® are registered trademarks in the United States, the United Kingdom, Europe and other countries.

ISBN-13: 978–0–230–53799–6 hardback

This book is printed on paper suitable for recycling and made from fully managed and sustained forest sources. Logging, pulping and manufacturing processes are expected to conform to the environmental regulations of the country of origin.

A catalogue record for this book is available from the British Library.

Library of Congress Cataloging-in-Publication Data
Ernest Dichter and motivation research : new perspectives on the making of post-war consumer culture / edited by Stefan Schwarzkopf, Rainer Gries.
    p.   cm.
  ISBN 978–0–230–53799–6 (hardback)
  1. Dichter, Ernest, 1907–1991.   2. Dichter, Ernest, 1907–1991—Influence.   3. Consumer behavior—Psychological aspects.
  4. Consumption (Economics)—Psychological aspects.
  5. Motivation research (Marketing)   I. Schwarzkopf, Stefan, 1976–
  II. Gries, Rainer, 1958–
  HF5415.32.E76 2010
  306.3—dc22   2010023955

10   9   8   7   6   5   4   3   2   1
19 18 17 16 15 14 13 12 11 10

Printed and bound in Great Britain by
CPI Antony Rowe, Chippenham and Eastbourne

Contents

Part I Introduction

Part II Dimensions of Ernest Dichter's Work and Personality

Part III The Branding of Consumer Life – Case Studies on Ernest Dichter's Work

Part IV   The European Theatre

Part V Conclusion

List of Figures and Table

Figures

Table

Preface and Acknowledgements

This book emanated from the papers and discussions at the first international conference on Ernest Dichter and Motivation Research, organised by the editors at the University of Vienna in December 2005. After a preliminary publication of some of the conference papers with a Viennese publisher, news was received in 2008 that Ernest Dichter's complete papers had been deposited at the Hagley Museum and Library in Wilmington, Delaware. In order to celebrate the life and work of Ernest Dichter and accession of the Dichter archive at Hagley Museum and Library, the museum has held a further workshop, 'Understanding Markets', in October 2009.

The editors of this collection would like to thank the staff of the Ernest Dichter Archive, University of Vienna, and in particular Roger Horowitz, Associate Director of the Center for Business, Technology, and Society, Hagley Museum and Library, Wilmington, for his generous help with tracing sources. The following institutions have kindly given permission to reproduce materials from their collections: Ernest Dichter Archive, University of Vienna, Austria; Hagley Museum and Library, Wilmington, DE. At Palgrave, Michael Strang and particularly Ruth Ireland proved immensely helpful and patient. Their help and advice is gratefully acknowledged.

Notes on Contributors

Regina Lee Blaszczyk is affiliated to the University of Pennsylvania. An award-winning historian and author, her six books focus on the history of innovation, with reference to design, consumer culture and fashion. Her publications include *Producing Fashion: Commerce, Culture and Consumers* (2007) and *Imagining Consumers* (2002).

Ronald Fullerton is Professor of Marketing at the American University in Cairo and holds degrees from Cornell, Harvard, Wisconsin and Rutgers Universities. He is a specialist on misbehaviour by consumers, the role of marketing in economic development and the historical development of marketing institutions and concepts. His publications include two scholarly books and over 30 scholarly articles.

Rainer Gries is a professor of Modern History at the University of Jena and a professor of Communications at the University of Vienna, Austria. He has written numerous books, book chapters and articles on the history of propaganda, advertising and product communication in Germany and Austria.

Kai-Uwe Hellmann is a senior lecturer in the sociology of consumption and economics at the Technical University of Berlin. He is a specialist in the history and sociology of consumption and of consumer behaviour. Among his many publications is the widely acclaimed monograph *Soziologie der Marke* (*Sociology of the Brand*) (2003).

Daniel Horowitz is a professor in American Studies at Smith College, Massachusetts. His PhD in History is from Harvard University, and he has focused on how American writers have responded to affluence and consumer culture since the 1830s. He has published *The Morality of Spending* (1985), *Vance Packard and American Social Criticism* (1994), *Betty Friedan and the Making of The Feminine Mystique* (1998) and *The Anxieties of Affluence* (2004).

Helene Karmasin is Austria's leading motivation and market researcher. She is the Head of Karmasin Motivforschung and a member of the management team of the Austrian Gallup Institute. Helene holds visiting professorships at various European universities and is the author of *Produkte als Botschaften* (*Products as Messages*), now in its fourth edition (2007).

Karina Krummeich graduated in 2008 with a Diploma in Communication Science from the University of Vienna. Her final year thesis was on the Centenary of Ernest Dichter and the accompanying exhibition at Ernest Dichter's uncle's former department store in the Brunnengasse (in the Ottakring district of Vienna).

Stefanie Lahm studied Communication Science and History at the University of Vienna and is now a doctoral student at the University's Institute of Communication Science. She works in the marketing department of a large Austrian property company and writes her PhD thesis on Ernest Dichter's global marketing consultancy work for tobacco products.

Andrea Morawetz studied Communication Science and Political Science at the University of Vienna and currently works as press officer at the Austrian Consumer Association (VKI). Her Master's thesis was on the history of the Austrian advertising industry in the interwar period, and the subject of her PhD is a cultural history of the product category of sparkling wine in the Habsburg Empire.

Katherine Parkin is Professor in Modern American History at Monmouth University, New Jersey. She works on the history of food consumption and gender. Her monograph *Food is Love: Advertising and Gender Roles in Modern America* (2006) won the Emely Toth Award for best book in feminist popular culture.

Véronique Pouillard is Assistant Professor at the Université Libre in Brussels, Belgium. Her 2005 dissertation received the prize of the Académie Royale de Belgique and has been published as *La Publicité en Belgique, 1850–1975* (*Advertising in Belgium*). During 2008–09, she was a postdoctoral fellow at Harvard University Business School.

Dirk Schindelbeck is Principal Lecturer at the University of Education in Freiburg, Germany. He has written and (co-)edited numerous books on the cultural history of German advertising and propaganda in the nineteenth and twentieth centuries, among them *Brands, Fashions and Campaigns: an Illustrated History of Consumption in Germany* (2003).

Stefan Schwarzkopf is Associate Professor in Business History and Marketing at Copenhagen Business School, Denmark. His PhD (Birkbeck College) charted the rise of a service-oriented advertising industry in Britain in the twentieth century. He has published widely on the history of advertising, marketing and political propaganda in twentieth-century Europe.

Gabriele Sorgo is a Reader in Cultural History and Marketing at the University of Vienna, Austria. She is Co-Director of the Institute of the Anthropology of the Senses and Everyday Culture in Vienna and has published widely on the religious connotations of modern consumer culture. She edited *Ascetism and Consumption* (2002) and is the author of *Mysteries of the World of Commodities* (2006).

Mark Tadajewski is Lecturer in Critical Marketing at the University of Leicester and has published numerous scholarly articles on the history and theory of marketing. He is the co-editor of *Marketing Theory* (2007), *The History of Marketing Thought* (2008) and *The Handbook of Marketing Theory* (2009). Mark is also the UK editor of the *Journal of Historical Research in Marketing*.

Part I
Introduction

1
Ernest Dichter, Motivation Research and the 'Century of the Consumer'

Stefan Schwarzkopf and Rainer Gries

1.1 Motivation Research as a political project

The autumn of 1938 was stormy and violent. All over the world, there was an air of anticipation, an atmosphere also filled with anxiety and uncertainty. Commentators in East and West divined change, disruption and upheaval. In Europe, many people desperately clung on to the hope of 'peace in our time' as Nazi Germany had enforced a political union with Austria (Anschluss) and now threatened to invade Czechoslovakia. In November, hundreds of synagogues and the shops and homes of thousands of Jewish people in Germany were burnt to the ground in murderous riots orchestrated by the Nazi regime. In the same year, the concentration camps Mauthausen and Neuengamme were opened. In late September, the notorious 'Long Island Express' hurricane struck Connecticut, New York, Long Island and Massachusetts. It damaged or destroyed 57,000 homes and buildings, knocked down 3 billion trees and left a path of devastation in which nearly 700 people lost their lives.

While Europe was in the midst of the preparations for a major war, the American people were more inclined to stay out of the troubled waters of world politics and instead rebuild consumer and investor confidence in a country shattered by the impact of the Great Depression. The DuPont company presented the synthetic fibre 'Nylon' to the world, in *Action Comics*, 'Superman' made his first appearance and Daffy Duck and Bugs Bunny had their screen debut. Yet underneath the apparent calm of a revived commercial culture, anxiety was rife. In October, Orson Welles's radio adaptation of *The War of the Worlds* was broadcast on CBS, which caused many thousands of frightened New Yorkers to believe in a Martian invasion of planet Earth. Although ensuing newspaper reports of a mass panic were later found to be wildly exaggerated, a young breed of psychologists and experts on 'crowd delusions' took the public reaction to the broadcast as a proof that even civilised, enlightened human beings of the Western world could still develop irrational fears from one moment to another. How could it be explained that the fantasy of Martian spaceships landing in the Bronx motivated people to call the police and leave their houses with shotguns to investigate the scenes of the 'landings' (Cantril et al. 1940).

In the midst of this tumultuous autumn, in September 1938, a young Austrian émigré descended from the jetty of an ocean liner that had brought him and his wife from Europe to New York. Clad in a simple suit, the young psychology graduate entered a new world that transformed him as much as he was about to transform his new home – America. Within the next two years, the young researcher worked on a number of marketing cases that today are part of the mythologies that modern consumer culture has created around itself. This young émigré was Ernest Dichter, an Austro-American psychologist and consumer researcher who pioneered the application of Freudian psychoanalysis and depth interviewing to marketing problems. Dichter's research techniques became part of what during the 1940s and 1950s was known as Motivation Research (MR). These techniques and their findings revolutionised mid-twentieth-century marketing and advertising practice in North America and in Europe as they directly aimed at finding out 'why' people were attracted to certain products and lifestyle choices.

Erroneously called the 'Father of Motivation Research', Dichter was hailed by many as the Sigmund Freud of the supermarket age. He famously advised Procter & Gamble that soap was used by consumers symbolically as a tool to rid themselves of sins and undesired character traits. What mattered for consumers was the symbolic ability of a soap to bring about a new start and prepare them for the daily challenges and excitements of urban life. He told Chrysler that male consumers understood cars in terms of relationships and that they formed quasi-personal bonds with specific brands and car makes, which they subconsciously likened to their sexual relationships with women. Thus, a cabriolet turned into a man's mistress and a sedan car into his more secure wife. Dichter is perhaps best remembered for his ability to see why women did not want to buy 'total product solutions' and food products with 'high usability' value, as in the case of the Betty Crocker Cake Mix brand. In a dawning age of technicised kitchens and ready-made meals, female consumers wanted to retain a sense of direct experience, a sense of influence and individual skill, when preparing family food. Dichter therefore advised General Mills to allow housewives to add an egg – of course seen by Dichter as a symbol of a housewife's ability to be sexually active and to give birth to new life (Dichter 1960a: 157). While these cases are now part of twentieth-century urban mythology and consumer capitalism's self-spun branding lore, Ernest Dichter's development over three decades as one of America's foremost marketing experts is a pivotal milestone in the emergence of interpretative consumer research and of modern consumer culture in a wider sense.

Dichter's research activities were first brought to the attention of a mass audience by the critical American journalist Vance Packard, whose bestseller *The Hidden Persuaders* chastised Dichter and other motivation researchers for their attempts at manipulating consumers and citizens (Packard 1957). Since Packard's epochal investigation into the working practices and social visions of the (M)ad Men who inhabited the marketing world of the late 1950s, the power fantasies of advertising men and the links between psychoanalysis and consumer behaviour have fascinated historians, social scientists and cultural critics on both sides of the Atlantic (Curtis 2002; Kirby 2008). Popular representations of the psychologist-cum-salesman have both attracted vocal support as well as increasing scepticism from different sections of the social science and humanities community. Yet these representations merely reflect a continuing debate as to the influence of persuasive communication on consumers, the meaning of 'motivation' and the role of the unconscious in the decision-making processes of consumers (Bowlby 1993; Dawson 2003; Ewen 1976; Frank 1998; Haineault and Jean-Yves Roy 1993; Schudson 1986; Twitchell 2000).

In the case of the motivation researcher Ernest Dichter, the fascination with the idea of marketers using psychoanalytic tools to make consumers happy meets the timeless fascination with people who transgressed social, cultural and national boundaries and whose actions forged a transatlantic, global culture. The Austrian-born Ernest Dichter, who like no other shaped American marketing and consumer research in the post-war era, joins the long line of Europeans who transformed the culture of the American market. From the German John Jacob Astor, America's first multimillionaire, James Gordon Bennett, the Scotsman who founded the *New York Herald* and helped popularise the idea of journalism for the 'penny' masses, to the Austrian architect Victor Gruen, the inventor of the American shopping mall, European immigrants have welded America as a consumer society and reminded us of the essentially European roots of the so-called American dream (Gruen 1960; Hardwick 2000; 2005; Mott 1941: 229–238; Rodgers 1998).

Ernest Dichter was born in Vienna on 14 August 1907, as the eldest of three sons. He grew up in an impoverished Jewish family of Polish and Sudeten-German immigrants. Studying psychology at the Sorbonne in Paris and with Charlotte Bühler at Vienna University in the early 1930s, Dichter met some of the last protagonists of Europe's cultural zenith of the late nineteenth and early twentieth centuries. After completing his university studies, Dichter underwent brief psychoanalytical training with a former pupil of Freud, Wilhelm Stekel. Stekel's interpretation of psychoanalysis, dominated by a quasi psycho-ethnological focus on the role of symbols and images, became an intellectual challenge for the young Dichter (Boos and Groenendijk 2007; Dichter 1979: 11–12). Increasingly pressurised by the police of the 'Austro-Fascist' state, he and his wife Hedy Dichter decided to emigrate to the United States in 1937. In New York, he was initially supported by another Austrian émigré working at Columbia University, the sociologist and market researcher Paul Lazarsfeld. Lazarsfeld had already introduced Dichter to the fundamentals of quantitative and qualitative social research back in Vienna at his Institute of Economic Psychology (Wirtschaftspsychologische Forschungsstelle). Beginning in the late 1920s, Lazarsfeld had done pioneering market research that focused on understanding the hidden dimensions of motivation and decision making. In an attempt to unite qualitative and quantitative approaches, Lazarsfeld called for research that relied on statistical information and direct observation, numbers as well as insight. Working on different research projects in New York in the late 1930s and early 1940s, Lazarsfeld revolutionised the understanding of the role of human motives in the market place (Fleck and Stehr 2007; Horowitz 1998; Kassarjian 1994; Lazarsfeld 1935; 1937; Levy 2003; 2005; Oberschall 1978).

Unlike Lazarsfeld, however, who stressed the statistical validity of his research results to such an extent that Dichter saw fit to dismiss him as a 'nose counter', Dichter created a far more colourful melange of theoretically less reflected research methods. While Lazarsfeld was no stranger to psychoanalytic ideas – his mother was a psychoanalyst – Dichter based his entire market and consumer research methodology on the basis of Freudian psychoanalysis. For Dichter this meant a discovery on two levels. On the one hand, he began to conceptualise the consumer soul as a hidden realm of desires, full of taboos, repression and secrets. On the other hand, Dichter discovered the 'soul of the products', which was also structured as a space of complexes and taboos

(Dichter 1960a: 96–98). Dichter realised that there was an enormous interest among American managers in interpretative, qualitative and explorative approaches to the dynamics of the consumption process and the communication between products and consumers.

Partially drawing on his own knowledge of Freudian psychoanalysis, partially copying Lazarsfeld's research practices, Dichter began to offer a unique form of marketing and consumer research. By 1939, he worked for *Esquire* magazine and the Chrysler Motor Corporation. In March 1940, *Time* magazine featured an interview with Dichter that presented him to a large audience of readers as the new star on the business horizon. Soon, the magazine prophesised, the American consumer would be directed in their choices by 'completely Dichterized advertisements' (*Time* 1940). At the same time, Dichter underwent language training in order to get rid of his Austrian accent. Before the end of the Second World War, Dichter had reinvented himself as the embodiment of the American Dream and as a revolutionary, who for the first time understood that consumers were driven by largely subconscious desires, fears and complexes. By the late 1950s, his global business reached an annual turnover of $1 million and magazines like *Time*, *Newsweek* and *Business Week* frequently presented him as the man who could get 'inside the consumer' and who was able to predict large-scale social changes. In June 1962, *Playboy* invited Dichter to discuss 'the Womanization of America' (*Playboy* 1962) and Vance Packard's bestseller immortalised him as the 'super-advertising-scientist'. In other words, Dichter advanced to become a symbolic figure of his time, who served as a projection screen for public criticism of marketing and post-war consumer culture (Bartos 1977; Bennett 2005; Dichter 1960a; 1964; 1977; 1979; Fullerton 2007; Fullerton and Stern 1990; Kreuzer et al. 2007; Stern 2004).

Ernest Dichter's role and that of Motivation Research in general in the making of twentieth-century consumer culture cannot be overestimated. Dichter arrived in the United States at a crucial moment during the late 1930s when Robert Merton and Paul Lazarsfeld at Columbia University's Rockefeller-sponsored Radio Project (later the Bureau for Social Research) developed the method of 'focus group' interviews; that is, qualitative consumer investigations with groups of people that were allowed to elaborate on their ideas and experiences, rather than just ticking boxes on research questionnaires (Lazarsfeld 1969; Lunt and Livingstone 1993; Merton et al. 1956; Morrison 1998; Platt 1996; Schramm 1997; Zeisel 1979). Once again supported by Lazarsfeld and working in the vicinity of the innovative social research group that emerged around Lazarsfeld during the late 1930s and early 1940s at Columbia University, Dichter developed a take on consumer research that stressed consumers' interaction with products and the importance of (brand) images and symbols in advertising communication.

In his first research project, the 32-year-old Dichter investigated people's uses of soap bars for Procter & Gamble's Ivory Soap. Based on his research, a new brand image and a new advertising slogan was developed which reflected consumers' recorded feelings that soap could wash away their old selves and prepare them for a new challenge: 'Be smart, and get a fresh start with Ivory soap.' In several dozens of open-ended research interviews with young men and women Dichter found that the ritualistic, anthropological significance of bathing as a symbol for getting rid of one's bad feelings, sins and immorality (baptism) broke through when consumers talked about their attitudes and cleaning habits. Showering and lathering also had a peculiar undertone of undressing and of erotic pleasure. Dichter realised that applying rich lather in the bath was one of the few occasions when the puritanical American was allowed to caress himself or herself (Dichter 1960a: 33–34; 1979: 35). In 1998, Hedy Dichter summarised her husband's approach to marketing research for Ivory Soap in the following way: 'My husband went to Y.M.C.A.'s and actually interviewed people about why they take baths and why they use soap. Lots of women told him that the Saturday night bath was very special: they said you never know what can happen, you have to be ready. That was the sort of thing he was interested in – the psychological, the sexual innuendos. So he saw that soap was more than soap, and a bath was more than a bath. He realised that it was a sort of cleansing ritual for many people, and he wrote a slogan keying into those feelings' (Ames 1998).

It has since been questioned whether the new advertising slogan was of any use to Procter & Gamble, the producers of Ivory Soap. Soon after its introduction, the slogan actually disappeared again from Ivory brand communication and the then research director of Procter & Gamble's advertising agency Compton, Dr Paul Smelser, is said to have found Dichter's research results rather useless (Battey 1981). But in these early research projects, a new type of understanding of consumer behaviour, one that focused not on statistically recording but on interpreting consumers' psycho-social involvement with the world of things around them, had been inaugurated. Likening himself to the famous TV detective, Ernest Dichter later wrote about his approach: 'Maybe I am a psychological Peter Falk. I observe the hidden clues; I listen with the third ear; I interpret. I see where others are too blind because they are too close to the trees. I find the solution and produce the sales increases. I have acted as a discoverer, as a general on the battlefield of free enterprise' (Dichter 1979: 147).

In his key work *The Strategy of Desire*, written as a rejoinder to claims that Motivation Research and modern marketing constituted 'hidden persuasion' and manipulation, Dichter attempted to convince his readers that products were marketed merely in order to allow people 'creative fulfilment' and that buying was in reality an 'expression of creativeness' (Dichter 1960a: 16, 170). As consumers expressed their personality through the product choices they made, brands merely became a part of the general strife of modern man for individuality (Dichter 1960a: 231). This creativity of consumers, according to Dichter, resided in their ability to merge the disparate pieces of information sent out by products, retail outlets, advertisements and other consumers into a consistent whole. Rather than assessing the various aspects of a product separately – that is, price, packaging, brand name, quality associations, smell and so on – consumers view products and brands holistically, as a totality ('Gestalt'). As a result, market researchers had to try and study how and why consumers perceived certain symbolic meaning in a brand and a product. In other words, in order to understand consumer behaviour, market researchers had to search for 'the soul, the meaning of objects' (Dichter 1958b; 1960a: 34, 95, 147) (see Figure 1.1).

Viewing products in terms of the holistic image they formed in the mind of consumers was a direct application of Wolfgang Köhler's and Karl and Charlotte Bühler's Gestalt-psychological theories. Dichter had been a student of the Bühlers at Vienna University and wrote his PhD dissertation with Charlotte Bühler in 1934 on people's ability for self-evaluating their own abilities and performance (Dichter 1934; 1960a: 85–98, 144–148). Having worked at Lazarsfeld's market research institute on patterns of milk consumption among the Viennese population, Dichter now merged the tools of consumer research with the idea that products were perceived by consumers in such a way that a subconscious dialogue emerged between consumer and product. Through this dialogue, consumers 'animated' products and brands and turned them into objects with a soul (lat. *anima*).

These insights ensured that Dichter became one of the most outstanding market and consumer researchers of his generation. Yet, unlike other, today largely forgotten, motivation researchers of his time, Dichter linked his research agenda specifically to the greater ideological battles of the day. By courtesy of Ernest Dichter, Motivation Research became above all a political project. In the wake of the Sputnik crisis,

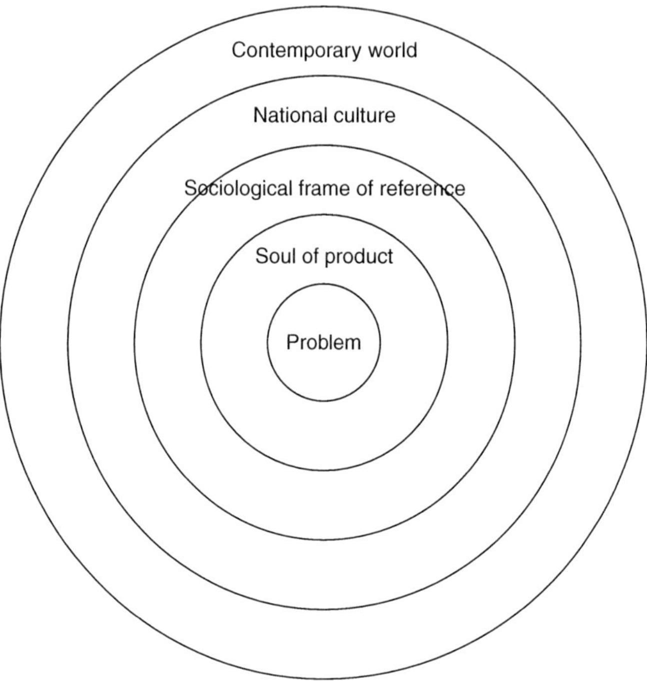

Figure 1.1   Dichter's Holistic View of the Product and of the Market Research Process (adapted from *The Strategy of Desire*, p. 145).

Dichter offered Motivation Research as a technique of social engineering to drag the American people out of their self-imposed standstill. In his key work *The Strategy of Desire*, published a year after the notorious 'Kitchen Debate' between Nixon and Khrushchev, as well as in numerous speeches and newspaper articles, Dichter claimed that the average American had become more complacent, fearful and fatalistic since the end of the Second World War. In Dichter's opinion, the Soviet Union launched one propaganda coup after the other; it embraced material wealth as sign of 'socialist progress'; Soviet citizens were less worried about consumption and material objects; and, above all, they had a collective plan, a vision for their national future. In all their prosperity, Americans seemed to lack these attitudes. He reminded his readers that they were in the middle of a 'silent war...on the outside with Russia and on the inside with our old concepts of thinking'. From the psychological point of view, he argued, 'the basic conflict we face is one between wanting to hold on to the status quo, wanting to return to the womb, to hide, to be fatalistic, or to face the world by accepting change as challenge' (Dichter 1958a; 1960a: 18, 21; 1970).

Dichter also enlisted his European audiences in this global struggle against complacency and inhibiting puritanism. In 1966, he told a group of supporters of European economic integration: 'Westerners berate themselves for their material goals and for leading a life of product acquisition. We feel that when we manufacture a new consumer product, it is somehow immoral. When the Russians do it, they consider it progress and morality. All over the world – in Russia with its sophisticated form of Communism and in Samoa with its primitive form of Communism, as well as in other countries – people are clamouring for more, not fewer consumer products.... We have to learn to reject the now so prevalent misconception: that Communism and Russia are more attractive to the uncommitted countries than capitalism and Western Democracy. Instead, wherever I went I found that it is the Western way of life which is held up as the desirable goal to be reached. Capitalist products are considered the desirable products to own and to use' (Dichter 1966: 12–13).

This fight that America and Western Europe led on the outside world against the totalitarian enemy of Soviet Russia had to be won at home, in the kitchen and at the supermarket, by helping, for example, suburban housewives overcome their fear of new ways of cooking and of new products: 'After an initial hesitation, [the housewife] has accepted canned food, instant coffee, frozen foods, etc., and she saves herself from guilt feelings' (Dichter 1960a: 184). By connecting Motivation Research to the political drama of the Cold War, Dichter took on his critics with canny fervour. While Vance Packard, John Kenneth Galbraith and William Whyte, author of the seminal study *Organization Man* (1956), claimed that modern industries, enlarged bureaucracies and sophisticated marketing had turned Americans into spineless and irresponsible comfort-seekers, Dichter hit back by arguing that Americans did not yet feel comfortable enough with their wealth and prosperity. Dichter attributed the fatalism, lack of initiative and sheer boredom exhibited by most Americans to their hidden, 'puritanical inhibitions', which prevented them from enjoying consumer capitalism to the full: 'Free enterprise and indeed our whole concept of modern economic life cannot survive unless we abandon the idea that a comfortable life is automatically an immoral one' (Dichter 1960a: 184, 227, 263; 1960b: 66).

For Dichter, Americans had to be instilled with the will to enjoyment through consumption if the nation was to have any chance as a future world power. The great aim of motivation researchers like Dichter was thus to implant consumption and the consumer brand more deeply in the collective project of an American future. The idea that there were secret communication channels between brands and consumers and that these communication channels could be strategically altered to serve societal needs became a mighty political weapon within the arsenal of post-war American marketing. It is not surprising, therefore, that Dichter finished his anti-Packardian and anti-Galbraithian opus magnum, *The Strategy of Desire*, with a kind of marketing communications plan that aimed at changing people's attitude towards 'Brand America'. The motivation-researcher-turned-cold-warrior proposed that if people were to understand the United States better the country had to act with more humility on the diplomatic stage and reawaken people's frustrated love for America. Further, he advised to showcase America's capacity for greatness by creating personal heroes and collective symbols to which people inside and outside the country could aspire. These heroes and symbols could also help remove fears of America's individualism and vitality which he believed had taken hold of foreign public opinion (Dichter 1960a: 272–282).

Another of Dichter's socio-political works, *Motivating Human Behavior* (1971) struck a similar chord. In the second half of this book, he proposed the potential application of motivation techniques to intervene in a wide range of social problems ranging from individual happiness to bringing about world peace. Openly labelling his practice as 'social engineering', Dichter admitted that motivational techniques could be used to manipulate consumers but he argued that what mattered was the use to which these techniques were put. Motivational techniques, according to Dichter, offered a set of devices through which individuals could overcome the gap between their natural inclinations (fear, laziness, nostalgia or prejudices) and their potential to self-actualise and become enlightened global citizens. Dichter suggested that there was a fear of using these techniques because of suspicions they could be turned into extreme forms of social control which then limited the rights of individuals. At the most unlikely of all times, in the 'critical' late 1960s and early 1970s, Dichter refused to accept these fears and instead proposed an optimistic view of global, American capitalism (Dichter 1971: 119–121, 230–242; 1987).

1.2   Motivation Research: its sources, its transfer and global export

Today, it has become accepted wisdom that products are created around people's character traits and are therefore seen as expressions of their personalities. It is for that reason that products seem to bear so much promise – of individual change and aspiration, of youth and freedom. It has become accepted knowledge that Coca Cola does not sell fizzy drinks but the *idea* of youth and refreshment and that Nike does not sell shoes but exhaustion, achievement and success. Cultural anthropologists of the Western world find more and more evidence of very intimate relationships between products and their owners (Hirschman 2007; McCracken 1988). While these relationships now feature heavily on the research agenda in social theory, consumer research and cultural anthropology, their discovery ultimately dates back to the mid-twentieth century and the work of a whole group of motivation researchers of whom Ernest Dichter was certainly one of the most innovative. Not without a sense of nostalgia, some within the advertising community today look back to the decades between the 1930s and the 1960s as an era of 'great personalities', of 'movers and shakers' in the world of marketing; as an era when 'advertising blockbusters' were still written (Fletcher 2006; Nelson 2008). In this book, we attempt to situate Ernest Dichter broadly within the wider culture of consumer research and consumer expertise that emerged during those years. We argue that Dichter's version of Motivation Research provides a unique vantage point from which to study the emergence during the twentieth century of a transatlantic research dialogue, the emergence and transfer of consumer cultures, and finally the making of 'us' as members of brand-driven market places that we cannot seem to escape (Fleck 2007).

These and other questions also kept Ernest Dichter awake at night. The young émigré, who was lucky to have escaped the anti-Semitic hell of Europe during the 1930s and 1940s, began his new career at an amazing speed. After having advised Procter & Gamble, the *Esquire* magazine, and, most famously, Chrysler during the late 1930s, Dichter attracted more and more high-profile clients. Among them were CBS, General Mills, DuPont and Exxon. Although he did not coin the famous 'Tiger' slogan, Dichter's work on consumer attitudes towards petrol brands led the oil giant Exxon to adopt the symbol of a tiger for the Esso brand. 'Put a tiger in your tank' symbolised to consumers the sheer power of Esso petrol (Dichter 1964: 274–277; 1979: 80, 93). The avalanche of research requests spurred Dichter to move out of the salaried project-researcher positions he held for years and to set up his own Institute for Motivational Research in 1946, first housed in Manhattan and later in a respectable mansion in Croton-on-Hudson near New York (Figure 1.2).

Only ten years later, in 1956, he founded Ernest Dichter Associates International, which allowed him to turn his research expertise into a global business. At that time, ironically, Vance Packard's exposure of the

Figure 1.2   The Ernest Dichter Institute for Motivational Research in Croton-on-Hudson, *c.*1955.

'hidden persuaders' helped him to gain further clients both in North America and in Europe. From the late 1950s, Dichter set up subsidiary companies and partner companies in Vienna, Munich, Frankfurt/Main, Zurich, Paris, Tokyo, London, Barcelona, Panama and Miami. Dichter inspired similar motivational research institutes in all parts of Europe, notably in Italy, and he became research active as far away as in South Africa, Japan and Australia, where he subcontracted work to other Motivation Research institutes (Dichter 1989; McLeod 2009). Among the global and international corporations which Dichter advised during the 1940s, 1950s, 1960s and 1970s were major American car companies (Chrysler, Ford), energy companies (Amoco, Shell, Exxon, Mobil Oil), branded food producers (General Mills, Cadbury's, Nestlé), household and consumer goods producers (DuPont) and travel companies (Air France, Japan Airlines, American Airlines). In addition, he was commissioned to conduct research for major advertising agencies, among them J. Walter Thompson, Young & Rubicam, McCann Erickson and N. W. Ayer, which they in turn used to counsel their own clients.

During the 1960s, Dichter also diversified into the market for political consulting and political advertising. Even before Dichter ventured into this field, an independent motivational research institute founded in Bremen in 1956 had conducted research into the 'motivational structure' of German voters in order to find the 'typical' conservative voter and advise the German Christian Democratic Union (CDU) on its image (Kruke 2007: 77, 122–123, 133). Dichter saw opportunities in this area of consultancy and, among others, advised the American Democrat presidential candidate Hubert H. Humphrey during the election year 1968 (Dichter 1979: 97–101). Humphrey, the former vice president, needed a clearly positioned image to help him move out of the over-bearing shadow of Lyndon B. Johnson, with whom the public was very familiar. Dichter advised Humphrey to focus public perception during the campaign on his ability to bring about social and political change ('Some talk change, others cause it'). Realising that Humphrey trailed in the polls heavily behind his opponent Richard Nixon, Dichter advised him to depict his Republican opponent as an embittered and miserable scaremonger and to instead promise a 'politics of joy'. In the midst of the culture wars of the 1960s and the riots that marred the campaign months, Nixon promised to restore 'law and order' and finally won the election by a small margin.

While the Humphrey 'brand' did not quite win the day, the success-ful Austrian chancellor Bruno Kreisky called on Dichter's services in order to sell his image to the collective psyche of the Austrian popula-tion as a trustworthy, forward-looking moderniser and champion of the European human rights agenda. Kreisky, a social-democrat, served for 13 years in office. In Italy, Dichter worked for the Christian Democrats who wanted to change their image and attract new voters. Dichter advised the party to present itself as youthful and open for change in order to take voters away from the socialist and communist parties, which at that time attracted a lot more younger supporters. Following Dichter, the Christian Democrats put a picture of a beautiful young woman on elec-tion posters under the slogan 'The Christian Democratic Party is only 20 years old', by that connecting the age of the Christian Democratic Party itself to the idea of youth, joy and future (Dichter 1979: 98–99).

There is a theme that emerges in all of Dichter's commercial and polit-ical recommendations, in his analyses and writings: the acceptance of change as a challenge and the full embrace of joyful, uninhibited opti-mism. Being a self-marketer of the highest order, Dichter connected this mindset to the idea of America and of modernity. Early on, he took language classes in New York in order to acquire an 'all-American accent' and he changed his name from 'Ernst' to 'Ernest'. In interviews, on his travels and research visits, in his publications and during his many speeches at conferences Dichter styled himself as a keystone in the structure of an 'American century' in the making. By the 1960s,

'Ernest Dichter' and 'motivation research' had become global brands which extended the reach of America's 'soft Empire' further into the social and cultural spaces of European marketing (Clarke 2008; de Grazia 2005; Mennell 2007). Although equipped with a keen eye for the differences in national cultures, Dichter was nevertheless very clear about the fact that he contributed to wide-ranging changes which restructured European societies along the lines of American-style consumer culture. In a sense, he extended the normal scope of marketing consultancy when he advised average citizens, housewives, voters, students and parents not to resist these changes but to embrace them.

Like many American marketing specialists before him, he targeted especially the French, whom he suspected to be mainly responsible for European cultural resistance towards Americanised mass culture, mass marketing and mass retailing. In 1974, Dichter wrote a series of children's books directed at French families. Originally intended for his own grandson Sasha, the four books introduced a little boy who discovered his emotions, his fears, the nature of social conflict and his own cognitive development. In *Sasha a tous les pouvoirs* ('Sasha has all powers'), he advised his French readers how responsible parenting could create more optimistic and open-minded children of the next generation, a generation that was better able to deal with the challenges and technological-material opportunities that the future was bound to offer (Dichter 1979: 188–189).

Wrapping the person Ernest Dichter into the narrative of American cultural imperialism and depicting him as an 'Americaniser', however, would not do justice to the story of a man and his research methods which were essentially about contradiction, conflict and the unseen, 'hidden', baggage of the past. The methods usually summarised under the term 'Motivation Research' are in themselves of profoundly European origins. They blend the holistic philosophy of Bühler's Gestalt psychology, which assumes that human beings perceive objects and events in images, as an amalgamated whole (Gestalt), with Freudian psychoanalysis and Lazarsfeld's social and market research methodology. In other words, the fascinating landscape of consumer, market and Motivation Research which emerged in the United States during the 1940s and 1950s would have been very bleak without the arrival of European immigrants (many of them of Jewish origin) like Paul Lazarsfeld, Ernest Dichter, Alfred Politz, Herta Herzog, Hans Zeisel, Leo Bogart and George Katona (Dichter 1979: 32; Heilbron et al. 2008; Schumann et al. 2008).

The essentially European origin of Dichter's Motivation Research puts a question mark behind the all-pervasive Americanisation narrative so often told (Schröter 2005: 111–120). Equally, Dichter's ascent in American society after 1938 and his global fame in the post-war era should not be mistaken as an all-out 'from cleaner to Millionaire' success story. His career was characterised by public objection, by attacks made on him in the press, by professional jealousies and personal rivalries that often hurt and demotivated the great motivator. Partly, of course, Dichter had to blame himself and his relentless self-marketing for being singled out as 'Mr. Mass Motivation himself' (Packard 1957: 32). As mentioned earlier, Dichter's research into the 'hidden' or subconscious communication between products and consumers was first exposed to a mass audience by a no-less-intriguing American: the journalist Vance Packard and his international bestseller *The Hidden Persuaders* (1957). Translated into all major European languages, Packard's polemic book branded Dichter as a dangerous marketing guru, whose skills in tapping the unsuspecting depths of consumer psyches could turn people into sexualised, aboulic marionettes of unscrupulous advertisers.

So powerful was the image of the marketer as 'hidden persuader' that Dichter had to continually defend himself. When the American media began to discuss James Vicary's experiments with subliminal advertising and Dichter's Motivation Research in one breath, Dichter issued public statements denouncing Vicary as a scandalous hypnotist. The bad image of Motivation Research, which gripped public perception in the wake of Vicary's faked experiments and Packard's blockbuster publication, affected the marketing profession as a whole. The German advertising manager Harry Damrow, for example, felt the need to entitle his memoirs *I have Not Been a Hidden Persuader* (Damrow 1981; Dichter 1979: 82–84; Rogers 1992). Contemporary market researchers therefore took on Dichter for what they perceived as his indefensible lack of interest in statistical, 'hard' data. Some found Dichter's interpretative openness difficult to accept (Alderson 1958; Levitt 1960; Paradise and Blankenship 1950: 286; Peterman 1956; Politz 1956–1957; Stryker 1956; Williams 1957; Woolf 1958), while others, like the British market researcher Mark Abrams, rubbished his *Strategy of Desire* for making generalised statements that 'reflect a totally insensitive approach to civilised culture' and for passing off commonplace observations as a 'substitute for careful statistical procedure' (Abrams 1960). The American researcher Edward Scriven warned by the mid-1950s that some marketing executives had begun to feel that 'the whole business of motivation analysis is simply a hodgepodge of jabberwocky, or the line of a glib psycho-salesman bent on selling fifty "depth" interviews for $50,000' (Scriven 1958: 65).

Attacks on Dichter shaped American and European public discourse throughout much of the post-war period. Betty Friedan, whose 1963 *The Feminine Mystique* became a key text for the second feminist movement, described Dichter as 'a man who is paid approximately a million dollars a year for his professional services in manipulating the emotions of American women to serve the needs of business' (Friedan 1963: 208). John Kenneth Galbraith and Martin Mayer, whose analyses of the causes and consequences of ubiquitous consumer marketing were widely read, provided powerful ammunition to those who believed that motivation researchers like Dichter were indeed to blame for the downfall of public-spiritedness and self-control in American life (Brown 1963: 176–193; Galbraith 1958; Mayer 1958). Much of today's research into the social evils of a fully fledged and 'uninhibited' consumer society still feeds from this anger and fear first unleashed by those who sought critical encounters with the original motivator in Croton-on-Hudson (Schor 2007).

Ernest Dichter's competitors and fellow consumer researchers were also far from welcoming. When Dichter returned to Europe during the late 1950s to seek new clients and publicise his research, leading figures in the European market research industries saw him as an intruder and branded him as a charlatan. At home, Paul Lazarsfeld remained friendly but increasingly sought to distance himself from the sexual connotations of the research interpretations produced by Dichter. Louis Cheskin, director of the Chicago-based Color Research Institute and one of Dichter's fiercest rival, triumphantly reported to Vance Packard that his adversary's 'almost complete preoccupation with Freudian symbolism and libidinous connotations' at times led him astray (Cheskin 1960: 155; Packard 1957: 35). In Britain and in Germany, the doyens of market and opinion research Harry Henry, Mark Abrams and Elisabeth Noelle-Neumann openly ridiculed Dichter's Freudian approach and gave him to understand in no uncertain terms that he was an embarrassment for the market research community (Henry 1958: 27; Noelle-Neumann 1963: 271; Schwarzkopf 2007). In Germany and in Austria in particular, old and very nasty animosities opened up once again between Dichter and those advertising and market researchers who had stayed in the German Reich during the war and who had often personally benefited from the expulsion and murder of Jewish advertising men.

One of them, Hanns F. J. Kropff, had co-organised the elimination of Jewish advertising and market research businesses in Vienna during the 1930s. Being favoured by the Nazis, Kropff advanced to become a major figure in the *Advertising Council of the German Industry* (Werberat der deutschen Wirtschaft), the main advertising control organ of the Nazi regime. Kropff also became a professor in advertising communication at Vienna's University of Economics (Hochschule für Welthandel) and was one of the main proponents of the idea that the German national character or Germany's racial constitution demanded a specific form of advertising communication and specific forms of advertising regulation. In his publications, Kropff defended the 'Führer Prinzip' (leader principle) and the idea that German advertising had to be part of the new totalitarian state (Kropff 1934: 17–78; 1939: 5; Semrad 2005; 2007).

Briefly disappearing after the war, Kropff made a starry comeback in the 1950s when he became Director of the Advertising Research Institute in Munich and Professor at the Goethe University in Frankfurt/Main. Sensing that Dichter was about to re-import Freudian approaches to the understanding of consumer behaviour, the former Nazi Kropff switched into attack mode and painted Dichter as a superficial charlatan who had essentially failed to keep up with the advertising research literature that had been published in Germany since 1930 (Kropff 1960: 410–411; Noelle-Neumann 1960). Members of the Nuremberg-based Society for Consumption Research (GfK – Gesellschaft für Konsumforschung) rallied together and set out to destroy Ernest Dichter at public debates at which they accused him of having stolen their ideas, developed during the early 1930s, of the wide-ranging psychological benefits of products, the products' 'soul' (Schindelbeck in this publication).

The very bitter irony cannot have been lost on Ernest Dichter: in the United States, he was being battered by the new Left for manipulating consumers and undermining traditional American puritanism, and in Europe he was attacked by the old Right for being a Liberal, a declared Freudian and an industrious global entrepreneur and relentless self-marketer. As if that was not enough, his brothers who had returned to Austria after the Second World War looked at him as a traitor to the cause of socialism and a lackey of American capitalism (Dichter 1977: 35). One does need a lot of optimism to withstand this onslaught and one cannot wonder why Dichter would have wanted to put himself through this harrowing experience when many other successful motivation researchers decided to remain outside the limelight of public attention. The answers to this question are to be sought in Dichter's background and upbringing. Although he was a very complex figure and a person full of contradictions, there are a number of factors that were essential for the making of Dichter as the great motivator of post-war consumer culture. These factors are Dichter's fear of poverty and connected to this his anxiety about comfort, his Jewishness and finally the importance of symbolic stories during his upbringing as a child in Vienna. All these factors help us interpret his unique approach to markets, products, brands and consumers, and they provide the key to so many apparent contradictions in his life.

Dichter's fear of poverty and his manic drive to avoid economic failure stemmed from early childhood experiences and from his experiences as an emigrant. Dichter's family was always in debt. Things were especially tough during and right after the First World War, when his father, a door-to-door salesman and sales representative, who earned money only from commissions, often had no income. The Jewish journalist and author Joseph Roth described the dreadful poverty of Eastern European Jewish people who had left Russia, Poland, Romania and what are today the Czech and the Slovak republics to live in Vienna. The poverty encountered by the Jews in the old capital of the Austrian Empire pushed the likes of Ernest Dichter's parents, who had come from Poland and the Sudetenland, to be constantly on the move ('Wanderschaft'); to expect the outbreak of a pogrom every so often; to see life as a constant struggle to make ends meet; and to abandon the hope of a glorious collective return to Jerusalem in favour of an individual journey to the new holy land, America (Hughes 2006; Roth 1930; 1985 [1927]).

When Dichter's father was in the Austrian army during the First World War, his mother fended off starvation by exchanging treasured items on the black market for flour, mixing it with straw to make barely edible bread. To provide fuel, Dichter and his brothers stole coal and cut down trees in a park. During those years, malnutrition and sheer hunger was a real and tangible experience in the life of young Ernest. At one point in 1918, his condition deteriorated so much that he was sent on a year-long holiday to Rotterdam in order to regain physical strength. Long-term exposure to hunger and deprivation engenders fantasies of houses made of sausages, of grilled chickens that fly into one's mouth and of gigantic cakes that can talk. Such fantasies must have developed in the brain of Dichter as a child and will have helped him to see more in food than just a source of nutrition.

In 1921, Dichter left school at age 14 to help support his family, working first as a secretary and then, from 1924 to 1927, as a sales clerk, sign painter and window decorator at his uncle's department store in Vienna. Dichter's department store in the Brunnengasse had been founded in 1890 by Leopold Dichter and by the 1930s it had become the largest department store outside Vienna's first district; that is, the immediate city centre (see Figure 1.3). In his uncle, Dichter found what his father did not offer: a man to look up to, someone

Figure 1.3 Leopold Dichter's Department Store, Brunnengasse Vienna, *c*.1930.

who encouraged his ambitions with new ideas about merchandising techniques, which his uncle had first encountered on a trip to the promised land of consumer plenty – the United States. While working at his uncle's department store, Dichter developed an interest in in-store and show-window design. Following his interests, Dichter developed a loudspeaker system for the department store in order to play music that enhanced the in-store shopping environment. When leaving Vienna in late 1937, he and his wife first went to Paris, where Dichter was hired as a commission salesman. Facing difficulty in making sales, Dichter realised that his success depended less on a product's quality and price and more on his ability to project the power and conviction of his own beliefs.

During the spring of 1938 came a critical turning point, a key moment in his reinvention. Fearing the expansion of Nazi Germany, Ernest and Hedy Dichter decided to leave Europe for good. The American Vice-Consul in Paris asked him why the Dichters should be allowed to immigrate to the United States. At this moment, Dichter articulated the mission of his career: standing before the Embassy official and fearing the denial of his visa request, Dichter said he 'made the best sales pitch of [his] whole life' (Dichter 1979: 28). He asserted that he could help inspire American citizens to solve problems by using depth psychology and, based on psychoanalytic theory, help in understanding the true reasons why consumers decided what to purchase. Dichter was so convincing, he later reported perhaps with some exaggeration, that the vice consul signed an affidavit indicating that he would personally support him if he ever encountered difficulties in the United States.

The constant experience of shortages, of being harassed and even imprisoned, of not having enough food and money for a living led to bizarre forms of status anxiety even when Dichter had already become a millionaire. While he made it his personal crusade to convince millions of American and European consumers to embrace comfort and luxuries, to 'let go' and remove their inhibitions about enjoyment of material goods, Dichter himself tended to remain outside the paradigms of the new consumer society he preached. Instead of spending money freely on enjoyments and home improvements, he devised complicated investment and saving plans that prevented him and his family members from spending money. He was stingy and at times annoyed his friends with the attitude of expecting them to invite him for meals instead of sharing bills. While he taught consumers to believe that temptations are a positive sign of a liberated mind, he himself resisted buying new household goods wherever possible. He also avoided expenditure for new cars or for more fashionable clothing for himself. While publicly glorifying consumption and optimism, he feared the return of poverty and often deliberately cut back on food consumption in order to retain the ability to rely on fewer calories; in other words, he trained hunger (Dichter 1979: 5–6; 137–138; 145–146).

This form of rigid self-governance also led to clashes with his children who could not see why the family should eat canned sausages when there was evidently enough money around for a Sunday roast. Dichter also deliberately gave small and simple presents to his children and grandchildren – and was deeply hurt by the attitude of some of them when they showed signs of disappointment at Christmas or birthdays about toys that turned out to be much smaller than expected. Consumerism creates higher expectations and, therefore, impatience and disappointment: a fact, that Dichter himself was evidently unwilling to concede. His children, Thomas and Susan Jane, in turn, left their parents' home embittered by the stingy attitude of their father. Thomas

Dichter, today a well-known and widely respected anthropologist and developmental economist, once reported that he felt his father played with his children and grandchildren mostly in order to use them as study objects (Dichter 1977: 355–357; Kreuzer et al. 2007: 105–106; Lahm 2007).

These attitudes of Dichter reveal a person who was tremendously insecure about his own position in life and who failed to find a stable psychological centre of his own existence. This inability to be comfortable with oneself and one's existence is another character trait of Eastern European Jews, first noticed by Joseph Roth back in the 1920s. As a child at school, Dichter felt constantly observed and was made to feel like an outsider by other schoolchildren who picked on his red hair, his awkward demeanour and, of course, his Jewishness. Although incredibly gifted, Dichter and many other young Jewish people who grew up in early twentieth-century Germany and Austria were led into a life as outsiders; thus their lack of piety towards their own names: a Grünbaum became a Greenboom once he/she arrived in America, and 'Ernst' became 'Ernest' Dichter (Dichter 1979: 48; Roth 1985: 65, 80).

In response to the anti-Semitism harboured by many of his contemporaries and the dreadful experience of poverty and widespread unemployment, the young student Ernest Dichter exhibited sympathy for socialist thought. Although he later downplayed his involvement in socialist circles, as a student in Paris he seemed to have been influenced by Leon Blum and belonged to a group of international students who regularly met to discuss Blumian socialism. After his return to Vienna in 1931, Dichter even published a small poem in the Austrian journal *The Young Worker*. In the poem, Dichter points at the crude inequality experienced by many younger people like himself, who felt excluded from mainstream society and who often had to suffer terrible poverty and hunger. Some of the lines of Dichter's poem are indeed moving: 'You live in marble palaces,…while we live in dirt and squalor.…We want to be human beings! Is that asked for too much?' (Dichter 1931; Duchkowitsch 2007).

Although Dichter's family does not seem to have been religiously active over and above the celebration of the typical Jewish holidays, his Jewish background provided him with two character traits that were to stay with him for the rest of his life. In the words of the author Joseph Roth, the Jewish religious experience is essentially based on the feeling of being left alone, or left behind by an angry god; a god who looks upon indulgence as sin and punishes the sinner by separating him from his people, his land, his home and his nearest and dearest. In that ever-present danger of separation and loneliness brought about by an avenging and punishing god, Jews are being called upon to search for more abstract forms of wisdom and for signs of god's greater plan in the apparent disorder and injustice of daily life.

This was but one side of Dichter's religious, spiritual and mythological heritage. In addition to Judaism as religion, Austria and Bohemia offered the young Dichter a fascinatingly rich heritage of fairytales, with which he will have been brought up at school and at home. Most of the fairytales of the area in which Dichter had his roots stressed poverty and self-control as great virtues. Theirs was a world structured by a 'moral economy', in which losing money and wealth was not problematic if overall community cohesion and total community welfare were secured and stable. In the world of central European fairytales, hunger and poverty were more often a sign of virtue, and riches more often a sign of moral decline and social danger. In this world, help often came from animated objects that talked in a human language, and riddles (as in the German word 'Rätsel') guided the way of ordinary humans to the real, invisible truth behind things. In other words, fairytales accustomed young Ernest Dichter to a reality that was hidden underneath material disguises.

Part of the Czech-bohemian tradition of fairytales were also the legends from the Jewish ghetto in Prague, the Josephstadt. These legends, too, often had a world view in which reality was hidden underneath a material cover that could mislead its onlookers. 'Real' reality, for want of a better word, was presented as a parallel world animated by spirits that defied measurement, technical manipulation or rational understanding. Under King Rudolf II, for example, there lived a rabbi in Prague by the name of Jehuda Loew ben Bezalel. He was wise, just, knowledgeable, and his skills allowed him to create an artificial human being made from clay, the Golem. The clay became alive when Rabbi Loew put the Schem – a piece of paper with the Hebrew name of God written on it – into the mouth of the Golem. On one Sabbath, Rabbi Loew forgot to remove the Schem from the Golem's mouth, and the Golem started wreaking havoc at the house of his master and threatened to destroy the houses of neighbours. When told about the disaster, the Rabbi came back from the Synagogue and removed the Schem from Golem's mouth, never to put it back again.

Some of the Jewish legends from central Europe read like a comment on Ernest Dichter's life itself. In Prague's Jewish cemetery lies a Jewish man, who during his lifetime, adopted the Christian faith and became a priest. On his deathbed, he uttered the wish to be buried among Jewish people and next to a woman whom he had loved in his youth. The Jews granted his wish and so reunited him with the object of his early love. His soul, however, could not find rest and to this day he gets up from his grave, goes to the Moldau River where the Grim Reaper ferries him on a boat across the river to the other side and to the cathedral, the Veitsdom. There, the former priest plays the organ and prays for his soul each night. He, like Dichter, is a wanderer between two worlds.

Jewish or Gentile, one cannot grow up in this mystical landscape between Vienna and Prague and not be influenced by the moral economy and non-positivist world view of these tales (Eidherr and Müller 2003; Feurstein and Milchram 2001; Idel 1990; Oxall and Weitzmann 1985; Petiška 1992; Rozenblit 1989). The most important fact they teach is that truth and purpose are hidden behind superficial activities and underneath the material forms that disguise the real meaning of things. One way or another, these folk tales point at the possibility of transubstantiation: the mystical act that transforms soulless material into something meaningful and often holy. Transubstantiation transforms reality as it brings to light what is hidden and mysterious (Scholem 1965: 158–204; 1970: 77–86). Later, as a controversial market researcher, the priest-like Ernest Dichter performed that magic of transubstantiation by revealing the true identity of products and brands in front of his astonished pilgrims who had come to seek an audience with the magus in the castle on Croton-on-Hudson.

1.3 Motivation Research and the disembedded consumer

Ernest Dichter's own transformation from an impoverished Jewish child from the social swamps of the late Austrian Empire into America's most popular market researcher of the post-war period is one of the most fascinating stories of the twentieth century. The cultural experience of American commercial life of the 1940s and 1950s was crucial for the making of Dichter as his generation's foremost consumer guru. Quickly leaving behind the tight moral economy of his birthplace, Dichter retained his ability to create in his mind a double-vision of reality. But instead of the virtue ethics of his homeland, he embraced the ethical utilitarianism of his new home, America, which in itself was going through a phase of rapid transformation in which traditional notions of self-control and respectability became softened (Lears 1994: 75–87; Offer 2006; Osgerby 2001; Parr 1999). The clash between these traditional notions of puritan self-control and the new self-seeking and self-actualising materialism brought about by post-war 'affluenza' produced a most contradictory decade, the 1950s; a decade, as well, when policy-makers decided to use economic and psychoanalytic theory more directly in order to turn their citizenry into a psychologically more balanced, more manageable and 'happy' population (Herman 1995: 241–275; Nuttall 2006; Thomas 2008; Thomson 2006: 251–288). As shown by David Bennett, the 1950s' American interpretations of Freudian psychoanalysis as 'ego psychology' produced a psychology of free enterprise that set out to make citizen-subjects fit for unrestrained consumer capitalism (Bennett 1999; 2005).

These shifts translated directly into a new popular image and a new cultural prominence for the stereotypical marketing professional of the 1950s and 1960s: the 'mad men' of Madison Avenue (Roman 2009; Stanley 2007; Warlaumont 2001). The circumstances of rapid rise in disposable incomes and increased competition between consumer brands now brought to the fore visions of the consuming subject and new forms of behavioural research that had been dormant in the advertising industry since at least the 1920s. It would be wrong to assume that the post-war period witnessed a sudden transformation of advertising and market research from a conventional, class-based and quantitatively driven understanding of consumer cultures towards a more qualitatively oriented engagement with lifestyles, cultures and the depths of consumer emotions (Arvidsson 2006: 50–62). This simplistic model is undermined by archival evidence which shows that advertisers realised as early as 1923 that, for example, 'soup can produce emotion' and that product advertising therefore had to create an emotional sales proposition (Lewis 1923). In the same year, Edward S. Jordan created his famous 'Cowboy' advertisement for the Chrysler 'Playboy Roadster'. Intuitively knowing that consumers buy cars depending on their sense of sexual self, Jordan filled the ad with a 'broncho-busting, steer-roping girl who knows what I am talking about' and the advice to use the new Chrysler to 'start for the land of the real living with the spirit of the lass who rides, lean and rangy, into the red horizon of a Wyoming twilight' (Curcio 2000: 339–340).

A year later, a copywriter at the J. Walter Thompson agency discovered that one could understand the way brands and consumers interact by describing a brand in terms of a person with distinct character traits. Lever's 'Lux' soap brand was thus envisaged by the JWT agency as a young, intelligent upper-class woman with a fast-paced lifestyle and an interest in latest fashion and clothing (Schwarzkopf 2009). This holistic idea of a brand as an image and a personality that offers individual fulfilment to consumers over and above mere utility had been developed in parallel by the Nuremberg School of market research around Alfred Vershofen at the GfK in the early 1930s. Vershofen and members of his circle already talked about the 'psychological-spiritual' attachment that consumers formed to specific products (Gries 2003: 53–60; 2004). From these beginnings it was a short step for market researchers to develop free-behaviour tests (as opposed to limited surveys of the 'yes–no' type) and techniques that aimed at finding out *why* consumers showed certain behaviour rather than just recording when, where and how much they bought (Lazarsfeld 1934).

Although consumers and the awareness of consumer emotions existed in Europe perhaps as early as the seventeenth century (McKendrick et al. 1982; Sombart 1967 [1913]), it was the twentieth century that turned into the 'century of the consumer'. On a scale unknown before, the twentieth century saw consumer behaviour becoming scientifically researched. This research not only turned into a new form of social technique and a new realm of knowledge for which 'experts' like Ernest Dichter became absolutely vital. This widespread turn towards consumer investigations also disembedded consumers and consumption as an activity from other forms of social existence and relationships behind which consumption normally disappeared. Using Martin Heidegger's terminology here, Dichter's Motivation Research turned 'being a consumer' from one of the many forms of social existence or social activity (dasein) into a concept that seemed to bring out the very essence of being human (sein). This great transition, in turn, meant that in Dichter's analysis consumption seemed to dominate all other social relationships within which it was once firmly embedded as a secondary activity. In Dichter's motivational research reports and his various other publications, being a consumer became *the* central form of human existence, the core of a person's *raison d'être*.

The general impetus behind Dichter's work was the idea that stable democracies needed self-aware and 'liberated' consumers. Although many other advertising and consumer experts of his age promoted the linkage between want-satisfaction and the state of guiltlessness and the achievement of social prestige, Dichter was one of the first to see very clearly that this technique brought about a new society. By 'liberating' consumers from the constraints of social or personal embarrassment and the ever-present sense of guilt, Dichter played a prominent part in the second 'Great Transformation' after the one that Karl Polanyi described for the nineteenth century, when the economic activities of production and trade first became disconnected from their initial social wiring and instead followed the anonymous incentives of the market (Buğra 2007: 1–10; Gemici 2008; Isaac 2005; Polanyi 1944).

The anthropologically inclined Austrian economist Karl Polanyi analysed the disembedding of economic and corporate activity from natural cycles, cultural restraints and the matrix of social networks. The anthropologically inclined Austrian consumer researcher Dichter, in turn, became part and parcel of the full psychological mobilisation of consumers which ultimately disembedded them from their social and cultural surroundings, and 'relieved' them of their culturally and socially formed inhibitions. Dichter unashamedly advised consumers to have it now and pay later, to ignore the inner voice of self-control and instead embrace 'a new freedom' (Dichter 1960a: 21). Unfortunately for those who looked for further philosophical substance in Dichter's ideas, his 'new freedom' really only meant getting a new sofa, a long-playing record or a new car if one desired.

Subconsciously fixed rationalisations and inhibitions were not seen by Dichter as useful or indeed necessary mental devices that allowed consumers to negotiate myopic choice and to hold a balance between genuine needs, income and wants and desires, but they were a 'danger' and merely a sign of 'superficial sophistication which prevents many people from admitting that they are influenced by advertising' (Dichter 1960a: 15). Getting, spending, enjoying and representing were elevated by Dichter to the rank of activities that allowed people self-actualisation and personal development. Critics who wondered how a hair dryer or a box of frozen fish-balls from a supermarket could be part of genuine human self-development were charged with being out of touch: 'If we want to get people to behave the way we think they should, we must stop making theological demands on them. Instead of embellishing the Ten Commandments, we must start worrying about why we have been unable to fulfil these demands....Heaven is wonderful, but for most of us too far off' (Dichter 1960a: 18, 114). Dichter aimed at nothing less than a complete overhaul of the way people lived their daily lives: 'What has become imperative for us is to revise our morality. Hedonism, as defended by the old Greeks, has to be brought to the surface again. We have to learn to forget the guilt of original sin' (Dichter 1960a: 263; 1976). Like the seventeenth-century Jewish pseudo-messiah Sabbatai Zevi, Dichter promised redemption through sin (Scholem 1971: 78–141; 1974: 244–286).

Companies were spurred on by Dichter to make the most of this consumer that he and others like Abraham Maslow had helped mobilise (Cooke et al. 2005; Miller and Rose 1997). Although Dichter fully recognised that consumers were actually embedded in culturally and socially very 'thick' relationships and could therefore not be fully rational, he nevertheless privileged the individualistic relationship between consumers and their chosen (or rejected) objects of desire. In this, Dichter constituted a form of secondary social transformation which followed on from the transformation first described by Polanyi in 1944. Following Polanyi, one could also argue that Motivation Research of the Dichterian type brought about a second 'double movement'; that is, the organised social response to the socio-moral disembedding of people as economic actors. Interpretations of advertising as a form of corporate mass manipulation and the perceived lack of consumer protection and consumer information triggered the disquiet of organised consumer groups, of legislators and intellectuals, who all began to react to the dangers of 'hidden persuasion'.

Unlike other market researchers of his generation, Ernest Dichter triumphantly recognised his role in this disembedding of the consumer; that is, the uncoupling of consumers from socially, religiously and culturally formed relationships and deeply internalised collective value concepts. Dichter believed that his work of reorienting the moral compass of consumers towards self-enjoyment and self-actualisation could help bring about a new human race fit for the marketplace of tomorrow. Scientifically less rigorous than other motivation researchers like Burleigh Gardner, Steuart Henderson-Britt and Herta Herzog, Dichter thus turned Motivation Research from an analytic tool into a new normative ethics of consumer society. His former mentor, the *éminence grise* of post-war social research, Paul Lazarsfeld tried to avoid a clash between the ethos of consumer-oriented market research in general and the pluralism of democratic visions that emerged during the war years. His collaborator at the Radio Project, Theodor W. Adorno, however, already sensed what was about to happen when he warned that the sell-out of social research to the corporate capitalist interests ('sneering empiricist sabotage') would only produce a body of powerful technocratic knowledge techniques that eventually undermined, not promoted, a humanistic and cultured society (Adorno 1993 [1962]: 11; Jenemann 2007: 8–32).

1.4 A guide for readers

This book can be read from cover to cover and its authors invite every reader to make that journey. Impatient readers can go directly to the Conclusion, where possible answers are outlined of how Motivation

Research as an academic subject and market research practice fitted into this 'Century of the Consumer' and how and why Motivation Research is important today in a research landscape awash with claims about emotional marketing and neuromarketing. Readers will be surprised to learn that Dichter's nemesis, Vance Packard, after having looked at the implications of Dichter's work, predicted the dawn of an age of control-obsessed 'bio-power'.

Readers can delve into particular sections of the book and discover aspects of Ernest Dichter's life and work in more detail. In the first section, they will learn about three crucial aspects of the making of Dichter as the great persuader of post-war consumers: America, consumer psychoanalysis and religion. Daniel Horowitz charts the ways in which Ernest Dichter became 'an American' and looks in more detail at the role of his critics in making Dichter an integral part of American post-war consumer culture. Ronald Fullerton and Mark Tadajewski both present an analysis of Dichter's work as a motivation researcher and his specific take on the psychology of consumer behaviour. Readers with a particular interest in how Dichter's research applied psychoanalysis and ethnography in analysing consumer responses will find much exciting material in these two chapters. Tadajewski and Fullerton provide a sober review of the alleged 'genius' of a great 'manipulator'. Both authors show how Dichter worked within the epistemological constraints of his time and discuss how these constraints defined what he saw – and what he failed to see. Also in this section, Gabriele Sorgo analyses Dichter's difficult relationship with religious thought and his strategies to replace religious beliefs with the maxims of secular salvation.

In the second section of the book, readers will find a collection of 'hands on' material about Dichter's market and consumer research practice. While most of us know some of Dichter's research results in their form as urban mythology (the convertible as 'mistress', the egg in the cake mix), relatively little is known about Dichter's actual research practice for American and European clients. Helene Karmasin, Regina Blaszczyk and Katherine Parkin remedy this by showing how Dichter perceived and drew out the qualities of certain product categories and how he attempted to produce particular styles of consumer behaviour with regards to automobiles, fashion products and food. Reading these case studies, it becomes clear that Dichter saw market and Motivation Research as an art form that combined quantitative research with a kind of semiotic analysis of consumer society that was later spearheaded by Jean Baudrillard (1970).

Karina Krummeich's and Stefanie Lahm's chapter on Dichter's analysis of 'female' products like cosmetics provides a fascinating glimpse at the difficult relationship between Ernest Dichter and the feminist movement in the United States. Following the exploits of Dichter, readers of this section will discover how this man of contradictions tried to sell the idea of mobility and transport in a rapidly changing market, make men more fashion-conscious, educate consumers and marketers alike about the differences between 'male' and 'female' foods (grilled steak vs soft cake) and, finally, how he shifted between encouraging women to further their professional careers while still trying to convince them that a stable social order needed to see them working at the cooker.

Section three will take the reader from a thematic analysis of Dichter's work back to Europe. The four contributions by Andrea Morawetz, Véronique Pouillard, Stefan Schwarzkopf and Dirk Schindelbeck review how Ernest Dichter and his research ideas were received in Europe after 1950. What they show is a continent both in awe and in anger. European attitudes towards Motivation Research conflated curiosity, suspicion, fervent support and ubiquitous anti-Americanism, a combination that made it very difficult for Dichter to set a foot into these markets and move beyond his 'hidden persuader' stereotype. The last section also shows how civil society, legislators and local businesses reacted to Ernest Dichter's ideas. Surprisingly, despite the widespread reservations against Dichter as a person, his style of consumer analysis became quickly absorbed into European market cultures, while the man himself was often rudely kept outside the various national 'inner circles'. In all, it seems that Dichter failed to inspire Europeans as much as he perhaps managed to do so in the more receptive and flexible United States. Nevertheless, as Kai-Uwe Hellmann argues in his chapter, Dichter and his widely publicised research findings acted as a kind of 'midwife' for a new set of European consumer societies. In order to test this hypothesis, Hellmann connects the recent research literature in consumer sociology to a thorough textual reading of how Dichter conceptualised and interpreted his own work during his lifetime.

References

Abrams, M. A. 1960. Review of Ernest Dichter 'The Strategy of Desire'. *Financial Times* [Mark Abrams Papers, Churchill Archive Centre, Churchill College Cambridge, Box 36].

Adorno, T. W. 1993 [1962]. Messages in a bottle. *New Left Review* 200 (July/August): 5–14.

Alderson, W. 1958. Advertising strategy and theories of motivation. In: R. Ferber, H. Wales (Eds), *Motivation and Market Behavior*. Homewood, IL: Richard Irwin, 11–20.

Ames, L. 1998. The view from Peekskill: tending the flame of a motivator. *The New York Times* (2 August).

Arvidsson, A. 2006. *Brands: Meaning and Value in Media Culture*. Abdingdon: Routledge.

Bartos, R. 1977. Ernest Dichter: motive interpreter. *Journal of Advertising Research* 17 (3): 3–9.

Battey, E. 1981. Compton Research Department, 1931–1961. Barton Cummings Papers, Box 8, Folder Compton Research, 1931–1961. Archives Center, National Museum of American History, Smithsonian Institution, Washington, DC.

Baudrillard, J. 1970. *La société de consommation*. Paris: Gallimard.

Bennett, D. 1999. Burghers, burglars, and masturbators: the sovereign spender in the age of consumerism. *New Literary History* 30 (2): 269–294.

——— 2005. Getting the Id to go shopping: psychoanalysis, advertising, Barbie Dolls, and the invention of the consumer unconscious. *Public Culture* 17 (1): 1–25.

Boos, J., Groenendijk, L. Eds. 2007. *The Self-Marginalization of Wilhelm Stekel. Freudian Circles Inside and Out*. New York: Springer.

Bowlby, R. 1993. *Shopping with Freud*. London: Routledge.

Brown, J. A. C. 1963. *Techniques of Persuasion: From Propaganda to Brainwashing*. Harmondsworth: Penguin.

Buğra, A. 2007. Introduction. In: A. Buğra, K. Agartan (Eds), *Reading Karl Polanyi for the Twenty-First Century: Market Economy As a Political Project*. Basingstoke: Palgrave Macmillan, 1–10.

Cantril, H., Koch, H., Gaudet, H., Herzog, H., Wells, H. G. 1940. *The Invasion from Mars: A Study in the Psychology of Panic*. Princeton, NJ: Princeton University Press.

Cheskin, L. 1960. *Why People Buy: Motivation Research and Its Successful Application*. London: Business Publications.

Clarke, P. 2008. Pacifying innovations and America's corporate colonizing: the Elias-Mennell civilizing thesis. *Prometheus* 26 (3): 277–290.

Cooke, B., Mills, A., Kelly, E. 2005. Situating Maslow in Cold War America: a recontextualization of management theory. *Group & Organization Management* 30 (2): 129–152.

Curcio, V. 2000. *Chrysler: The Life and Times of An Automotive Genius*. Oxford: Oxford University Press.

Curtis, A. *Century of the Self*. BBC Documentary. Broadcast April 2002.

Damrow, H. 1981. *Ich war kein geheimer Verführer: aus dem Leben eines Werbeleiters*. Rheinzabern: Gitzel.

Dawson, M. 2003. *The Consumer Trap: Big Business Marketing in American Life*. Urbana: University of Illinois Press.

de Grazia, V. 2005. *Irresistible Empire: America's Advance Through Twentieth-Century Europe*. Cambridge, MA: Belknap.

Dichter, E. 1931. Ist das zuviel? *Der jugendliche Arbeiter*, November: 15.

——— 1934. Die Selbstbeurteilung der eigenen Fähigkeiten und Leistungen. Dissertation, University of Vienna.

—— 1958a. A goal for American foreign policy as seen by a psychologist. Discussion paper, Ernest Dichter Archive, University of Vienna, Report No. 4693.

—— 1958b. Toward an understanding of human behaviour. In: R. Ferber, H. Wales (Eds), *Motivation and Market Behavior*. Homewood, IL: Richard Irwin, 21–31.

—— 1960a. *The Strategy of Desire*. Garden City, NY: Doubleday.

—— 1960b. Motivation research and depth communication. In: Green Meadow Foundation (Ed.), *Motivation Research and Depth Communication*. Zurich: Green Meadow Foundation, 63–73.

—— 1964. *Handbook of Consumer Motivations: The Psychology of the World of Objects*. New York: McGraw-Hill.

—— 1966. Needed: a psychological bridge over the English Channel. Discussion paper, Ernest Dichter Archive, University of Vienna, Report No. 4742.

—— 1970. Communicating internationally. Discussion paper for the United Transportation Union Conference, Chicago. Ernest Dichter Archive, University of Vienna, Report No. 4834.

—— 1971. *Motivating Human Behavior*. New York: McGraw-Hill.

—— 1976. Hedonism: the philosophy of rediscovering the pleasures of life. Discussion paper for the Philip Morris Company, Munich (Germany). Ernest Dichter Archive, University of Vienna, Report No. 4899.

—— 1977. *Motivforschung – mein Leben: die Autobiographie eines kreativ Unzufriedenen*. Frankfurt/Main: Lorch.

—— 1979. *Getting Motivated by Ernest Dichter: The Secret Behind Individual Motivations by the Man Who Was Not Afraid to Ask 'Why'*. New York: Pergamon.

—— 1987. Americanization of Europe and Europeanization of the U.S.: creating the 'Fourth World' through innovative competition. Discussion paper for the Forum for Economy and Development Congress, Alpbach (Austria), July. Ernest Dichter Archive, University of Vienna, Report No. 5054.

—— 1989. Motivating the Japanese consumer. *Journal of International Consumer Marketing* 1 (2): 121–133.

Duchkowitsch, W. 2007. War Ernst Dichter in jungen Jahren ein Sozialist? Ein Beitrag zur Erkundung seiner Autobiographie. In: R. Gries, S. Schwarzkopf (Eds), *Ernest Dichter: Doyen der Verführer*. Vienna: Mucha Verlag, 43–48.

Eidherr, A., Müller, K. Eds. 2003. *Jiddische Kultur und Literatur aus Österreich*. Klagenfurt: DRAVA Verlag.

Ewen, S. 1976. *Captains of Consciousness: Advertising and the Social Roots of the Consumer Culture*. New York: MacGraw-Hill.

Feurstein, M., Milchram, G. 2001. *Jüdisches Wien*. Vienna: Böhlau.

Fleck, C. 2007. *Transatlantische Bereicherungen: Zur Erfindung der empirischen Sozialforschung*. Frankfurt/M.: Suhrkamp.

Fleck, C., Stehr, N. 2007. Von Wien nach New York. In: Fleck, C., Stehr, N. (Eds), *Paul F. Lazarsfeld: Empirische Analyse des Handelns. Ausgewählte Schriften*. Frankfurt/M: Suhrkamp, 7–58.

Fletcher, W. 2006. Ex Libris. *International Journal of Advertising* 25 (1): 121–123.

Frank, T. 1998. *The Conquest of Cool: Business Culture, Counter Culture and the Rise of Hip Consumerism*. Chicago: University of Chicago Press.

Friedan, B. 1963. *The Feminine Mystique*. New York: Norton.

Fullerton, R. 2007. Mr. Mass Motivations himself: explaining Ernest Dichter. *Journal of Consumer Behaviour* 6 (6): 369–382.

Fullerton, R., B. Stern. 1990. The rise and fall of Ernest Dichter. *Werbeforschung und Praxis* (June): 208–211.

Galbraith, J. K. 1958. *The Affluent Society*. Boston: Houghton Mifflin.

Gemici, K. 2008. Karl Polanyi and the antinomies of embeddedness. *Socio-Economic Review* 6: 5–33.

Gries, R. 2003. *Produkte als Medien: Kulturgeschichte der Produktkommunikation in der Bundesrepublik und der DDR*. Leipzig: Leipzig University Press.

——— 2004. Die Geburt des Werbeexperten aus dem Geist der Psychologie. Ernest Dichter: der Motivforscher als Experte der Moderne. In: H. Berghoff, J. Vogel (Eds), *Wirtschaftsgeschichte als Kulturgeschichte: Dimensionen eines Perspektivenwechsels*. Frankfurt/Main: Campus, 353–375.

Gruen, V. 1960. *Shopping Towns, USA: The Planning of Shopping Centres*. New York: Reinhold.

Haineault, D.-L. and Jean-Yves Roy Eds. 1993. *Unconscious for Sale: Advertising, Psychoanalysis and the Public*. Minneapolis: University of Minnesota Press.

Hardwick, J. 2000. *Mall Maker: Victor Gruen, Architect of an American Dream*. Philadelphia, PA: University of Pennsylvania Press.

——— 2005. A Viennese refugee and the re-forming of American consumer society. *Jahrbuch für Wirtschaftsgeschichte* 2: 89–113.

Heilbron, J., Guilhot, N., Jeanpierre, L. 2008. Toward a transnational history of the social sciences. *Journal of the History of the Behavioral Sciences* 44 (2): 146–160.

Henry, H. 1958. *Motivation Research: Its Practice and Uses for Advertising, Marketing and Other Business*. London: Crosby Lockwood.

Herman, E. 1995. *The Romance of American Psychology: Political Culture in the Age of Experts*. Berkeley: University of California Press.

Hirschman, E. C. 2007. Metaphor in the marketplace. *Marketing Theory* 7 (3): 227–228.

Horowitz, D. 1998. The émigré as celebrant of American consumer culture: George Katona and Ernest Dichter. In: S. Strasser, C., McGovern, M. Judt (Eds), *Getting and Spending: European and American Consumption in the Twentieth Century*. Cambridge: Cambridge University Press, 149–166.

Hughes, J. 2006. *Facing Modernity: Fragmentation, Culture and Identity in Joseph Roth's Writing of the 1920s*. Leeds: Maney.

Idel, M. 1990. *Golem: Jewish Magical and Mystical Traditions on the Artificial Anthropoid*. Albany: State University of New York Press.

Isaac, B. L. 2005. Karl Polanyi. In: J. Carrier (Ed.), *A Handbook of Economic Anthropology*. Cheltenham: Edward Elgar, 14–25.

Jenemann, D. 2007. *Adorno in America*. Minneapolis: University of Minnesota Press.

Kassarjian, H. 1994. Scholarly traditions and European roots of American consumer research. In: G. Laurent, G. Lilien, B. Pras (Eds), *Research Traditions in Marketing*. Boston: Kluwer, 265–279.

Kirby, T. 2008. *Selling the Sixties: How Madison Avenue Dreamed the Decade*. BBC Documentary. Broadcast March 2008.

Kreuzer, F., Prechtl, G., Steiner, C. Eds. 2007. *A Tiger in the Tank: Ernest Dichter, An Austrian Advertising Guru.* Riverside: Ariadne Press.

Kropff, H. F. J. 1934. *Psychologie in der Reklame als Hilfe zur Bestgestaltung des Entwurfs.* Stuttgart: Poeschel.

—— 1939. *Die Totalität der Werbung. Ein Beitrag zur Vorbereitung ihrer Rationalisierung und zum Einbau in die neue Absatzlehre.* Berlin: C. Heymann.

—— 1960. *Motivforschung: Methoden und Grenzen.* Essen: Girardet.

Kruke, A. 2007. *Demoskopie in der Bundesrepublik Deutschland: Meinungsforschung, Parteien und Medien, 1949–1990.* Düsseldorf: Droste.

Lahm, S. 2007. Motivation ist alles. *Extradienst* 9: 86–114.

Lazarsfeld, P. 1934. The psychological aspect of market research. *Harvard Business Review* 13: 54–71.

—— 1935. The art of asking 'Why' in marketing research. *National Marketing Review* 1 (1): 32–43.

—— 1937. The use of detailed interviews in market research. *Journal of Marketing* 2 (1): 3–8.

—— 1969. An episode in the history of social research: a memoir. In: D. Fleming, B. Bailyn (Eds), *The Intellectual Migration: Europe and America, 1930–1960.* Cambridge, MA: Harvard University Press, 270–337.

Lears, T. J. Jackson. 1994. *Fables of Abundance: A Cultural History of Advertising in America.* New York: Basic Books.

Levitt, T. 1960. The M–R snake dance. *Harvard Business Review* (November–December): 76–84.

Levy, S. 2003. Roots of marketing and consumer research at the University of Chicago. *Consumption, Markets and Culture* 6 (2): 99–110.

—— 2005. The evolution of qualitative research in consumer behaviour. *Journal of Business Research* 58: 341–347.

Lewis, E. 1923. The emotional quality in advertisements. *JWT News Bulletin* April: 11–14.

Lunt, P., Livingstone, S. 1993. Rethinking the focus group in media and communication research. *Journal of Communication* 46 (2): 79–98.

Mayer, M. 1958. *Madison Avenue, USA.* New York: Harper.

McCracken, G. 1988. *Culture and Consumption: New Approaches to the Symbolic Character of Consumer Goods and Activities.* Bloomington: Indiana University Press.

McKendrick, N., Plumb, J., Brewer, J. 1982. *The Birth of a Consumer Society: The Commercialization of Eighteenth-Century England.* Bloomington: Indiana University Press.

McLeod, A. 2009. 'Pseudo-scientific hokus pokus': motivational research's Australian application. *Journal of Historical Research in Marketing* 1 (2): 224–245.

Mennell, S. 2007. *The American Civilizing Process.* Cambridge: Polity.

Merton, R., Fiske, M., Kendall, P. 1956. *The Focussed Interview.* New York: The Free Press.

Miller, P., Rose, N. 1997. Mobilising the consumer: assembling the subject of consumption. *Theory, Culture and Society* 14 (1): 1–36.

Morrison, D. 1998. *The Search for a Method: Focus Groups and the Development of Mass Communication Research.* Luton: Luton University Press.

Mott, F. L. 1941. *American Journalism: A History of Newspapers in the United States Through 250 Years, 1690–1960.* New York: Palgrave Macmillan.

Nelson, M. 2008. The hidden persuaders: then and now. *Journal of Advertising* 37 (1): 113–126.

Noelle-Neumann, E. 1960. Motivation research in relation to public opinion research and market analysis. In: Green Meadow Foundation (Ed.), *Motivation Research and Depth Communication*. Zurich: Green Meadow Foundation, 75–89.

—— 1963. *Umfragen in der Massengesellschaft: Einfuehrung in die Methoden der Demoskopie*. Reinbek: Rowohlt.

Nuttall, J. 2006. *Psychological Socialism: The Labour Party and Qualities of Mind and Character, 1931 to the Present*. Manchester: Manchester University Press.

Oberschall, A. 1978. Paul F. Lazarsfeld and the history of empirical social research. *Journal of the History of the Behavioural Sciences* 14: 199–206.

Offer, A. 2006. *The Challenge of Affluence: Self-Control and Well-Being in the United States and Britain since 1950*. Oxford: Oxford University Press.

Osgerby, B. 2001. *Playboys in Paradise: Masculinity, Youth and Leisure-Style in Modern America*. Oxford: Berg.

Oxall, I., Weitzmann, W. 1985. The Jews of Pre-1914 Vienna: an exploration of basic sociological dimensions. *Leo Baeck Institute Year Book* 30: 395–434.

Packard, V. 1957. *The Hidden Persuaders*. New York: MacKay.

Paradise, L. M., Blankenship, A. B. 1950. Depth questioning. *Journal of Marketing* 15 (January): 274–288.

Parr, J. 1999. *Domestic Goods: The Material, the Moral and the Economic in the Postwar Years*. Toronto: University of Toronto Press.

Peterman, J. 1956. Ten critical questions about motivation research. *Industrial Marketing* (April): 45–48.

Petiška, E. 1992. *Der Golem: jüdische Sagen und Märchen aus dem alten Prag*. Prague: Martin.

Platt, J. 1996. *A History of Sociological Research Methods in America, 1920–1960*. Cambridge: Cambridge University Press.

Playboy. 1962. The Playboy Panel: the Womanization of America (June).

Polanyi, K. 1944. *The Great Transformation*. Boston, MA: Beacon Press.

Politz, A. 1956–57. 'Motivation research' from a research standpoint. *Public Opinion Quarterly* 20 (Winter): 663–673.

Rodgers, D. 1998. *Atlantic Crossings: Social Politics in a Progressive Age*. Cambridge, MA: Belknap.

Rogers, S. 1992. How a publicity Blitz created the myth of subliminal advertising. *Public Relations Quarterly* (Winter): 12–17.

Roman, K. 2009. *The King of Madison Avenue: David Ogilvy and the Making of Modern Advertising*. New York: Palgrave Macmillan.

Roth, J. 1930. *Hiob: Roman eines einfachen Mannes*. Berlin: Kiepenheuer.

—— 1985 [1927]. *Juden auf der Wanderschaft*. Köln: Kiepenheuer & Witsch.

Rozenblit, M. 1989. *Die Juden Wiens: 1867–1914. Assimilation und Identität*. Vienna: Böhlau.

Scholem, G. 1965. *On the Kabbalah and its Symbolism*. London: Routledge.

—— 1970. Der Golem von Prag. In: G. Scholem (Ed.), *Judaica II*. Frankfurt/M: Suhrkamp, 77–86.

—— 1971. Redemption through sin. In: G. Scholem (Ed.), *The Messianic Idea in Judaism*. London: George Allen, 78–141.

—— 1974. *Kabbalah*. Jerusalem: Keter.

Schor, J. 2007. In defense of consumer critique: revisiting the consumption debates of the twentieth century. *The Annals of the American Academy of Political and Social Science* 611 (May): 16–30.

Schramm, W. 1997. *The Beginnings of Communication Study in America: A Personal Memoir* (S. Chaffee and E. Rogers, Eds). Thousand Oaks, CA: Sage.

Schröter, H. 2005. *Americanization of the European Economy: A Compact Survey of American Economic Influence in Europe since the 1880s*. Dordrecht: Kluwer.

Schudson, M. 1986. *Advertising, the Uneasy Persuasion: Its Dubious Impact on American Society*. New York: Basic Books.

Schumann, D., Haugtvedt, C., Davidson, E. 2008. History of consumer psychology. In: C. Haugtvedt, P. Herr, F. Kardes (Eds), *Handbook of Consumer Psychology*. New York: Lawrence Erlbaum, 3–28.

Schwarzkopf, S. 2007. 'Culture' and the limits of innovation in marketing research: Ernest Dichter, motivation studies and psychoanalytic consumer research in Great Britain, 1950–1970. *Management and Organizational History* 2 (3): 219–236.

——— 2009. Discovering the consumer: market research, product innovation and the creation of brand loyalty in Britain and the United States in the interwar years. *Journal of Macromarketing* 29 (1), 8–20.

Scriven, L. E. 1958. Rationality and irrationality in motivation research. In: R. Ferber, H. G. Wales (Eds), *Motivation and Market Behaviour*. Homewood, IL: Richard Irwin, 64–72.

Semrad, B. 2005. Vertrieben, verdrängt oder vergessen? Die 'Wiener Schule' der Werbeforschung und ihre fachhistorischen Implikationen. *Medien & Zeit* 4 (December): 50–64.

——— 2007. Ein Jude im Wien des frühen zwanzigsten Jahrhunderts: der junge Ernst Dichter. In: R. Gries, S. Schwarzkopf (Eds), *Ernest Dichter: Doyen der Verführer*. Vienna: Mucha Verlag, 32–40.

Sombart, W. 1967 [1913]. *Luxury and Capitalism*. Ann Arbor: University of Michigan Press.

Stanley, A. 2007. Smoking, drinking, cheating and selling. *The New York Times* (19 July).

Stern, B. 2004. The importance of being Ernest: commemorating Dichter's contribution to advertising research. *Journal of Advertising Research* 44 (June): 165–169.

Stryker, P. 1956. Motivation research. *Fortune Magazine* (June): 144–147, 222–226.

Thomas, N. 2008. Will the real 1950s please stand up? Views of a contradictory decade. *Cultural and Social History* 5 (2): 227–236.

Thomson, M. 2006. *Psychological Subjects: Identity, Culture, and Health in Twentieth-Century Britain*. Oxford: Oxford University Press.

Time. 1940. Psychoanalysis in advertising. 25 March: 46–47.

Twitchell, J. 2000. *Lead Us into Temptation: The Triumph of American Materialism*. New York: Columbia University Press.

Warlaumont, H. G. 2001. *Advertising in the 60s: Turncoats, Traditionalists, and Waste Makers in America's Turbulent Decade*. Westport, CT: Praeger.

Whyte, W. 1956. *The Organization Man*. New York: Simon & Schuster.

Williams, R. J. 1957. Is it true what they say about motivation research? *Journal of Marketing* 22 (2): 125–133.

Woolf, J. D. 1958. Depth interviewing useful but overglamorized. In: Advertising Age (Ed.) *The Pros and Cons of Motivation Research.* Chicago: Advertising Age, 81–83.

Zeisel, H. 1979. The Vienna Years. In: R. K. Merton, J. S. Coleman, P. H. Rossi (Eds), *Qualitative and Quantitative Social Research: Papers in Honor of Paul F. Lazarsfeld.* New York: Free Press, 10–15.

Part II

Dimensions of Ernest Dichter's Work and Personality

2
From Vienna to the United States and Back: Ernest Dichter and American Consumer Culture

Daniel Horowitz

2.1   Introduction

Hundreds of thousands of émigrés, most of them Jews, fled Europe in the 1930s and early 1940s as Hitler swept across the European continent. Of those who arrived on the shores of the United States, thousands contributed to key developments in American culture. Typically, their contributions drew on European high culture and they frequently remained aloof from or critical of American culture, which many of them found debased by obedience to the dictates of the mass market. Many intellectuals gave serious attention to an understanding of popular culture but most of them did so with an elitist disdain towards American culture. The most important and critical émigré observers of American culture were members of the Frankfurt School – Herbert Marcuse, Leo Löwenthal, Erich Fromm, Theodor Adorno, Max Horkheimer among them. In their now classic essay *The Culture Industry: Enlightenment as Mass Deception*, first published in 1944, Horkheimer and Adorno asserted that what they called the culture industry had succeeded in shaping taste, as intermediary institutions such as the family had weakened. Capitalism in their eyes powerfully formed consumer culture which, in turn, promoted a false consciousness among consumers, degrading their lives and lulling them into passivity. Adorno and Horkheimer held out the possibility that 'Culture', by which they most prominently meant that inspired by avant-garde creativity, had a critical function in holding up an alternative version of reality. Culture was the only vehicle that could save society from the power of capitalism to shape consumer society. Like Adorno and Horkheimer, most émigrés cast a sceptical eye on American commercial culture. They preferred high culture – whether classical or avant-garde – which they juxtaposed to what they saw as a corrupt American mass culture.

Seen in the context of how other émigrés responded to American consumer culture, Ernest Dichter's distinctiveness is striking. To be sure, he was not the only émigré who responded positively to American culture. From an earlier generation, Edward Bernays, son of Viennese Jewish immigrants and nephew of Sigmund Freud, beginning around the First World War developed a successful career in public relations promoting American goods and services. Paul Lazarsfeld used the techniques of market research he had developed in Vienna to analyse, for the most part dispassionately, American consumer culture. For over a quarter of a century beginning, during and after the Second World War, George Katona, drawing on his surveys of consumer finances and expectations, celebrated intelligence and creative power of the middle-class American consumer. Moreover, in *The Lonely Crowd* (Riesman 1953) native-born David Riesman, drawing on the work of Fromm and Löwenthal, offered an appreciative and nuanced, but often ambivalent understanding of popular culture. Over time Riesman helped legitimise the study of popular culture, a subject on which one of his students, Herbert Gans, another émigré, made major contributions.

Nonetheless, of all the émigrés Ernest Dichter offered the most positive, appreciative and unbridled understanding of American consumer culture, something he promoted relentlessly as a market researcher and writer. More than anyone else, he appreciated and celebrated emerging patterns of mass consumption. He found himself living in his adopted nation, one with a strong, puritanical tradition that saw affluence as a harbinger of immorality and declension. Instead, like millions of Americans, Dichter emphasised the way consumer goods offered pleasure. He linked democracy with purchasing and choice, redefined the roles of middle-class women, and asserted that affluence would aid his adopted land in the fight against Communism abroad. In books, in articles, and in thousands of studies carried out for corporations, he promoted a decidedly anti-puritanical vision, as he called into question the wisdom of social critics such as Vance Packard and John Kenneth Galbraith, whose popular books chastised Americans for their excessive consumption. Drawing on both European psychology and popular Americans beliefs, Dichter offered a vision of a world filled with consumable goods that were symbols of personal growth and creative self-expression. Several of the most influential critics of advertising, including Vance Packard and Betty Friedan, attacked Dichter's work and in the process unwittingly confirmed the centrality of his position in his adopted nation. However, they often shared with him characteristic tenets of American ideology in the 1950s: a focus on white, middle-class America and a sense that the problems of consumer culture could be solved by self-actualising humanistic psychology. In his professional work and in his role as a self-made American man, Dichter absorbed key elements of American consumer culture while still living in Europe, promoted a vividly American view that linked consumption, pleasure and democracy and then, through his role in Americanising European patterns of consumption in the post-war period, gave back to his continent of origin what he had practised in his adopted homeland (Horowitz 1998a; 2004).

2.2 Dichter becomes an American

How Dichter came to make such contributions can be best understood by examining a few key points in his life. Childhood poverty imbued in him an appreciation for a world filled with pleasurable goods. Although there was wealth among his father's relatives, with his father's failure as a travelling salesman, young Dichter faced poverty at least well into his teens. His early encounters with the pleasures of consumer culture in Vienna instilled in him a sense of how to link commerce, pleasure and sexuality. Eager to experiment in developing a sound system for his uncle's department store in the early 1920s, Dichter drew on information in an American magazine and 'flooded the store with music' and thus 'brought a new atmosphere into the cold commercial display of merchandise'. Dichter was thus able to satisfy his father's insistence that his son earn money and contribute it to the household, turning himself into the provider that his father could not be. Through his work in his uncle's store, Dichter later wrote, his uncle had furnished him with 'objects' for his nephew's 'sexual training course'. On company time, he had sexual experiences with a female employee. 'Since all this exploration had to be carried out somewhat hurriedly', Dichter recalled of a time when he was about 17, he and his partner had to be 'very inventive' as they stood 'up behind rows of kitchen utensils and sundry chinaware, glasses, and, around Christmas time, behind dolls and electric trains, waiting to be given a place in the visible shelves at the front of the store' (Dichter 1979).

In addition, Dichter's formal university education provided him with the ideas that would enable him to celebrate American consumer culture. At the University of Vienna, he studied with Charlotte Bühler, one of his principal mentors in psychology. Bühler emphasised self-realisation, personal fulfilment, the process of continuous development, purposefulness and a motivation-based theory of personality. In addition, he was trained by Paul Lazarsfeld in the techniques of commercial market research, which Dichter applied in studies on the milk drinking habits of the Viennese (Dichter 1979: 17; Miksch 1957). With his departure from Vienna in 1937, Dichter began the process of reinventing himself that would be so crucial to his success in America. He and his wife first went to Paris from where they emigrated to the United States in September 1938. By the time he left Europe, he had begun the transformation into a keen interpreter of consumer culture. Selling goods and selling himself were already inextricably linked – through his reaction to his father, through the influence of both his uncle and Lazarsfeld, through his absorption of Bühler's ideas about self-fulfilment, and through his seemingly spontaneous but hardly accidental ability to pitch himself successfully to the vice consul in Paris, who issued the Dichters with their visa. Particularly telling were the processes by which American consumer culture inspired him. Dichter's experience at his uncle's department store was critical. Through what his uncle had learned on his visit across the Atlantic, as well as from Dichter's pouring over American magazines, young Dichter mastered how to connect the spread of consumer goods with pleasure, sexuality and expressiveness.

Dichter began the process of repaying his debt to America by drawing on what he had discovered in Europe. In a particularly revealing incident, Dichter completed the reshaping of his identity shortly after his arrival. A professor of phonetics asked him if he wanted to learn how to drop his Viennese accent. 'The best way to describe what he did with me', Dichter later wrote in a way that drew on the American dream of rebirth through success, 'is to compare it to the kind of job that Prof. Higgins did with Liza in *My Fair Lady*.' When given the choice of what kind of accent he wanted, Dichter decided on 'an all-American one. That way', he asserted, 'people would not be able to quite locate my origin, but would not be suspicious of my foreign background' (*Printers' Ink* 1959; Dichter 1979: 41–42). Yet as a Jew and émigré, Dichter faced resistance from employers. In the 1930s, advertising agencies were bastions of white Protestants with elite college educations. Even when an agency sought Jewish employees, it did so in revealing ways. In 1929, an agency placed an advertisement in *Printers' Ink* for 'Jewish brains', claiming that experience of merchandising was 'inborn' and 'in the blood' (*Printers' Ink* 1929). Early in his American career, when he pushed for adoption of more sophisticated market research methods, his employer responded with 'You refugees and greenhorns are all alike. You barely

Figure 2.1   Ernest Dichter: The Viennese Émigré, Researcher and Intellectual (*c*.1959).

master the language and off you go, trying to change things.' Drawing on American appreciation for entrepreneurship and innovation, Dichter responded angrily. 'I thought this was particularly appreciated in this country. Do things differently and build a better mouse-trap' (Dichter 1979: 33; see Figure 2.1).

2.3   Dichter shapes America

Dichter's success in the United States came quickly and spectacularly, though not always smoothly. Lazarsfeld, who had arrived in 1933 and by 1938 was rapidly earning a reputation as America's most sophisticated market researcher, recommended Dichter for his first job, which Dichter obtained three days after his arrival with a firm called Market Analysts, Inc. at a salary of $30 a week. Dichter's first assignment was a study of milk drinking habits, a topic he had studied under Lazarsfeld in Vienna. Though he did not always acknowledge the influence of his fellow Austrian, Dichter's debt to Lazarsfeld was considerable. The organisation of Lazarsfeld's applied contract work under the auspices of an interdisciplinary research centre in Vienna may have served as a model for Dichter's work after 1946, building on Lazarsfeld's later description of himself as a 'managerial scholar'. Though Lazarsfeld would eventually earn a reputation for rigorous scientific research, in the late 1930s some of his most important work was largely qualitative. In December 1937, he convened a meeting with major American psychoanalysts to explore how Freudian notions of free association and formative childhood experiences might contribute to communications research (Lazarsfeld 1969). Dichter concentrated mainly on developing the qualitative side of Lazarsfeld's approach to psychological market research while neglecting his mentor's emphasis on the quantitative approach (Fullerton in this book; Lazarsfeld 1969).

Determined to find a position that would enable him to try out his ideas, Dichter wrote six companies simple letters: 'I am a young psychologist from Vienna', he noted, 'and I have some interesting new ideas which can help you be more successful, effective, sell more and communicate better with your potential clients.' Aided by Lazarsfeld's recommendations, Dichter received four replies and took a position with *Esquire*, the men's magazine that was in important ways the precursor of *Playboy*. Using depth interviews, Dichter discovered what people at the magazine knew but would not admit – that what attracted subscribers was *Esquire's* pictures of nude women. Dichter later claimed that he had turned this realisation into a sales pitch that emphasised the connection between the impact of the pictures and the readers' receptivity to the visual appeal of advertising. This led him, he argued with some exaggeration, to be the first person to develop the concept of a product's image, or Gestalt (Dichter 1979: 33–35).

While at *Esquire*, Dichter did another study in which he further developed his methods. Carried out for the Compton Advertising Agency in 1939, a contact that Lazarsfeld also was instrumental in making, Dichter's study of Ivory Soap relied on extensive, non-directive interviews where people talked about their experience of bathing. He focused less on the product itself than on people's relationship to it. This market research tactic stood in contrast with the more widely used one of tabulating why people did or did not buy an item. Dichter's extended conversations revealed the importance of a bath or shower as an event preceding a special occasion. Moreover, they demonstrated to Dichter an erotic element in bathing, 'one of the few occasions when the puritanical American was allowed to caress himself or herself'. In addition, Dichter explored the bath as a cultural anthropologist might, as a ritual that involved purification. Finally, the interviews strengthened Dichter's insight into the Gestalt of a product: that aside from the specifics of price, smell and convenience, a bar of soap had a personality that advertisements could elaborate upon. His insights contributed to a new approach in an Ivory advertising campaign: 'Be Smart and Get a Fresh Start with Ivory Soap' (Dichter 1960: 33–34; 1979: 34–35).

Armed with the insights he was developing and again aided by a stroke of good luck, in 1939 Dichter began a study that launched his career. His boss at *Esquire* invited Dichter to go with him to Detroit to help Chrysler with a marketing problem. As a relatively new line, the Plymouth car faced the resistance of people who were loyal to more established brands. Making his presentation to executives from Plymouth and its advertising agency, J. Stirling Getchell, Dichter promised to bring his skills to the situation. Chrysler hired Dichter and he left his job at the magazine. Now he began his work on Plymouth's marketing problem by listening to one hundred consumers. He made two important discoveries. One concerned the importance of women in the decision to buy automobiles, something that knowledgeable people had not always understood and that led Chrysler to place ads in women's magazines – for the first time, he claimed incorrectly, in the history of the automobile industry. In addition, Dichter's interviews revealed the importance of convertibles as items that tempted consumers to look at a wider range of cars. Though they accounted for only 2 per cent of sales, convertibles had tremendous symbolic significance: their display in the showroom brought in customers who often leaned up against one as they discussed buying a less sporty vehicle. Dichter emphasised how frequently consumers connected a convertible with youth and freedom. This was especially true with middle-aged men. They connected a convertible with the thrill they assumed a mistress would bring them, even though they ended up buying a sedan, which reminded them of the comfort and familiarity of their wives.

The Plymouth study launched Dichter's career in the advertising business. Trade magazines picked up the narrative of the car as wife or mistress, and *Time* followed suit with an article, one that contained a photograph of Dichter, who had been in the United States for less than two years. In March 1940, the news magazine described him as 'a small, neat, emphatic man who speaks almost perfect English' who claimed 'that he is the first to apply to advertising the really scientific psychology', one that tapped 'hidden desires and urges'. The Getchell advertising agency, *Time* predicted, would soon issue 'its first completely Dichterized advertisements, for Plymouth cars. Probable motif: the subconscious lure of adventure on the open road, the deep passion to master a machine' (*Time* 1940).

Notoriety brought Dichter numerous offers and a well-rewarded job as a director of psychological research with J. Stirling Getchell, who more than anyone else shaped American advertising in the 1930s. The firm earned a $1.5 million contract with Chrysler and Dichter used his $600 bonus to buy his first car. By 1940, his salary was $150 a week, equivalent to about $100,000 a year in 2006 dollars. The Dichters were now also secure enough, financially and from Hitler's reach, to start a family. When his son Thomas William was born in June 1941, during the days when Hitler invaded Russia, Dichter announced to his wife, 'This is it. Hitler has lost the war!', a remark that meant that the invasion was a mistake and that the family was now safe. Their daughter Susan Jane was born two years later. It was no accident that the Dichters gave both children what their father acknowledged as 'unmistakeably [sic] American names' (Dichter 1979: 14).

Thus, remarkably soon after his arrival in the United States, Dichter had established himself as a player in the games played by promoters of consumerism. In less than three years after he stepped off the boat in 1938, he had virtually lost his Austrian accent and given his children an American birthright. Icons of American consumer culture – *Esquire*, Madison Avenue, *Time*, Ivory Soap and Chrysler automobiles – had all played key roles in both his success and his connection to his adopted nation's commercial culture. Ambition, luck, optimism, connections and skill turned his life into a distinctive version of the American success story. Already apparent was his articulation of key elements that underscored the 'Americanness' of his contribution. He tapped into the nation's penchant for believing that forces and people operating in secret conspired to shape history even as he turned the conspiracy of motivational researchers into an engine of frictionless material and even spiritual progress.

Like American Freudians, he turned Freud's deeply pessimistic credo into an optimistic one. In the process, Dichter transformed dark and tragic sexual urges into pleasurable ones linked to individual self-fulfilment. His emphasis on pleasure – served up in a way that combined sexuality and masculinity – countered the puritanical tradition long articulated by American intellectuals and embraced an equally American emphasis on pleasures and affluence. He well understood that the pursuit of a higher standard of living was central to the nation's experience of the 1930s. In working on campaigns that promoted the pleasures of using soap while taking a bath or shower with hot water, and of taking the family for a ride in an automobile, he connected the purchase of goods with participation in democratic consumption communities. Above all, he succeeded in linking the chase after a higher standard of living with self-fulfilment and the pursuit of the American dream of making it in an abundant society.

2.4   America encounters Dichter

Nothing more tellingly underscores how central a figure he was in American life than the criticism of him that two writers – Vance Packard and Betty Friedan – levelled against him in the late 1950s and early 1960s. Although by the mid-1950s Dichter had established himself as a major figure in American advertising, it was Vance Packard's publication of his bestselling *The Hidden Persuaders* (1957a) that was successful in bringing Dichter notoriety and business. *Hidden Persuaders* was an exposé of the way market researchers and advertisers used depth psychology, especially motivational research (MR), to probe the emotions of consumers so that appeals could play upon hidden and irrational desires. Acknowledging that some people called him 'Mr. Mass Motivations Himself', Packard mentioned Dichter, 'the most famed of these depth probers', much more frequently than his principal competitors, Louis Cheskin, Pierre Martineau and Burleigh Gardner. Packard had two principal objections to Dichter's work. One was that his use of MR was undermining Americans' resistance to mass consumption, bringing in its wake commercialism, an empty abundance and self-indulgence. Secondly, Packard worried that MR involved a gross invasion of privacy and provided a dangerous example of the way experts and corporations were manipulating a largely innocent American public as they encouraged their irrational behaviour. As Packard argued during a 1957 radio debate with Dichter, given his own commitment to 'self-guidance and individuality', that he had serious misgivings about the way 'advertisers are learning to play upon these subconscious needs without our awareness' (Horowitz 1994; Packard 1957b).

Although Packard's bestselling book offered a critique of MR, it had an unintended effect. Once people involved in advertising read *Hidden Persuaders*, Dichter's phone rang from across the nation and some people assumed that he had paid Packard for the useful publicity. Packard's criticism gave Dichter celebrity status, with radio, television and speaking appearances in the United States, as well as invitations from around the world. Dichter established small franchised offices in more than a dozen cities in the United States and abroad. In the late 1950s and early 1960s, Dichter's operation had about $1 million in revenues, equal to roughly $7.5 million in 2006 dollars. Shortly after *Hidden Persuaders* appeared, Dichter answered Packard's charges. At first, he did so in the monthly publication of his Institute for Motivational Research, responding that persuasion was a normal part of life, with the psychological seduction of children, which Packard had blamed on MR, being 'a natural process which starts on the very first day of the child's life' with the child's dependence on the mother (Dichter 1957b).

However, Dichter was not satisfied with defending himself only to his clients. Yearning to realise his desire to become accepted as a social philosopher, and to defend MR from its detractors, he was soon at work on a more ambitious response geared to a larger audience, one that answered Packard's *Hidden Persuaders* and Galbraith's *Affluent Society* (1958). Already with the publication of *The Psychology of Everyday Living* ten years before the appearance of Packard's book in 1957, Dichter had begun to articulate his social ideology in broad terms. Now, in *The Strategy of Desire* (1960), he brought together much of his previous work and provided the most ambitious, if still unsystematised, synthesis of his outlook. Here Dichter moved more fully than he had done before to translate the findings of market research into social philosophy. In the process, he articulated how he hoped to recast American society in the post-war period. More so than he had done before, he now connected the spiritual and the material. He asserted that the purchasing of commercial goods and services rested on creative discontent and connected to personal self-fulfilment. He celebrated American middle-class consumers as a group that countered the evils of both Nazi and Soviet society. To him, consumer culture offered Cold War American democracy progress, pleasure and self-realisation.

2.5   Dichter and the American woman

While Vance Packard in *Hidden Persuaders* had criticised Dichter for the way he celebrated commercialism and eroded personal selfhood, Betty Friedan in *The Feminine Mystique* attacked him for being 'this most helpful of hidden persuaders' who connected the purchase of things with the way the housewife achieved personal satisfaction, selfhood and sexual fulfilment (Friedan 1963: 208; Horowitz 1998b). In the chapter of her book called 'The Sexual Sell', she began her discussion of Dichter's work with his 1945 study of the marketing of household appliances. With this study, Friedan reported, Dichter advised manufacturers that the most promising market they should exploit was not among career women or committed housewives but among what he called 'The Balanced Homemaker', women who worked at home but maintained outside interests, including the memory of or hope for a career. These women, Friedan reported Dichter as saying, could be convinced to treat home-making as a career as advertisers persuaded them to gain a sense of achievement and creativity from cleaning, cooking and child care. By the mid-1950s, Friedan argued, Dichter's surveys 'reported with plea-sure' the disappearance of the career woman. Market research could now concentrate, she reported, on encouraging the housewife to find 'in housework a medium of expression for her femininity and individ-uality' by associating creativity with consumer products (Friedan 1963: 209–210, 213). Friedan relied on Dichter's construction of womanhood, and on other sources, to launch her scathing and influential depiction of middle-class American women trapped in what she called the suburban 'concentration camp'. Her publication of *The Feminine Mystique*, read by millions of captivated readers, helped revive American feminism – some-thing confirmed in 1996 when Friedan was chosen as the president of the National Organization for Women, the first major feminist women's organisation in the post-war world.

Friedan had most of the basic elements of the story right but the chronology and some elements wrong. The pressure for women to asso-ciate consumption with creativity, which she tended to see as a post-war phenomenon, had been going on for a long time. It is impossible to understand Dichter's vision of the role of women in a consumer society without recognising the larger intellectual context in which he worked. If Dichter's relationship with those who hired him necessitated that he pay minimal attention to race and class, the opposite was the case with gender. With women as the purchasers of a very high percentage of the kinds of goods Dichter worked to promote, they comprised a similarly high proportion of the people he interviewed. Moreover, men in the advertising business had traditionally seen women consumers as easily swayed by emotional appeals, a tendency that Dichter's emphasis on the irrational seemed to reinforce. In addition, Dichter's discussion of the relationship between his work and women's roles was inseparable from his larger vision. Central to his response to women's situation was his emphasis on consumption as therapy; his insistence on the central-ity of the creative discontent of the consumer; the stress on realistic solutions to relieve frustration; and his belief that his job was to show corporations how to link pleasure with purchases in order to overcome the heritage of puritanical self-restraint.

If Friedan did not recognise the pre-1945 origins of Dichter's vision, she nonetheless correctly realised that it was Dichter's 1945 study of home appliances that set the stage for his post-war reconstruction of American womanhood. Here, Dichter developed his classification of three types of women that would dominate his analysis of the female market for at least the next 15 years. The first group was 'Career Woman'. Even though many of them never had careers, they believed 'they would be happier if they were not "imprisoned" in their homes'. This group did their housework 'only under protest and felt they are wasting their energies'. Consequently, their expectations for products were 'usually unreasonable and unrealistic', in good measure because they had 'no vital, personal relationships' to what they purchased. Although Dichter did not wish to pursue 'the neurotic basis' of their rejection of the role of homemaker, he made it clear that because their attitudes were not 'very healthy' they were not 'the ideal type of consumer'. The 'Pure Housewife' was also apt to be too critical of products, but for a different reason: 'Because her housewife role is her whole life she has to prove to herself and others that she is absolutely indispensable and that nobody else could take over her job.' As a consequence, she tended to be too fearful and critical in her response to appliances, nostalgically preferring the familiar ways (Dichter 1945a).

Finally, there was the 'Balanced Woman', Dichter's favourite, whom he described as the most fulfilled emotionally and 'a mature and responsible member of society'. This type of woman, Dichter wrote, 'combines the desire to compete with other women in jobs with a keen interest in an individual and well cared for home managed by herself'. What made this type appealing to Dichter was her 'feeling of confidence which comes with knowing that she is capable' of both housework and career. For some, career might be in the past or future; for others, the outside interest involved being a student or volunteer, activities that 'broaden the basis of the woman's life and give her the feeling of satisfaction'. Dichter predicted that over the coming years this group would become more common, principally because two world wars and a depression had convinced Americans that women 'are not economically safe if they are not able to perform some type of work in addition to being a housewife'. Still, even though this balanced type derived pleasure from activities outside the home, she placed considerable emphasis on the home as 'an end in it itself ... a center to which to return from the city's adventures and activities … a cozy shelter from an indifferent outside world' (Dichter 1945a: 7–10, 16).

If Friedan did not realise that before 1945 Dichter had developed a framework that would help reshape women's lives in the post-war world, she cogently told how Dichter worked to squelch women's independence, and how he set out to manipulate women's desires in order to increase sales. She also well understood how he used the language of science and professionalism to give women the illusion of achievement; how he promoted labour-saving methods that did little to relieve drudgery; and how he played on women's guilt over not being perfect housekeepers. She understood that by the mid-1950s Dichter had stopped interviewing the career woman in order to focus on the Balanced and Pure types and that he linked creativity with housework.

It was this analysis of the types of housewives that provided the basis of Dichter's advice to corporations on how to take advantage of his findings. Because it was the wave of the future, manufacturers should target the balanced type, 'educating women to have outside interests and better themselves intellectually', with the time for such interests made available by labour-saving appliances. Secondly, products should be designed for this type of woman, so that a homemaker could lighten her household duties and, at the same time, 'make her home more individual and more home-like'. Women, he wrote, wanted 'to have their cake and eat it too'. On the one hand, they wanted to save time, eliminate dirt and gain comfort. On the other hand, 'they do not want to give up their feeling of personal achievement and pride in a well run household which "doing it yourself" provides'. This woman 'finds beauty, sense and balance in housework', Dichter asserted, through 'intelligent planning and organization' (Dichter 1945a: 10). Dichter thus told his clients

> to make more and more women aware of the desirability of belonging to this group. Educate them through advertising that it is possible to have outside interests and become alert to wider intellectual influences (without becoming a Career Woman). The art of good homemaking should be the goal of every normal woman.
>
> (Dichter, quoted in Friedan 1963: 210)

Throughout the 1950s, Dichter focused his attention on teaching American women how to find creativity in housework. He advised women to relieve their tensions by solving specific problems. Much of what he focused on was ways to make housework palatable to housewives. In a 1945 study of the new medium of television, he argued that to work against women's guilt for watching, it was necessary to provide programmes that would help in housework and shopping, thus providing a 'legitimate excuse for tuning in daytime programs' that did not require full concentration (Dichter 1945b). In *The Psychology of Everyday Living* (1947), he told women to make their housework interesting by introducing 'numerous variations and surprises'. He praised cooking at home as a job not to be scorned: on close examination, he argued, women 'will discover that, compared with other fields requiring skill and years of training, the preparation of food is a highly respectable occupation'. He advised women to use bulletin boards and filing cabinets to help make the kitchen 'the center of household management'. By organising kitchen work, using modern recipes, and developing 'a production plan', he told women, they would be on the road to acquiring 'your kitchen degree' (Dichter 1947: 18, 27, 230–231; 1957a). As late as 1964, Dichter urged manufacturers of household products to 'establish genuine communication with the housewife' by sympathising 'with her problems and feelings', emphasising with 'her kingpin role in the family' and helping 'her be an expert' (Dichter 1964: 126–127).

Nowhere was Dichter's strategy more revealing than in the study for which he became most famous: his advice that the food company General Mills promote their Betty Crocker-branded flour mix 'Bisquick' as a product through which women could express their creativity. After the Second World War, General Mills developed a version of 'Bisquick' to which women had to add only water because powdered milk and eggs were included. In fact, women added eggs and milk because they could not believe a cake could be made without these ingredients. As *Newsweek* reported in 1955, Dichter convinced General Mills 'that cooking was not just a chore to most housewives but an important symbol of their status in the family and an outlet for their creativeness' (*Newsweek* 1955). Dichter recommended that in its advertisements General Mills should emphasise that women and Betty Crocker's 'Bisquick' would do the job together, leaving some room for the housewife's creativity.

In his efforts to shape women's identity, Dichter focused not only on housework but also on ways corporations could reshape women's images of their bodies. In this endeavour, his work on cosmetics played a central role. In 1947 he wrote that women use make-up as a 'form of psychological therapy' in order 'to get rid of an awareness of personal inferiority, real or imagined' (Dichter 1947: 143). In 1949, he noted that advertisements for deodorants could help women 'consider themselves smart body technicians' (Dichter 1949). A 1956 study identified emerging notions of beauty but persisted in aiding corporations to take advantage of women's emotional insecurities. Here Dichter underscored the challenge cosmetic manufacturers faced because of the conflicts that resulted from the tension between old and new values. In place of an emphasis on 'pure sex per se' was coming a stress on 'fantasy, whimsy, or poetry' that involved 'more subtle and passive sex symbols'. Moreover, the vacuum created by the demise of 'sex as the chief meaning of beauty' meant that women wished 'to gain attraction as a more complete human being'. Rather than pitching cosmetics to women in 'extreme emotional situations', the time when they usually purchased them, Dichter urged advertisers to play on their subconscious awareness of the 'beneficent effects of cosmetics' by telling them that 'taking care of their appearance will do marvels for them *every* day'. In all these ways, it was possible to promote cosmetics as the woman's 'intimate allies' in building a 'favorable self-image' (Dichter 1956).

2.6 Dichter: unique among outsiders?

As far as can be determined, Dichter never responded directly to Friedan's *Feminine Mystique*. Just as she had written her chapter on 'The Sexual Sell' without mentioning her adversary by name in the text, referring to him only as 'the manipulator', Dichter returned the favour when he attacked women's liberation without using the name of the person whose book and organising revived the women's movement. Friedan, herself educated by émigrés at Smith College, never mentioned Dichter's Viennese background or remnants of his Austrian accent. In contrast, in *The Hidden Persuaders* Packard, quintessentially American in his transformation from a son of a farmer to a self-made successful writer, remarked that in the 1940s Dichter still spoke 'broken English'. Yet as figures who were among the most influential social critics of the late 1950s and early 1960s, Packard and Friedan confirmed Dichter's position as a major force in shaping American post-war consumer society.

In a whole range of ways, Ernest Dichter's take and impact on American consumer culture remained distinctive, especially when measured with that of other émigrés. Compared with all the others who fled Europe as Nazism spread across the continent, Dichter celebrated commercial culture, salesmanship and the good life as defined by the increasing spread of materialism. While most other émigrés embraced an elevating culture or an adversarial idea of avant-garde, Dichter linked democracy, capitalism, a rising standard of living and consumer culture. He promoted and confirmed the crucial role of suburban, middle-class women in the post-war American economy. He challenged those who, like Friedan, Galbraith and Packard, equated the pursuit of a higher standard of living with moral declension. Instead, Dichter used a tamed version of Freudian psychology to connect pleasure, purchases and personal growth. Trained in Europe but influenced by American culture from an early age, he drew on a range of American traditions – the quest for self-improvement and success through material pleasures the chief among them.

Like most of the émigrés who arrived in the United States in the 1930s and early 1940s Dichter remained in the country even when it became possible to return to Europe. To be sure, there are notable exceptions, like Theodor Adorno, Thomas Mann and Max Horkheimer, who returned to Germany in the late 1940s and early 1950s. However, the great majority of émigrés stayed on. They remained even though many of them, unlike Dichter, kept their distance from American popular culture, taking refuge in émigré communities or in the hope that refined or adversarial culture would enable them to keep their distance from what many of them saw as the crass and soporific qualities of America as a mass society. Dichter rarely gave serious consideration to returning to Vienna to live. However, during the early 1950s when McCarthyism held sway, perhaps sensing a similarity between hysterical American anti-communism and the Nazism that drove him from Europe, Dichter considered returning to Europe to live. Instead, he remained, and celebrated a democracy that was tough minded and realistic – more interested in reducing frustration by solving specific problems than in chasing after abstract and what he felt were unachievable goals. And yet, he acknowledged the importance of his Viennese years when he donated his papers to the University of Vienna – just as this book of essays recognises the transatlantic nature of his inspiration and contribution.

References

Dichter, E. 1945a. Electrical appliances in the postwar world: a psychological study of women's attitudes. Report for Crowell Collier Publishing Corporation, Ernest Dichter Archive, University of Vienna, Report No. 4164.
——— 1945b. Studies in television. *Tide* 19 (1 April): 110.
——— 1947. *The Psychology of Everyday Living*. New York: Barnes and Noble.
——— 1949. A psychological view of advertising effectiveness. *Journal of Marketing* 14 (July): 61–67.
——— 1956. The five new meanings of beauty. *Motivations* 1 (May): 8–11.
——— 1957a. The psychology of house cleaning products. *Motivations* 2 (May): 10–13.

———— 1957b. Persuasion: to what end? *Motivations* 2 (June): 15–16.

———— 1960. *The Strategy of Desire*. Garden City, NY: Doubleday.

———— 1964. *Handbook of Consumer Motivations: The Psychology of the World of Objects*. New York: McGraw-Hill.

———— 1979. *Getting Motivated by Ernest Dichter: The Secret Behind Individual Motivations by the Man Who Was Not Afraid to Ask 'Why?'*. New York: Pergamon.

Friedan, B. 1963. *The Feminine Mystique*. New York: W.W. Norton.

Galbraith, J. K. 1958. *The Affluent Society*. Boston: Houghton Mifflin.

Horowitz, D. 1994. *Vance Packard and American Social Criticism*. Chapel Hill, NC: University of North Carolina Press.

———— 1998a. The émigré as celebrant of American consumer culture: George Katona and Ernest Dichter. In: S. Strasser, C. McGovern, M. Judt (Eds), *Getting and Spending: European and American Consumer Societies in the Twentieth Century*. Cambridge: Cambridge University Press, 149–166.

———— 1998b. *Betty Friedan and the Making of 'The Feminine Mystique': The American Left, The Cold War, and Modern Feminism*. Amherst, MA: University of Massachusetts Press.

———— 2004. *The Anxieties of Affluence: Critiques of American Consumer Culture, 1939–1979*. Amherst, MA: University of Massachusetts Press.

Lazarsfeld, P. 1969. An episode in the history of social research: a memoir. In: D. Fleming, B. Bailyn (Eds), *The Intellectual Migration: Europe and America, 1930–1960*. Cambridge, MA: Harvard University Press, 270–337.

Miksch, B. 1957. Inside Dr. Dichter. *Sponsor* 3 August: 36.

Newsweek. 1955. Inside the consumer. The new debate: does he know his own mind? 10 October: 92.

Packard, V. 1957a. *The Hidden Persuaders*. New York: McKay.

———— 1957b. Transcript for NBC radio programme 'Conversation'. 6 May 1957: 13. Vance Packard Papers, Penn State University Library, University Park, Pennsylvania.

Printers' Ink. 1929. Jewish Brains. 11 April: 193.

———— 1959. Ernest Dichter of Croton: a doctor for ailing products. 26 June: 72.

Riesman, D. 1953. *The Lonely Crowd: A Study of the Changing American Character*. Garden City, NY: Doubleday.

Time. 1940. Psychoanalysis in advertising. 25 March: 46–47.

3
Ernest Dichter: The Motivational Researcher

Ronald Fullerton

3.1 'Mr Mass Motivations'

Dr Ernest Dichter was more, much more, than people now think; and he was less, much less, than he claimed to be. During the 1950s and into the 1960s, he was one of the best-known individuals in the Western world. No business consultant was better known, more highly paid – or more controversial. Fellow motivation researchers denounced him, social critics saw his work as dangerous manipulation; his business thrived. In this chapter, I want to show what he was, and what he was not. Dichter was a gifted practitioner of observation and in-depth interviewing (at least until he decided that he did not need to use them anymore), and an unusually imaginative interpreter of his research findings. He provided real value to clients for many years. He was extremely adept at securing publicity for himself. On the other hand, Dichter was neither the founding father of 'Motivation Research' nor its only significant practitioner. He utilised only a few of the many tools and concepts associated with Motivation Research. He left no methodological legacy – nothing that could be passed onto future adherents of Motivation Research.

Dichter's claims of unique psychoanalytic insight into the unconscious depths of consumers' minds helped him build a lucrative consulting business. Business leaders, advertising professionals, journalists, even academics, attributed to Dichter near-magical powers to penetrate to the very heart of consumer motivations. Seeking audience with 'Mr Mass Motivations', as he liked to call himself, many made their way up a steep dirt road to his castle-like headquarters on a hill in Croton-on-Hudson, some 50 kilometres north of New York City. During his visits to Germany in 1955 and 1958, business people queued up like patients for a miracle doctor, awaiting the chance to press money into the hands of 'The King of the Market Researchers' (Kropff 1960), hoping to receive a few words of advice. He opened branches in the United Kingdom, in France, in Austria and in Italy. He earned a million dollars a year.

Dichter himself liked to claim that his own unique genius underlay his success. Even as a young immigrant to the United States he claimed to the mass-circulation *Time* news magazine in 1940 to be 'the first to apply to advertising really scientific psychology. . . . in tapping hidden desires and urges' (*Time* 1940). Addressing an advertising convention in Miami Beach 15 years later, Dichter proclaimed that his insights into consumers' motivations were part of the 'major revolution in thinking [which] has been taking place . . . in atomic science . . . [and] in the biological sciences' (Dichter 1956). All pre-Dichter market research had been, he continued, 'somewhat like the medicine man of a primitive tribe who concluded that dark nights cause pregnancy because he had observed a perfect correlation between dark nights and the consequent pregnancy of the tribal maidens who walked out on such nights'. Repeatedly, he belittled conventional market researchers as 'nose counters' and 'census takers' (Dichter 1956). He alone could decipher 'the human facts which explain the dynamics of communication' (Dichter 1961). Boasting to the journalist Vance Packard in the mid-1950s (Packard 1957), in his autobiography in the late 1970s (Dichter 1977), and again to the advertising executive Rena Bartos (Bartos 1986) during the 1980s, Dichter portrayed himself as the founding genius of Motivation Research. During the 1940s and 1950s, Dichter was able to exploit his own background to portray himself as a master of two enormously popular, related intellectual trends, psychoanalysis and 'Motivation Research'. By associating himself with the most titillating, sexually oriented, variant of psychoanalysis, he was able to demonstrate operationally that 'sex sells'.

3.2   Dichter and Freudian psychoanalysis

Dichter had studied psychology in France and Austria, but his knowledge was eclectic rather than specialised. He was clever, however, to portray himself as the master of using Freudian sexual psychoanalytic insights to elucidate consumer motives. He was thus able not only to capitalise on the attention-arousing power of sexual explanations, but also to exploit the esteem of psychoanalysis, which was at its peak during the 1940s and 1950s. Among the educated it became a given that psychoanalysis offered profound insights into human behaviour. Psychoanalysis had been developed to help miserably tortured, dysfunctional people, for example, hysterics and kleptomaniacs. One of Freud's most famous cases involved the 'Rat Man', who fantasised rats gnawing at his anus. During the 1940s and 1950s, however, it was widely assumed that psychoanalysis offered profound insights even into 'normal' behaviour – an attitude that Dichter gleefully exploited. Having lived and worked on the same street in Vienna as Sigmund Freud himself, although he had never once met the great man, and having been given some lessons in psychoanalysis in Vienna by an early disciple of Freud, Dichter claimed that his Viennese background had given him unusual psychoanalytic understanding: the ability to penetrate far below consciousness and defensive mechanisms, into the very heart of human motivation.

Dichter had attempted to make a living as a lay psychoanalyst for a few years after 1934 but had to work in market research to supplement his income. He had undergone neither extensive training in psychoanalysis nor medical training, then considered essential for psychoanalysts. His doctorate, a first-level European doctorate closer to an American Masters than to an American doctorate, at the University of Vienna was done under Charlotte Bühler, whose work was closer to German experimental psychology than to psychoanalysis. Associating himself with psychoanalysis contributed mightily to Dichter's reputation, but the depth of his grounding in it was questionable.

Much of Dichter's career appears to reflect the influence of the 'rogue' psychoanalyst from whom he actually had taken lessons. Dr Wilhelm Stekel (1868–1940) gave Dichter some lessons in psychoanalysis, presumably at some point during the early 1930s. Stekel had been an early follower of Freud; his intuitive understanding of symbols inspired Freud to add a section on symbolism to the third edition of his famous *The Interpretation of Dreams.* By the time that Dichter worked with him, however, Stekel had long since been banished from Freud's circle. Like his pupil, Dichter, he over-relied upon intuition and exhibited cavalier attitudes towards both accuracy and scientific integrity. After about 1915, Freud considered him a pleasant fellow but a disgrace to psychoanalysis, eventually describing him as an example of 'moral insanity' (Jones 1964).

Nonetheless, Dichter could with some justification claim to have learned something at the feet of one of the pioneers of psychoanalysis. He was hardly the first to apply psychoanalytic thinking to business issues. That consumer motives were often veiled, even unconscious, and needed psychological interpretation had been stressed on both sides of the Atlantic by the early 1930s, for example, by the German Otto Breyer

(Breyer 1929), by the Austrian advertising consultant Hanns F. J. Kropff (Kropff 1934), by the Austrian émigré Paul F. Lazarsfeld (1935) and by the American Donald Anderson Laird in his 1935 book *What Makes People Buy*, which explained to business executives that 'the dynamics of human nature is in its unconscious' (Laird 1935).

Freud's version of psychoanalysis emphasised the sexual roots of much conduct. Other versions of 'depth psychology', such as those of Alfred Adler and Carl Jung, did not. Adler and Jung had begun as disciples of Freud but then broke away to establish their own theories about the unconscious drivers of human thought and conduct. Dichter emphasised sexual interpretation, no doubt out of conviction – yet there is no denying that sex is more compelling to most people than Adler's inferiority complexes or Jung's collective unconscious. Dichter's pronouncements, issued during an era when movies had to show married couples having twin beds, had prurient appeal. The lure of cigarette smoking, Dichter argued in 1947, had to take into account that 'Smoking is oral pleasure. [Part of the pleasure derived from smoking comes from] the powerful erotic sensitivity of the oral zone' (Dichter 1947b). Katherine Parkin has shown how *Motivations*, Dichter's monthly newsletter, was filled with sexual explication of market phenomena (Parkin 2007). Read closely, many of Dichter's analyses are based on Adler's inferiority complex. But his public persona flaunted Freudian sexuality. Dichter could find sexuality in the most astounding places, as in his descriptions of asparagus and wood in his seminal *Handbook of Consumer Motivations* (Dichter 1964): asparagus, because of its peculiar shape, easily acquires a phallic significance and in its very cultivation and growth makes this sexual significance possible; wood is sensuous, and as people typically pick up samples of wood they turn them over and over in their hands, allowing their palms and fingers to move over the surface.

3.3 Dichter and Motivation Research

Motivation Research (MR) was considerably more than merely the use of psychoanalytic insights in market analysis. It drew upon several behavioural social sciences, including schools of psychology that were quite distinct from Freudian psychoanalysis. MR utilised several ways of interpreting market information. It attracted growing attention from both academics and business executives. Motivation researchers strove to uncover the underlying motivations that were believed to govern much of buyer behaviour. 'In motivational research', explained the

Columbia University sociologist Paul F. Lazarsfeld in 1943, 'we change our focus to sub-surface phenomena'. This was essential, he continued, because some buyer motivations were unconscious, others only partly conscious. Buyers might have forgotten, or they might have rationalised their motives (Lazarsfeld 1943). Motivations were presumed to be closely linked to attitudes. 'What people do is intimately related to their inner feelings and perceptions', wrote the Rutgers University psychologist Smith. 'The motivation researcher', he continued, 'seeks to reinterpret product features and communications material through the eyes of the consumer' (Smith 1954: 3). By the late 1940s, marketers were showing considerable interest in using the newer social science techniques to improve both their marketing and their internal relations with employees. Advertising researchers were prominent, but hardly the only marketers interested. MR had great promise, concluded a task force of the American Marketing Association in 1950: the 'best brains in all the social sciences' could be of enormous aid to marketing executives (Woodward et al. 1950).

By the mid-1950s, several large-scale commercial organisations were conducting motivational studies. The researchers included respected social scientists such as Steuart Henderson Britt, Burleigh B. Gardner, Herta Herzog, Pierre Martineau and Dr W. Lloyd Warner. Many were affiliated with advertising agencies. Herta Herzog, Paul Lazarsfeld's second wife, had conducted psychological research with the Lazarsfeld organisation in Vienna before 1934. Rejoining her husband in New York during the mid-1930s, she became the most powerful woman in the American advertising community. Her work was more careful than that of Dichter, utilizing a series of stages that included structured questionnaires after depth-interviewing 300–400 consumers (Collins and Montgomery 1969). The social class studies of Martineau and Warner were used for decades by advertising firms and other market analysts. Stuart Henderson Britt, who had one of the most dynamic Motivation Research units in American advertising, had been an active motivation researcher since the second half of the 1940s. Burleigh B. Gardner was the head of Social Research, Inc., a firm that specialised in the application of social science to practical matters. He had begun motivational research by conducting personnel research for the Western Electric Company (Collins and Montgomery 1969). Several independent marketing consultants also played major roles. These included Louis Cheskin, who pioneered the study of consumer responses to colour, James Vicary, who famously claimed to have subliminally manipulated movie theatre patrons to buy popcorn and of course Ernest Dichter,

Table 3.1 Major Motivation Research leaders and organisations (*c.* 1954)

Principle Investigator	Organisation Affiliation	Location
Britt, Dr Stuart Henderson	Needham, Lewis, Brorby Advertising	Chicago
Dichter, Dr Ernest	Institute for Motivational Research	Croton, NY
Gardner, Dr Burleigh B.	University of Chicago; Social Research, Inc.	Chicago
Herzog, Dr Herta	McCann-Erickson Advertising	New York
Martineau, Pierre	Chicago *Tribune* (newspaper)	Chicago
Stevens, William	Young and Rubicam Advertising	New York
Twedt, Dr Dik Warren	Needham, Lewis, Brorby Advertising	Chicago
Warner, Dr W. Lloyd	University of Chicago; Social Research, Inc.	Chicago

Source: Fullerton 2005.

who was believed to be the most commercially successful of them all (Table 3.1).

3.4 The origins of Motivation Research

Evidently, Dichter was hardly the only prominent motivation researcher. Nor was he the 'Father of Motivation Research', as his methods had really been developed by others. What became Motivation Research began in Europe during the 1920s and 1930s, first in the group surrounding Wilhelm Vershofen at the Society for Consumption Research (GfK – Gesellschaft für Konsumforschung) in Nuremberg (Vershofen 1937; 1940), and secondly in the work carried out by Paul F. Lazarsfeld and his colleagues at the University of Vienna after 1927. Lazarsfeld had established the Institute for Economic Psychology (Wirtschaftspsychologische Forschungsstelle) in 1927, which funded itself by conducting commercial market research studies. The work done by this institute was, particularly in its psychological depth, far in advance of that done then in the United States and elsewhere in Europe. Lazarsfeld avoided the simplistic, later-discarded typologies of 'innate' psychological instincts that dominated American literature under the influence of the mechanistic notions of Watson's 'Behaviourism'. Lazarsfeld's institute conducted studies of long-term unemployment and other non-marketing activities, but commercial market research studies constituted the bulk of its efforts. At least 40 commercial studies were done by 1934, for a variety of companies stretched across German-speaking Europe, especially in Vienna, Zurich and Berlin. In addition, conceptual papers describing the institute and its workings were produced (Fullerton 1990; 1994). By 1933, 20,000 consumers had been interviewed by the institute's researchers. Some 16 full market studies, and excerpts and summaries of 21 others, are preserved in archives at Columbia University and the University of Vienna.

The institute's primary method of investigation was a 'systematic questioning of the buyer [in order to] determine all of the factors which play a role in the purchase of a specific product' (Lazarsfeld 1933: 3). In other words, in-depth interviewing was used. All interviews were done face to face. Lazarsfeld and his associates believed that every purchase was subject to a variety of influences. This was even true of habitual purchases: 'Central to our investigations is the task of uncovering all of the connections between a specific group of customers and a specific product… [so that] the full structure of the relationships between the consumer and a particular product category is illuminated' (Toffler 1933: 7–8). If questioned systematically and in psychologically informed ways which enabled them to recall the details of the buying process, Lazarsfeld and his colleagues believed, consumers could actually and accurately explain the buying process – a view which few held at the time. True, some of those questioned might give inaccurate or confused answers, but the large number of respondents, between 300 and 1,500 for each report, assured overall accuracy. The questioning process would produce solid data only if it 'proceeds in the least constrained way possible, in the form of a relaxed and impartial conversation' (Lazarsfeld 1933: 4). The fact that respondents were questioned about the factual details of the process before being asked about their opinions and attitudes increased the objective accuracy of their 'buying biographies'.

Considerable effort was devoted to interpreting these 'buying biographies'. Reflecting the soon-to-vanish intellectual vitality of Vienna in the 1920s and the early 1930s, the analysis drew upon social psychology, Marxism, Freud, behaviourism, introspection, statistics and psycholinguistics. Lazarsfeld himself had completed doctoral studies in statistics. Herta Herzog, one of his key associates, had received advanced training in introspection. Several of the institute's researchers, including Lazarsfeld and Herzog, had studied psycholinguistics with Karl and Charlotte Bühler and were thus able to evaluate the intensity of needs by analysing consumers' verbalisation. The more words consumers would evoke to describe a product, the greater their positive need. To an extent which may seem striking today, Lazarsfeld and his colleagues blended quantitative and qualitative analysis. The studies were among the earliest to make extensive use of cross tabulations, for example.

3.5 Moving Motivation Research to the United States

Motivation Research in the United States began with the publication of Lazarsfeld's article on psychology in market research in the influential *Harvard Business Review* in 1934. By then a recent émigré to the United States, Lazarsfeld drew upon his own considerable experience. The examples presented in the article included psycholinguistic interpretation of adult attitudes towards milk and the role of the Adlerian inferiority complex among customers in shoe stores. Although psychological insight was crucial for interpreting market research 'and the formal analysis of the act of purchase' market researchers had neglected it. Psychological insights could not only improve understanding of market research data but also secure better data through the development of questionnaires based 'on better knowledge of the structure of the purchasing act'. Deeper questions would yield more actionable results (Lazarsfeld 1934a). The article offered a new perspective to both business executives and marketing academics. The perspective was not the use of psychology per se – there existed several disparate schools of psychology – but rather of the rich 'depth' psychologies that had recently been developed in central Europe by Freud, Jung, Adler and others. Lazarsfeld strongly implied that behaviourist and mechanistic approaches to psychology were simplistic. Motive lists, as they appeared in several American handbooks on consumer psychology, were based on the assumption that businesses knew exactly what drove their customers and merely had to match the motive with the response. But how could businesses have such knowledge in view of buyers' tendencies to rationalise, to be ignorant of and to forget what motivated them? Even in the 1920s there was a growing awareness in the United States of the importance of unconscious motivations in human conduct. Behaviourism eschewed attitudes in favour of a simple, direct, stimulus-response paradigm. Lazarsfeld posited attitudes between stimuli and responses.

Between 1934 and 1937, Lazarsfeld threw himself into a frenzy of market research and methodological projects including now-classic writings on market research and framing questions done for the fledgling American Marketing Association (Lazarsfeld 1935; Wheeler et al. 1937: chs 3, 4, 11, 15). A 1934 proposal for a study of consumer buying stressed pin-pointing 'to what extent emotional factors influence the purchase and use of commodities in addition to purely economical and technical factors which [until now were the sole] consideration' (Lazarsfeld 1934b). A collaborative article with Arthur W. Kornhauser, who had criticised motive lists since the 1920s, proclaimed that: 'Market research is aimed predominantly at knowledge by means of which to forecast and control consumer behavior. . . . The attitudes that lead to buying hence lie at the very heart of market research problems' (Kornhauser, Lazarsfeld 1935: 393, 395). Lazarsfeld's chapter on psychology and market research in Wheeler et al. (1937) recapitulated the criticism of motive lists and showed how psychologies such as those of Freud and Adler could help interpret research findings.

After about 1940 Lazarsfeld's interests broadened and he grew more conventionally academic and less likely to seek commercial ventures. One of his last significant papers about Motivation Research was an unpublished talk given at the Market Research Council in New York City on 15 October 1943. He never bothered to publish it, but Dichter did, drawing very heavily, and without attribution, upon it for his 1947 article on 'Depth Interviewing' in the *Harvard Business Review* (Dichter 1947b; Lazarsfeld 1943). In any event, by the time that Dichter had begun his work in the United States as an executive for the small New York advertising agency of J. Stirling Getchell in 1939, the foundations of Motivation Research had already been well established.

'Depth Interviewing' would today be termed 'long interviewing'. Although Dichter told Vance Packard that he had pioneered depth interviewing as an aid to merchandising as early as the 1930s, before all others, this was typical Dichter hokum. He learned it at Lazarsfeld's Institute for Economic Psychology. Dichter did not learn the methodology until he worked as an interviewer for one of this institute's last studies in 1936. Dichter was a skilled depth interviewer, but not the only one and certainly not the inventor of the technique. In the mid-1950s, Dichter's Institute for Motivational Research claimed to employ open-ended qualitative interviews, observation, and 'depth' interviews in which 'people were encouraged to talk freely in a conversational manner' (Newman 1957: 345–347). Lazarsfeld's researchers had been using open-ended questions from the late 1920s, when Dichter was still a student.

Projective techniques were, along with depth interviews, one of the mainstays of most Motivation Research. Like depth interviews, these techniques elicited people's inner feelings, as in a famous study in which

American women judged other women by their grocery shopping lists: women whose list contained instant coffee were seen as lazy and irresponsible; good women took the trouble to brew regular ground coffee (Haire 1950). Dichter had nothing to do with their development. They had been shaped by academic psychologists during the 1930s and 1940s. These psychologists had in turn built upon Sigmund Freud, his early Swiss disciple Carl Jung, pioneering studies in Gestalt psychology by the German Max Wertheimer around 1910 and by the Swiss Hermann Rorschach in 1922 (Sargent 1945). Sometimes, Dichter said that his organisation used psychological projective techniques, other times he did not. Though, as Helene Karmasin shows in this book, Dichter did use projection techniques in studies conducted for automobile companies. Dichter's reports and research papers seldom utilised the full range of concepts developed and used by other motivation researchers. Dichter slighted body image and colour; he ignored culture and subcultures; he ignored social class, which was effectively analysed by W. Lloyd Warner, Burleigh B. Gardner and Pierre Martineau. He also did not necessarily probe as deeply as several other leading motivation researchers. Comparing Dichter's interpretations of brand symbolism with the classic 1955 *Harvard Business Review* analysis of brand meaning by the then well-known motivation researcher Burleigh B. Gardner and the young Sidney Levy, we see that both advocated 'conversational'-style depth interviews. Yet Gardner and Levy also advocated a sophisticated battery of projective methods to probe 'the main dimensions of a brand or product character' (Gardner and Levy 1955).

3.6   Dichter seen from 'the Outside'

From the early 1950s onward, Dichter drew furious criticism from within the marketing research community. Professional jealousy accounts for some of this as, for example anything written by the veteran quantitative researcher Alfred Politz. These men were competing for big business clients and Dichter had dismissed experts like Politz as simplistic 'nose-counters'. But long-standing advocates of Motivation Research such as the advertising executive Alfred Blankenship were also caustic. Blankenship argued that Dichter's methods did not uncover respondents' hidden attitudes, but rather stimulated them to invent stories (Paradise and Blankenship 1951). The real 'Father' of Motivation Research, Paul F. Lazarsfeld, publicly criticised the tendency of some motivation researchers – explicitly mentioning Dichter – to generalise grandly from small samples, to ignore basic statistical safeguards in favour of glib bravado (Lazarsfeld 1955). In private, Lazarsfeld was even more critical of Dichter, according to a close colleague (Neurath 1990).

Dichter claimed not to care about critics. He vigorously defended his approach, sometimes with mere rhetorical bluster, at other times with arguments like this one from 1960: A 'really thorough understanding of a basic motivational pattern', for example, one found in 80 housewives out of 100, is 'large enough to indicate that the pattern is significant and lends itself to practical applications' (Dichter 1960: 77). Two to five thousand interviews were simply unnecessary. While statisticians would have blanched at such reasoning, businessmen under pressure to produce results would have appreciated it. Into the early 1960s, in any event, his consulting business grew even as more and more controversy swirled about him. Dichter grew arrogant and bragged to academic audiences that he knew all answers without using any research. Dichter claimed that he had research done only because the clients wanted and paid for it (Hollander 1997).

Dichter rescued companies but he inadvertently threatened society. In 1949, Dichter had asserted that the 'goal [of advertising was] the mobilization and manipulation of human needs as they exist in the consumer' (Dichter 1949). The preface to the British edition of Vance Packard's *The Hidden Persuaders* warned Britons that 'the kind of tomorrow we may be tending toward…may be exemplified by the depth probing of little girls to discover their vulnerability to advertising messages. No one, literally no one, evidently is to be spared from the all-seeing, Big Brotherish eye of the motivational analyst.' An international bestseller, Packard's book led millions to consider Motivation Research a big menace and Dichter the most menacing of the 'depth boys'. Packard showed how, through the sinister counsel of Dichter and other 'depth boys', the friendly folks who proffered prunes, pancake mix and coffee to American tables were cynically manipulating them. Even the foodstuffs that one could stock in the family backyard bomb shelter were part of the danger (Packard 1957). Instead of trying to hide away from such criticism or shyly defending himself, Dichter bragged that Packard had helped increase his business. Within a few years after *The Hidden Persuaders*, he willingly unloaded a great deal of fodder for the American feminist author Betty Friedan and her idea of the *Feminine Mystique* (1963). Again, a great deal of publicity for Ernest Dichter.

But was this the sort of figure with whom consumer product executives would want to consort? Business began dropping, albeit slowly. In the world of business consulting, there are always new trends and fads emerging. Anyone who follows the panaceas relentlessly presented in popular business magazines such as *Business Week* will have encountered any number over time: synergy, zero-based budgeting, corporate re-engineering and so on. Some are solid, others more fluff, but all eventually fade, either to be forgotten or to be absorbed into the management research mainstream. After about 1960, new methods for researching consumer attitudes came to the fore in the United States. While Dichter's research style remained the same, that of some others seemed to progress to create new magic. In America, the prevalent style of marketing analysis increasingly reflected the 'hard' sciences: formal experimental designs, operations research, mathematical modelling and multivariate analysis – both aided by Lazarsfeld's later work – all became widely used, especially as access to computers spread. Not only did these approaches promise greater scientific 'purity', they also allowed researchers to probe, analyse and test research results with new power. In the market research community, Dichter's flamboyant version of qualitative research simply became less fashionable. Some newer qualitative researchers drew upon cultural anthropology to develop better questioning techniques; others on qualitative work to generate mathematically actionable concepts.

Even in the advertising business, where Dichter had had his strongest influence, quantitative 'management science' techniques were being increasingly used by the mid-1960s: 'Mathematical programming, simulation, Baysian analysis, multivariate analysis, and Markov analysis have become everyday production and research tools to the Advertising Industry', wrote Stanley Cohen in 1966. Who needed Dichter? Despite his attempts to reinvent himself as a management guru, he gradually faded into quaint irrelevance, outliving his fame by at least 20 years. He rose, he crested for 15 years, he fell – but he had enjoyed a long run as a major independent consultant, celebrity and symbolic bogeyman. His ability to market himself was extraordinary: Dichter got to know journalists, to whom he provided fascinating copy and who in turn provided outlets for Dichter to a wider world. He was, for example, by far the most accessible of the many motivation researchers whom the journalist Vance Packard interviewed for *The Hidden Persuaders*. Dichter made his by-then huge archive of research studies available to Betty Friedan during the early 1960s. Friedan (1963: 208) subsequently wrote:

The headquarters of his institute for motivational manipulation is a baronial mansion in upper Westchester. The walls of a ballroom two-stories high are filled with steel shelves holding a thousand-odd studies…[and with], 300,000 individual 'depth interviews', mostly with American housewives. He let me see what I wanted, said I could use anything that was not confidential to a specific company.

3.7   Dichter as a consultant: a man of his times

To an unusual extent, Dichter's skills meshed with the Zeitgeist of the later 1940s and the 1950s. We have seen how he linked himself with Freudian psychoanalysis and Motivation Research. He was also a cheerful celebrant of the fruits of post-Second World War affluent consumer society. 'Possessions expand our personality', he wrote in 1947. This line of thought meshed perfectly with the mass prosperity enabled by the post-Second World War US economic boom. Later it would mesh with Italy's post-1960 boom. Dichter found playful, happy, highly creative symbolism – iconic evidence of joyful moments in life – in everyday products. Dichter offered such examples as the idyllically happy ice-cream consumers '[who] often eat it as if they want the ice cream to run down their chins. It is associated with love and affection [and]…childhood memories' (Dichter 1964: 339). Ice cream is a happy symbol here. In his charming, popularly written 1947 book *The Psychology of Everyday Life*, Dichter explained how we are influenced in everyday consumer life, and hence how to avoid being gulled. There was so much to buy, and emotions were a big part of consumer thinking, but one had to use them positively: 'Skill in buying has a profound influence on our everyday living' (Dichter 1947a: 211). One could reasonably think that the book was commissioned by a consumer protection organisation to help American consumers avoid the emotional dangers of the marketplace.

He believed that he could aid the businessmen who were catering to as well as stimulating mass affluence; his conviction would have enhanced his appeal to business clients. Among those who followed Motivation Research there was concern about the ability of academic social scientists and business executives to work together. Some executives felt uncomfortable with academic social scientists (Smith 1954: Chapter 17). But with Dichter there were no such problems. Vance Packard found that businessmen found it worthwhile to pay to talk with Dichter even if they did not follow his counsel. His informed guesses could be 'brilliant' (Packard 1957: 204). Consulting more than one consultant is a way of reducing risk, particularly among the larger companies which made up most of Dichter's clientele. His success as a consultant was founded on the belief that he gave good value, not the belief his advice alone was enough. Even during its heyday few believed that Motivation Research would ever supplant conventional, quantitative market research. An internal 1953 survey by the advertising agency Dancer-Fitzgerald-Sample, which was involved in MR, showed that only 7 per cent of the agency's research projects under way at that time involved motivational research (Smith 1954: 205). Conventional large-scale quantitative surveys continued to constitute the bulk of the market intelligence upon which firms relied.

What companies could get from Dichter was his ability to combine observation and common sense with imagination. His skill at observation is evident in the chapter on why people smoke in his *Psychology of Everyday Life:* 'the way we smoke is characteristic of our whole personality. The mannerisms of smokers are innumerable.' Observation of people holding and smoking cigarettes had shown how important they were in smokers' self-presentations. He could deliver similar suggestive insights without end. Like other motivation researchers, Dichter assumed that products, especially branded ones, were suffused with powerful unconscious symbolism in consumers' minds. 'We have to penetrate to the deeper meaning which products, services, and objects that surround us have for the individual....We buy...symbolic meaning,' Dichter explained in his *Handbook of Consumer Motivations* (1964). No other motivation researcher wrote as much, or as colourfully, about product symbolism as did Dichter. Some of his best-known examples are baking, which he saw as an expression of femininity: 'The most fertile moment occurs when the woman pulls the finished cake, bread loaf, or other baked product out of the oven. In a sense it is like giving birth' (Dichter 1964: 21). In prunes, Dichter saw a 'symbol of old age; they are like dried-out spinsters; they have none of the soft pleasurableness of plums. Prunes are devitalized...they are felt to be dried out, to have nothing to offer' (Dichter 1964: 59).

Dichter's creative use of symbolism was his greatest substantive achievement and helps explain why his 1964 *Handbook of Consumer Motivations*, a compendium of Motivation Research cases and findings, still inspires the creators of advertising today. The moving symbolism that Dichter intuited in mundane items, could be used in promotion to make these items interesting, even exciting. Some of the biggest advertising accounts are for mass-market consumer goods such as toothpaste, detergent and floor wax, which are not easily made interesting and memorable.

Above all, Ernest Dichter was a master myth-maker. Dichter's stories make Vance Packard's *The Hidden Persuaders* an extremely interesting book, even today. Methodologically, Dichter's 'findings' were questionable – replication was not even mentioned – and of course Dichter seldom reported any failures. He left no body of explicit techniques that could be passed on, his genius was in his own imagination. Nobody else could offer such great stories. Thus, the convertible as mistress, the prune as a terrifying reminder of old age, the cake mix as symbol of parturient motherhood. These and many more stories became part of the mythology of twentieth-century consumer life. As one of Dichter's many critics, the venerable Austrian advertising psychologist Hanns F. J. Kropff, conceded, this was 'a highly intelligent, intellectually flexible, pragmatically oriented advertising consultant – better said a copywriter of genius' (Kropff 1960: 47). Dr Ernest Dichter was more, much more, than people now think, and he was less, much less, than he claimed to be.

References

Bartos, R. 1986. Ernest Dichter: motive interpreter. *Journal of Advertising Research* 26: 15–29.

Breyer, O. A. 1929. Arbeitsmethoden und Arbeitsgebiete der Marktanalyse. *Die Reklame* 640–650.

Cohen, S. I. 1966. The rise of management science in advertising. *Marketing Science* 13: B10–B28.

Collins, L., Montgomery, C. 1969. The origins of motivation research. *British Journal of Marketing* 3: 103–113.

Dichter, E. 1947a. *The Psychology of Everyday Living.* New York: Barnes and Noble.

——— 1947b. Psychology in marketing research. *Harvard Business Review* 25 (4): 432–443.

——— 1949. A psychological view of advertising effectiveness. *Journal of Marketing* 14 (1): 61–66.

——— 1956. A credo for modern research in advertising. Speech given at Advertising Federation of America Meeting. Miami Beach, 11 June 1956. Paul Lazarsfeld Collection, Butler Library of Columbia University, Box 157, Folder 6.

——— 1960. *The Strategy of Desire.* Garden City, NY: Doubleday.

——— 1961. Seven tenets of creative research. *Journal of Marketing* 26 (2): 1–4.

——— 1964. *Handbook of Consumer Motivations: The Psychology of the World of Objects.* New York: McGraw-Hill.

——— 1977. *Motivforschung, Mein Leben: die Autobiographie eines kreativ Unzufriedenen.* Frankfurt/Main: Lorch.

Friedan, B. 1963. *The Feminine Mystique.* New York: Dell.

Fullerton, R. 1990. The art of market research: Paul F. Lazarsfeld. *JAMS: Journal of the Academy of Marketing Science* 18 (4): 319–329.

———— 1994. Tea and the Viennese: a pioneering episode in the analysis of consumer behaviour. In: C. T. Allen, D. R. John (Eds), *Advances in Consumer Research*, Vol. 21: 418–421.

———— 2005. The devil's lure (?): motivation research, 1934–1954. In: L. C. Neilson (Ed.), *The Future of Marketing's Past: Proceedings of the 12th Conference on Historical Analysis and Research in Marketing*. Long Beach, CA: Association for Historical Research in Marketing, 134–143.

Gardner, B., Levy, S. 1955. The product and the brand. *Harvard Business Review* 33 (2): 33–39.

Haire, M. 1950. Projective techniques in marketing research. *The Journal of Marketing* 14: 649–656.

Hollander, S. C. 1997. Talk to the Advisory Board of the Conference on Historical Research in Marketing, Kingston, Ontario.

Jones, E. 1964. *The Life and Work of Sigmund Freud*. Edited and abridged by L. Trilling and S. Marcus. Harmondsworth: Penguin.

Kornhauser, A. W., Lazarsfeld, P. F. 1935. The techniques of market research from the standpoint of a psychologist. *Institute of Management* 16: 3–15, 19–21.

Kropff, H. F. J. 1934. *Psychologie in der Reklame*. Stuttgart: C. E. Poeschel.

———— 1960. *Motivforschung: Methoden und Grenzen*. Essen: W. Giradet.

Laird, D. A. 1935. *What Makes People Buy*. New York: McGraw-Hill.

Lazarsfeld, P. F. 1933. Neue Wege der Verkaufspsychologie. Typescript report. Paul Lazarsfeld Collection, Butler Library of Columbia University, Box 33, Folder 3.

———— 1934a. The psychological aspects of market research. *Harvard Business Review* 13: 54–71.

———— 1934b. Psychological aspects of marketing. Biography Folder 1933–1946, Paul Lazarsfeld Archive, University of Vienna.

———— 1935. The art of asking WHY in marketing research. *National Marketing Review* 1: 32–43.

———— 1943. Depth interviewing. Talk given to the Market Research Council, New York City, 15 October 1943. Paul Lazarsfeld Archive, University of Vienna.

———— 1955. Progress and fad in motivation research. Proceedings of the Third Annual Seminar on Social Science for Industry – Motivation. Paul Lazarsfeld Archive, University of Vienna.

Neurath, P. 1990. Personal interview by the Author.

Newman, J. W. 1957. *Motivation Research and Marketing Management*. Boston, MA: Harvard Graduate School of Business Administration.

Packard, V. 1957. *The Hidden Persuaders*. New York: David McKay Co.

Paradise, L. M., Blankenship, A. B. 1951. Depth questioning. *Journal of Marketing* 15 (3): 274–288.

Parkin, K. 2007. *Food is Love: Advertising and Gender Roles in Modern America*. Pennsylvania: University of Pennsylvania Press.

Sargent, H. 1945. Projective methods: their origins, theory, and application in personality research. *Psychological Bulletin* 42: 257–293.

Smith, G. H. 1954. *Motivation Research in Advertising and Marketing*. New York: McGraw-Hill.

Time 1940. Psychoanalysis in advertising. 25 March: 46–47.

Toffler, R. 1933. Untitled dissertation on the influence of advertising, Paul Lazarsfeld Collection, Butler Library of Columbia University, Box 35, Folder 1.

Vershofen, W. 1937. Absatzwirtschaft und Verbraucher. Typescript manuscript, Paul Lazarsfeld Archive, University of Vienna.
——— 1940. *Handbuch der Verbrauchsforschung, Vol. 1: Grundlegung.* Berlin: Carl Heymann.
Wheeler, F. C., Bader, L., Frederick, J. G. Eds. 1937. *The Technique of Marketing Research.* New York: McGraw-Hill.
Woodward, J. L. et al. 1950. Depth interviewing. *The Journal of Marketing* 14: 721–724.

4
Ernest Dichter, Religion and the Spirit of Capitalism: An Exegete of Pure Cult Religion Serves Consumer Society

Gabriele Sorgo

4.1 Introduction

Sociologists refer to those actions as 'religious' whose meaning is marked by references to supernatural powers (Riesebrodt 2007: 115). Ernest Dichter distanced himself personally from all religion and belief in a supernatural being, although journalists often referred to him as 'advertising guru' and 'Pope of advertising' (Kreuzer et al. 2007). However, not all supernatural powers are otherworldly, and not every religion publishes its teachings in books. Transcendental phenomena may be encountered in everyday life, such as in those abysms of the psyche that remain out of reach of the conscious will both in oneself and in others, while exercising a strong influence on action (Luckmann 1996: 128–153). Moreover, transcendental experience may occur in encounters with worldly powers: while these may not be responsible for generating rain or droughts, they may still decide on hunger or satiety. From the perspective of social anthropology, it seems only clear that people tend to behave religiously vis-à-vis supernatural powers no matter what their origins may be. We idolise or demonise such powers, we adore or fear them. Vance Packard, who in 1957 warned against invisible practices of seduction carried out by advertising experts and against their illicit reach for the unconscious, was indirectly expressing a critique of religion (Packard 1957). In line with the tradition of the Enlightenment, Packard intended to enlighten unsuspicious consumers about possible manipulations and psychological tricks on the part of a new priestly cast – a cast providing a payable mediation service between the heights of industrial capitalism and the depths of consumer life.

Ernest Dichter belonged to a generation which believed that human-made tools and systems of production were expressions of a transhistorical current called 'progress'. To Dichter, serving this current was comparable with a mission – a mission whose external sign of success was an income of millions of dollars. He understood his work as a form of communication in the service of progress, and aimed at liberating people from traditional, mostly religiously motivated reservations against material enjoyments. In order to convert people to this idea of progress, Dichter, a Doctor of Psychology, believed he was acting as social anthropologist and as depth manager who sought to short-circuit the abysms of the human soul with the blessings of modern industry, by that creating what the philosopher and theologian Max Brod called an 'inner-worldly miracle'. Brod applied this term to Jewish inner-worldliness, which separates Jewish spirituality from the Christian disregard for matter (Brod 1939).

In the 1920s, at a time when Dichter still decorated shop windows to finance his degree, his contemporary Walter Benjamin already studied the social and cultural misery that modern systems of production and sales were generating in the shadow of an abundance of goods. Benjamin compared arcades and shopping streets with hell instead of paradise (Benjamin 1983, vol. 1: 135, vol. 2: 1010). In 1940, when Dichter began to successfully apply motivational research methods in New York, the Jewish intellectual Walter Benjamin took his life in a small town on the French–Spanish border in fear of being persecuted by the German secret police. Benjamin, while trying to flee to the United States, never thought of the 'land of plenty' as an attractive destination, though.

Taking his cues from Karl Marx, Benjamin referred to capitalism as a belief system without a body of teachings or a dogma. As a 'pure cult religion', capitalism transformed everything into flows of capital (Benjamin 1985: 100–103). In Thomas Aquinas's terms, the complex of labour and consumption that make up the cult in Benjamin would be considered as a purely exterior cult (*cultus exterior*), such as religions usually couple them to a *cultus spiritualis,* that is to a teaching or a revelation (*Summa theologiae* I II 102, 4. 1952: 476–481). If, then, as Benjamin asserted, the spiritual cult was missing from what he called the religion of capitalism, there was no teaching to be interpreted (exegesis) or to be performed in a religious service. All that remained was an incessant transformation of goods into money and back into goods – a cultish activity of production and consumption without any ethical additions. Exegetes of this type of religion would therefore not concern themselves with texts, commands or interdictions, but instead with techniques, forms of action and motives that spur the circulation of money and goods.

Benjamin related the fact that new technologies of reproduction could transform works of art into goods through their departure from the 'womb of the ritual' (Benjamin 1977: 20). He may have been among the first to understand that the loss of ritual and artisan authenticity was going to be compensated for by techniques of advertising and presentation. In order for consumer goods to be admired and bought they still needed an aura, albeit one that now had to be put into place artificially. Therefore, with more goods being produced and competition among brands becoming more intense, the end of the nineteenth century brought new professions dedicated to the advertising of mass products. From his youth, Dichter studied the same phenomena as Benjamin, although not as a critic, but as a promoter of the new practices of consumption. His intention was to provide goods with a 'soul' (Dichter 1961: 99–129), and to weave them into discourses, myths and fantasies in order to increase their 'selling appeal'. In what follows, I will try to narrate the biography of Dichter as influential marketing consultant against the background of the development of consumerism. My *leitmotiv* is the hostile kinship between religion and marketing as it is reflected in Dichter's personality, methods and publications.

4.2 Anti-ritualism and expectations of salvation

Dichter's autobiography tells us that his father was very religious (Dichter 1977: 366). Consequently, there were frequent conflicts between his 'symbolically non-Jewish' mother, who had little regard for rituals, and Dichter's father. Dichter never said as much as a good word about his father. A distancing from the heritage of the fathers, of his biological father in particular, clearly marked Dichter's life and work. The only reason Dichter provided for this rejection is his father's failure to achieve economic success.

Dichter's rejection of the paternal role model went hand in hand with his dismissal of his father's religion and of ritualised forms of action. Dichter always claimed to question habits and to break with routines, and not only to see things differently, but to put them upside down (Dichter 1971: 224). In later years, he often underlined that he could not care for things religious and that he specifically disliked traditions: 'I am not sufficiently familiar with Jewish history or theology as to know exactly […]. Perhaps the strict observation of kosher rituals was one of the reasons why in spite of all the idealised circumstances I never felt really at home in Israel.' (Dichter 1977: 13). Dichter considered laws and sermons as entirely outdated and as poor methods of educating people to be good. Over several decades, he repeated in talks and in books that Moses's method of outlawing and sanctioning moral tres-pass had not been successful (Dichter 1977: 146; 1989a: 14b). Thus, Dichter in some ways entered into a competition with the most impor-tant Jewish–Christian father figures. In fact, the difference between the Ten Commandments chiselled into rock, and the *zeitgeist*-driven sug-gestions contained in Dichter's studies could hardly be more radical. Dichter's focus was permanent change. His anti-ritualism and his scep-ticism vis-à-vis social traditions spurred his success at a time when European societies fell to pieces during the 1930s and 1940s, and the United States, too, experienced enormous social and economic change.

Dichter's status of a misfit, put down to his Jewish origin and his red hair, strengthened his interest in all managerial and technological innovations that seemed capable of relativising or even unhinging peo-ple's ingrained habits and attachment to traditions. After all, Dichter still experienced first-hand the adverse results of such attachments in the form of Vienna's anti-Semitism. Consequently, Dichter's autobiog-raphy does not begin with his childhood or youth, but with a successful 'sales negotiation' at the American consulate in Paris, where the 30-year-old applied for a visa and explained his ideas. Choosing a specific kind of vocabulary for describing a non-commercial negotiating situa-tion, Dichter proudly pointed out that the American clerk 'bought' him. He bought the message that Dichter's Motivation Research might be of use to his new host country. Even if Dichter had not been Jewish, he would probably never have been able to expect a similar career in Europe as awaited him in the United States. In Austria, where patriarchal eco-nomic leadership had little regard for marketing strategies, his messages would have fallen on deaf ears. By contrast, in the United States the year 1938 marked the return of consumer spending to pre-depression levels. Moreover, the advertising industry was seeking to improve its reputa-tion by adopting scientific methods, which in turn resulted in excellent career opportunities for Dichter, who had already been involved in mar-ket research in Vienna (Fullerton 2007: 64–67; Lears 1994: 234). Dichter knew how to make use of these opportunities. In his later years, when addressing his customers, he would speak of 'us Americans' as if he had been born there and brought up in a Protestant ethic: 'We Americans have historically been utilitarian, pragmatic' (Dichter 1965).

Dichter was endowed with a psychological sensitivity that made him soon realise where the difficulties in selling luxury items such as cars and gentlemen's magazines might be located. He made it his task to liberate the Americans from a certain kind of guilt that seemed to prevent them from enjoying shopping. In his *Findings* – the monthly newsletter of his Institute for Motivation Research – he repeatedly proclaimed the 'Death of Puritanism' (*Findings* April 1966: 1). The bottom line of his consulting work was simple: consuming makes you happy, more consuming makes you even happier. He was so focused on increasing sales that he even wished the Vietnam war might not end so soon, so that arms production could continue to flourish and people would continue to shop (*Findings* 1967: 1). Dichter did not hesitate to denounce religion as the source of a dangerous reluctance against shopping. 'If people come to believe that a recession is inevitable (seven fat years, seven lean years), they may actually talk themselves into it.' (*Findings* 1967: 1).

Dichter's cursory remarks on religion reveal that he thought of religious teachings, the Jewish and Christian ones in particular, as a threat to the economy. The threats of punishment contained in religion generated feelings of guilt. Dichter's idea was to 'absolve' people from their guilt through 'motivational' advertising. Sure enough, this placed Dichter into the position of a priest. Although his research method of in-depth interviews represented an attempt to reveal value orientations and symbolic references rooted in the subconscious, most of the 'enlightenment' remained reserved for his customers, who wanted to use it for profit. Dichter described his work as a 'more profound type of education' (Dichter 1977: 139). Yet, what was the objective of this education? Although Dichter liked to compare his work with anthropological research, he mostly worked on behalf of businesses. Dichter would have had something to put against the purely negative view of American consumer society expressed by Theodor. W. Adorno and Max Horkheimer. His insights concerning the playful and creative potentials of the commercial world preceded cultural anthropological research by several decades. Dichter claimed for example that 'shopping is an expression of creative potential' (Dichter 1961: 201). Similar views, matched with a differentiated critique of capitalism and empirical evidence, were later expressed by Csikszentmihalyi and Rochberg-Halton (1981), Löfgren (1994: 47–70) and Miller (1998).

Dichter's personal goal to reveal himself as the best of all sales strategists coincided with the restructuring of American society into a 'consumers' republic'. Both employers' and workers' representatives identified the good consumer with the good citizen (Cohen 2006: 47).

Dichter's good news concerning an approaching supermarket paradise was eagerly adopted in the post-war years: 'When she first steps into a supermarket she is confronted with a paradise of choice, variety, quality, etc.' (Dichter 1956: 79). In Dichter's view, both the economy and consumers would benefit from a mutual cooperation, from a smooth integration of human desire and its objects, and from increasing sales through accelerated consumption, impulse buying, and rapidly switching fashion trends. In his *Findings* in 1969, he argued that 'the industry should present the impression of being in touch with the needs and desires of the modern family…of constantly creating new and ingenious products' (*Findings* March 1969: 3). Dichter considered it his mission to help two formerly separated spheres getting in touch more closely. He claimed that his Motivation Research was capable of putting the soul of humans in touch with that of goods, strengthening social bonds as well as economic and national welfare.

In order for this to be possible, what needed to be overcome was distrust vis-à-vis producers and alienation vis-à-vis growing amounts of consumer goods. The estrangement from mass products was to be overcome by the right sales stories, attractive packaging and symbolic associations. In some of Dichter's reports, supermarkets are considered 'contact zones' and treasure chambers (Dichter 1986: 14). According to his optimistic view, supermarkets would be part of people's homes, being wonderlands and larder in one, and representing places where lonesome housewives would establish contacts with new goods and possibly find new friends. For Dichter, the slogan 'A cup of coffee for the road', for instance, 'displaced fear of an insidious enemy by confidence in and gratefulness to a protective friend' (Dichter 1963a: 10).

Dichter thus considered himself the redeemer of a society that he largely equated with the economy. Frequently, in cases when his advice was urgently required, he was flown to Europe like a saviour (Haupt 1990). In Dichter's view, the shopping process had healing properties because possessions promised security (Dichter 1961: 104). Dichter, a restless person, turned established views on their heads by claiming that all bad things came from religion and philosophy and their belief that paradise would be somewhere at the end of life or after (ORF 1984: 27). However, Dichter's inversion of traditional value hierarchies and his criticism of a Christian work ethic that moved all enjoyments to the afterworld never touched the fundamental structures of political order. His ideas remained embedded in a meritocratic model of society and focused on a white middle class with high spending power. The absolution Dichter recommended his clients to offer did not refer to the whole life of the shoppers and did not result in a purely hedonistic lifestyle:

> One easily forgets that people, unless properly motivated to constantly buy new things, would soon stop pushing themselves and would start working less, resulting in decreased productivity.
>
> (Dichter 1977: 350)

Dichter's goal was not the abolishing of the Protestant ethic but the promotion of the labour–consumption cycle. He implicitly considered productivity as the most important service to progress and the source of all good. Consumption and its carnivalesque enactments represented the second, complementary component of cult actions.

4.3   Instead of sermons: entertainment and amusement

'Why should the devil have all the good tunes', Dichter asked, arguing that good ideas must have good marketing in order to become effective. Even at an advanced age Dichter spoke out against the Ten Commandments and championed a mass media-based 'education' of the public by advertising specialists. 'Mass communications are paying considerable attention to the format, the skilful often insinuating and slyly seductive manner, in which the message is dramatized and "played"' (Dichter 1989a: 6b). He even went so far as to denounce political and religious guidance altogether:

> Asking the people to change whether by giving them ten or more commandments or haranguing them in sermons or speeches, the purpose is the same. A person, a group, a religion or political party is convinced that they know the answer to the world evils. If only the uneducated masses were to be ready to accept the gospel and the truth according to the one and true apostle.
>
> (Dichter 1989a: 1)

According to Dichter, teachers, preachers and politicians were meant to learn from advertising specialists how the masses could be motivated to more democracy. Shopping in a supermarket could be considered a 'training ground' for democratic behaviour, which to Dichter was the same as being able to take decisions: 'Advertisers can help people educate for better Citizenship' (*Findings* 1973: 1; see also Dichter 1961: 199; 1989b: 8). 'The shopper for goods is not any different from the voter choosing between political candidates, or from the lover who picks a bride' (Dichter 1963b). American advertising specialists had promoted similar ideas already before the First World War (Lears 1994: 160). Dichter's line of reasoning thus blurred any difference between social and profit-orientated acting.

However, in his work as contracted advertising consultant Dichter left no doubt that the ultimate goal was for people to shop as much as possible. More often than not, Dichter's measures were meant to encourage customers not to carry out rational acts of consumption but rather to succumb to impulse purchases (Dichter 1956: 82). While the motivation researcher Dichter sometimes suggested that morally good ideas should be better packaged and presented in more entertaining ways, he insisted at other times that politicians should not be elected only because of their fashionable suits. While, on the one hand, he advised that supermarkets should have entire sections with special offerings for children (Dichter 1956: 88; 1986: 3) and that sweets should be marketed as high-protein children's snacks (*Findings* 1967: 4), he expressed dissatisfaction about the lack of regard his spoiled grandchildren had for his presents (Dichter 1977: 356). Yet Dichter was not a cynic. He was a deeply faithful disciple of the religion of capitalism. As 'depth manager', he attempted – surely unconsciously rather than consciously – to take up the heritage of traditional religious authorities. The second stage of industrialisation had increased both the mobility and the purchasing power of workers. New discourses around new goods and services were able to compensate for the loss of social bonds and to create new lifestyles. For him, 'in-depth marketing may satisfy psychological and spiritual needs by other methods' (Dichter 1991: 169). Like a 'gold digger' (Dichter 1991: 9) Dichter was able to draw from the stock of old structures of meaning that he uncovered in his depth interviews. Depth management then meant to weave new textures of meaning based on goods and their 'stories' in order to cajole faithful consumers into the cult of consumption that had created the supermarket as its temple.

4.4   Advertising substitutes religion

As a representative of the world of commerce, Dichter was in a position that had traditionally competed with religious dignitaries specialising in the *sacrum commercium* with the world beyond all things material (Herz 1958). Dichter dealt with more limited forms of transcendentalism and preferred to refer to the near future instead of eternal life (Dichter 1979). Ever since the Middle Ages, priests had been railing against the distraction of mass attendants by market events (Sorgo 2006: 97–111). Even at the beginning of the twentieth century, priests tried to accomplish a closure of shop windows on Sundays (Reinhardt 1995: 116–125). While the Church in early modern Europe was still able to exercise a temporal and ritual control over the hustle and bustle of carnivals, the weekly, monthly and yearly markets slid from the Church's control once the world markets began to develop. However, market life is related to carnival life. A market place usually displayed a contradictory hotchpotch of things and people, reflecting carnivalistic inversions and mixtures (Stallybrass and White 1995: 39). Chamber pots were offered next to cooking pans, fresh bread next to old fish. At the markets, members of different social and professional groups mingled, as did local residents and travellers.

According to the criteria of the cultural anthropologist Victor Turner (1995: 137), spheres of commerce in which foreign people and foreign goods are brought together are fundamentally liminal; that is, they are removed from established structures of order. In pre-industrial society, therefore, so-called rituals of transition (van Gennep 1999) protected the social system from the disorder that was feared to emerge from the fissures between regulated periods and secure social roles, as well as from outside one's own cultural context. Traditionally, the carnival, a typical ritual of transition, had bridged the threshold between the old and the new ecclesiastic year. When in the seventeenth century in the bigger cities most goods that had previously been offered at fairs and yearly markets became available on a daily basis, carnivalesque phenomena began to cluster around these new commercial locations (Minichton 1979). The goods from around the world spoke of cultural difference and the corresponding transgressions of boundaries.

Since markets develop when there is a discrepancy between demand and supply they present themselves – like the carnival – in the niches of order, in the in-between space among individuals, objects and social structures. A market represents a sphere in which goods as well as potential buyers are 'liquid', which means their roles and duties are not determined but are in a threshold state between desire and gratification. In as much as this is the case, a permanent global market, such as it first appeared in urban European centres in the eighteenth century, offers diversion and entertainment because it allows people to step out of their everyday roles and to experiment with new forms of action. The colorful hustle and bustle on major fairs and markets often resembled the chaos of a crazy world and therefore attracted projections of the land of milk and honey, of paradise and of hell (Braudel 1986: 81). They represented liminal locations *par excellence*. Whatever barkers, buffoons, actors, faith healers and prostitutes did on pre-modern marketplaces, drawing on an array of tricks and spectacles in order to attract clients, is done by advertising specialists using mass communication techniques on today's stage of the permanent market (Lears 1994).

Starting from the idea that pre-industrial markets took place on public streets and squares and therefore helped fill governmental treasuries, supporters of free trade have been eager to charge the market with symbols of political participation and public welfare ever since the eighteenth century. At that time, organological concepts of state and economy drew on the notion of the market as the 'heart' that set everything in motion and that nourished and invigorated the body politic by circulating merchandise (Sorgo 2006: 313–332). From that point, the path leads into the twentieth century and its fusion of economy and society, resulting in a vision of the consumer as citizen (Trentmann 2006). In the first four decades of the last century, American advertising specialists succeeded in creating a permanent link between business and public welfare in the public discourse (McGovern 1998: 244–247). It was the advertising specialists who constructed the American way of life as a kind of secular religion whose articles of redemption were held for sale at department stores. Dichter, inspired by a sense of mission, took up this notion of consumption and belonging and elevated producers – his clients – to the rank of selfless benefactors:

> The general store is part of American history, its folklore and nostalgia. It is a warm personable congregate that belongs to the community. The owner does not manage it, he is the focal point, often the benefactor and the arbiter.
>
> (Dichter 1986: 2)

With regard to consumer practices of the year 2000, he speculated:

> Will it not rather be a matter of wanting to create a kind of permanent carnival of the senses, a collective enterprise brightening and embellishing everyday life, and a communication tool for all those who will join in this great festive dance of the year 2000?
>
> (Dichter 1979: 117)

Although modern supermarkets offer a release from everyday life and a carnivalesque experience, there are no longer any common excesses and no collective reflection as they existed in early modern carnival (Handelman 1982). Everyone has to choose, limit and justify their own diversions on an individual basis. Instead of making use of a carnival king, a puppet acting as scapegoat and burnt after the feast, the customer remains king on his/her own account. 'We have surrounded ourselves, and still do, with the scepter and crown of tangible royalty bought with the symbol of our mighty arsenal – the Dollar', reports Dichter (1965). In an achievement-oriented society with a puritan work ethic and a carnivalesque enacting of recreational consumption, money is enough of a justification for pleasure. In any case, bills will be settled at the cash desk, as Dichter recognised (1956: 80).

4.5   The prophet of the new capitalist spirit

Dichter's *oeuvre* clearly mirrors the development of the work and consumer societies of the twentieth century. When Dichter established his institute, American consumers were mainly concerned with 'keeping up with the Joneses'. The 'American way of life' had already been put into place as the transcendental objective (Lears 1994: 244). Being well integrated into society meant possessing certain goods and working for them. The motto was: working for shopping. However, this changed in the late 1950s. Using the catchphrase 'the inner Joneses', Dichter predicted that customers would turn away from mass consumption and embark on a search for more individuality (Dichter 1963b). Advertising should reflect that: 'The advertiser […] sells culture and spiritual enrichment' (Dichter 1965). Dichter recommended that goods should be furnished with a non-material added use.

Sociologists Luc Boltanski and Eve Chiapello (2003) compared management literature of the 1960s with that of the 1990s in order to show that capitalism changed its 'spirit' in between these periods. By 'spirit' they mean the essence of those discourses developed both by the leaders and the less-powerful participants in the capitalist system of production in order to give meaning to economic processes and to define their own place in this system in such a way as to reconcile economic goals with a personal quest for meaning. Although their studies are based on French sources only, the authors' frequent references to American management techniques make it reasonable to assume that what happened in France was a delayed repercussion of what had occurred in the United States before. Boltanski and Chiapello's comparative study shows that in the 1960s the main goal was that of motivating leaders, which meant to give 'meaning to dependent employment and providing capitalism with a spirit' (Boltanski and Chiapello 2003: 99). Managers were supposed to be assigned autonomous spheres of responsibility and a certain amount of autonomy within the organisation. Moreover, France, following the American model, aimed for a performance-based assessment of employees and was no longer ready to reward non-creative, doggish loyalty (Boltanski and Chiapello 2003: 104).

During the 1960s, Dichter, too, provided such advice in 'How to recruit and keep good personnel' (*Findings* 1966: 3). 'Ego involvement' ranked number one on his 1966 to-do list: 'Call it a "partnership feeling", a sense of participation.' A personal involvement of the employees was thought to strengthen their interest in their work and render it more pleasant. In a 1971 communication headlined 'Motivating the "new" employee', Dichter asserted: 'Money still has its attractions of course. But its motivating power over employees is giving way to a new system of values' (*Findings* 1971: 1). Dichter viewed this as a turn towards inner values and immaterial enjoyments, just as it had occurred in consumers. He believed that the new quest for meaning made employees want to 'spiritually grow' in their work. Dichter died in 1991, yet the new spirit of capitalism found by Boltanski and Chiapello in 1990s management manuals already made itself felt in his later writings, when he was only occasionally contracted for consultancy services. Dichter represented what we today would call a trend scout. However, he only functioned as amplifier, not as the originator of certain trends. For example, his prediction of a reduction in working time did not materialise (Schor 1992: 28–32).

From the late 1960s onwards, Motivation Research lost its importance. Increasingly, companies adopted more precise quantitative research methods in studying consumer behaviour (Fullerton 2007: 71). In the face of more demanding consumers and more segmented markets, Dichter's interpretative method no longer seemed reliable enough. Following the oil crisis of 1973 and the transfer of many production plants to low-wage countries, there was a shortage of jobs and consequently an increase in work efficiency among the middle classes. Once again, the consumer society revealed itself as an achievement-based society in which people did not work in order to live, but in which work had become life itself. Longer working hours and promotion of worker responsibility were tools used by companies with middle-class employees in their attempt to convert the corporation into a community of meaning (Bell 2008). Dichter had understood the key themes of post-Fordism as early as 1975 and thus shifted his area of emphasis to management consultancy. His writings during the 1970s and 1980s are focused on self-realisation, flexibility and trust. He found it liberating that there was a turn away from the previous company structures and their relatively secure jobs and careers, the subject of most 1960s management literature. His remedy against mounting stress at the workplace consisted in improved (self-)management. The 'manager of the future should be subjected to stress tests' (Dichter 1975a: 100) and would ideally be his/her own therapist, as well as being the therapist of his/her employees. This seems to be an anticipation of the 'coach' who since the 1990s has been supporting middle and higher management in emergency situations (Boltanski and Chiapello 2003: 119).

In his book *The Second Career* (1975b), Dichter championed life-long learning. However, he did not see changed economic conditions as a motive for career changes. He saw it in the boredom and lack of fulfilment of people remaining in positions without individual responsibility. In entertaining ways, Dichter reinterpreted the disadvantages of accelerated capitalism as possible advantages. 'Self-realisation' and 'professional polygamy' sounded a lot more attractive than the fact that decreasing real income and part-time employment forced many to work in several jobs at once. In his book on success factors in leadership, published in 1984, Dichter already adopted the jargon Boltanski and Chiapello consider characteristic of the 1990s. Passing responsibility on to consumers yet another time, Dichter declared supreme the continual retraining, self-realisation, team work, brainstorming and cutting of bureaucracy: 'high-speed management is becoming increasingly necessary in order to keep up with rapidly changing consumer requests and the aging of new products' (Dichter 1984: 179). Boltanski and Chiapello describe the new management aims in more objective terms: 'Workers are able to organize themselves. Nothing is forced upon them. Instead, they identify with their project by themselves. The key character within this structure is the leader whose strength consists in having a vision, to communicate it and to win the support of others for it. [...] This vision has the same advantages as the spirit of capitalism, for it secures the commitment of the workers without applying violence, and it gives meaning to everyone's work.' (Boltanski and Chiapello 2003: 115).

If this description of the mouldable spirit of capitalism is applied to the work of Ernest Dichter, the reasons for his success become more tangible. After the Second World War, he was able to supply urgently needed visions both in the United States and in Europe (Haupt 1990: 54). Visions provide meaning. In the realm of the supernatural, visionaries have either founded religions or reformed existing ones. Dichter's sphere of action was the economy, although in the course of the twentieth century this realm acquired some essentially religious functions. Zaretsky and others have stressed that Fordism favoured the spread of psychoanalysis in North America (Zaretsky 2006: 201). Mass production was based on consumer demand that was supposed to be controlled by psychological techniques. In this context, Dichter was able to offer his services as a therapist of the masses in the 1940s. He communicated to his clients and to the public that the human soul harbours a fathomless potential of desires that he could help convert into fuel for the economy. Since at the same time the economy and the nation merged into a sacred whole, Dichter helped to turn the formerly sinful activity of spending money into a socially useful activity. In a period of accelerated mobility and increasingly fragile social embedding, Dichter offered goods as ties between people and imagined communities. An anti-Communist, he called for a fetishisation of goods and markets, portraying consumption as an activity that stabilised identities and provided meaning to the citizens of industrialised nations. Dichter's success remained intact until these grand, quasi-religious constructions of meaning were rocked by the new post-Fordist spirit of capitalism. In the 1970s, companies began to rely on less interpretative marketing research based on quantitative methods without any prior Motivation Research. Dichter's depth management seemed no longer necessary for the new syncretism of short-term, individualised constructions of meaning.

References

Aquin, Thomas von. 1952. *Summa Theologiae. Pars I^a^ et II^ae^*. Rom: Marietti.

Bell, E. 2008. Towards a critical spirituality of organization. *Culture and Organization* 14 (3): 293–307.

Benjamin, W. 1977. *Das Kunstwerk im Zeitalter seiner technischen Reproduzierbarkeit*. Frankfurt am Main.: Suhrkamp.

—— 1983. *Das Passagen-Werk*. In: R. Tiedemann, H. Schweppenhäuser (Eds), Gesammelte Schriften, vols 1 and 2. Frankfurt am Main.: Suhrkamp.

—— 1985. *Kapitalismus Als Religion*. In: R. Tiedemann, H. Schweppenhäuser (Eds), *Gesammelte Schriften* , vol. VI. Frankfurt am Main.: Suhrkamp, 100–103.

Boltanski, L., Chiapello, E. 2003. *The New Spirit of Capitalism*. London: Verso.

Braudel, F. 1986. *Sozialgeschichte des 15.–18. Jahrhunderts. Der Handel*. München: Kindler.

Brod, M. 1939. *Das Diesseitswunder oder die jüdische Idee und ihre Verwirklichung*. Tel-Aviv: Goldstein.

Cohen, L. 2006. *The Consumer's Republic: An American Model for the World?* In: S. Garon, P. McLachlan (Eds), *The Ambivalent Consumer: Questioning Consumption in East Asia and the West*. Ithaca/London: Cornell University Press, 45–62.

Csikszentmihalyi, M., Rochberg-Halton, E. 1981. *The Meaning of Things: Domestic Symbols and the Self*. Cambridge: Cambridge University Press.

Dichter, E. 1956. A pilot motivational research study on the psychology of supermarket-shopping in Binghampton, New York, for The Great Atlantic &

Pacific Tea Company. Report for Paris & Peart, Inc. Ernest Dichter Archive, University of Vienna, Report No. 892.

——— 1961. *Strategie im Reich der Wünsche* [*The Strategy of Desire*]. Düsseldorf: Econ-Verlag.

——— 1963a. Creativity: what it is and how it works. Article written by the Institute for Motivational Research and first appearing in its publication *Motivations*, New York. Ernest Dichter Archive, University of Vienna, Report No. 4305.

——— 1963b. The mass market is dying out. Copy from an US newspaper, title not mentioned. Ernest Dichter Archive, University of Vienna, Report No. 4308.

——— 1964. *Handbuch der Kaufmotive. Der Sellingappeal von Waren, Werkstoffen und Dienstleistungen* [Handbook of Consumer Motivations]. Wien/Düsseldorf: Econ-Verlag.

——— 1965. Discovering the 'Inner Jones'. *Harvard Business Review* 43 (3): 6–12.

——— 1969. Bericht einer Motivleitstudie über Tampons, speziell Camelia-Tampons für Vereinigte Papierwerke. Nürnberg. Durchgeführt von Ernest Dichter International, Ltd. Institute for Motivational Research, Croton-on-Hudson, NY, USA und Zürich/Schweiz. Ernest Dichter Archive, University of Vienna, Report No. 3039.

——— 1971. *Überzeugen nicht verführen. Die Kunst, Menschen zu beeinflussen*. Düsseldorf/Wien: Econ-Verlag.

——— 1975a. *Der nackte Manager. Erfolgreiches Management ohne Systemzwang*. Frankfurt am Main.: Lorch-Verlag.

——— 1975b. *Die zweite Karriere*. Wien/Düsseldorf: Econ-Verlag.

——— 1977. *Motivforschung – mein Leben. Die Autobiographie eines kreativ Unzufriedenen*. Frankfurt am Main.: Lorch-Verlag.

——— 1979. *Comment vivrons-nous en l'an 2000?* Paris: Hachette.

——— 1984. *So führen Manager ihr Unternehmen zu Spitzenleistungen. Auf der Suche nach den Erfolgsfaktoren der Führung*. Landsberg am Lech: Verlag Moderne Industrie.

——— 1986. What makes people buy? From supermarket to human market. Ernest Dichter Archive, University of Vienna, Report No. 5071.

——— 1989a. Why should the devil have all the good tunes? Unpublished Article, Ernest Dichter Archive, University of Vienna, Report No. 5067.

——— 1989b. Vortrag Vorarlberger Wirtschaftsforum, 16 November 1989 in Dornbirn. Ernest Dichter Archive, University of Vienna, Report No. 5068.

——— 1991. *Neues Denken bringt neue Märkte. Analyse der unbewussten Faktoren. Umsetzung ins Marketing. Anregungen und Beispiele*. Wien: Ueberreuter.

Findings. 1966. 2 (4), April.

——— 1967. 3 (2), February.

——— 1969. 5 (3), March.

——— 1971. 7 (6), June–July.

——— 1973. 9 (9), September.

Fullerton, R. 2007. Ernest Dichter, der Motivforscher. In: R. Gries, S. Schwarzkopf (Eds), *Ernest Dichter. Doyen der Verführer*. Wien: Mucha Verlag, 58–76.

Handelman, D. 1982. Reflexivity in festival and other cultural events. In: M. Douglas (Ed.), *Essays in the Sociology of Perception. Collected Works, Vol. VIII*. New York: Routledge, 162–190.

Haupt, K. 1990. The rise and fall of Ernest Dichter – Aus der Sicht eines psychologischen Marktforschers aus Deutschland. *Werbeforschung & Praxis* 6: 54–55.

Herz, M. 1958. *Sacrum commercium. Eine begriffsgeschichtliche Studie zur Theologie der Römischen Liturgiesprache.* München: Zink.

Kreuzer, F., Prechtl, G., Steiner, C. Eds. 2007. *A Tiger in the Tank: Ernest Dichter, an Austrian Advertising Guru.* Riverside: Ariadne Press.

Lears, T. J. J. 1994. *Fables of Abundance. A Cultural History of Advertising in America.* New York: Basic Books.

Löfgren, O. 1994. Consuming interests. In: J. Friedman (Ed.), *Consumption and Identity: Workshop on Commodities and Cultural Strategies.* Chur: Harwood, 47–70.

Luckmann, T. 1996. Religion – Gesellschaft – Transzendenz. In: H.-J. Höhn (Ed.), *Krise der Immanenz. Religion an den Grenzen der Moderne.* Frankfurt am Main.: Fischer, 128–153.

McGovern, C. 1998. Consumption and citizenship in the United States, 1900–1940. In: S. Strasser, C. McGovern, M. Judt (Eds), *Getting and Spending: European and American Consumer Societies in the Twentieth Century.* Cambridge: Cambridge University Press, 37–58.

Miller, D. 1998. *A Theory of Shopping.* New York: Cornell University Press.

Minichton, W. 1979. *Die Veränderungen der Nachfragestruktur von 1500 bis 1750.* In: C. Cipolla (Ed.), *Europäische Wirtschaftsgeschichte. Vol. 2: Sechzehntes und siebzehntes Jahrhundert.* Stuttgart/New York: Fischer, 51–111.

ORF (Österreichischer Rundfunk). 1984. *Warum? – Warum nicht? Franz Kreuzer im Gespräch mit Ernest Dichter und Peter R. Hofstätter.* Wien: Franz Deuticke.

Packard, V. 1957. *The Hidden Persuaders.* New York: D. McKay & Co.

Reinhardt, D. 1995. *Beten oder Bummeln? Der Kampf um die Schaufensterfreiheit.* In: P. Borscheid, C. Wischermann (Eds), *Bilderwelt des Alltags. Werbung in der Konsumgesellschaft des 19. und 20. Jahrhunderts.* Stuttgart: Steiner, 116–125.

Riesebrodt, M. 2007. *Cultus und Heilsversprechen. Eine Theorie der Religionen.* München: C. H. Beck.

Schor, J. B. 1992. *The Overworked American: The Unexpected Decline of Leisure.* New York: Basic Books.

Sorgo, G. 2006. *Abendmahl in Teufels Küche. Über die Mysterien der Warenwelt.* Wien: Styria.

Stallybrass, P., White, A. 1986. *The Politics and Poetics of Transgression.* London: Methuen.

Trentmann, F. 2006. *The Evolution of the Consumer: Meanings, Identities, and Political Synapses Before the Age of Affluence.* In: S. Garon, P. McLachlan (Eds), *The Ambivalent Consumer: Questioning Consumption in East Asia and the West.* Ithaca/London: Cornell University Press, 21–44.

Turner, V. 1995. *Vom Ritual zum Theater. Der Ernst des menschlichen Spiels.* Frankfurt am Main.: Fischer.

van Gennep, A. 1999. *Übergangsriten (Les Rites de Passage).* Frankfurt am Main.: Campus.

Zaretsky, E. 2006. *Freuds Jahrhundert. Die Geschichte der Psychoanalyse.* Wien: Zsolnay.

5
Ernest Dichter and Consumer Behaviour: Intellectual Primacy and Interpretive Consumer Research

Mark Tadajewski

5.1 Introduction

In this chapter, I propose that we look at the values underpinning Motivation Research. Specifically, I will focus on the axiology, ontology, epistemology and view of human nature that underscores much writing on Motivation Research in marketing, but particularly that of Ernest Dichter. My intent here is not to homogenise the work of scholars involved with Motivation Research. My point is to indicate that we might consider Motivation Research to be primarily associated with the interpretive research tradition (Tadajewski 2006).

To turn to the task at hand, by the time Dichter arrived in the United States Motivation Research was already well developed (Fullerton and Stern 1990; Lazarsfeld 1969). Appropriate reference points for similar scholarly endeavours would be the pioneering work conducted by Paul Lazarsfeld at the University of Vienna from the late 1920s onwards (Fullerton 1999); Dichter's own work at this institution in 1936 and later in the United States with Market Analysts, Inc. (Dichter 1979); the studies being conducted by Social Research, Inc. by Burleigh Gardner and Sidney Levy from the mid-1940s (Karesh 1995; Levy 2003, 2005). Equally important was Louis Cheskin's research at the Color Research Institute which was, in turn, a further development of research he had begun to conduct in the 1930s when he was working with the Chicago Board of Education (Cheskin 1957: 42, 46, 58, 101).

Further back in time, we could gesture to the work of J. George Frederick – the editor at *Printers' Ink*, who did much to promote Motivation Research – and who, it was claimed, had 'nearly half a century of professional experience with marketing and motivation research' by 1959 (Frederick 1959). Outside of the United States, the work of Wilhelm Vershofen promoted Motivation Research and qualitative market research via his studies at the Gesellschaft für Konsumforschung in Nuremberg, a consultancy which focused on empirical consumer research commensurate with Motivation Research (Bode 2007). It appears, therefore, that Motivation Research first emerged around 1909, developed further through the 1920s and 1930s, rising to prominence in the public consciousness with the publication of Packard's (1957) *The Hidden Persuaders*.

Certainly, as the above brief review indicates, the intellectual primacy of who first engaged in Motivation Research is contested. By Motivation Research, I mean an attempt to understand the motives underpinning consumer buying behaviour, and central to this task is the sorting out of the 'real' motives given by consumers from those that they espouse. Broadly speaking, these motives are classifiable, as Converse et al. proposed in 1958, into three broad categories: (1) those of which the consumer is consciously aware and willing to disclose to the researcher; (2) those of which they are aware, but are unwilling to divulge to the researcher; and (3) those motives of which the consumer is unaware and thereby unable to declare.

It is these unconscious or hidden motives that posed the greatest difficulties for conventional market research at the time. Generally involving the use of experimental-statistical tools, pre-coded questionnaires and large samples, this approach sought to discover the 'what and how explanations' so that the '*what* factors' could be manipulated by the marketer (Williams 1957: 128; emphasis in original). The prevalence of this scientific style was apparently communicated to Dichter just prior to his move to the United States: 'The worship of percentages has been held up to me as a typical American affliction by Paul Lazarsfeld. He predicted that I would never be successful with any of my new fangled ideas. They were too European. Luckily he was wrong' (Dichter 1979: 46).

In the main body of the chapter, I will examine Motivation Research in terms of its axiology, ontology, epistemology and view of human nature as these are represented in the Motivation Research literature. Although my focus is predominantly on the work of Ernest Dichter, other relevant sources will be drawn on.

5.2   Axiology – the values of Motivation Research

Marketing theory in the 1950s was predominantly logical empiricist, and this orientation is represented in the central values underpinning this discourse (Dichter 1979). Awareness of the limitations of current research practice and the growing use of Motivation Research among marketing practitioners led to intense academic interest (Blake 1954). Given the willingness to borrow the conceptual tools of other disciplines by marketing and consumer researchers, it was not long before Freudian theories and their implications for the conceptualisation of the consumer were being seriously discussed by marketing scholars (Collins and Montgomery 1970).

Dichter, however, was quick to question interpretations of his work that labelled him a Freudian, preferring instead to stress the 'eclectic' nature of his own axiological, epistemological and methodological influences (cf. Blankenship 1965): 'I have often been accused of being a Freudian. I don't see quite why this should be an accusation rather than a compliment. In reality I am not; I am much more of an eclectic. By popular opinion Freud is always associated with sex' (Dichter 1979: 92). What Dichter's remarks serve to forewarn here is the complex constellation of epistemic values that underpin Motivation Research. Even so, as a discreet community of discourse its main focus is on 'why' questions and answers; that is, on establishing a better understanding of why consumers engage in certain types of behaviour and why they view particular products in the manner that they do (Dichter 1961, 1978, 1979; Yoell 1950, 1952): 'It is not enough to know that young women use more hand lotions than older women. The point is to find out *why* people have these preferences' (Britt 1950: 669; emphasis in original).

In various attempts to understand why consumers purchase particular goods and services, there is far more nuance to the axiology of Motivation Research than would make this an exemplar of 'positivist' or 'interpretive research', when compared against Laurel Hudson and Julie Ozanne's (1988) review of the various ways of seeking knowledge about consumers. Dichter, for example, was not convinced that it is possible to explain consumer behaviour by subsuming it under a universal law. What motivation theorists actually proposed was that it is possible, given the appropriate research, for consumer behaviour to be explained and from such explanations that it will become possible to predict what a given cohort of consumers will do in any specific consumption situation. But their attempts to do so are not consistent with what Hudson and Ozanne (1988) suggest would be the case if this paradigmatic community were positivist.

Instead, motivation researchers look for some underlying thematic association between various consumer segments in order to explain why any given community will view, using the example provided by Haire (1950) for instance, a buyer and consumer of instant coffee as lazy, a bad wife, single and so forth. This type of thematic analysis is undertaken so that the motivation researcher can 'understand' the phenomena that they are investigating. They seek to do this by identifying the individual associations, meanings and symbolism that a consumer attaches to a given product or consumer environment (department store) and, over the process of conducting between 50 (Yoell 1952), 100–150 (Yoell 1950), 200 (Frederick 1959), 200–250 (*Business Week* 1955), 500 (Dichter 1960) 2,000 (Dichter 1964) and 3,000 (Frederick 1959) interviews, attempt to discern the pattern of shared meanings in the chosen sample.

The 'patterns' that the motivation researcher excavates are not expected to remain stable in the sense of a law-like generalisation. In spite of occasional reference to 'causal laws' or 'psychological laws', Dichter (1961: 79) did not speak in terms of the law-like generalisations now associated with logical empiricism. He used these terms to describe the way that general motivational patterns emerge from qualitative data, and he indicates that there are certain norms adhered to by a substantial proportion of the population.

Consistent with the pattern metaphor he invoked, Dichter reiterated the need for a contextualist world view when undertaking Motivation Research. This said, some similarity can still be discerned between motivation and logical empiricist research in the sense that Motivation Research does aim to generate an account that demonstrates the underlying systematic association between variables. And at its point of *tentative* conclusion, a piece of Motivation Research should provide 'a really thorough understanding of a … motivational pattern among a group large enough to indicate that the pattern is significant' (Dichter 1961: 77). Although, I should add, motivation researchers do place very concrete bounds on the extent to which generalisation is possible: 'Things that may be learned about one buyer situation in one locality with respect to one kind of product may have little or no applicability to another buyer situation in another locality with respect to another kind of product' (Britt 1960: 20). Emphasising these limitations further 'Actually, every social situation is different from every other and requires a separate analysis' (Britt 1950: 667).

One consequence of this limited generalisability is that the research process can never authoritatively conclude. As Dichter illustrated: '*Re-search* is a continued search with the emphasis on the search' (Dichter 1961: 2; emphasis in original). The task for motivation researchers is that they accept 'the need for continuous testing and observation' (Dichter 1960: 2). Here emphasis is placed on the ability and willingness of the researcher to bracket previous 'stereotypes' of consumer behaviour. The researcher must enter the field adopting a research strategy that bears resemblance to 'cultural anthropology' whose major axiological tenet 'considers that the day-to-day behavior of twentieth-century man – even when he lives in Brooklyn, on the outskirts of Paris, or in the south of Italy – is as worthy of study as the Samoans or the Trobrianders' (Dichter 1971: 2).

The demand that consumer researchers leave textbook stereotypes behind is an important axiological precept because these representations are believed to be wholly unrealistic: 'The people I encountered in the textbooks were nice, [and] rational. . . . No wonder we are disappointed and depressed when we meet the walking and talking master mold' (Dichter 1979: 113). What is required is careful observation of the consumption phenomena of interest and, as an example, Dichter recalls how he used observation supplemented with extensive photography when he was interested in the 'why' and 'how' people smoked. This was a 'scientific discovery trip' that aimed to understand how certain buying behaviours were influenced by the social context in which they were performed and by the consumers' own attitudes, beliefs, desires and budgetary considerations (Britt 1960; Dichter 1979).

Human behaviour, on this reading, is not only determined by outside forces acting on the individual. Instead, Dichter stressed the complex interplay between the individual, the group and the society in which they are emplaced. This is not to say that Motivation Research entirely distances itself from supporting a degree of determinism that, for one cultural critic, borders on being 'antihumanistic' in its potentiality for manipulation. Writing about the use of depth psychology to probe consumer consciousness, Packard argued, 'All of this probing and manipulation has its constructive and its amusing aspects; but also, I think it is fair to say, it has seriously antihumanistic implications. Much of it seems to represent regress rather than progress for man in his long struggle to become a rational and self-guiding being' (Packard 1960: 13).

Dichter, by contrast, exhibited a clear subscription to some mid-point between determinism and voluntarism, which is illustrated by comments such as 'We have something called willpower and even if, at times, I have expressed doubts about it, [the consumer] usually has a working brain and controllable emotions' (Dichter 1979: 192). So, where Packard presented motivation researchers as using advanced psychological techniques to probe the inner workings of the consumer's mind which, in conjunction with subliminal advertising (the two were often seen to be related), could motivate consumers in ways that were advantageous to the specific organisation funding the research (Klass

1958), Dichter (1960) dismissed such a view, as did the motivation researcher Steuart Henderson Britt (1960). Packard's interpretation of Motivation Research is, Britt argues, 'just so much hogwash' (1960: 228). There are, as the advertising researcher Bauer reminded us, clear 'limitations to persuasion', to quote the title of his chapter, since if it were true that motivation researchers were able to uncover, and thereby formulate, appeals which tapped unconscious and repressed motives then this, if psychoanalytic thought is correct, would 'produce intolerable anxiety. Hence, appeals to such motives may backfire and backfire violently' (Bauer 1964: 47). What Motivation Research may connect with, Bauer suggested, is not unconscious motives per se, but rather 'non-economic', 'non-essential' motives.

5.3   Ontological assumptions of Motivation Research

Although little discussed in the literature, there are brief ontological references relating to the nature of reality for motivation researchers. Conventional research at this time subscribed to naïve realism and the view that the external, physical world had an existence independent of human perception (Bayton 1958). In this historical context, among some marketing scholars, theories were not considered to impinge on observation, which was presupposed to be pure and untainted by mediating influences. Subscription to this view, while largely implicit, led consumer researchers to assume that the description of behaviour based on 'directly observable [and] directly ascertainable collections of facts' is likely to corroborate current hypotheses (Dichter 1978: 54). There is little, if any, ontological depth presumed here with surface phenomena connected in directly observable, causal fashion and whose empirical regularities are assumed to be measurable: 'It relies on observations, answers to questions, and recording and registrations of various forms of behaviour. It is, in the sense of modern semantics, based on naïve empiricism' (Dichter 1978: 55). In practice, this meant consumer researchers emphasised the utility of direct questions in the research process with causal relationships assumed to be identifiable between what consumers say they do and their actual behaviour (Politz 1957).

In contrast to this empiricism, motivation researchers espouse an ontological position that is closer to 'interpretivism' than to 'positivism', although it shares certain aspects of each, seeing the social world as embodying emergent, historically and temporally stable properties with certain behaviours dating 'back tens of thousands of years'

(Dichter 1979: 107). As Dichter registered, human behaviour is influenced 'by instinctive responses and social norms, or cultural values' and in response to the complexity of their lives consumers create cognitive shortcuts that enable them to move through and manage their everyday activities (Dichter 1960: 80). One pertinent example of what Dichter is gesturing towards here can be found in a discussion of consumer choice behaviour.

Studying the choice behaviour associated with purchasing soap, the Chicago-based motivation researchers Cheskin and Ward attempted to explain the popularity of one package over another. They concluded: 'it is self-evident that the average housewife does not consciously go to the grocery store to buy package designs; she goes to buy ham, vegetables, soap, canned fruit, and so on. Only rarely does she consciously consider the container in which these items are sold' (Cheskin and Ward 1948: 573). That is, the consumer is not necessarily a rational information processor or wholly beholden to deterministic forces that dictate appropriate behaviours, but is instead capable of exhibiting a degree of voluntarism in that they can refuse their extant consumption categorisation systems. Even allowing that this is possible, many consumers will not engage in an extended refusal of all previous knowledge, since as Britt (1960) suggested, this kind of individual would be in need of serious therapy given the decision-making paralysis that such a state would induce. More likely, as a consequence of environmental complexity, consumers will remain willing to engage in sub-optimal behaviours – what Szmigin and Foxall (2000) equate with a mid-point between the determinism of 'positivist' research and the voluntaristic perspective of 'interpretivism' – because it serves a useful purpose in enabling them to negotiate the complexity of everyday life.

In line with this mid-point position, the primary interest for the motivation researcher is how consumer behaviour is determined in part by the environmental conditions and the subjective perception of the consumption situation for their respondent(s). Consistent with this view of the social, whenever we are interested in understanding why a consumer, a group or a cultural unit behaves in the way that they do, Dichter wrote, 'I must use interpretative research. I cannot exclusively rely on asking the people or groups involved why they are doing what they are doing' (Dichter 1978: 54). Where research seeks to ask a 'why' question (in contrast to the 'what' questions asked by conventional marketing researchers), what they are asking for is an '*interpretation* of human behaviour' (Dichter 1978: 54; emphasis in original). 'We want to find out what motivated, what moved, what influenced these people to do what they did' (Dichter 1978: 54). Clearly motivation researchers do not ask these 'why' questions directly given that a very clear methodological aim of Motivation Research is concerned with sidestepping those rationalisations that are likely to emerge when the respondent feels that they have been placed in a position where they are being prejudged by the researcher. In methodological terms (which are discussed below), this involves the formulation of hypotheses, that are

> ...developed for the purpose of theoretically explaining a particular behavior. It then tests the validity of these various hypotheses, rejecting those which are not confirmed through further research and substituting others until several reasonable and supportable explanations for the behavior to be interpreted have been established.
>
> (Dichter 1978: 55)

After the initial sets of hypotheses have been determined, it is into the field that the motivation researcher shifts their attention, with the two most commonly used methods being the depth interview and various projective tests that could be used to elicit a description of the subjective process that a consumer goes through when purchasing goods or services (Haire 1950). Here the 'objective' external world is ontologically marginalised in favour of the subjective interpretation of the individual behaviour of the consumer (Dichter 1960). The espoused interpretations of their own behaviours by the respondents will not 'always correspond with reality', and it is the task of the motivation researcher to negotiate consumer espoused beliefs in favour of their repressed 'real', subjective beliefs, opinions and motivations (Britt 1960).

In a reflection on this process of ontological co-creation where both the interviewer and interviewee negotiate the nature of the social, Dichter proffered what appears to be an ontological position more in line with social constructionism than logical empiricism. Reflecting on the last stages of the research process, Dichter noted how those involved play a central part in the social construction of the 'world in which we live, the motivation researcher and the communicator who applies his findings are at the same time participants and formulators of the future world' (Dichter 1960: 63). And these players in the business community are ultimately responsive, Britt (1960) maintained, to the consumer, who is consequently a central participant in the ontological creation of the consumer society that Dichter (1960, 1971) applauded and Packard (1957) lamented.

5.4 Epistemological assumptions of Motivation Research

Dichter was extremely critical of the 'naïve empiricism' that underpins much 'nose counting research' (Dichter 1979) and the belief that research can be objective in the sense that it is free from any interpretation (Bayton 1958). What is more scientific is to acknowledge that motivation researchers, as the primary research instrument, will introduce certain assumptions into their projects: 'To state the existence of these assumptions, instead of pretending that they are not there, frees the researcher from naïve empiricism' (Dichter 1961: 2).

In order to illustrate a clear divergence between the epistemological presuppositions associated with the 'naïve' empiricism of the 1950s, it is appropriate to note the use of free association in Motivation Research. While free association is used in a clinical environment to treat maladjusted patients, when translated into Motivation Research, it is used to encourage the spontaneity of response in the interviewee, since allowing 'or encouraging a person with some slight guidance to simply pour out his feelings about a particular subject brings out true motivations in a much more reliable fashion than predetermining the framework in which the answers are to be given' (Dichter 1960: 285). Here the respondent is asked 'to summarize for us his own motivations and to give us the interpretation of what he considers normal, usual, average, etc. [and then] what we insist instead is that he report actual events' (Dichter 1960: 284). This process needs further qualification because regardless of the openness of the interpretive framework, and although Dichter and his fellow motivation researchers paid close attention to the introspective recall of the consumer, motivation researchers did not trust their respondents responses, but in actual fact subscribed to an 'epistemology of suspicion'.

In *Freud and Philosophy: An Essay on Interpretation*, Paul Ricoeur (1970) called Freud a 'master of suspicion'. By this, Ricoeur is trying to position psychoanalysis as a form of suspicious interpretation where the object of interest is distorted in some fashion, whether this is in the sense of the repression of sexual or aggressive wishes that societal convention places outside the bounds of acceptable behaviour and which consequently find themselves manifested in dreams, where the censorship of the ego is less influential. According to Freud (1900/1965), it is the task of the dream analyst to translate the dream language and the complexity and ambiguity that will be inherent in the complex network of meaningful associations that are condensed in the dream, so that it can be understood. With this in mind, Dichter's epistemological standpoint bears resemblance to Freud's 'suspicion'. For instance, Dichter referred to his own research position vis-à-vis his interviewees as similar to that of an 'archaeologist', while the personality of the respondent is akin to an 'onion' (Dichter 1979: 159, 188). What he meant is that the espoused responses elicited from the consumer might not reveal very much because people prefer to make their behaviour appear more rational and more reasonable. The motivation researcher therefore has to peel away the various layers of social, ego protection, much like one would peel an onion, in order to reveal the 'true', 'real' beliefs and behaviours.

This is not to say that consumers always behave irrationally, or that all behaviours have to be explained in terms of emotion. Rather, what this epistemological stance holds is that 'people do behave rationally. But rational behaviour also includes acceptance of emotions, such as the fear of embarrassment, as a motivator' (Dichter 1979: 114). This is not necessarily a function of consumer irrationality, but highlights that the motivation researcher must devote greater time to making what would otherwise be dismissed as irrational consumption behaviour understandable in terms of the standards of rationality acceptable at the time, assuming, of course, a certain degree of cultural relativism (Britt 1960). In an analogous manner to the concept of *verstehen* that underwrites interpretive research, motivation researchers see buying behaviour as never irrational in itself, but only from a particular point of view.

5.5 Methodological assumptions of Motivation Research

The realisation that the subjective beliefs of consumers might not mirror those they espouse heralded an important turn within marketing and consumer research regarding the conception of 'man'; that is, the understanding of human nature that was adopted as a methodological presupposition. Eliasberg (1954), for example, made the point that since the popularisation of Veblen's (1934) conspicuous consumption thesis it had become clear that consumers are not simply satisfied with the 'essential' products they must consume to sustain physiological life, such as food or shelter. Rather, their consumption becomes a way of satisfying other socially related ego needs and from this, he reasoned, the latest psychological and psychiatric techniques are of particular relevance for those interested in marketing and consumer behaviour (Eliasberg 1954; Vicary 1951). One way that these techniques can be acquired and utilised efficiently, Eliasberg suggested, is for companies to employ psychologists, sociologists and other trained behavioural experts in their consumer research departments. As an illustration of the contribution that such disciplines can make to consumer research he discussed Freud's views on personality development.

According to Eliasberg, Freud postulated 'three provinces in the human personality. They are the subconscious, the conscious ego and the superego' (Eliasberg 1954: 46). The term 'superego' is used to describe the influence of conscience and ego ideals as they are derived from parental or cultural example throughout childhood. Conscious ego, in Eliasberg's formulation, is used to refer to the more rational aspects of personality and like the super ego before it, is a mixture of both conscious and unconscious elements. Here the ego's task is to monitor and control the more primitive aspects of personality: the id impulses that violate social convention.

As an example of this theory in practice, the marketing and motivation researcher Bayton (1958) discussed the willingness to consume credit. Attempting to explain the growing readiness of consumers to use credit facilities as a means to postpone present expenditures at the same time as increasing discretionary spending today, one possible psychoanalytic interpretation of this will-to-consume is that there has been a modification of superego control over attitudes towards credit availability (Bayton 1958: 285).

Whereas in the past, the 'ego-ideal' was oriented towards expanding 'savings', with debt seen as somehow 'immoral' and something to 'hide' from the neighbours, beliefs and motivations towards credit had gradually shifted towards the control of the ego, which emphasises caution but within certain bounds (Bayton 1958: 285). Provided debt could be managed, it could be consumed. Bringing his interpretation in line with the changing nature of consumption habits, Bayton suggested that the implication of this increased disposable income and the relaxation of superego control were that the individual consumer had become psychically more able to consume both the necessities of everyday life alongside a small, but satisfying, selection of luxury goods without feeling too guilty, particularly where these catered to ego-ideals (Bayton 1958).

Although Bayton directly imported Freudian theory to interpret consumer behaviour, in general Motivation Research did not import psychoanalytic theory or method *in toto* into consumer research, regardless of accusations otherwise (Rothwell 1955; Scriven 1958; Westfall et al. 1957; Williams 1957). Nor was it an attempt to uncover and repair neuroses implanted in childhood (Dichter 1979). A 'much better'

Figure 5.1 Ernest Dichter at a Group Discussion, *c.*1966.

description of the relationship between psychoanalysis and Motivation Research is that both are forms of 'psychological detective work' where the researcher is viewed as a 'psycho-detective' charged with uncovering consumer motivations through extended in-depth interviews (Dichter 1979: 79). The kind of 'detective work' that this involves and the environment in which it takes place does not resemble a 'proper' psychoanalytic counselling session but bears more resemblance, Dichter asserted, to a form of 'mini-psychoanalysis' utilising qualitative research and small samples (Dichter 1979: 45, 49).

When a particularly 'interesting' behaviour had been uncovered in the initial exploratory research, these themes were examined further through 'lengthy interviews' with 100–300 participants selected from various groups 'in order to prove or disprove our original hypothesis' (Dichter 1979: 49). Each of these interviews were recorded verbatim and 'every phrase, every gesture, and every intonation of the respondent' noted by the researcher (Dichter 1960: 285; see Figure 5.1). The logic of this approach is explicated by Newman (1958). Newman proposed that free association encourages the consumer to avoid recourse to any extensive logical analysis of the narrative they espoused, permitting the skilled interviewer to uncover those thoughts that have somehow been repressed by the respondent. In a project that sought to understand why men read the magazine *Esquire*, which 'at that time resembled *Playboy* or *Penthouse*', Dichter explained his research approach:

> I would go out and talk at great length to a number of men, but I would not ask them why they did or did not read *Esquire*. I would simply let them tell me their associations, their experiences, their ideas and thoughts while talking and thumbing through the magazine.
>
> (Dichter 1979: 34)

In the interview situation, the task of the motivation researcher is to reassure the respondent by 'developing rapport...inserting delicate probes, where necessary, to encourage fuller discussion' (Dichter 1958: 28). The respondent was asked to provide a description, at length, of a specific time when they actually used the product or service. Discussing the in-depth interview, Dichter reminds us how distinct Motivation Research remains from psychoanalysis: 'it isn't really putting somebody on the couch.... It's very simple. We don't tell our interviewer what we are interested in, just as the physician does not tell the lab assistant that he suspects that the patient has liver disease' (Bartos 1986: 17).

Here the emphasis is on the analysis of the subjective accounts that are generated by researcher immersion in the consumption history of the individual concerned. Importance is placed on letting the emergent nature of the phenomena reveal its characteristics to the researcher rather than, as we would expect with a 'positivist' study, the researcher imposing a conceptual framework, identified prior to the fieldwork on consumer behaviour. Instead, the guiding epistemological assumption framing the discussions of the research strategy appropriate for Motivation Research is that an emergent research design is favoured, and an ethos of openness and sensitivity to the nature of the phenomena is all pervasive: 'Researching is a process where open-mindedness, the ability to see seemingly unrelated things as related and in a new light, is the major requirement' (Dichter 1960: 70).

5.6   Conclusion: the marginalisation of Motivation Research

Admitting that bias is introduced into research as a function of our own historical and cultural position was never likely to be a popular view in an academy that remained wedded to empiricism. Moreover, when such comments come from outside of the academy, primarily from practitioners who failed to have the institutional legitimacy that academics desired (Martineau 1955, 1961) and who also deliberately flouted the existing rules of discursive formation by criticising the excessive quantification of marketing research, Motivation Research was ripe for discipline.

This tendency was compounded by the fact that the scholarly Dichter of his early writing became subsumed under the 'messianic' (Collins and Montgomery 1970) figure of Ernest Dichter marketing man and believer of his own hype, with comments such as the following appearing in print: 'I could cure cancer, solve international conflicts eliminating wars, or to put it very modestly, become a messiah who could use his talents in almost all areas' (Dichter 1979: 13). And this, Collins and Montgomery (1970) maintain, was one cause of the active turn against Motivation Research in the 1960s (cf. Tadajewski 2006); with Dichter's 'Pentecostally fervent advocacy of Motivation Research ... [obscuring] its possible usefulness' (Collins and Montgomery 1970: 10). Certainly, the time came when marketing and consumer scholars were simply not seeing what Motivation Research had to offer apart from the discursive pyrotechnics that Dichter continued to perform.

References

Bartos, R. 1986. Ernest Dichter: motive interpreter. *Journal of Advertising Research* 26 (1): 15–20.

Bauer, R. A. 1964. The limits to persuasion: the hidden persuaders are made of straw. In: M. M. Grossack (Ed.), *Understanding Consumer Behavior*. Boston, MA: The Christopher Publishing House, 39–52.

Bayton, J. A. 1958. Motivation, cognition, learning – basic factors in consumer behaviour. *Journal of Marketing* 22 (3): 282–289.

Blake, J. K. 1954. Consumer motivation research. *Dun's Review and Modern Industry* (July): 30–46.

Blankenship, A. B. 1965. Freud in consumerland. *Journal of Marketing* 29 (1): 116.

Bode, M. 2007. How the Germans invented interpretive consumer research and forgot all about it. The rise and fall of the qualitative Nürnberg School of Consumer Research in Germany. Paper Presented at the 4th Interpretive Consumer Research Conference, April 26th and 27th, Marseille, France.

Britt, S. H. 1950. The strategy of human motivation. *Journal of Marketing* 14 (5): 666–674.

——— 1960. *The Spenders*. New York: McGraw-Hill.

Business Week 1955. Research rivals trade blows. 29 October: 56–60.

Cheskin, L. 1957. *How to Predict What People Will Buy*. New York: Liveright.

Cheskin, L., Ward, L. B. 1948. Indirect approach to market reactions. *Harvard Business Review* 26 (5): 572–81.

Collins, L., Montgomery, C. 1970. Whatever happened to motivation research? End of the Messianic hope. *Journal of the Market Research Society* 12 (1): 1–11.

Converse, P. D., Huegy, H. W., Mitchell, R. V. 1958. *Elements of Marketing*. 6th Edition. London: Sir Issac Pitman and Son.

Dichter, E. 1958. Toward an understanding of human behavior. In R. Ferber and H. G. Wales (Eds), *Motivation and Market Behavior*. Homewood, IL: Richard D. Irwin, 21–30.

——— 1960. *The Strategy of Desire*. New York: Doubleday.

——— 1961. Seven tenets of creative research. *Journal of Marketing* 25 (4): 1–4.

——— 1964. *Handbook of Consumer Motivations: The Psychology of the World of Objects*. New York: McGraw-Hill.

——— 1971. *Motivating Human Behavior*. New York: McGraw-Hill.

——— 1978. Interpretive versus descriptive research. In: J. N. Sheth (Ed.), *Research in Marketing*, Vol. 1. Greenwich: JAI Press, 53–78.

——— 1979. *Getting Motivated by Ernest Dichter: The Secret Behind Individual Motivation by the Man Who Was Not Afraid to Ask 'Why?'*. New York: Pergamon Press.

Eliasberg, W. 1954. Freud, Veblen and marketing. *Printers' Ink* 12 February: 46–52.

Frederick, J. G. 1959. *Introduction to the New Science and Art of Motivation Research*. Liverpool: The Bell Press.

Freud, S. 1900/1965. *The Interpretation of Dreams*. J. Strachey (Trans.). New York: Avon.

Fullerton, R. 1999. An historic analysis of advertising's role in consumer decision-making: Paul F. Lazarsfeld's European research. *Advances in Consumer Research* 26 (1): 498–503.

Fullerton, R., Stern, B. 1990. The rise and fall of Ernest Dichter. *Werbeforschung und Praxis* (June): 208–211.

Haire, M. 1950. Projective techniques in marketing research. *Journal of Marketing* 24 (5): 649–656.

Hudson, L. A., Ozanne, J. L. 1988. Alternative ways of seeking knowledge in consumer research. *Journal of Consumer Research* 14 (4): 508–521.

Karesh, M. A. 1995. The social scientific origins of symbolic consumer research: Social Research, Inc. In: K. M. Rassuli., S. C. Hollander, T. R. Nevett (Eds), *Marketing History: Marketing's Greatest Empirical Experiment*. Fort Wayne, IN: Association of Historical Research in Marketing, 95–111.

Klass, B. 1958. The ghost of subliminal advertising. *Journal of Marketing* 23 (2): 146–150.

Lazarsfeld, P. 1969. An episode in the history of social research: a memoir. In: D. Fleming, B. Bailyn (Eds), *The Intellectual Migration: Europe and America, 1930–1960*. Cambridge, MA: Harvard University Press, 270–337.

Levy, S. J. 2003. Roots of marketing and consumer research at the University of Chicago. *Consumption, Markets and Culture* 6 (2): 99–110.

——— 2005. The evolution of qualitative research in consumer behavior. *Journal of Business Research* 58 (3): 341–347.

Martineau, P. 1955. It's time to research the consumer. *Harvard Business Review* 33 (4): 45–54.

——— 1961. Respectable persuasion. *The Journal of Marketing* 25 (4): 108–110.

Newman, J. W. 1958. *Motivation Research and Marketing Management*. Boston, MA: Harvard Business School, Division of Research.

Packard, V. 1957. *The Hidden Persuaders*. New York: MacKay.

——— 1960. *The Hidden Persuaders*. Harmondsworth: Penguin.

Politz, A. 1957. Science and truth in marketing research. *Harvard Business Review* 35 (1): 117–126.

Ricoeur, P. 1970. *Freud & Philosophy: An Essay on Interpretation*. D. Savage (Trans.). New Haven, CO: Yale.

Rothwell, N. D. 1955. Motivational research revisited. *Journal of Marketing* 20 (2): 150–154.

Scriven, L. E. 1958. Rationality and irrationality in motivation research. In: R. Ferber, H. G. Wales (Eds), *Motivation and Market Behavior*. Homewood, IL: Richard D. Irwin, 64–74.

Szmigin, I., Foxall, G. 2000. Interpretive consumer research: how far have we come. *Qualitative Market Research: An International Journal* 3 (4): 187–197.

Tadajewski, M. 2006. Remembering motivation research: toward an alternative genealogy of interpretive consumer research. *Marketing Theory* 6 (4): 429–466.

Veblen, T. 1934. *The Theory of the Leisure Class*. New York: Random House.

Vicary, J. M. 1951. How psychiatric methods can be applied to market research. *Printers' Ink* 11 May: 39–48.

Westfall, R. L., Boyd, H. W., Campbell, D. T. 1957. The use of structured techniques in motivation research. *Journal of Marketing* 22 (2): 134–139.

Williams, R. J. 1957. Is it true what they say about motivation research? *Journal of Marketing* 22 (2): 125–133.

Yoell, W. 1950. Base your advertising on the true buying motive. *Printers' Ink* 8 September: 38–39.

——— 1952. Make your advertising themes match consumer behavior. *Printers' Ink* 21 March: 82–87.

Part III

The Branding of Consumer Life – Case Studies on Ernest Dichter's Work

6
Ernest Dichter's Studies on Automobile Marketing

Helene Karmasin

6.1 Introduction

Dichter's reception by the general public in the United States and in Europe was mainly determined by his analyses of a few product areas which provided material for some rather popular myths that are known also to people who do not have much knowledge about Dichter's specific work in market research and consumer psychology. These myths of course include the *topos* of the convertible car being a man's 'mistress' and the sedan car being his wife, which Dichter first developed in January 1940 for Chrysler and their Plymouth brand (Dichter 1960a: 289–297). Based on Dichter's advice to bring the dream of a 'mistress' a little bit closer to a man who still ends up 'marrying his wife' by buying the sedan, the Chrysler corporation developed the hardtop car (Packard 1957: 77–78; Twitchell 1997: 111–113). The remarkable career of Dichter's gendered mistress–wife metaphor and the fact that it has remained a part of Western cultural memory for so long indicate that in some way his ideas reflect a distinct set of cultural beliefs. They also show that cars as objects of consumption are a unique area of symbolic production in the wider field of consumer interaction with objects and marketing messages (Holbrook 2006; Karmasin 2007; Martineau 1958; Wilson 2002). A large number of market analyses carried out today show that more than ever the symbolic and communicative 'meaning' of cars can be used to sell them and that their market value actually depends on that meaning to a large extent. The success of off-road vehicles (SUVs) is just one example that shows how the image of manliness, family protection and outdoor lifestyles can justify car-makers' pricing strategy. Few marketers would agree that the price of an average SUV was based on its material production costs or its actual use value in consumers' daily lives.

Ernest Dichter never bothered to develop a coherent and – crucially – testable model of consumer motivations. But his eclecticism was in great demand among American and European car-makers between the 1950s and the 1980s, like Chrysler, Ford, General Motors (Pontiac, Chevrolet) and Nash in the United States, and Citroën and Renault in France (see Pouillard in this book), and Saab, Volvo, Vauxhall, the British Motor Corporation, Ford, Volkswagen, and Mercedes Benz in Great Britain and Germany. He studied the sales opportunities and psychological barriers to certain American car brands in Canada, Australia and virtually all parts of non-Communist Europe. At the Dichter Archive at Vienna University (Austria), there are around two hundred studies by the Dichter Institute for various car-makers, but also for makers of tyres and other spar parts producers that make up the global automobile industry. In his handbooks on Motivation Research, Dichter devoted large sections to the analysis of the various motives that drive consumers to accept or reject a car (Dichter 1960a: 33–36; 1964: 262–285).

Moreover, Dichter developed research projects *around* cars as highly symbolic and laden consumer objects. Like other market researchers, he realised that modern lifestyle changes of the 1960s, 1970s and 1980s, like the gradual disappearance of the 'nuclear family', growing urbanisation, the increased demand on employees to commute longer distances to and from work and the rising environmental and economic concerns of government planners about private mobility and petrol consumption, could be studied by engaging with people's uses of cars (Dichter 1966, 1971). He also used the car as a symbol and object of symbolic material practices when he asked in 1967 whether we live our life as a 'series of cars' (Dichter 1967b).

An analysis of the available archival material helps correct a number of public myths about Ernest Dichter. All car-related studies were carried out with high precision and care and were based on a number of well-founded hypotheses and techniques. They were anything but a stroke of genius of a 'depth psychology nerd'. The fact that the automobile industry was dominated by engineers with a practical knowledge about statistical techniques might have spurred Dichter on to pay greater attention to the validity of the data he produced. In addition, the automobile industry contributed a major share of his annual research income so he would have been wise not to offend any of his clients with shoddy market research. All of Dichter's findings and analyses were accompanied by very pragmatic suggestions about their market-oriented use; in other words, all studies advised clients very clearly on what they should do in order to solve their problems. In the individual studies, the car is not only seen as a means to make individual and hidden desire come true, and it is not only interpreted as an answer to 'everybody's unconscious' – as the familiar quote about the sports car being a mistress and the sedan being a wife would suggest. Although this was a novel and spectacular statement, Dichter's conceptualisation of the car was one of an object that conveyed meaning and embodied the values of a society. For Dichter, a car was thus a semiotic system, a sign system. This is in fact an important finding since Dichter's semiotic ideas were acknowledged only much later in the literature on the semiotics of marketing and product cultures (Barthes 1964; Eco 1976; Valentina 2007; Williamson 1978).

6.2 Basic methods and techniques used for the studies

Dichter's studies used a holistic approach with comprehensive questionnaires being prepared in advance. When offering a new study to an existing or a prospective client, Dichter always included a detailed list of questions in the proposal which had to be asked in order to solve the client's specific problem. If, for example, a client asked: 'Why do people buy or not buy a Nash/Chrysler/Ford/General Motors car?', then Dichter's project proposal included the following questions (Dichter 1950, 1962):

- Which trends do characterise present-day society?
- Which groups are the focus of attention and what are their demands on their car?
- Which different groups of drivers are there

  - with respect to their general values: conformists versus non-conformists
  - with respect to their lifestyles: singles, families, business people
  - with respect to the significance that their car has for them

- Which types of cars are there in the market: American/foreign cars?
- What is the car-maker's corporate brand image? How do the company's image, the brand image and the image of a given make of car interact?
- How do buyers, non-buyers think?

- What does the decision-making and purchasing process look like, if one takes into account friends and the dealer's activities?
- Which technical features of the car are perceived and in what way?
- What effect do product names have? Do some car names sound masculine, feminine, American, foreign?
- What impact did past advertising have on brand and product utility perception among the car's target group?

These and other questions were worded as hypotheses. In addition, there were also questions which were derived and formulated from an in-depth research with few, sometimes as few as twenty, consumers. Yet, crucially, all hypotheses were subjected to a quantitative analysis. Dichter's automobile projects usually comprised a comprehensive and team-oriented set of research activities. For example, a team of psychologists, social scientists, psychiatrists and anthropologists would consider the problem before it was dealt with and their work was included in the analysis of findings. All reports included careful documentation and their conclusions were based on discernible and verifiable research results, not lofty 'insights'. They also contained conclusions which were directly relevant to marketing strategies. These activities of course reflected state-of-the-art market research practice of the post-war years. What was unique, however, was the considerable personal, or 'guru', element in the filed reports. Rather than presenting his institute's findings as detached and objective research data, Dichter was careful to add himself and his private opinion as the actual bonus of the research the client purchased. It was this subjective component which differentiated Dichter's research services from that of his competitors and finally justified the high service fee his clients paid.

What was also new and unique was Dichter's heavy reliance on depth interviews with selected consumers. These were largely unstructured interviews and – unfortunately for the historian – their questions were never really documented. The results from these interviews were often presented in the form of literal quotes. However, Dichter never specifically explained or justified why these quotes were selected or which method of analysis was used when deciding whether a recorded consumer insight was research-relevant or not. Nevertheless, Dichter's conclusions were often far-reaching and convey very interesting ideas about the meanings and uses of cars in post-war Western societies. In essence, they show a meticulous understanding of the desires, fantasies and needs of consumers at the time, but also their way of thinking and the cultural values on which these needs, wants and desires were based. One can assume that Dichter did not base his work on any explicit theory whatsoever – and certainly not only on 'depth psychology' – but that he had an imaginative way of arriving at and interpreting his conclusions, based on subtle cultural knowledge, which apparently was what made him so attractive to managers from Detroit to New York and Paris. This knowledge could have been based on the theories of structuralism or cultural theory; that is, on Roland Barthes (1958), Claude Lévi-Strauss (1958), Mary Douglas (1975) and Mary Douglas and Isherwood Baron (1996), who, however, were probably not known to him. In a very practically minded way, Dichter nevertheless developed structuralist and semiotic theories in parallel, without really spelling out the theoretical implications of his findings. In the absence of anthropological or social theoretical foundations, Dichter often resorted to Freudian psychoanalysis in order to provide his research results with a quasi-scientific grounding.

Other novel research techniques that Dichter applied at various times included projective techniques and tests, such as polarity profiles, allocation of values and completion of sentences. When testing the significance and impact of advertisements, consumers were presented with a journal of thoughts from which the researcher concluded to what extent a person identified with the advertised products (Dichter 1965, 1967a). Dichter also sent out research staff to observe consumers and sales personnel during the processes of a car purchase. In some instances, research staff acted as consumers, pretending to be interested in a particular car, in order to detect possible flaws in the sales techniques of his clients' sales staff. Today, of course, we know this technique as 'mystery shopping'.

The following pictures visualise some of Dichter's techniques and show them 'at work' (Figures 6.1–6.5; from Dichter 1959, 1972a). Some of them engage directly with consumers' actual uses of cars (Figures 6.2 and 6.5) and measure what purposes a specific car is serving within a particular family setting. Conveniently, as both pictures show, Dichter used respondents from his local Peekskill area on the Hudson River. A polarity profile (Figure 6.1) helped Dichter to find out about people's feelings about the car they would like to drive in the future. In another exercise (Figure 6.3), consumers were asked to describe a 'typical' Ford, General Motors, Chrysler or AMC car. This allowed Dichter to discern attitudinal descriptors that consumers used to 'order' the world of cars; for example, in terms of 'fast' or 'large cars', those with 'boring designs' or 'family',

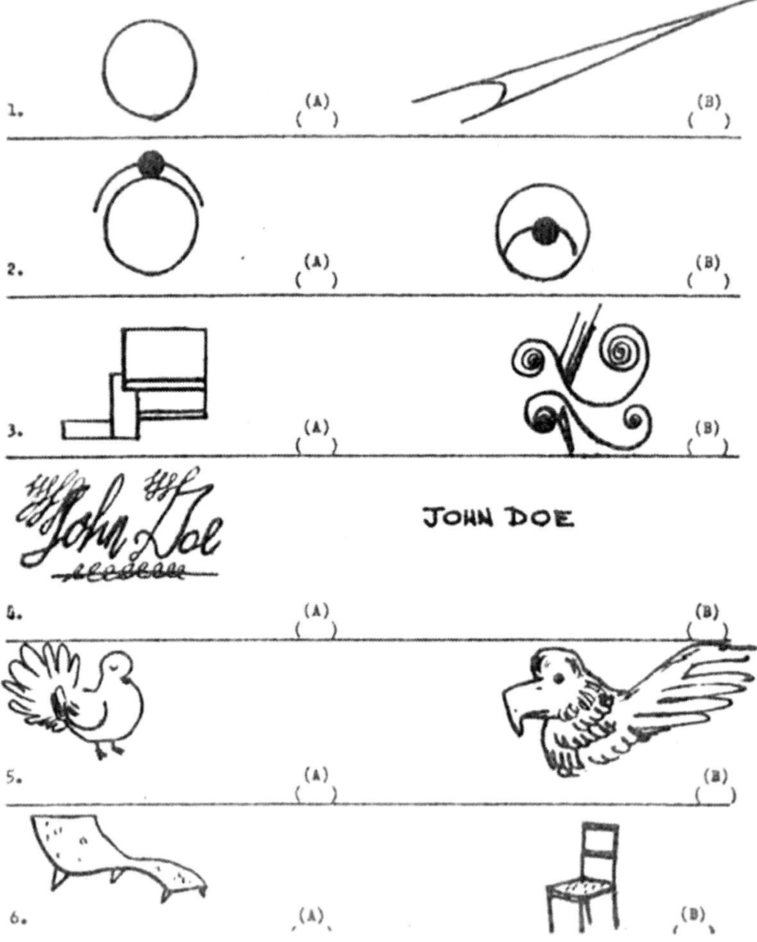

Figure 6.1   Projective Technique (from Dichter 1959).

'expensive' or technologically 'refined' cars. Figure 6.4, in turn, shows that Dichter early on worked with the idea that not just demographic factors (income, age, sex, family status) determined a consumer's choice of car brands but also wider behavioural and psychographic factors like

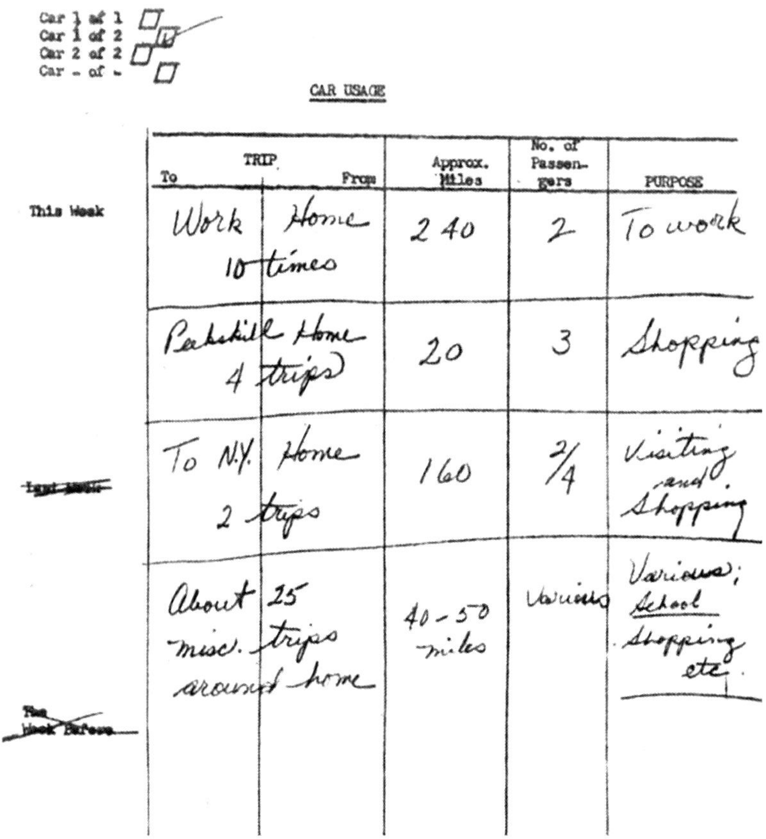

Car ½ of 1 ☐
Car 1 of 2 ☐
Car 2 of 2 ☐
Car _ of _ ☐

CAR USAGE

	TRIP		Approx. Miles	No. of Passengers	PURPOSE
	To	From			
This Week	Work 10 times	Home	240	2	To work
	Peekskill 4 trips	Home	20	3	Shopping
	To N.Y. 2 trips	Home	160	2/4	Visiting and Shopping
	About 25 misc. trips around home		40–50 miles	Various	Various; School Shopping etc.

Figure 6.2   Care Usage (from Dichter 1959).

self-concept, time orientation, moral attitudes towards expenditure and credit, status orientation and education.

6.3 Dichter's concept of consumer motivations and the symbolism of a car

The essential factor in all of Dichter's research conclusions was that the non-functional values of a car were the defining factors that drove consumers' decision making. In other words, car brands had to acquire the right type of meanings in order to resonate with consumers and in order to be perceived as attractive by them. It was only later, much later in fact, that anthropologists like Grant McCracken began to write about how consumer products form a language of meaningful symbols into

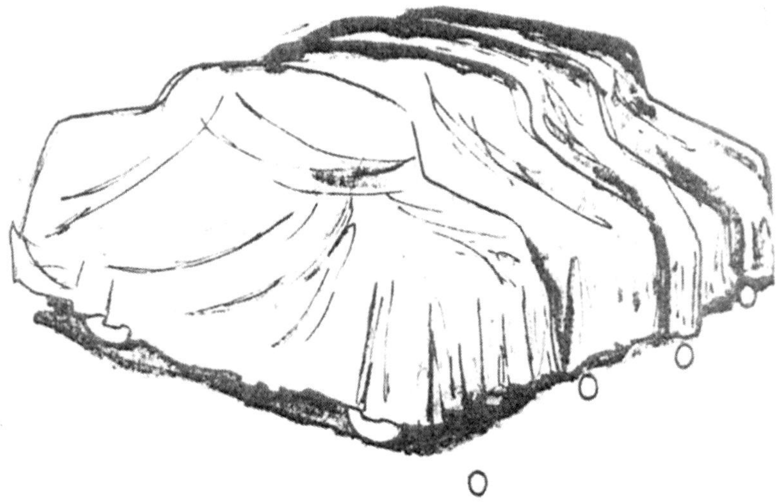

Figure 6.3   Elicitation of Responses (from Dichter 1959).

which consumers actively buy in and from which they actively choose (McCracken 1988, 2005: 53–92).

Dichter studied how those symbolic values aroused feelings in consumers' minds, how they interacted with hopes and fears, and what they could compensate. In this respect, Dichter's recourse to depth psychology is best noticeable. In Dichter's research, it was clear that car brands had extraordinarily high sign value and that cars were thus purchased to reaffirm a consumer's social status that either signalled conformity or nonconformity, youth or tradition. While Dichter's contemporaries acknowledged that cars were bought for their prestige value, Dichter widened the scope of researchable value factors that signified important symbolic meaning for consumers. Particularly, his 1960s studies on Ford show how he attempted to identify the complex network of desirable objects, values and behaviours that resulted in the purchase of a specific

Faces the product

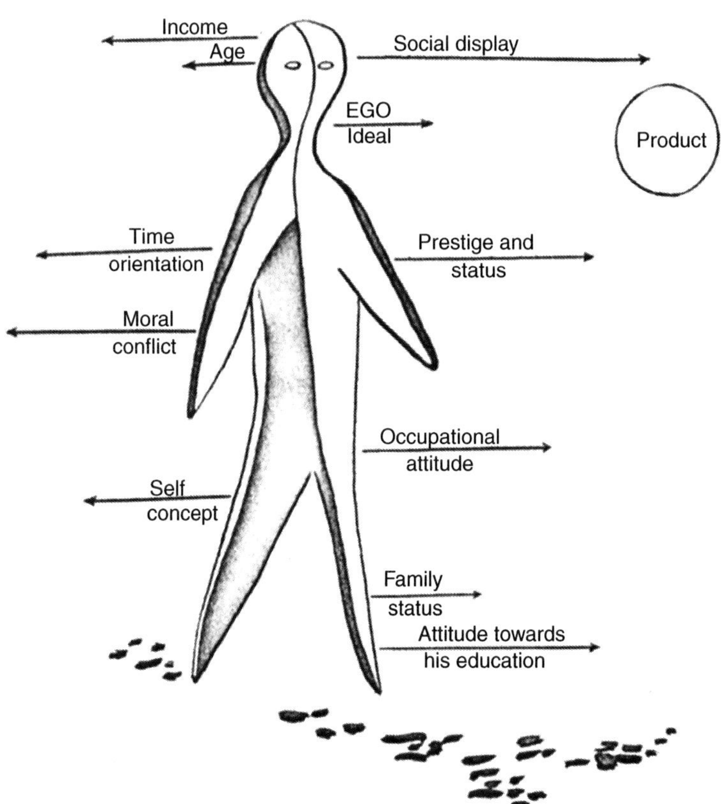

Figure 6.4   Consumer Attitude Categories (from Dichter 1972a).

car brand. It is therefore not surprising that he began to describe himself as a cultural anthropologist.

Another remarkable result of his analyses is the attention he gave to the communication of significance. He described in much detail that the significance of a car and a brand is communicated on several levels. The physical characteristics of the car (size, motor, design, interior, acoustic code, colour code), the sign system that has been created through the corporation's brand and car names, its advertising and its pricing strategy all play a part in how consumers build associations that translate into measurable attitudes towards a particular car. Dichter made

118

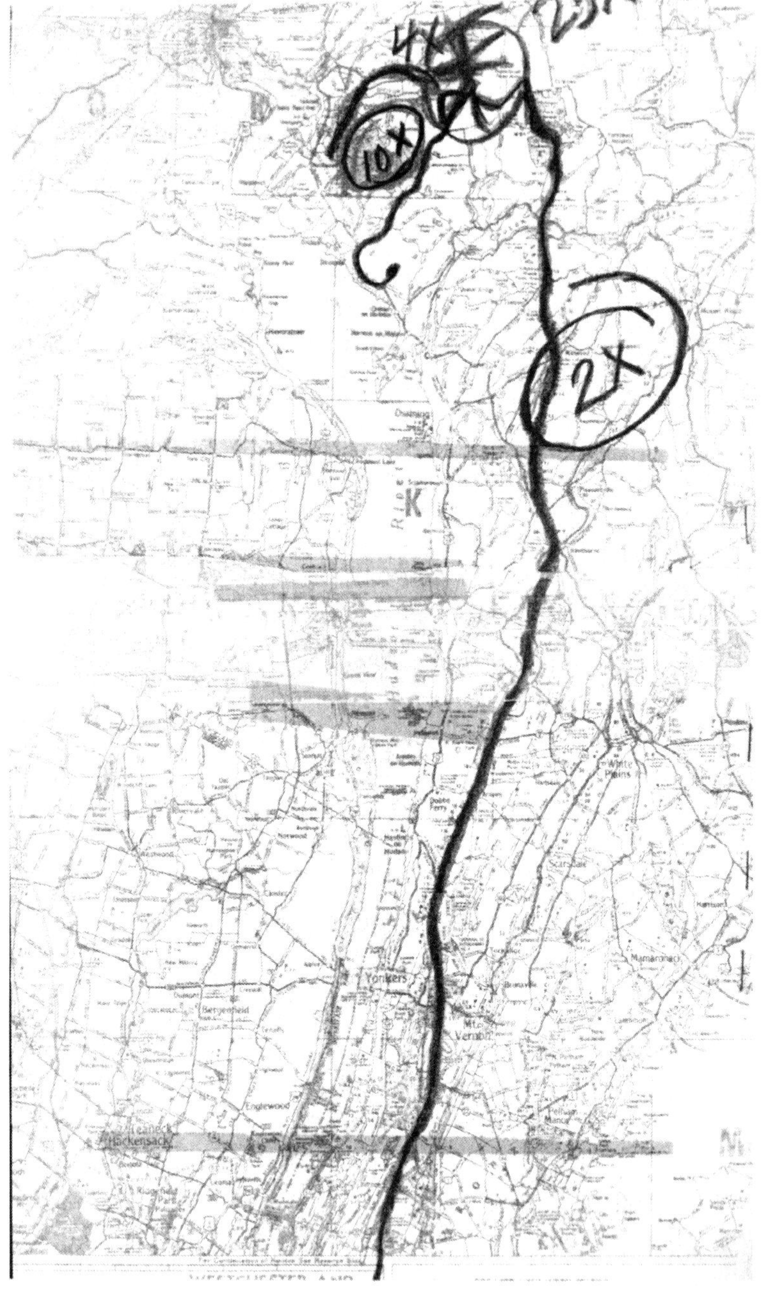

Figure 6.5   Care Usage (from Dichter 1959).

his clients aware that all of the above aspects were condensed into an image that controlled the perception and assessment of information by consumers. Dichter thus worked on an implicit semiotic theory which, however, he never explicitly described or theoretically codified. He thus advised his clients to build motivational appeals that fuelled the flames of desire not so much through exciting words and pictures but through psychological excitement engendered by the promise of dreams coming true.

Dichter's car studies specified some such motives that could be translated into consumer appeals. In his idea, a car fulfilled a man's dream of seven-league boots and was thus an extension of his ego and a possible compensation for low self-esteem. A car allowed a man to buy energy, power, strength and success. A car could also collectively stand for power and strength. For example, he described how Volkswagen and Mercedes contributed to re-establishing Germany's reputation after the war and how such symbolic stories could identify these German car brands with the idea of power, recovery, strength and success. A car could be an expression of a social revolution, a symbol of mobility and a symbol of the middle class as it separated developed from underdeveloped nations. The very mobility of cars allowed them to stand for youth, virility, 'youthful lifestyle' and, in an extrapolation, for life itself as people could live their life as 'series of cars' or often fondly remembered their 'first car' (Dichter 1967b). Driving was thus a symbol of life, fight and flight. It made possible ruling, discovery, speed and the mastery of destiny. Moreover, cars had a personality. Consumers often described their cars as 'my companion', 'my valued friend, a being that belongs to me' or an extension of 'my home'. By touching it, by cleaning it and by repairing and refitting it with new accessories, consumers made cars their homes and turned it into a 'person' they felt they knew.

Consumers filled the car with a 'soul' and animated it (Latin: anima = soul). Each car and each brand therefore had a unique personality that was different from other cars and other brands. When buying a car, consumers wanted to feel that the car was made 'for them' and that it took into account individual needs. Rather than merely being a bland symbol of social status or income, a car said a thousand things more about its owner, and consumers implicitly knew that. A car, naturally, also had a more obvious use value and consumers wanted their cars to be reliable and 'unproblematic' – the 'silent servant' that so many middle-class families began to remember after the Second World War. These silent servants were entrusted by their owner with a family's safety and security. A car therefore had to communicate 'stability' and 'permanence'. Other factors that Dichter's research elicited included the perceived drama of choice for consumers who were faced with an ever-larger number of cars they were invited to buy. Moreover, cars – and choice – seemed to get more complicated as more and more technical details required the consumer's attention. Because more and more car models were launched year after year, consumers feared the loss of value after having made the purchase (buyer remorse). In other consumers, Dichter detected an astonishing eye for detail. Minute aspects of a car, like the window lift or the position of the rear-view mirrors, came into play when choosing between cars. In addition, consumers of course paid attention to the question whether they were made to feel important in the car dealer's showroom and whether the dealer was able to negotiate on price and conditions of service.

Based on these research insights, Dichter developed a number of consumer typologies that were of use to car manufacturers in segmenting their markets. One of these typologies assumed that a car was an expression of a general pattern of living and that it corresponded to a 'personality make-up'. Different consumer personalities preferred different types and makes of cars. Today, we know this as VALS typology, within which consumers are segmented according to identifiable and measurable values, attitudes and lifestyles (Solomon 2007: 213–222). Consumers could also be segmented on the basis of lifecycle analysis. A car was a companion and marked a stage in a consumer's linear career. Often, they started with a small model, then moved to a family car and later 'bought their way up' to more prestigious and more expensive models. Consumers' general attitudes towards social and political life could also be used for typologies. There was, for example, the 'quiet conservatism' of some consumers, who preferred conventional behaviour. Their car had to be permanent, and it had to be worth its price. On the other hand, there were social innovators or 'radicals' with a distinctive, confident individuality. Their cars were a part of the expression of individuality and it had to provide joy of driving and distinct feeling. This typology was used by Nash, which in the 1950s began to split up its market into the 'Nash apostles' and the 'Nash pioneers' (Dichter 1950, 1958a).

In his research, Dichter also distinguished between a company's image, the brand image and the image of individual makes. Chrysler, for example, was found to be equated with 'being a pioneer' and technical excellence, but also with a having a slightly 'cold' and distanced image. In order to correct a company's and/or a brand's image, Dichter recommended comprehensive measures including advertisements, revised training of dealers (after sales calls), the integration into local networks and engineering a car's appearance on popular television programmes like the *Ed Sullivan Show* (product placement) (Dichter 1939). His image-focused research, for example, also allowed him to develop a typology of Chrysler sub-brands based on image characteristics. A Dodge was a 'practical, sexless, trusted servant'; a Chrysler was a 'status symbol, a finely accounted companion to a successful careerist'; a Plymouth in turn was a 'neurotic trouble-bringer' (Dichter 1972a).

Dichter used often detailed semiotic analyses when describing and interpreting different elements of the appearance and designs that conveyed meaning. He was, for instance, aware of the significance of the acoustic code of cars, for example, the noise the door made when it closed, the significance of a car's engine sound, and of the significance of the design of the cockpit. Generally, when pictures of a car were shown in advertisements, he advised to use the cockpit rather than a front view as consumers wanted to see interiors. Advertisements provided a kind of classification system that helped consumers translate the chaos of different brand names and makes into a manageable order. A car's power could be made visible through designs that made it look like a boat, a horse or an airplane, which were all powerful signals that communicated speed and acceleration. Connected to this was the problem of finding appropriate names for cars. Names had to express speed, drama and movement. He thus advised the Australian subsidiary of Ford to introduce the name 'Falcon' and Chevrolet to use the name 'Corvair'. Other names he recommended were based on rocket and missile projects ('Discoverer', 'Explorer') and appealed to the American pioneering spirit (Dichter 1958b).

Automobiles were also reactions to cultural changes in value systems, and Dichter realised that cars had to move with the times and were different in different social circumstances. For the 1970s, for example, he identified a number of challenges. As young liberal trendsetters, women and non-European immigrants ('black is beautiful') gained in importance, smaller cars and simpler tastes would come to the fore. Instead of 'keeping up with the Joneses', a new generation of cars would offer satisfaction to the 'inner Joneses'. Interestingly, Dichter argued that non-American cars, especially from Europe, were better prepared to meet these new consumer expectations. In response to the threat from European and Japanese car-makers, Dichter advised the industry captains in Detroit to strengthen the feeling of 'Buy American' among consumers, while working harder on changing their range of makes (Dichter 1971, 1972a, 1972b).

When the oil crisis of 1973 finally began to sound the end of America's global manufacturing dominance, Dichter detected a more general change. What he called the 'post-affluent age' was beginning with more ecologically minded actors starting to dominate the stage. Dichter now realised that environmentalists, 'samurais who defend honor, morality, work with their swords', had moved in and changed people's assumptions about what 'real' needs actually were and how many things one could do without. For this new group, shortages had a ring of biblical retribution. But they opened up markets for bicycles and organic food and DIY products. While in the new 'post-affluent' era cars had lost their overt status-signalling function, Dichter predicted that the bond between car and consumer would actually become closer and social attitudes towards the car in the United States would become more similar to those in Europe. In Europe, the car had always been an 'adored mistress'; it was given a name by consumers, and cars were adorned with trees and images of saints (Dichter 1979).

6.4   The Ford Taunus 1958

One of Dichter's greatest advantages in the American advertising and market research scene was his familiarity with the differences between America and Europe and the differences between the various European markets. The Ford company made use of this unique set of skills in 1958 when Dichter tried to help the company's German subsidiary to rescue its Ford 'Taunus' model. In his study for Ford, he first described the 'German car dealer', his motives and the significance the car had for him (which was different to the American car dealer). But also the German consumer seemed to be unlike the US consumer: 'The German car buyer is calculating, rational and deeply sentimental' (Dichter 1958c). Value was important to him, value for money, and he hated series of makes which – like in America – changed every year and thus decreased the reselling value of his car. This rational self, however, was accompanied by a highly emotional self. To the German customer, buying a car was like 'looking for a bride' and a completed purchase was 'a dream come true'. To him – and Dichter made clear that the buyer always was a 'him' – the car was like a living being, which was also often given a nickname ('Peterle').

Unlike the American buyer, German car consumers actually read instructions carefully and observed technical guidelines. Although the average German car buyer longed for a large Mercedes Benz that would impress his neighbours and colleagues at work, he would never take out a bank loan as was usual in the United States. He wanted 'a bit of a Mercedes' without the financial risks that an expensive car involved: a medium-sized vehicle, with a rich sound the door made when it closed, a nice interior and a comfortable all-round 'feel'. The ideal car was a comfortable German 'Wohnzimmer' (living room) transplanted onto the road. Dichter also felt that this was the major problem of Volkswagen, a car-maker from Protestant north Germany that favoured a very Puritan design and always had a bit of a 'plebeian stamp' (Dichter 1960b). In addition, Ford was regarded as 'American' by many German consumers. Although America was en vogue in 1950s Cold War West Germany, it also meant 'tycoon', 'bad quality', 'bad outfit', 'cold and distant'. Although Ford tried to embed itself into local societies by adopting national designs and local names, it worked to the disadvantage of Ford in the case of the Ford Taunus. The name 'Taunus' referred to a hilly region in the *very* German state of Hesse, which was characterised by small towns with cobbled streets and small inns. Romantic, but also with a strong whiff of provinciality and lack of promise. Accordingly, consumers perceived the car's design as 'hilly', ridiculous and not worthy of serious attention. Ford also forgot to take into account that consumers usually bought their way through a range of cars, beginning with a small model and then climbing up the ladder of increasingly better and more expensive models. The Ford Taunus was thus the German equivalent of the British Leyland company in the United Kingdom: well meaning, but utterly unattractive.

Dichter recommended comprehensive PR- and HRM-related measures. All Ford managers should learn German and engage in local civic associations. Ford had to be seen to do something for Germany and German society. Ford had to adapt its range of models to the German taste and ensure that its models and their marketing communication were more 'emotional'. The design of the Ford Taunus had to be changed, especially its 'acoustic code' (the closing door) and its interior design. In due course, Ford changed the design of its 'Taunus' model and introduced a new, much softer and less 'American' car design (17M P3) in 1960 with three engine sizes ranging from 1.5 litre to 1.8 litre.

6.5 Conclusion

Dichter's contributions were both state-of-the art market research and a creative performance of an individual who based his ability to advise clients on his ability to recognise the role of goods in modern culture and society. Each society produces objects that have symbolic functions based on their actual purpose, and which illustrate the ways of thinking of a given culture. No culture has produced more objects than the industrial societies of our 'modern age'. We need and use all these goods for symbolic and communicative purposes: they contribute to our identity, they illustrate our culture's way of thinking, they represent our main concept of what is desirable and they act as sign systems (Karmasin 2007). Dichter recognised the car as a central cultural artefact, which stands for central concepts of our collective desire: mobility, individuality, self-determination, autonomy and creation of distinction.

Several important sub-systems of a society play a role in the making of cars as carriers of symbolic meaning, like technology, politics, economy, design, marketing, advertising, communications, urban and regional planning. Dichter was a pioneer to notice this significance and he excellently translated this into marketing strategy. Many of his observations are still valid today, which is probably also due to the central role of the car. However, he never explicitly codified his theories and never seemed to notice or quote the relevant anthropological theories which existed in his day. His research, however, is proof of his cultural sensitivity.

References

Barthes, R. 1958. *Mythen des Alltags* [*Mythologies*]. Frankfurt am Main.: Suhrkamp.
——— 1964. *Elements of Semiology*. A. Lavers, C. Smith (Trans.). London: Jonathan Cape.
Dichter, E. 1939. Motion picture tie-ups. Ernest Dichter Archive, University of Vienna, Report No. 12.
——— 1950. A psychological research survey on the sales and advertising problems of Nash Cars. Ernest Dichter Archive, University of Vienna, Report No. 33.
——— 1958a. Typology: the classification of consumers by psychological types as a tool for advertising and merchandising. Ernest Dichter Archive, University of Vienna, Report No. 4567.
——— 1958b. Memo on the sales potential for Ford in Australia to Ford International Division, Ford Motor Company. Ernest Dichter Archive, University of Vienna, Report No. 1199.
——— 1958c. A motivational research study of the sales problems of the Ford Taunus in Germany. A progress report. Ernest Dichter Archive, University of Vienna, Report No. 1198.
——— 1959. A pilot summary on automobile usage and the automobile of 1962 to the M-E-L Division, Ford Motor Company. Ernest Dichter Archive, University of Vienna, Report No. 3171.
——— 1960a. *The Strategy of Desire*. Garden City, NY: Doubleday.
——— 1960b. A problem analysis and proposal on public attitudes toward new directions for Volkswagen. Ernest Dichter Archive, University of Vienna, Report No. 1719.
——— 1962. A motivational research study of the Rambler image among owners of competitive cars. Phase II: the impact and influence of 1962 car models. Ernest Dichter Archive, University of Vienna, Report No. 2005.
——— 1964. *Handbook of Consumer Motivations: The Psychology of the World of Objects*. New York: McGraw-Hill.

——— 1965. Test of an advertising campaign. Ernest Dichter Archive, University of Vienna, Report No. 2613.

——— 1966. The car – your friend or foe. Ernest Dichter Archive, University of Vienna, Report No. 4778.

——— 1967a. Report on the test of an advertising campaign for Vauxhall Viva (Bericht zu einem Anzeigentest für Vauxhall Viva). Ernest Dichter Archive, University of Vienna, Report No. 2806.

——— 1967b. Do we live our life as a 'series of cars'? (Wird das Leben in 'Autoabschnitten' gelebt?) Ernest Dichter Archive, University of Vienna, Report No. 4463.

——— 1971. The challenge of the 1970s: marketing automobiles in a rapidly changing society. A proposal for a motivational research study. Ernest Dichter Archive, University of Vienna, Report No. 3492.

——— 1972a. Marketing Chrysler automobiles in a rapidly changing society: a motivational research study. Volume I. Ernest Dichter Archive, University of Vienna, Report No. 3499.

——— 1972b. A motivational research study on Chrysler's image in the seventies. Summary of key findings of progress report. Ernest Dichter Archive, University of Vienna, Report No. 3495.

——— 1979. What comes after the affluent society (Was kommt nach der Überflussgesellschaft). Ernest Dichter Archive, University of Vienna, Report No. 4979.

Douglas, M. 1975. *Implicit Meanings: Essays in Anthropology*. London: Routledge.

Douglas, M., Isherwood, B. 1996. *The World of Goods: Towards an Anthropology of Consumption*. Oxford.

Eco, U. (1976). *A Theory of Semiotics*. London: Palgrave Macmillan.

Holbrook, M. 2006. Consumption experience, customer value and subjective personal introspection. *Journal of Business Research* 59: 714–725.

Karmasin, H. 2007. *Produkte als Botschaften*. Frankfurt am Main.: Ueberreuter.

Lévi-Strauss, C. 1958. *Anthropologie Structurale*. Paris: Plon.

Martineau, P. 1958. A case study: what automobiles mean to Americans. In: R. Ferber, H. G. Wales (Eds), *Motivation and Market Behavior*. Homewood, IL: Richard Irwin, 36–49

McCracken, G. D. 1988. *Culture and Consumption: New Approaches to the Symbolic Character of Consumer Goods and Activities*. Bloomington: Indiana University Press.

——— 2005. *Culture and Consumption II: Markets, Meaning, and Brand Management*. Bloomington: Indiana University Press.

Packard, V. 1957. *The Hidden Persuaders*. London: Longmans.

Solomon, M. R. 2007. *Consumer Behavior: Buying, Having, and Being*. Upper Saddle River, NJ: Pearson Prentice-Hall.

Twitchell, J. 1997. *Adcult USA: The Triumph of Advertising in American Culture*. New York: Columbia University Press.

Valentina, V. 2007. Semiotics: what it is and what it can do for market research. In: M. van Hamersveld, C. de Bout (Eds), *Market Research Handbook*. Chichester: John Wiley, 447–67.

Williamson, J. 1978. *Decoding Advertisements: Ideology and Meaning in Advertising*. London: Boyars.

Wilson, T. 2002. *Strangers to Ourselves: Discovering the Adaptive Unconscious*. Harvard, MA: Belknap.

7
Ernest Dichter and the Peacock Revolution: Motivation Research, the Menswear Market and the DuPont Company

Regina Lee Blaszczyk

7.1 Introduction

'We've all heard of the colonial revolution, the cultural revolution, the population revolution,' Ernest Dichter told a group of menswear manufacturers meeting in Scottsdale, Arizona, in February 1966. 'Today, I would like to describe to you another revolution that is about to explode – the peacock revolution.' Among animals, the male is normally the more colourful sex, Dichter explained, except in the human world, where 'men are the drab ones'. For generations, the clothing industry had exhibited 'a schizophrenic personality', with the 'vital, constantly changing women's apparel market in dramatic contrast to the lethargic men's apparel market'. Dichter saw a bright future as a generation of male baby boomers, aged 16–29, rejected sartorial drabness for creative expression. These affluent young 'peacocks', he asserted, had the potential to transform the menswear trade into a fast-moving business, dominated by changing styles, bright colours and novel designs. 'Young men are ready for and expect designers to bring out fashions and fads … that will appeal to various personality types and provide a variety of mood experiences.' Menswear manufacturers, he warned, had better pay attention (Dichter 1966).

Dichter delivered his speech on the peacock revolution at a Young Men's Market Workshop sponsored by E. I. du Pont de Nemours & Company, a major American chemical manufacturer and the world's largest producer of synthetic fibres (*Philadelphia Daily News* 1966). For the past decade, Dichter's Institute for Motivational Research (IMR) had been earning more than \$1 million annually as a consultant to American firms like DuPont, which wanted to know the reasons why people made certain choices in the marketplace. While DuPont did not produce textiles or garments, the fibre-maker needed to connect with manufacturers and retailers in those industries, which channelled large quantities of its high-tech products – Nylon, Dacron polyester, Orlon acrylic and Lycra spandex – to consumers as finished products. Dichter's 1966 study of the peacock revolution – one of about ten projects completed for DuPont's Textile Fibres Department between 1956 and 1975 – was part of the chemical company's effort to gain a deeper understanding of the menswear industry, which was changing dramatically as baby boomers grew up. While fashion historians have argued for the important influences of British style and the youth market in this era, Dichter's research on the peacock revolution shows that the post-war menswear story was far more complex, owning much to a mixture of local and global forces, including shifts in American blue-collar tastes.

This essay on the peacock revolution examines the relationship between Dichter and DuPont, with reference to men's attitudes towards textiles and clothing, and the cultural symbolism of these materials and products. Often, historians look elsewhere – to variables such as religion, politics, gender and race – to explain the evolution of post-war consumer culture. However, business historians have demonstrated how much can be learned by examining the firm, its relationships with customers and consumers and the complex processes of design, development and marketing. My contributions to this research have stressed the importance of keeping one's eyes on the prize: the artefact. This approach is sympathetic with Dichter's own methods, which put the *things* and the people who bought them at the centre of analysis.

7.2 Consumers, customers and identity kits

As post-war prosperity opened the portal of consumer society to ever more Americans, DuPont sought to expand the market for synthetic fibres in home furnishings and apparel. For decades, these industries had been fragmented, localised and dominated by small family firms. After the Second World War, the textile trade consolidated and moved from the north-east to the south, while the garment business, centred on Seventh Avenue in New York, flourished during a golden age of women's mass-market fashion. By the late 1950s, DuPont had mechanisms for probing these markets – an extensive technical service network, a substantial marketing division and a sales office in the Empire State Building – but it was always seeking more and better information.

As one of the founders of motivational research, Dichter was well equipped to help DuPont understand the psychological dimensions of various market segments, from textiles and seat belts to home furnishings and apparel. An astute observer, gifted with intuition, he believed that some products carried more cultural and symbolic weight than others and carefully crafted his career around this perception. Within his theoretical framework, certain types of goods were more important in the creation of personal meaning and group identity. More often than not, people used those particular types of things as they constructed their personal spaces, linked themselves to affinity groups and positioned themselves culturally. This basic way of relating to the material world, in which people privileged some artefacts over others, was true for both consumers and customers.

In the case of ordinary consumers who acquired goods for personal use, Dichter understood that for many Americans 'buying actually means living', and purchases were powerful cultural symbols of accomplishment. In a 1940 report for the De Soto automobile company, he noted 'the strongest visible manifestation of living in our modern world is through purchasing and owning.' The practice of identifying oneself through possessions has a long history dating back at least to Renaissance Europe, but industrialisation augmented the standard of living and extended this cultural phenomenon to greater numbers of people. In the post-war era, mass consumption became a hallmark of the American lifestyle, as major transformations in the political economy extended middle-class tastes and purchasing power to the vast majority. At the time of the De Soto survey, Dichter's interviewees already equated consumption with the good life. 'You know how it is,' one man confessed. 'The average person has a feeling he is progressing in life if he owns more things and better things.' In a world where possessions delineated achievement, every purchase could be equated with 'living', but 'certain objects' carried more cultural weight (Dichter 1940). As I have elsewhere explained, durable and semi-durable goods that required substantial financial, emotional or symbolic investment, like houses, appliances, bric-a-brac, furnishings, high-tech devices and clothing, were part of the identity kits that consumers used to define themselves (Blaszczyk 2009). Dichter never used the term 'identity kit', but his *oeuvre* reflects an implicit understanding of this important concept at the heart of consumer society.

Dichter also acknowledged that customers, businesses which purchased raw materials, designed new lines and selected merchandise for stores, played a big role in determining whether products succeeded or failed. Like consumers, business representatives were shaped by their environment, bringing private experiences to bear on professional decisions. A retail buyer might decide not to stock coloured towels because his mother always used white, while a sales clerk might not push a particular brand of shoes to shoppers because his commission was low. Workplace politics also affected how business professionals responded to suppliers, their own customers and the ultimate consumer. In department stores, internecine rivalries might have an impact on the morale of the retail buyer and the sales clerks, who could respond to new products with enthusiasm or indifference (Dichter 1958b). Layers of decision makers separated a manufacturer from the ultimate consumer, each exerting influence that could have consequential ramifications. Acknowledging the important role of the customer, Dichter designed research surveys that would identify and describe these otherwise hidden variables to his clients.

Dichter did not invent the practice of scoping out the marketplace – a strategy that I have called 'imagining consumers' – but elaborated on techniques that had been evolving since the Victorian era. Entrepreneurs like John Wanamaker, Marshall Field and Frank W. Woolworth created retailing empires by catering to strivers who crafted middle-class identity through the judicious purchase and display of certain goods: the single-family home, porcelain bric-a-brac, parlour suites, bustles and corsets, and three-piece business suits. In the 1920s, marketing scientist Paul T. Cherington at the J. Walter Thompson advertising agency helped clients understand their customers by gathering data from door-to-door surveys and 'man-on-the-street' observations. Big businesses like General Motors internalised the marketing function, hiring analysts to chart dealers' statistics and artists to interpret them in new designs. These marketing pioneers knew how to divide the American population into countless segments based on factors like age, ethnicity, gender, geography and income. Yet while they identified market segments and described different tastes, these early practitioners did not explain the psychological motivations that led customers and consumers to act (Blaszczyk 2000).

Dichter belonged to a new generation of market researchers who borrowed tools from anthropology, sociology and psychology to analyse the reasons why people made certain choices. He believed that consumers valued the material world and affixed meanings to objects based on myriad factors: private experiences, family traditions, peer-group pressure, neighbourhood trends, workplace interactions and popular culture. No one could actually get inside the shopper's head, and consumers themselves were often unable to articulate the reasons for their choices. To figure out what motivated people, the Institute for Motivational Research used demographically representative focus groups to probe consumers' thoughts, exploring the meanings they ascribed to products. Dichter put representative individuals in a simulated kitchen, and his research staff watched them wash dishes with different brands of soap while trying to discern what 'clicked' or not. In other instances, the institute queried people in stores, streets or homes about different appliances, sheets or retailers. In any group study, the trick was to identify commonalities and differences in taste, try to explicate the reasons behind them, and apply this knowledge to products or environments that would sell better. For additional fees, Dichter helped corporate clients to design marketing programmes and advertising campaigns that reflected the product's psychological dimensions.

7.3　DuPont as a marketing pioneer

DuPont dominated the post-war synthetic fibres business by combining first-mover advantages, laboratory research and the industry's most advanced marketing effort (Blaszczyk 2006, 2008b; Hardin 1988, 1990; Holmes 1982; Hounshell and Smith Jr 1988; Smith Jr 1986). Formed in 1952, the Textile Fibers Department oversaw product development, technical service, sales and marketing for DuPont's entire family of synthetic fibres. Department managers gave marketing a prominent place on their organisational chart, building extensive in-house expertise in apparel, fabrics and home furnishings. By the late 1950s, DuPont had a large staff of marketing specialists with experience in women's wear, menswear, draperies, carpets, tyres and other target markets for fibres. DuPont had achieved world leadership in fibres when a large investment in industrial research led to the invention of Nylon, the first synthetic fibre. An overnight success in hosiery, Nylon became DuPont's most profitable product, with cumulative operative earnings of $4.27 billion from its 1940 commercialisation through 1967. Initially, the firm tried to emulate the 'Nylon model' by investing heavily in R&D on other fibres, but discovered the inadequacies of this strategy with Orlon acrylic and Dacron polyester (Busche 1968; Hounshell and Smith 1988: 274). Confronted by agile competitors and the highly volatile fashion and home-furnishings trade, DuPont learned that it could not simply invent new materials and wait for sales to materialise (Arora and Rosenberg 1998; Chandler 2005). In an environment where style mattered, the fibre giant needed to imagine the wants, needs and desires of consumers, creating products that met public demand (Blaszczyk 2006; Handley 1999; O'Connor 2005, 2008a).

Every year, the Textile Fibers Department conducted hundreds of formal market research surveys to determine how DuPont fibres fared in the marketplace and how they might be adapted to new uses. The department invested in several types of market research, from conventional market surveys to approaches that probed lifestyle choices. Conventional surveys measured the potential size and scope of a market. Other such studies tested new products, evaluated proposed changes to an established product, measured the effectiveness of an advertising campaign or determined the optimum pricing of a product. In contrast, newer types of surveys, like those completed by Dichter, examined shifts in consumer lifestyles, purchasing power, shopping habits and expectations about material life, probing the scope and dimensions of particular markets.

One surviving DuPont market survey on 'The Shirt Industry' shows how the Textile Fibers Department approached the menswear business in the early post-war era. In 1952, researcher W. H. Ayers alerted fibre managers that the American penchant for casual living and the influence of the California fun-in-the-sun aesthetic was the most significant factor in men's apparel, offering the best opportunity for market development. The men's shirt trade was enormous, using as much fabric as women's dresses. In dress shirts, cotton was still the dominant fibre, accounting for 95 per cent of the market because of its superior appearance, washability, comfort and price. Businessmen who wore suits to work were cotton snobs, turning up their noses at nylon, polyester or acrylic dress shirts. The real opportunity for DuPont fibres thus lay in sports tops, a growth segment of men's and boy's apparel. Here, male consumers were willing to experiment, to try something new and fashionable. In 1947, menswear manufacturers had produced 73 dress shirts for every 27 sports tops. Three years later, the ratio was reversed, with 47 dress shirts for every 53 sports shirts. Influenced by the Californian casual aesthetic and blessed with rising disposable incomes, male consumers saw sports shirts as personal indulgences, buying them 'on impulse'. Those who donned grey flannel suits to work as travelling salesmen, engineers and corporate middle managers had personal satisfaction in their showy weekend apparel (Ayers 1952).

Cultural trends thus dictated that DuPont's menswear future rested in sportswear, a new field 'characterized by a lack of any traditional fiber' (Ayers 1952). Synthetics like Orlon acrylic and Dacron polyester, with their quick-drying properties and durability, had excellent prospects in this market where style, variety and price determined whether or not a consumer would make an impulse purchase. 'Individuality,' Ayers reported, 'keynotes the demand in sports shirts.' DuPont could help manufacturers and retailers sell more shirts by developing technologies that would augment their fashion appeal. Improved dyeing techniques, new fabric constructions and moderate-priced yarns would give shirt-makers competitive advantage. The boy's sports shirt market, burgeoning due to the baby boom, was particularly significant. While cotton still dominated this trade with a 90 per cent market share, man-made fibres had the potential to make inroads, providing the materials could be improved to compete on price and washability (Ayers 1952). Based on such research, the Textile Fibers Department developed an aggressive end-use marketing programme aimed at the menswear trade. The firm's menswear marketers worked closely with textile mills and apparel manufacturers to explain what synthetics could or could not do. The advertising department developed high-profile campaigns for magazines like *Playboy* and *Esquire*, using testimonials by celebrity golfer Arnold Palmer to tout synthetic sportswear as masculine active wear. The public relations staff in the Empire State Building circulated press releases and fashion photographs of sexy male models in tight-fitting sportswear, all made from DuPont fibres.

7.4   The rising tide of individuality

DuPont's Textile Fibers Department augmented this in-house marketing expertise by hiring consultants with special know-how, networking capabilities and public relations value. Along these lines, prominent hand weaver Dorothy Liebes spent 15 years helping DuPont's home-furnishings marketers navigate the interior decoration field, creating 'idea fabrics' that exposed decorators, designers and architects to what could be done with synthetics (Blaszczyk 2008a). Under contract with DuPont, members of La Chambre Syndicale de la Couture Parisienne, the French trade association for haute couture, created new lines using fabrics made from synthetics, glamorising the new miracle materials (Blaszczyk 2007). In turn, DuPont publicists promoted these elite French connections to augment the company's cultural capital and recast synthetics in high style.

Beginning in December 1956, Ernest Dichter contributed to DuPont's overall marketing efforts in two ways: (1) bringing to the table his specialised knowledge about the symbolic meaning of goods (2) and his reputation as the self-styled 'founding father' of motivational research. His institute compiled detailed research reports for DuPont, providing fibre marketers with anthropological insights about social trends and consumer behaviour, which they could share with clients. Dichter's personal appearances, such as the lecture on the peacock revolution, were designed to educate customers, stimulate media interest and engage consumers. The Institute for Motivational Research's studies for DuPont included reports on Nylon sheets (1956–1957), Nylon carpets (1957–1958), tyres (1963), seat belts (1965), men's hosiery (1966), the peacock revolution (1965–1967), pantyhose (1972–1974) and ladies' girdles (1975). Dichter's foreign office also completed a handful of studies for DuPont International, S. A., which managed European sales of synthetic fibres from Geneva in Switzerland.

By the time Dichter started working for DuPont, his consulting firm had some 700 market studies under its belt, including research on the textile industry, the garment trade and the consumers who bought their products (Dichter 1956a). Dichter publicised his work in feature articles for trade journals like *Hoisery Merchandising Magazine* and applied his knowledge to other clients' problems, as when he advised Young & Rubicam, the New York agency for Cannon Mills, on advertisements for Nylon stockings (Dichter 1952a, 1952b). In 1955, his institute ventured into the menswear territory, helping Norman, Craig & Kummel, a New York apparel manufacturer, to develop a brand identity for its Manhattan shirts (Dichter 1955). The next year, Dichter discussed the challenges of the menswear market in a feature for *Apparel Arts*, a fashion magazine for men's clothing retailers (Dichter 1956b).

Dichter's article for *Apparel Arts* grappled with the conundrum of under-consumption, which stood out against the backdrop of post-war prosperity. In 1955, American spending had reached record heights, encouraged by rising incomes and liberal consumer credit. While certain types of goods were in great demand, apparel sales remained stagnant, due primarily to the poor performance of the menswear trade. Although men splurged on cars, purchasing 7 million vehicles in a single year, they were decidedly indifferent towards new clothes. Like DuPont's W. H. Ayers, Dichter identified informality as a force that was breaking down sartorial traditions that dated to the nineteenth century. Whereas Ayers had simply identified the sportswear trend, Dichter urged clothing manufacturers to think more carefully about the issue. 'It is…by far not sufficient to observe and state that there is this trend toward informality,' he wrote. 'If the clothing industry wishes to do something ... it must be able to comprehend the deeper meaning of the new vogue of slacks, sports coats, sports shirts, etc.' Was informality a fad, or did it reflect a fundamental shift in human needs? Was it a 'translation of our political democracy, a tendency to egalitarianism'? Was the trend based on new ideas about health or comfort? What were the deeper implications for American culture? How did informality line up with new aesthetic concepts in other areas of material life? (Dichter 1956b).

Writing on the heels of Sloan Wilson's *The Man in the Gray Flannel Suit* (Wilson 1955), Dichter used the novel's popularity as a springboard for further discussion. While the sack suit was certainly a status symbol for New York professionals, it was not the only type of menswear used to convey social position. Elsewhere in American culture, men followed local traditions, inspired less by the national media and more by local leaders. Whereas television, magazines and movies promoted the cultural authority of actors, baseball players and prominent politicians, most men looked to their immediate surroundings for role models. By stressing the sustained importance of the local, Dichter reminded apparel stores that consumers learned by looking, developing a highly personal sense of what was appealing and stylish by watching their neighbours (Dichter 1956b). Dichter's observations were remarkably prescient. In the next decade, men's fashions would be reconfigured by a mixture of the local customs, national trends and global influences.

In 1958, Dichter further explored the interplay of national and local forces in a discussion of informality for *American Fabrics and Fashion*, a major trade journal for the fibre, textile and garment industries. In his view, the major demographic transformation of the decade – the rise of the new middle class – would reshape consumers' purchasing habits in the years ahead. Dichter explained the expansion of the American middle class, which swelled as former members of the 'upper lower class' increased their earnings, education and geographic mobility, enabling them to move up the class ladder. Uneasy about their toehold on this social ladder, these upwardly mobile consumers were 'anxious to purchase not merely products but roots in the middle class'. The ownership of certain goods could signal a household's familiarity with mainstream values and behaviour, yet these newcomers also wanted possessions that reflected their unique desires. They shopped 'not as members of the anonymous masses, but as individual human beings who [were] now able to follow their own tastes and whose personal needs have been considered by the manufacturer' (Dichter 1958b). In 1963, Dichter reiterated these points: 'The American market... relies more and more on psychological segmentations. U.S. manufacturers may produce ... on a mass scale, but individuality has become the decisive appeal in many products and services' (Dichter 1963).

7.5 How the peacocks fanned their tails

How did the rising tide of individual taste play out in the menswear market? By the 1960s, manufacturers and retailers clearly understood that baby boomers constituted the largest market cohort in history. This generation had more discretionary income than previous generations as they moved from youth to adulthood. For the women's apparel industry, this translated into a higher demand for teen styles, as famously epitomised by the sweater girl and bohemian look of the previous decade. As Ayer and Dichter had suggested, change transpired more slowly in menswear, sometimes at a glacial pace. By the mid-1960s, however, a confluence of national and transnational forces appeared to have had a dramatic effect on young men's clothing. On 13 May 1966, *Life* magazine's cover story, 'Face It! Revolution in Male Clothes', spotlighted the new European-style fashions: the rakish, thin-shanked, high-heeled booted, broad-belted, narrow-hipped and epauletted variations of attire that had changed 'the fashion habits of the U.S. male'. Like resplendent peacocks, four mop-topped teens posed for the *Life* photographer against the Chicago skyline in their 'new mod gear'. Here, *Life* journalists declared, was the influence of London's Carnaby Street with its hip boutiques and innovative designers (*Life* 1966).

By the time *Life* hit the news-stands, Dichter's Institute for Motivational Research had already completed its study of the young men's clothing trade for DuPont, where menswear marketers had their fingers on the pulse of innovation. Seeing that change was afoot, DuPont market experts recognised the need for an in-depth analysis of what made boomer boys tick, and who exactly within the cohort was driving new trends. To find out, Dichter's staff interviewed 100 young men, talked to clothing salesmen and observed youthful shoppers browsing in stores. Through this fieldwork, they identified a significant demographic group: the highly independent man who rejected bureaucratic organisations and refused to 'dress for a job'. Instead, these nonconformists wore clothes for their role as 'a man – a rebel, a "swinger," hot-rodder, surfer, beatnik, etc. – expressing their own individuality'. These boomers were not only 'less respectful of traditions and less inhibited' but were also 'very verbal about their likes and dislikes in wearing apparel' and exerted a 'major influence on the dressing styles of older men' (Dichter 1966).

Who exactly were these showy birds? Were they the mod teens who proudly took a Beatle-like pose for *Life*'s photographers? While high-school students were part of the flock, Dichter's team found that they were not the only birds in the nest. Several factors like age, education, marital status and occupation influenced a young man's clothing choices, and whether or not he would dress as a conformist, an individualist or something in between. Among students, high-school boys and college men constituted two discrete groups, with younger consumers more willing to experiment with the playful sensuality of fashion. Like the Chicago teens on the cover of *Life*, the high-school students interviewed by Dichter's researchers were less inhibited and more adventurous than their elders, thinking of shopping as 'an exciting tactual orgy – a new adventure'. Conversely, the college man was 'the most conforming of all male creatures', inhibited by an 'academic atmosphere' that discouraged spontaneity. The competition for female attention encouraged bachelors to experiment with new clothing ideas that would differentiate them from their peers and perhaps impress single women. Finally, young married men relied on their spouses for permission to experiment with stylish garb, wary that personal indulgences might be seen as profligate for a man with a new family. None of this will surprise today's historians, given what we know about the birth of the teen market, bachelor culture and the gendered dimensions of American consumer society (Dichter 1966).

On the other hand, Dichter's findings about social class and male consumption habits open the doors on to a nuanced understanding of post-war consumer culture. As employees, young men divided into three groups: white-collar workers with college or graduate degrees; other white-collar workers; and blue-collar workers. Taste-wise, the most conservative men sat at the top of the social ladder, where the ambition to succeed within a bureaucracy mandated the sack-suit uniform. These consumers operated not under the age-old premise that the clothes make the man, but that the 'successful man makes the clothes'. With a promising future, a 29-year-old junior executive felt most comfortable in loose-fitting wool clothes, which symbolised the security and substance of his achievements. On the rung below, office workers without a college education – 'the most status conscious of all groups' – eyed their superiors and emulated the successful corporate look. For them, the suit was a personal statement of 'having arrived'. As one young man put it: 'When I put on a suit I feel like one of the boys.' The end result was the grey flannel army satirised by Sloan Wilson (Dichter 1966; Wilson 1955).

One of the most adventurous sartorial groups consisted of 'the great working masses' that needed and wanted 'to express individuality'. The blue-collar consumer was a 'very sensuous being' who, in contrast to the young executive, was 'most likely to live by the philosophy that clothes can make the man'. He avoided clothes worn by the 'higher...more stuffy class, such as the button down collar, the gray flannel suit, the uniform of Wall Street and management'. Ethnicity, class and taste meshed to shape him into a distinctive type of fashion individualist. Dichter told the menswear trade:

> While the average blue collar man does not have the available income of management types, a sizeable proportion of our blue collar group in this country are of either Italian or Latin descent, representing groups who tend to be more concerned with personal appearance and to spend proportionately more on it, whether married or single.
>
> (Dichter 1966)

7.6 Conclusion

Dichter's research for DuPont is wonderfully suggestive for what it tells us about relationships among big business, marketing practice and fashion culture in post-war America. For decades, fashion scholars and historians have credited journalist George Frazier with coining the term 'peacock revolution' in a 1968 article on menswear for *Esquire* magazine (Frank 1998: 269; Frazier 1968; Schoeffler and Gale 1973). Yet, Frazier's oft-quoted article came two years after Dichter's Scottsdale speech, which was publicised in DuPont press releases and widely quoted in newspapers across the land. The point is not to quibble over the origins of the term, but to state the important role of big business and motivational researchers like Dichter in creating, analysing and promoting fashion and consumer culture.

Dichter's research on the peacock revolution highlights another salient aspect of post-war consumer society, with particular reference to taste. Many curators and fashion historians have stressed the influence of Pierre Cardin's Edwardian Look and London's Carnaby Street on American menswear in the mid-1960s. Like DuPont researcher W. H. Ayers, other scholars have argued that the main consumer for peacock fashions was the man in the grey flannel suit, who tried to escape his humdrum existence by living out playboy fantasies on weekends.

However, Dichter's analysis of men's consumption habits points to multiple ebbs and flows, to peacocks up and down the social ladder. If we follow the actors, we can acknowledge the importance of the teen market, the corporate bureaucrat and the blue-collar individualists. While critics of *Saturday Night Fever* (1977) decry John Travolta's white polyester suit as the ultimate expression of poor taste, it may be more appropriate to see this flamboyant ethnic style as the final gasp of the blue-collar peacock revolution. With his eyes fixed on the consumer and the artefact, Ernest Dichter would probably have agreed.

References

Arora, A., Rosenberg, N. 1998. Chemicals: a U.S. success story. In: A. Arora et al. (Eds), *Chemicals and Long-Term Economic Growth: Insights From the Chemical Industry*. New York: Wiley, 71–102.

Ayers, W. H. 1952. The shirt industry. Box 78, Papers of the Textile Fibers Department, E. I. du Pont de Nemours & Company, Hagley Museum and Library, Wilmington, DE.

Blaszczyk, R. L. 2000. *Imagining Consumers: Design and Innovation from Wedgwood to Corning*. Baltimore: Johns Hopkins University Press.

——— 2006. Styling synthetics: DuPont's marketing of fabrics and fashions in post-war America. *Business History Review* 80 (Autumn): 485–528.

——— 2007. Du Pont de Nemours: mode et révolution des textiles synthétiques. In: D. Veillon, M. Ruffat (Eds), *La Mode des Sixties: L'entrée dans la modernité*. Paris: Éditions Autrement, 202–219.

——— 2008a. Designing synthetics, building brands: Dorothy Liebes, interior decoration, and post-war American interiors. *Journal of Design History* 21 (1): 75–99.

——— 2008b. Synthetics for the Shah: DuPont and the challenges to multinationals in 1970s Iran. *Enterprise and Society* 9 (December): 670–723.

——— 2009. *American Consumer Society, 1865–2005: from Hearth to HDTV*. Wheeling, IL: Harlan Davidson.

Busche, R. M. 1968. Memorandum to E. B. Yelton: Development and Commercialization of New Products. 22 July 1968. Box 15, Series 8, Acc 2091, E. I. du Pont de Nemours & Company, Executive Committee Papers, Hagley Museum and Library, Wilmington, DE.

Chandler, A. 2005. *Shaping the Industrial Century: The Remarkable Story of the Evolution of the Modern Chemical and Pharmaceutical Industries*. Cambridge, MA: Harvard University Press.

Dichter, E. 1940. The psychology of car buying in the De Soto class. Report by J. Stirling Getchell, Research Department, June 1940, Ernest Dichter Papers, Hagley Museum and Library, Wilmington, DE.

——— 1952a. What Makes the Lady Buy. *Hoisery Merchandising Magazine* (February).

——— 1952b. Memorandum to Charles Feldman, Young and Rubicam: 'Cannon Nylons'. 26 May 1952. Ernest Dichter Papers, Hagley Museum and Library, Wilmington, DE.

——— 1955. Creative memo on Manhattan Shirts. Submitted to Norman, Craig & Kummel Inc., New York. November 1955. Ernest Dichter Papers, Hagley Museum and Library, Wilmington, DE.

——— 1956a. Typescript of speech to National Association of Wool Manufacturers, Waldorf-Astoria, New York. 3 May 1956. Ernest Dichter Papers, Hagley Museum and Library, Wilmington, DE.

——— 1956b. Let's find out why men buy. *Apparel Arts: The Fashion Magazine for Men's Stores*. Tearsheet, in Ernest Dichter Papers, Hagley Museum and Library, Wilmington, DE.

——— 1958a. A motivational research study of the sales and advertising problems of Nylon carpets on the retail level. Ernest Dichter Papers, Hagley Museum and Library, Wilmington, DE.

——— 1958b. Nine ways to vitalize textile sales. *American Fabrics* 43 (Summer): 54.

——— 1963. The world customer. *American Fabrics* 50 (Spring): 89.

———1966. The Peacock Revolution: the psychology of the young men's market. Speech given at Scottsdale, Arizona, 18 February 1966. Copy at Beeghly Library, Ohio Wesleyan University, Dublin, OH.

Frank, T. 1998. *The Conquest of Cool: Business Culture, Counterculture, and the Rise of Hip Consumerism*. Chicago: University of Chicago Press.

Frazier, G. 1968. The Peacock Revolution. *Esquire* (October): 207–209.

Handley, S. 1999. *Nylon: The Story of a Fashion Revolution*. Baltimore: John Hopkins University Press.

Hardin, A. L. 1988. Miracle fiber to commodity: polyester, 1950–1975. M.A. Thesis, University of Delaware.

——— 1990. Industry structure and the marketing of synthetic fibers. *Business and Economic History* 19 (2nd ser.): 213–222.

Holmes, D. F. 1982. The history of the Textile Fibers Department. Revised Edition, Box 81, acc. 1771, Papers of the Textile Fibers Department, E. I. du Pont de Nemours & Company, Hagley Museum and Library, Wilmington, DE.

Hounshell, D. A., Smith Jr, J. K. 1988. *Science and Corporate Strategy: DuPont R&D, 1902–1980*. New York: Cambridge University Press.

Life. 1966. Face It! Revolution in male clothes. 13 May.

O'Connor, K. 2005. The other half: the material culture of new fibres. In: S. Küchler, D. Miller (Eds), *Clothing as Material Culture*. New York: Berg, 41–59.

——— 2008. The body and the brand: how Lycra reshaped America. In: R. L. Blaszczyk (Ed.), *Producing Fashion: Commerce, Culture, and Consumers*. Philadelphia: University of Pennsylvania Press.

Philadelphia Daily News. 1966. Young men lead peacock rebellion. 6 April. Acc. 2407, Ernest Dichter Papers, Hagley Museum and Library, Wilmington, DE.

Schoeffler, O. E., Gale, W. 1973. *Esquire's Encyclopedia of 20th Century Men's Fashion*. New York: McGraw-Hill.

Smith Jr, J. K. 1986. Innovating in synthetic materials: case studies in DuPont R&D, 1900–1940. PhD Thesis, University of Delaware.

Wilson. S. 1955. *The Man in the Gray Flannel Suit*. New York: Simon & Schuster.

8

The 'Sex of Food': Ernest Dichter, Libido and American Food Advertising

Katherine Parkin

8.1 Introduction

No history of American advertising would be complete without a consideration of Ernest Dichter's contribution to the field and the European influence he brought to it in the mid-twentieth century. Although his influence can be considered as part of a larger whole, as one of a group of European émigrés who shaped American society with their arrival in the 1930s and 1940s, Dichter's unique influence as a leading practitioner of Motivation Research touched all Americans. One of the more distinctive aspects of his work concerned his promotion of sex and gender differences in advertising, and this chapter considers his admonitions to food advertisers in particular. Drawing on his European background and training, Dichter was perhaps more comfortable than most in encouraging advertisers to consider sexuality when marketing their goods. Ernest Dichter was aware of the complexity of the word sex, noting in 1957: 'In the American parlance [sex] has a number of uses. It may mean simply "male" or "female" or it may mean something lascivious or obscene. It may stand for a biological urge and it may denote a challenging or provoking quality.' Drawing on his training as a psychologist and making full use of the American embrace of Freud in the 1950s, Dichter encouraged advertisers to promote a food's imagined sexual qualities (Dichter 1957).

His biographer Daniel Horowitz found that Dichter 'packaged himself by using controversial, speculative, and Freudian remarks to capture the attention of image-hungry clients and audiences. . . . [He] focused on hidden, irrational, and often sexualized reasons for consumers' behaviour' (Horowitz 1998: 157–162). The height of Dichter's power as psychiatrist to the American consumer coincided with the 'Golden Age' of the American popularisation of Freud. According to Nathan Hale, Freud's status reached its peak on the 100th anniversary of his birth in 1956, the same year that Ernest Jones's three-volume study of Freud appeared (Hale 1995). Dichter's approach to market research reflected his roots in Austrian psychology and psychiatry. Moreover, he wanted to cut a Freudian figure, hoping it lent credence to his work. In his 1979 auto-biography, *Getting Motivated*, Dichter proudly asserted his association, noting that for about 20 years he lived 'across the street from Sigmund Freud' and that he owed his success as a public speaker to a public-speaking course offered by Freud's daughter-in-law, Esti Freud (Dichter 1979: 79, 131–2) Suggesting this European connection was critical to his success, 'since Freud's stature among educated Americans (including business leaders) was second only to that of Einstein then' (Fullerton and Stern 1990: 208–211).

8.2   The power of sex

In his company's newsletter, distributed to American corporate clients, he made it clear that Americans had a unique problem. He argued, 'The trouble with American advertising is that it hasn't enough sex and the little that it has is the wrong kind.' Armed with this credibility, Dichter based his analyses on thousands of surveys and interviews conducted with consumers. He promised that he would bring a European correc-tive, 'analyzing this situation and offering psychologically correct ways to put back the power of real, unadulterated sex into American ads' (Dichter 1957). In Dichter's assessment of American advertising, he did not just make the common argument that sex sells. Indeed, his analysis included examples of attempts by American advertisers to present men and women together in sexy settings, so he was not responding to a lack of sex in advertising per se. Instead, Dichter contended that the kind of imagery being employed was vapid. He contended that in its current expression, the ads not only missed the mark in capturing sexuality, but also veered perilously towards being 'unreal, inhuman and tedious'. Dichter sought to increase sales by ostensibly deepening the sensuality that existed between women and men. In his chapter on 'Tickling the Palate' in his 1964 *Handbook of Consumer Motivations*, he complained that 'Though it sounds obvious to say that appetite, for food or for sex, is sparked by the suggestion of inner lusciousness, both women and advertisers err in appealing through a surface brightness which actually repels the thought of inwardness' (Dichter 1964: 16). Dissatisfied with the superficial, stereotyped portrayals of sensuality, Dichter argued again and again for deeper, richer, more meaningful representations of the fullness of human sexuality.

Genuine sensuality sold to a mass market is perhaps a paradox, yet it is evident throughout his writings that Ernest Dichter believed in fundamental and marketable differences between women and men. He argued that one reason for the missing sexuality – the right kind of sexuality – was that Americans portrayed men and women too similarly. Dichter charged that similarity removed the tension between women and men. If there was no difference, he claimed, there could be no romantic love, and certainly no sexual desire. He contended that, 'Democracy and the feminist movement have made man and woman equal. Advertising went one step further: it has made them identical' (Dichter 1957: 15). Tellingly, Dichter was chagrined with a feminist movement that was dormant in American society at the time and considered advertisers' portrayal of men and women in partnership roles as evidence of equality between the sexes. Clearly, *difference* was paramount in his understanding of gender and sexuality.

In his assessment of American society generally and advertising in particular, Dichter noted a history of taboos that stifled the creative expression of sexuality. While he decried the absence of sexuality in advertising, he was even more dismayed by what he considered pseudo-sexuality in America. He tried to persuade advertisers that their portrayals of sexuality had been reduced to such pathetic stereotypes that they had lost all power to affect consumers and stimulate sales. Of particular concern to Dichter was the loss of women, particularly accessible, distinctive, 'physical' women. While he appreciated the youth appeal, he maintained that there was nothing 'warm, outgoing, womanly about these beauties'. In describing one advertisement, for example, he bemoaned her 'mannish vest' and yelped, 'look at her body, look at her clothes! Her figure is that of an adolescent boy' (Dichter 1957: 13–19). He maintained that narcissism pervaded images of women and left consumers cold.

One of Dichter's striking suggestions to promote sexual interest and sales was that advertisers should also affirm consumers' gender roles. He encouraged advertisers to promote foods, for example, as feminine or masculine, so that they could position their products as a validation of the masculinity or femininity of the person eating their foods. Dichter believed that people categorised a food's sex, considering it either female or male. His own subscription to a gendered taxonomy of food was evident in his reports to clients and monthly newsletters. For example,

Dichter posited, 'Perhaps the most typically feminine food is cake … the wedding cake's … the symbol of the feminine organ. The act of cutting the first slice by the bride and bridegroom together clearly stands as a symbol of defloration.' He offers no evidence that he culled this insight from surveys, but presents it matter-of-factly as truth. He did proffer evidence that women were dissatisfied with dry cakes, but then argued 'Women's demand for moistness in a cake reinforced its feminine symbolism.' Dichter was not content to just summarise the findings and draw conclusions about their significance. After several examples of cake mixes 'tasting like sawdust', he went on psychoanalyse the respondents. He believed that distaste for dry cake 'may represent a projection onto the cake of the woman's feelings about herself. She wants to be moist and fresh, dewy-eyed and moist-lipped, not a dried up, barren old crone' (Dichter 1955c: 17).

Dichter's gendered notions about food lay bare the calculated ways in which he encouraged advertisers to create food and sex associations, predicated on their alleged gender differences (Dichter 1955b). He called on pseudo-science to provide what he considered conclusive evidence of a gendered physiologic response. Dichter recounted in a 1955 memo that in

> an experiment conducted by a famous surgeon, it was discovered that food has sex. While administering barium during the examination of the esophagus, the good doctor found that, when he mentioned the word 'salad' to his female patients, their esophagi dilated, permitting the passage of the chalky compound. When the word 'steak' was suggested to the male patients, their esophagi reacted similarly. But when the words were reversed, the esophagi of both sexes remained unchanged. Food advertisers should take the consumer's sex into account, in order to execute the most effective appeals as a basis of recognition.
>
> (Dichter 1955c: 18)

In this case, Dichter did not suggest that the food actually had a sex, but instead that people had a physiologic response to certain foods based on their sex. He also called on advertisers to 'find out its gender' before they tried to market their foods. Indeed, Ernest Dichter is one of the earliest to use the term gender in this modern manner, which did not enter popular discourse for several years to come. It is telling that Dichter had to find and use this word to describe foods that had no scientific sex, but were believed to have a sex role.

Motivation research's goal was to find new ways for corporations to achieve greater profits and one of the most consistent suggestions from Dichter was to tap into or create a food's sex role. In a 1955 study for General Mills, for example, in addition to asking 'How can teenagers be influenced to continue to eat cereal?' and 'What chances would low-calorie cereals have?', Dichter also asked 'Could there be masculine and feminine cereals?' Dichter noted a number of traditional ideas that the company could develop, but also encouraged General Mills to make something of his finding that some cereal brands had a gender. In addition to the many symbolic meanings cereals imbued, he argued that some cereals also had clear personalities, ages and genders. Wheaties, for example, was found to be 'More masculine', 'For teenagers', 'For poor people' and 'Nutritious'. In describing his findings, Dichter wrote, 'Rice Krispies are essentially feminine' (Dichter 1955a: 2–3, 7–9, 73–76).

Dichter described a consumer perception of the cereal, not really *as* female, but as eaten by females. He found that 'the number of respondents who thought that Rice Krispies would be eaten by women was over four times larger than the number of respondents who thought that Rice Krispies would be eaten by men. No other cereal drew a similarly one-sided reaction.' His own description of the responses affirms that consumers had a clear sense of the sex of the eaters, not the cereal per se. The consumers described the cereal as 'light-hearted, fun to eat, amusing'. Dichter took this and claimed the cereal was a 'bubbling, vivacious, young woman'. He concluded that 'further tests also revealed, that anthromorphically Rice Krispies were seen not only as a cheerful woman, but as one who had an even temper, was not addicted to extremes, and "wore well" every day' (Dichter 1955a: 12–13).

Of rice generally, he asserted that the 'evidence proves unmistakably' that rice was conceived as a feminine food. He noted: 'Rice is a strong female. It is young and healthy. And it is blessed with great fertility.' It was on the issue of fertility that Dichter added some flourish to his analysis. Many respondents noted the change in rice while it cooked, but Dichter claimed that they also

> ...subconsciously associate it with biological phenomena. Rice is something that gains life while it cooks. It expands and swells. It is as if little eggs were maturing fast, ready to burst with new life at any moment. The babbling, boiling water contributes added realism to this process of pseudo-birth.
>
> (Dichter 1955c: 7)

Dichter also found that many people remembered 'that rice is grown in water'. He framed it in the context of pregnancy, claiming that rice is 'enveloped and nourished by warm mud, and this is a basic biological picture directly leading to conscious and subconscious associations with the placenta'. To the predominantly male world of advertising, whose understanding of pregnancy and birth undoubtedly came from passing out cigars in the waiting room, Dichter may again have found a receptive audience.

A year later, in a 1956 article in Dichter's monthly newsletter, *Motivations*, he alerted readers to the 'fascinating contrasts in the sex attributes of food'. His studies found that 'Rice is felt as being feminine, but potatoes as masculine; tea is feminine, coffee is strongly masculine. The two most extremes are meat and cake, the latter being the most feminine of foods.' Some foods, however, did not readily yield up their associations to Dichter, so he proclaimed: 'Some foods are bisexual, among them roast chicken and oranges' (Dichter 1956: 4).

8.3   The steak as phallus projection

Findings like these occasionally led some to dismiss motivational research as quackery. The marketing field periodically reflected on questions about its validity and value to the profession. For example, between 1955 and 1958, *The Journal of Marketing* featured a series of articles and letters to the journal on the question that headlined one, 'Is Motivation Research *Really* an Instrument of the Devil?' (Rothwell 1955; Wells 1956; Wiebe 1958; Williams 1957). Acknowledging the tremendous influence of Motivation Research, Vance Packard published a runaway bestseller, *The Hidden Persuaders*, which alerted Americans to a new reality: social scientists were recording and selling consumers' thoughts and feelings to major corporations. Not only were pollsters surveying consumers' age, sex and income; not only were store spies observing the products they bought; but psychologists were now using depth interviews to try to determine *why* they bought what they did. Moreover, these scientists were also watching how many times consumers blinked in the aisles of the grocery store, determining what colours attracted them to products on the shelf, and employing countless other invasive practices that riled Americans, even as they intrigued them (Packard 1957).

In his critical exposé of the practice of motivational research, Packard repeatedly underscored the significance of his findings: this was a very big business. Major blue-chip corporations were paying hefty sums to motivational researchers to better market their products. In the mid-1950s, *Fortune* magazine reported that the largest advertisers and their advertising agencies spent almost one billion dollars on Motivation Research. Packard tried to impress upon his readers that this was not a fly-by-night trend as those businesses were not only after their money, they also wanted their hearts and minds. In spite – or because – of the criticism, Dichter was a respected figure in the advertising world. His ideas helped make him a successful businessperson and he played an important role in shaping advertising strategies for many large corporations. In an article in June 1961 in the *New York Times* on Dichter's testimony in front of the Senate Antitrust and Monopoly subcommittee investigating packaging disclosures, reporter Alvin Shuster proclaimed him 'an expert on why people buy what they do'. Dichter argued to the subcommittee that better labels would be ineffective because 'consumers, despite their growing sophistication, invariably succumbed to human emotional weaknesses no matter what they purchased. "What people actually spend their money on in most instances," he said, "are psychological differences, illusory brand images" ' (Shuster 1961: 10).

By 1962, journalist Peter Bart reported in the *New York Times* that the use of motivational research had 'died down' and Dichter acknowledged 'that the field has lost much of its electricity' (Bart 1962: 11). Yet, in 1963, according to Betty Friedan in her watershed classic, *The Feminine Mystique*, even without the 'electricity', Dichter earned about one million dollars a year for his work as a motivational researcher. Friedan's chapter on 'The Sexual Sell' used Dichter's studies to analyse some of the ways in which motivational researchers and advertisers targeted women. Building on Packard's analysis, she alerted women to some of the practices used to lure them into purchases, and further helped them see how advertisers were also trying to shape and limit their gender roles (Friedan 1963).

Coincidentally, much of Dichter's early work focused on foods he argued were feminine, but in the later 1960s and early 1970s, his research began to focus on foods he claimed were masculine. It is in his analysis of meat that the most obvious popular Freudian associations between sex and food are evident. In a 1968 study submitted to Bonsib, Inc., an advertising agency based in Fort Wayne, Indiana, Dichter laid out his findings. He noted that:

> Our research reveals that shape is perhaps the most fascinating attribute of wieners and luncheon meats. Despite the fact that shape may suggest and reinforce the artificiality of these products, it

also tends to stimulate sexual symbolism. On a subconscious level, wieners – and luncheon meats, to some extent – are perceived as phallic representations.

(Dichter 1968: 16)

Again blurring the line between the food's sex role and the consumer's gendered response, Dichter found that women and men had different responses to meat. For example, he found that 'Men do not appear to be as "embarrassed" in eating wieners as women appear to be.' Dichter suggested that women's discomfort arose because they were 'spellbound and definitely attracted by the meats'. Dichter also found that 'little boys, in particular, exhibit a stark preference for wieners. Psychologically, this suggests an expression of their desire to emulate the male parent' (Dichter 1968: 17). As an example of how meats could be successfully portrayed in advertising to capture subconscious sexual desire, Dichter cited the popular 1960s Oscar Mayer jingle (Wyman 1993: 128–130):

> I wish I were an Oscar Mayer wiener.
> That is what I'd truly love to be.
> For if I were an Oscar Mayer wiener,
> Everyone would be in love with me.

Nor was this analysis limited to meat. Dichter also argued in his *Handbook of Consumer Motivations* that 'fruits, roots, and foods of elongated shape', such as asparagus, had phallic significance. Asparagus was believed to increase 'sexual potency' and even to 'have originated on the grave of a rapist'. He vied to legitimate his analysis by proclaiming, 'This is not an invention of Freud but derives from many different societies. Asparagus in its very cultivation and growth makes this sexual significance possible. Asparagus is grown in tomblike culture beds and pushes through in the spring in a rather sudden fashion, growing rapidly, almost visibly' (Dichter 1964: 19–20). Still, every time he wrote about the sex of food, meat was his prime example of masculine food. Dichter always listed steak as the most clearly identifiably male food. The category of meat clearly illuminates how Dichter tried to convince advertisers to designate foods as male or female.

As he described meat industries struggling with sales in 1971, however, Dichter threw back the curtain and revealed that gender was ascribed to the food, not found inside it. He discovered, for example, that 'women wouldn't buy lamb for their families because it was considered a weaker, less virile food than other meats. Only when we began to masculinise the image and to describe cuts of lamb in more exciting terms did we begin to succeed' (Dichter 1971: 140–141). He offered another example with fish. Earlier, in his 1964 *Handbook of Consumer Motivations*, Dichter had argued that ancient people and modern psychologists had long associated fish with fertility (Dichter 1964: 41–42). This association would, by his logic, therefore, make fish a feminine food. Yet in 1971, in a section on 'What to do when people won't eat, or won't eat the food you want them to eat', he 'recommended promoting fish as a man's food, featuring big, powerful game fish such as swordfish in ads and fish "steaks" for an aura of strength'. Dichter's ambiguity about fish stemmed from the reality that fish is not a gendered product, any more than cake or rice or cars. He understood that it was the trappings that sold a food's gender identity. To sell fish, then, he suggested, 'surrounding the product with the appetite appeal of hearty vegetables and beer or ale, and eliminating dainty, feminine connotations in serving dishes or settings' (Dichter 1964: 41–2; 1971).

Dichter encouraged advertisers to embrace and create cultural associations between gender and food. Referring back to the case of women and rice, for example, he found that many women preferred rice over potatoes – the man's food. They found it less 'filling', less 'choky', less 'bulky'. Rice was also a useful staple in the kitchen because, as one respondent pointed out, it 'can be used for any and all courses from soup to main dish to stuffing to desserts'. Female consumers also reported that rice allowed them to fulfil their expected sex roles within their family. Its tremendous versatility (suggested above) and its healthfulness meant that women could use it to make foods for babies and older people, to provide healthy meals and to liven up their family's menu. Dichter concluded that rice offered all of this – and more. Not only was rice perceived as healthy and easy to work with,

> …now the grain of rice is just about the tiniest food that appears in the dining room on the plate. In addition, it is often white too, which is a feminine color. This combination makes for a dainty impression and symbolizes the more formal, more restraint [sic], less heavy-handed feminine approach to food.
>
> (Dichter 1955c: 10)

In a later collection of his food analyses, Dichter concluded about rice: 'It doesn't have the stubborn logic and limited use of most vegetables and cereals, but yields to the moment's impulse and caprice. It is the woman herself' (Dichter 1964: 61–62).

8.4   The gospel spreads

Motivational researchers and advertisers also suggested that certain foods had a sensual identity. Most analysis of sex in advertising has centred on categories like automobiles and cigarettes, but the history of food advertising is surprisingly rich with a tradition of food's connection with the sensual. Moreover, while historian Michael Schudson argued that generally 'advertisements did not become markedly more sexual as time went on', his findings were not true of food advertising. While in the first half of the century, some ads suggested food's sexual power. In the post-war era, food advertisements became increasingly overt in their sexual claims. Dichter supported making advertising more sexual and believed that Americans had taken the fun out of sex and advertising (Parkin 2006; Reichert and Lambiase 2003; Schudson 1986: 55–60).

Food advertisers had always tried to convince consumers that their foods would help them to be good looking and healthy. To keep pace with changing norms of behaviour and shifting employment patterns for women, in the 1940s and 1950s food advertisers began to use more explicitly sexual images. Advertisements for Kellogg's Pep cereal appearing in the 1940s, for example, played on the word 'pep', asking readers, 'How's your "Pep Appeal"?' Suggesting that Pep cereal could positively affect one's sex appeal, the advertisements starred male and female actors being photographed or filmed who did not convey enough 'oomph' for the camera. Advertisers wanted consumers to believe that they could purchase sex appeal, and that it was an essential trait for success on the stage of life. With barely coded language, they sent a clear message that Pep cereal would deliver sexiness to men and women (*American* July 1940: 97; August 1940: 95; September 1940: 69).

Even when they targeted a younger female audience, food advertisers appealed to female sexuality. Food advertisers targeted girls as consumers, entreating them to both entice and please males with their cooking. For example, a 1960s campaign featured attractive females and males holding a Wonder Bread sandwich. With bold headlines like 'BOY TRAP' and 'DATE BAIT', the advertisements blurred the line between the female sandwich and the girls, and encouraged girls to seduce boys with Wonder Bread (*Seventeen* March 1967: 171; May 1967: 185; February 1969: 170; April 1969: 203; August 1969: 341).

Diet foods were the most likely to emphasise the triad between food, health and sexiness. Yogurt ads used attractive, vivacious young women to sell their yogurt. One 1966 advertisement asked: 'Why do teenagers with bikini figures eat yogurt?' The text promised: 'It tastes good', but advertisers wanted consumers to take away several reasons. The image suggested that if women ate yogurt, they could keep or achieve a thin figure. Further, the advert suggested that eating the yogurt would make women coy and playful. Another 1966 advert employed the words 'slim' and 'sexy', leaving nothing to chance (Dannon Yogurt 1966). Advertisers focused on women's sensuality and encouraged a belief that foods themselves were playful and sexy.

Advertising experts today also contend that gender is critical to their marketing strategies. In August 2002, Marianne Oglo, a Senior Brand Planner at J. Walter Thompson's New York office, reported that 'gender association plays a fundamental role in our discussions with consumers when exploring their perceptions and associations with various brands'. The words and imagery that Oglo extracted from early twenty-first-century tea consumers, for example, mirrored consumer responses Dichter recorded 50 years earlier. Oglo found that

> Almost unanimously, consumers associate tea with feminine and nurturing qualities, compared to coffee, which they consider to be masculine and virile. You see this pattern in product development as well: take for example two products you can buy in the store, Mr. Coffee, or Ms. Tea!…We believe that in the case of Lipton, it does not help the brand at this point in time. The tea category has shown a steady decline over the past thirty years (with the exception of a slight bump last year). When trying to make Lipton tea more relevant and contemporary to a younger target, words like 'weak', 'for when you're sick', or 'what grandma gave me' only hurt us.
>
> (Oglo 2002)

Advertisers and manufacturers struggling to enhance the market for their products find themselves hemmed in by the same gendered constructs they helped build and solidify. In the case of tea, advertisers previously used visual and verbal markers to help signify the tea as feminine. Juxtaposing the tea-drinking habits of Europe and Asia and those of the United States reveals the extent to which American advertisers constructed tea drinking as female. Now, facing a declining market, they want to reposition their product to attract men. J. Walter Thomson's

Marianne Oglo assessed the dilemma faced by advertisers today, when she reflected:

> Of course, we would never think to rebrand Lipton as the tea for weight lifters, but we are conscious of this ubiquitous perception and as a result, considering ways to subtly tweak visual and other cues that would further perpetuate a weak, feminine persona. Take for example the packaging evolution over the past few years. The colors are much more bold and confident than ever before. Lipton 'Soothing Moments' has been dropped off the herbal tea packs.
>
> (Oglo 2002)

Advertisers had been so successful in promoting and solidifying tea's image and gender identity that they now find it difficult to broaden their consumer base. Oglo used 'weight lifters' to signify an extreme masculinity that advertisers believed would never seriously consider tea, but they remained hopeful that they could enjoin men in general to drink tea. Recounting an effort to analyse potential consumers, she suggested one way they hoped to tip the gender scale:

> We observed a classic example of [gender association] during a down & dirty 2-week coffee deprivation study we conducted in New Jersey this past spring. We asked approximately 30 consumers to replace all but one cup of coffee with a premium Lipton tea, and to record their day-to-day feelings and experience in a little customized diary. One of the consumers, a fireman, admitted to putting the tea into a cooler so his colleagues at the firehouse wouldn't think of him as being a wimpy tea drinker! Afterwards, some of the men talked about feeling more bonded with their wives because they had a chance to spend 'tea-time' with them…and in doing so, show their partners a softer side.
>
> (Oglo 2002)

Writing in 1985, Dichter claimed that he worked on an advertising campaign in 1952 that sought 'to change the image of tea as a women's drink'. He suggested that 'We changed the image of tea by showing husky men drinking hot, hearty tea.' The new slogan was 'Take tea and see!' Sales increased considerably. Tea had become a 'masculine' beverage (Dichter 1985: 76). Modern-day advertisers are still employing motivational research, hungry for the information they hope can make the difference in sales. They are focusing their efforts not just on taste-tests or nutritional data, but also on motivating human emotions to compel or inspire people to buy their products. One of the most critical areas to target continues to be gender. In the late twentieth and early twenty-first centuries, advertisers persisted in asserting that consuming appropriate foods was an important way to affirm appropriate sex roles.

In a symposium on the 'Future Study of Public Opinion' that appeared in *Public Opinion Quarterly* in 1987, more than 40 years after he began his pioneering work, Dichter continued to reject the long-standing criticism that motivational research put too much stock in psychological findings. He claimed defiantly: 'Attitude research in the future will learn to take itself even more seriously.' He also sustained a belief that 'Rather than snapshots, we need 3D movies capable of registering the multivariates of human motivations – anger, hope, and disappointments' (Dichter in Bogart 1987: S180–S181).

8.5   Conclusion

The current food advertising climate still reflects the imprint of Ernest Dichter. The merits of taste, smell and appearance were only avenues to exploit what he thought were food's true selling point – its gender. Dichter tried to persuade advertisers and Americans that foods did have sex roles. With his Freudian cachet and European background, Dichter sought to bring sexuality to American shores. He wanted advertisers to embrace a mature sexuality in their marketing strategies. Beyond overt sensuality, Dichter intended the differences between women and men to extend to a parallel distinction in foods, further enabling an affirmation of gender differences through food consumption. By arguing for clear lines between men and women and for the benefits of tension and difference, Ernest Dichter promised advertisers that sexuality would be lucrative. Dichter's findings were clearly influenced by his own notions of sexiness and gender roles, and were a force in shaping American advertisers' attitudes for decades to come.

References

The American Magazine. 1940. Crowell Publishing.
Bart, P. 1962. Advertising: 'M.R.' use is dwindling. *New York Times* 18 December: 11.
Bogart, L. 1987. The future study of public opinion: a symposium. *Public Opinion Quarterly* 51 (2) (Supplement: 50th Anniversary Issue): S173–S191.

Dannon Yogurt. 1966. J. Walter Thompson Archives, Competitive Advertisements 1966, Box 20.43, Hartman Center for Sales, Marketing and Advertising History, Duke University, North Carolina.

Dichter, E. 1955a. A motivational research study on present and future psychological trends in cereal. Submitted to General Mills. Ernest Dichter Archive, University of Vienna, Report No. 712.

—— 1955b. Creative research memo on the psychology of food. Submitted to the Fitzgerald advertising agency. Archive of the Institute for Motivational Research. Peekskill, NY.

—— 1955c. Creative research memo on the sex of rice. Submitted to the Leo Burnett Co., Inc. Archive of the Institute for Motivational Research. Peekskill, NY.

—— 1956. The sex and character of food. *Motivations* 1 (2): 4.

—— 1957. Put the libido back into advertising. *Motivations* 2 (5–6): 13–19.

—— 1964. *Handbook of Consumer Motivations: The Psychology of the World of Objects*. New York: McGraw-Hill.

—— 1968. A motivational research study of luncheon meats and wieners. Submitted to Bonsib, Inc. Ernest Dichter Archive, University of Vienna, Report No. 2945.

—— 1971. *Motivating Human Behavior*. New York: McGraw-Hill.

—— 1979. *Getting Motivated by Ernest Dichter: The Secret Behind Individual Motivations by the Man Who Was Not Afraid to Ask 'Why?'*. New York: Pergamon Press.

—— 1985. What's in an image. *Journal of Consumer Marketing* 2 (1): 75–81.

—— 1987. The future study of public opinion: a symposium. *Public Opinion Quarterly* 51 (2) (Supplement: 50th Anniversary Issue): S180–S181.

Friedan, B. 1963. *The Feminine Mystique*. New York: W.W. Norton & Company.

Fullerton, R., Stern, B. 1990. The rise and fall of Ernest Dichter. *Werbeforschung und Praxis* (June): 208–211.

Hale, N. 1995. *The Rise and Crisis of Psychoanalysis in the United States: Freud and the Americans, 1917–1985*. New York: Oxford University Press.

Horowitz, D. 1998. The émigré as celebrant of American consumer culture: George Katona and Ernest Dichter. In: S. Strasser, C. McGovern, M. Judt (Eds), *Getting and Spending: European and American Consumer Societies in the Twentieth Century*. New York: Cambridge University Press, 149–166.

Oglo, M. 2002. Interview with author on 15 September. (Email transcripts in author's possession.)

Packard, V. 1957. *The Hidden Persuaders*. New York: McKay.

Parkin, K. 2006. *Food is Love: Food Advertising and Gender Roles in Twentieth-Century Advertising*. Philadelphia, PA: University of Pennsylvania Press.

Reichert, T., Lambiase, J. Eds. 2003. *Sex in Advertising: Perspectives on the Erotic Appeal*. Mahwah, NJ: Lawrence Erlbaum.

Rothwell, N. D. 1955. Motivational research revisited. *Journal of Marketing* 20: 150–154.

Schudson, M. 1986. *Advertising, The Uneasy Persuasion: Its Dubious Impact on American Society*. New York: Basic Books.

Seventeen Magazine. 1967–1969. Triangle Publications.

Shuster, A. 1961. Consumers held led by emotions. *New York Times* 30 June: 10.

Wells, W. D. 1956. Is motivation research *really* an instrument of the devil? *Journal of Marketing* 21 (2): 196–199.
Wiebe, G. D. 1958. Is it true what Williams says about motivation research? *Journal of Marketing* 22 (4): 408–410.
Williams, R. J. 1957. Is it true what they say about motivation research? *Journal of Marketing* 22 (2): 125–133.
Wyman, C. 1993. *I'm a Spam Fan: America's Best-loved Foods*. Singapore: Longmeadow Press.

9
Patriarch or Promoter of the Women's Movement? Ernest Dichter and his Interpretation of the Female Image

Karina Krummeich and Stefanie Lahm

> The husband cares for material security, the wife fulfills her household duties, and both compete with each other for a co-operative goal. True competition safeguards the individual because it insists that every member of the society do his best in his own field, without encroaching upon the field the other member has chosen.
>
> Ernest Dichter, *Strategy of Desire* (1960): 241

9.1 Introduction

At first, this statement by Ernest Dichter seems to reveal a social traditionalist who puts men and women into their 'appropriate' spheres of work and household, respectively. Looking behind the scenes of Dichter's research and writing strategies, however, a more complicated picture is revealed. In order to unpick Dichter's uneasy relationship it is not only necessary to analyse his research studies, articles and main works but also to incorporate the historical and social environment of the motivation researcher. At the time of Dichter's birth in 1907, the so-called first women's movement was internationally concerned with the issues of female suffrage. For Austrian (as well as German, English and American) women the years 1918–1920 finally brought their right to vote in democratic elections. At a time when European and American middle- and working-class women were fighting for their political rights and social equality, the issue of contested gender roles was relevant for Dichter's family, too. His autobiography clearly shows that his mother

155

was not only responsible for the family income but was also recognised as the 'head' of the family. Although this was rather due to his father's failure at work and his financial distress than to any feminist inclinations, Dichter was doubtlessly influenced during his childhood by a dominant mother.

The situation for female employees in Austria before the First World War was hardly comparable to the social position that men could claim for themselves in the public sphere. Moreover, the remuneration of women was based on completely different standards even if they had to earn their own living and maybe even support other family members (Appelt 1985: 51). While the number of male employees declined during the war years, the status of the working woman was conveniently tolerated. Although often considered mere replacements for men who were on military service, women were now able to reach a higher position within their respective companies. The fact that this was a temporary solution in order to keep the economy going and allow for efficient administration of the collective war effort seemed to go without saying. A woman's career in the work environment was always considered a temporary affair even if the employment lasted for several years. Thus, the majority of women returned to house and home quite naturally after the war was over without any noteworthy attempts to preserve their newly won public status. And yet, a first incentive was given as women had found out that they could accomplish a great deal more than they had thought themselves capable of until then.

During the emerging Austrian version of Fascism in the 1930s ('Austro-Faschismus'), the generally accepted female image began once more to conform to patriarchal views. In order to integrate all aspects of society into a 'national community', women were once again required to fulfil the twin roles of housewife and mother. Thus, Fascist misogyny became in a sense the point of culmination of the previous, 'traditional' misogyny that had structured much of Austrian society. The female public of the 1930s was addressed by the propaganda machinery using a large range of female stereotypes, such as the 'German Gretchen', the (working-class) 'female comrade' and the (middle-class) 'factory owner's wife', and thereby integrated into the National-socialist objectives. Although Fascist social rhetoric played upon a variety of women's identities, the only characteristic that was of interest to unify these various personalities was the idea of 'motherliness'. The image of Austrian and German women during the Second World War was largely restricted to this characteristic (Wittrock 1983: 3–13).

In stark contrast to the Austrian and German public image of the social role of women during the 1930s and 1940s, there seemed greater willingness in the United States to redefine the role of women along more equal and experimental lines. Ernest and Hedy Dichter arrived in the United States at a point in time, however, when the duties of a woman were still restricted to the household, the bringing-up of children and activities that assured a happy marriage. Due to the exceptional economic circumstances of the Second World War, the American government mobilised the home front by means of political propaganda and advertised a new type of woman – the 'working patriot'. Thus, carrying the burden of their dual role, women found themselves between the function of a caring housewife and mother on the one hand and the factory or office worker on the other. The latter role was epitomised by Norman Rockwell's character of 'Rosie the Riveter' who appeared on the cover of the *Saturday Evening Post* in May 1943. 'Rosie' represented the strong matron, who, as a working woman, helped her country, thereby contributing to the victory of the beloved homeland. However, a majority of Americans believed that this new freedom and the new public responsibilities of women would find their end with the return of the men from war (Dabakis 1993; Matthaei 1982).

Nevertheless, the newly won freedom of decision and the freshly awakened sense of awareness could not be banned from the minds of some women, although many returned to their traditional lifestyles. For many women, the challenge to fight for equal rights and to take on social responsibility became at least imaginable – a thought that should finally manifest itself in the civil rights movement of the 1960s. Ernest Dichter would use this background during his professional heyday in the 1950s and 1960s by directly addressing the enormous target group of women whose state of tension between socially dictated behavioural roles and the wish for self-realisation remains a polarising issue to this day.

9.2   The psychological consultant – Ernest Dichter as 'life coach'

As a motivational researcher, Dichter combined a fascinating array of public roles, which provided for a myriad of touch-points with the female world. During the late 1940s, for instance, Dichter began to offer insight into his psychoanalytical knowledge by acting as a readers' consultant for the *Real Story Magazine*. In seven editions of the magazine, the self-appointed social anthropologist answered readers' letters, written by both male and female readers who sought advice on issues regarding life, relationships and love.

Although the magazine's topics as well as the advertisements published next to the articles suggested that this was a magazine with a mainly female audience, the publication at times also answered men's enquiries. Dichter's advice published in the *Real Story Magazine* exhibits his still largely traditionalist views on gender roles. His response to a letter carrying the title 'Should unfaithful husbands be forgiven?' is a prime example. The desperate question of a female reader about how to deal with her unfaithful husband was answered by Dichter very rationally and without any empathy – quite in contrast to his basic principles. By giving her the advice to approach the problem from a certain distance in order not to morally judge but to understand the husband, Dichter performed a remarkable conversion of guilt and defended the husband. In Dichter's world, the unfaithfulness of a man was an understandable reaction to missing love and lack of care at home.

> In all likelihood, the responsibility lies with both of you – even though your role and your faults have only been those of passive neglect. [...] It may be your only way of learning how and where you have failed to hold him.
>
> (Dichter undated a)

The solution for the woman's problem lies in an open and honest conversation, which should, however, take place without any tears and reproaches. Dichter, the psychoanalyst, demands the 'talking through' of things on a rational basis – a character trait he attributed to the man and denied the woman in that relationship.

In this same edition of the magazine, Dichter also gave advice to a young woman who was faced with the decision between two possible husbands. Surprisingly, Dichter used a wholly different approach in her case. The person seeking advice should not – as in the previous example – distance herself from the problem but should internalise the issue in order to reach a decision. Without getting involved with the woman's problem any further, Dichter referred directly to predominant social norms. While in the first case fully understanding the man's extramarital affairs, Dichter seemed to condemn the wavering woman's behaviour in a similar situation. The Puritan guidelines of American social behaviour, which Dichter purported to analyse in his research, played a major role when advising the woman that she could only reach happiness by making a quick and careful decision or otherwise risk being permanently exposed to moral and social judgement by her friends and relatives.

It is remarkable that the gender-specific moral responsibility was in both cases entirely left with the woman. Somewhat in contrast to the paradigm of the passive woman, it is she who is left with the responsibility of solving family problems and of ensuring the success of the marriage. The question arises of course whether Dichter was 'forced' to follow the magazine's editorial policy; whether he was trying to adhere to social parameters; or whether the young motivation researcher was allowing insight into his personal opinion. Definite conclusions about the background of these statements cannot be drawn. Dichter's private life, however, helps shed light on the motives that drive his reasoning. Decades later, Dichter reported about his extramarital activities for which he got permission from his wife Hedy (Figure 9.1). His statement that these affairs probably hurt Hedy implies that there obviously was a certain imbalance within this 'half-open marriage' (Dichter 1979: 89). The discrepancy between the 'modern' way of leading a married life and

Figure 9.1   Ernest and Hedy Dichter, *c*.1965.

traditional values were also reflected in his advisory activities. While surely under some editorial guidance and attempting to respond to the moral expectations of the magazine's readers, it seems understandable that Dichter wanted to distribute his knowledge most profitably and thus subordinated his analysis to the expectations of his respective client. Hence, it can be assumed that the motives behind Dichter's argumentation in the advice columns were a conglomerate of a number of social factors.

Dichter, however, escapes easy social stereotyping by historians as some of his statements seem to contradict the image of a 'traditionalist'. While at times exculpating himself and other unfaithful husbands, he also presented himself as an advocate of the women's movement at other times. The following example shows that Dichter's moral and social judgement changed over time. In his autobiography, he proudly exclaimed:

> Telling Procter & Gamble to utilize their detergent commercials to influence family relations by showing the husband and the son taking care of the laundry can achieve more than a well-planned president's committee resolution on equal rights or even a pronouncement from Gloria Steinem.
>
> (Dichter 1979: 191–192)

During the 1960s and 1970s, Dichter thus developed himself into a 'progressive' critic when realising that changing market conditions demanded new forms of social analysis from him. During those years, a second wave of international women's movements quite radically challenged social assumptions that Dichter had been happy to employ in the decades before.

9.3   From Barbie Doll to Betty Friedan

In 1958, Dichter became involved in the commercial launch of Matell's Barbie doll. This product launch must have been a tempting challenge for him. Rather than delegating this survey to his assistants as he did with many other projects at that time, he put himself in direct charge of the study, which included a survey of 357 children and 58 parents. Dichter's advice to equip the doll with a personality, a very unusual decision at that time, proved to be the basis of the toy's global commercial breakthrough. Today, every half a second a Barbie doll is sold somewhere in the world (Bennett 2005). Dichter recognised the true psychological significance of toys as consumer products and chose the Barbie doll to make a point of this insight. He understood toys as a means of handling psycho-social impressions and as social tools that established ethic principles. The decisive element of the new Barbie doll was her seemingly unlimited freedom as she had the possibility to achieve everything she ever dreamt of. It was this message which Dichter wanted to communicate to the 'small female buyers' (Dichter 1959). For Dichter, the doll's image served as a projection screen for the American dream – a dream that this Austrian immigrant himself lived and propagated. Dichter turned Barbie into an object of attribution of human, especially female, needs. This corresponds very precisely with Dichter's maxim that consumption could be a vehicle for the free development of people's personalities.

However, this message was not accepted enthusiastically by everyone. Dichter's critics used it to unmask consumption as a power that ran counter to the idea of emancipation. The Barbie doll, whose ever 'feminine' appearance in pink was obviously designed for girls, was seen as stabilising the traditional role allocation between the sexes. Many of these objections were expressed by Betty Friedan in her *The Feminine Mystique* (Friedan 1963). Friedan caused great uproar with her book, which was regarded by many as the starting point of the second women's movement in the United States. As Friedan's biographer Daniel Horowitz summarised:

> It has become commonplace to see the publication of Betty Friedan's 'The Feminine Mystique' in 1963 as a major turning point in the history of modern American feminism and, more generally, in the history of the postwar period. And with good reason, for her book was a key factor in the revival of the women's movement and in the transformation of the nation's awareness of the challenges middle-class suburban women faced. The 'Feminine Mystique' helped millions of women comprehend, and then change, the conditions of their lives.
>
> (Horowitz 1998: 197)

In her profound examination of the mystification of the female image, Friedan wrote against the often hidden oppression of women in American everyday life. The cleaning and cooking and child-minding housewife, Friedan argued, may be a legitimate role. But this role could not be expected of all women, as a large number of them did not want to be housewives or mothers and could never pursue happiness in exercising these stereotypes. It was Friedan's intention to make clear to women that the traditional image of the female might not be the only image to strive for and that it was not immoral not to find fulfilment in house-keeping: 'I, like other women, thought that there was something wrong with me because I didn't have an orgasm waxing the kitchen floor' (Friedan 2001: 43).

By presenting such provocative statements, Friedan fought against the female isolation within the four walls of the house and propagated the 'new woman', a self-dependent woman with her own interests and own needs. Friedan thereby wanted to create a collective awareness that freed the public debate about gender roles. With his own take on the idea of the 'new' post-war female, Dichter created the Barbie doll with a personality that was characterised by being a single, independent woman, beaming with self-confidence and happiness. Predictably, Betty Friedan interpreted Dichter's ideal of a 'new woman' as diametrically opposed to hers. In the chapter 'The Sexual Sell' of her landmark book, without even once mentioning his name, she criticised his work directly as typical for the entire sector of advertising and Motivation Research. Her main point of criticism was the manipulation by Dichter of female emotions for economic purposes. Exploiting the increased purchasing power of women merely in order to increase the turnover of the companies he advised, Dichter found himself charged with denying female consumers' quest for 'true felicity': 'Somehow, somewhere, someone must have figured out that women will buy more things if they are kept in the under-used, nameless-yearning, energy-to-get-rid-of state of being housewives' (Friedan 2001: 299).

Friedan's clear words did not fail to have the desired effect. The American women's movement celebrated the pamphlet as a feminist manifesto and drew from it new energy and inspiration. While, at first, Friedan's reproaches did not seem to harm Dichter himself or Motivation Research directly, they did form the basis of more widespread societal change of opinion. In the course of the feminist rebellion, the Barbie doll was criticised as representing a type of female stereotype that should be burnt together with bras and 'How-To' handbooks that taught women to be good housewives. Other people, however, regarded the Barbie doll as a kind of 'feminist pioneer' (Lord 1994: 10) and therefore as an antagonist to Betty Friedan's vision of a new woman:

> In her independence Barbie defies the feminine mystique. Thereby she also partakes of the male privilege to be an individual unto one's self and to forswear self-sacrifice in favor of self-actualization.
>
> (Rogers 1999: 39)

Based on the social conditions described here, the question of Dichter's perception of women arises. It is not immediately clear whether Friedan's invectives were legitimate and whether Dichter really was a representative of the conservative, patriarchic wing of society. In order to approach these issues, it is necessary to analyse why Dichter, at a time when the man was no doubt seen as the head of the family, focused so strongly on the woman as consumer in his advisory activities. It was of course a common assumption that women ran the household and, therefore, many advertisements focused on a female target group. Post-war advertising campaigns for fast-moving consumer goods usually emphasised that women should fulfil their household duties and make sure that the needs of their husbands and children were considered above all. Dichter took up this idea by extending women's role as housekeeper and manager of the 'company home'. But his focus went a lot further. He acknowledged women's individual needs and thereby regarded the woman as a self-dependent character whose desires were at least as important as that of her family: 'Women are not just buying a soap for the family – even after they are married they still buy a soap for themselves' (Dichter 2002 [1960]: 240). Dichter did not only consider the female consumer as being responsible for the daily shopping. He also recognised her as a decisive power regarding larger purchases and luxury items. Thereby, he encouraged and authorised not only her right to have a say in these matters, but also subtly questioned male dominance and authority.

9.4 The model woman

Dichter's most popular categorisation of types of women was developed at the beginning of the 1940s and was referred to by him throughout his career. His 'basic model' of womanhood (Dichter 2002 [1960]: 182–185) was used for various products, categories and sectors, like sanitary pads and cleaning products. The various types of women that Dichter defines in his model can be described as follows. The primal and traditional type of woman is recognised by Dichter as the conventional housewife, who finds total fulfilment in her role as caring wife and mother. Regarding consumption, this pure housewife is rather problematic, as her constant bad conscience does not allow her to use time-saving household and food products. Everything she does not control herself makes her seem dispensable and endangers her status within the family. The number of women whose fear of progress and change were regarded as their main motif, according to Dichter, decreased over the years, which of course was very convenient for the advocate of progress and innovation.

Dichter's second type, the 'career woman', was also characterised as an insecure person, to whom household duties were not more than a non-essential burden and who looked for her recognition outside of her house and home. Her independence, also from her husband, was her utmost concern. According to Dichter, one of her main characteristics was a certain state of unhappiness. Due to her constant search for the 'magic' product, she would never be satisfied, which is why she was considered a less relevant consumer for advertising and consumer researchers. For Dichter, this group was also in continuous decline.

In Dichter's opinion, neither the housewife nor the 'career woman' symbolised the future of modern womanhood. The modern woman was instead embodied in the idea of the 'balanced woman'. Her main feature was her wish to find happiness both in her family as well as in extra-domestic activities. This woman considered housework as a means of expressing individuality and creativity. This aspect was used by Dichter to sell various products to female target groups by calling on the modern woman's creative abilities regarding housekeeping and interior design. According to Dichter, the fact that women now had more social contacts also meant that they could be considered an equal conversational partner and also a better partner altogether by their husbands, as well as a better mother. In order to have more time for herself and the family, 'modern woman' would also accept ready-made and pre-packed products without being haunted by guilt.

> The 'woman of the day', and probably of the decade, perhaps even of the century, is the balanced woman. Although she is one of three basic types, she appears, from the evidence compiled over some twenty years by the Institute, to be the type who is emerging as dominant.
>
> (Dichter 1964a: 2)

Arguably, the 'balanced woman' was the perfect consumer as she was happy to try out new things yet always acted with caution. Unlike the archetypical housewife, the 'modern' woman never consumed without asking questions. At the same time, the 'modern' woman's brand loyalty promised to be far greater than that of the 'career woman'. All this led Dichter to regard the new type of woman as ideal – an ideal to which also his wife Hedy belonged. She followed her extra-domestic interests at the Institute for Motivational Research, while at the same time fulfilling her roles as wife and administrator of the motivator's castle in Croton-on-Hudson. Already earlier, when the two of them were still living in Vienna, Dichter commented on his marriage as follows:

> Hedy, long before Women's Liberation, was the breadwinner, but she still remained the devoted wife who would never allow me to wash the dishes, if this is a symbol of equality between the sexes.
>
> (Dichter 1979: 13)

His 'trisection' of the female sex was not limited to the United States as Dichter applied this model internationally and worked with it in numerous studies in America, Britain, France and Germany during the 1960s. While the model might seem to us a drastic simplification, it must be regarded as rather progressive given the circumstances at that time. In the majority of 1950s and 1960s market research surveys, women were either not considered at all or were generally regarded as housewives (Bartos 1989: 7). Furthermore, this model was of course only a basic framework. In order to extend and improve it, Dichter constantly searched for sub-categories that allowed him to enlarge his scope of interpretation. Over the course of many years, however, he realised that there was no generally valid image of the female gender and that women want to be regarded as individuals with a personality.

9.5   Latent female images

Numerous surveys shed light on Dichter's complex approach in characterising different female images. Although no specific definitions can be found, a clear picture emerges regarding the mutual influence of the self-image of interviewed women and Dichter's approach to various aspects of the female psyche. Some of these principles will be illustrated briefly in the following sections. Even when he attributed women in different situations with different character traits, he at the same time attempted to crystallise motivating factors that characterised general 'types' of women. For instance, by describing the 'suffering' (Dichter 1969: 20–25) and the 'insecure' (Dichter 1968: 47–48) woman, he referred to the cliché of the weaker sex. Moreover, vanity, self-abandonment and dependence were – at least for the self-styled expert on women consumers – to be associated with womanhood. However, it must be stressed that Dichter's ambiguity concerning the female image also became increasingly evident in many of his research studies as he repeatedly referred to the development, the independence and, in close connection with that, the upgrading of the public status of women. Especially latent characteristics are important here, which reveal the revolutionary approaches of Dichter as marketing psychologist. While clearly describing women as the weaker sex, he also seemed to want to distance himself from this point of view:

> Incidentally, it is a male mistake or an old prejudice, to regard women as weak or discriminated by nature. Modern anthropology proves the opposite: Women are more resistant concerning health and body! The modern woman does not want to be considered as a weak creature.
>
> (Dichter 1965: 6)

In contrast to the common gender-specific separation between the 'rational' character of the male and the 'emotionality' of the female, the motivation psychologist confirmed that females were also capable of instrumental orientation and practical thinking (Dichter 1971: 182). The most significant description of women emerges from their characterisation by Dichter as anti-fatalistic individuals. Referring to this idea, Dichter regarded womanhood in general as optimistic and future-oriented: 'There are many indications emerging that the modern woman, and even more so the woman of the future, will become much more anti-fatalistic and wants to be in greater control of her destiny' (Dichter 1964a: 20). Furthermore, Dichter argued:

> Today's woman is no longer willing to accept a drab existence in a masochistic, suffering fashion. [...] The breaking down of traditional cultural taboos on women, not only to work, but to obtain and utilize higher education or simply to operate as an individual even within the family circle, has opened up a myriad of new potentials and opportunities in the search for satisfaction.
>
> (Dichter 1964a: 24)

Especially regarding Dichter's constantly recurring criticism of the fatalistic behaviour of Americans and Europeans, the motivation researcher's evaluation of gender images is of great relevance. His 'Memorandum on the Changing Role of the American Woman' (Dichter 1964a) can be seen as one of the most significant research studies concerning Dichter's progressive social views. The interesting aspect of this survey, which was carried out for the Lever Brothers Company, is that it did not focus on a specific product but centred on a social phenomenon. While Dichter began the survey by introducing his basic, three-pronged model of womanhood, he then concentrated mainly on the 'balanced woman' in the course of the survey – now, however, presenting a far more diverse personality profile. Apart from this woman's attitude towards married and family life as well as consumption, Dichter described the aspect of professional occupation as one of the most prominent ones. To reinforce his theses, he referred to one of the pioneers of the women's movement, Simone de Beauvoir, whose bestseller *The Second Sex* defined work as a determinant of woman's place in society (de Beauvoir 1953). Not only did Dichter make this feminist manifesto a topic of discussion. He is also unmasked as a visionary thinker in the following statement:

> The next decade should see the emphasis change from 'should women work and if they do so are they not denying their families for the sake of their egos?' to, 'what are the things that society, business and industry, educational institutions and government bodies do to help women do the best possible job of carrying this double burden?
>
> (Dichter 1964a: 12)

9.6 Women and technology: 'The Other Sex' meets the car

In contrast to this progressive survey, Dichter's studies on car-buying behaviour again present a very contradictory perception of women. For example, Dichter complained about women's lack of technical knowledge, but managed to put this statement into perspective by adding that this deficit also applies to most men. On the one hand, he was of the opinion that women – following their usual interests – mainly focused on superficial criteria such as colour and upholstery. On the other hand, he attributed them with more rationality than men when buying a car:

> That's why a married car buyer, whether he admits to it or not, usually likes to have his wife's opinion before making up his mind. This is because he knows deep down that his wife is inclined to think more rationally than he does and would therefore keep him from making a foolish choice.
>
> (Dichter 1971: 182)

Apart from the question of decision-making powers of women when buying a car, Dichter also appreciated the freedom a woman gained by owning her own car. As the car was a status symbol and metaphor for power and independence, it offered women the possibility of symbolically being on the same level as men. He therefore gave the following advice: 'Gas stations have to accept the fact that they are catering not only to men but also to women, and not only to women as family buyers, but as individuals with their own cars' (Dichter 2002 [1960]: 240). While recognising this social trend, Dichter nevertheless stressed traditional clichés and advised petrol stations to adapt their services to 'female' needs by, for example, offering vacuum cleaners. Again, this example shows the ambivalence of Dichter's attitudes towards the distribution of roles between men and women.

9.7   Women in the land of the free and the home of the brave

In many areas of his life, Ernest Dichter was a man of contradictions and this tendency can also be seen in his perception of women. While, at least from today's point of view, many of his statements can be considered as being patriarchal or even misogynist, other declarations were emancipatory and present Dichter as an enthusiastic proponent of the women's movement. Although he concerned himself with the problems of female managers (Dichter 1975: 127–130) and discussed the preconditions for a female American presidency (Dichter, undated b), other research aspects and statements seem reactionary. While he spoke against gender-specific toys – 'Adults frown upon doll play on the part of little boys as "sissy" behaviour, in actuality, this type of play is emotionally as important for little boys as for little girls' (Dichter 1959: 5) – he was also involved in the planning and market launch of the girls' toy *par excellence*, the Barbie doll. It must be stated here that Dichter's contradictory perception of women did change to a limited extent over the course of his life and career. Yet, the lack of systematised thought ran through Dichter's entire life and work. He avoided systematisation as he wanted to be seen as the 'all-round adviser' whose analyses were ultimately meant to change and improve entire societies.

This wide scope may have also been the reason why Dichter described the United States as a path-breaking ideal for all other nations. The most significant difference in his analyses of the American and the European woman can be found in his general belief that American society represented an advanced state of development. In some of his surveys, Dichter argued that social developments in Europe took place about ten years later than in the United States. Regarding emancipation, he therefore described America as 'the most advanced country in freeing women from a purely household role' (Dichter 1958: 11). Social and cultural developments in his adopted country, where he found personal happiness, were compared by Dichter to the circumstances in 'old Europe':

> The British woman's emancipation is a reluctant one. Possibly here is one of the major differences between the British woman and the American. The American woman has put emancipation first, and has then wondered how exactly to use it; the British woman has a feeling that this emancipation is partially forced on her; she finds it more readily available than her mother did. Quite a lot of women are not at all sure that they want it, much less know what to do with it.
>
> (Dichter 1964b: 19)

Although Dichter can be regarded as a representative of an optimistic view of women's emancipation, he did not trust the individual without social guidance. The general ambivalence of the motivational researcher became most clear when his own self-conception is considered. His aspiration to be marketing 'guru', social analyst and futurologist at the same time does imply a certain contradictory world view. It is difficult, for example, to reconcile the social anthropologist, who – in advertising research – swims with the masses, with the activities of a revolutionary thinker and social reformer. It is also not clear to what extent Dichter was aware of this fact. While Dichter referred to himself as a promoter of women's emancipation, he also sponsored conservative and patriarchal views in his studies on consumer products. In retrospect, Dichter once again emerges as an uneasy and deeply complex figure: both European and American, patriarch and social visionary.

References

Appelt, E. 1985. *Von Ladenmädchen, Schreibfräulein und Gouvernanten. Die weiblichen Angestellten Wiens zwischen 1900 und 1934*. Vienna: Verlag für Gesellschaftskritik.

Bartos, R. 1989. *Marketing to Women Around the World*. Boston, MA: Harvard Business School Press.

Bennett, D. 2005. Getting the Id to go shopping: psychoanalysts, advertising, Barbie dolls, and the invention of the consumer unconscious. *Public Culture* 17 (1): 1–25.

Dabakis, M. 1993. Norman Rockwell's 'Rosie the Riveter' and the discourse of wartime womanhood. In: B. Melosh (Ed.), *Gender and American History since 1890*. London/New York: Routledge: 182–204.

De Beauvoir, S. 1953. *The Second Sex*. London: Cape.

Dichter, E. 1958. A summary of a report on the Canadian woman. Ernest Dichter Archive, University of Vienna, Report No. 4602.

——— 1959. A motivational research study in the field of toys for Mattel Toys, Inc. Institute for Motivational Research, Croton-on-Hudson.

——— 1964a. Memorandum on the changing role of the American woman. Ernest Dichter Archive, University of Vienna, Report No. 2390.

——— 1964b. A motivational research study on the British woman in today's culture for 'Woman's Own'. Ernest Dichter Archive, University of Vienna, Report No. 2432.

——— 1965. Kritische Stellungnahme zur OKASAGOLD-Broschüre: Das schwache Geschlecht steht seinen Mann ('Critical comment on the OKASAGOLD-brochure: the weak sex asserts itself'). Ernest Dichter Archive, University of Vienna, Report No. 2527.

——— 1968. Bericht zu einer Motivleitstudie über die unbefriedigten Modebedürfnisse der 'Frau um 40' ('Memorandum on a motivational research study on the unsatisfied fashion requirements of the woman in her forties'). Ernest Dichter Archive, University of Vienna, Report No. 2820.

——— 1969. Bericht zu einer Motivleitstudie über Tampons, speziell Camelia-Tampons ('Memorandum on a motivational research study on tampons, especially Camelia tampons'). Ernest Dichter Archive, University of Vienna, Report No. 3039.

——— 1971. *Motivating Human Behavior*. New York: McGraw-Hill.

——— 1975. *Der Nackte Manager. Erfolgreiches Management ohne Systemzwang.* Frankfurt am Main.: Lorch Verlag.

——— 1979. *Getting Motivated by Ernest Dichter: The Secret Behind Individual Motivations by the Man Who Was Not Afraid to Ask 'Why?'* New York: Pergamon Press.

——— 2002 [1960]. *The Strategy of Desire*. New Brunswick, NJ: Transaction.

——— Undated a. The psychological consultant. *Real Story Magazine*. Ernest Dichter Archive, University of Vienna, File No. 4643.

——— Undated b. The making of a woman president. Ernest Dichter Archive, University of Vienna, Report No. 5101.

Friedan, B. 2001 [1963]. *The Feminine Mystique*. New York: W.W Norton & Company.

Horowitz, D. 1998. *Betty Friedan and the Making of 'The Feminine Mystique'. The American Left, the Cold War, and Modern Feminism.* Amherst: University of Massachusetts Press.

Lord, M. G. 1994. *Forever Barbie. Unauthorized Biography of a Real Doll.* New York: William Morrow & Co.

Matthaei, J. 1982. *An Economic History of Women in America. Women's Work, the Sexual Division of Labor, and the Development of Capitalism.* New York: Schocken Books, Inc.

Rogers, M. F. 1999. *Barbie Culture*. London: Sage.

Wittrock, C. 1983. Weiblichkeitsmythen. Das Frauenbild im Faschismus und seine Vorläufer in der Frauenbewegung der 20er Jahre. Frankfurt am Main.: Sendler Verlag.

Part IV
The European Theatre

10
Ernest Dichter as Midwife and Educator: Post-war European Consumer Societies and the Sociology of the Consumer

Kai-Uwe Hellmann

10.1 The cultural construction of social agency

This chapter studies how Ernest Dichter described his work as a researcher and writer through metaphors. I argue that the metaphors used by Dichter to present and interpret his work reveal a number of interesting insights into his vision of the consumer. By referring to himself as a 'midwife', an educator and social reformer, Dichter prepared the stage for continuous self-presentation as a public mentor who enabled consumers to recognise themselves as independent actors in society.

Within the scope of our subject, neither Dichter's complete works nor his life as such is of specific interest. Instead, the following question will be crucial: to what extent did Dichter's research actively contribute – in the sense of Michel Callon's performativity thesis – to the emergence and denotation of the consumer's role as an agent and actor in society. Two presuppositions will be guiding. First, I argue that it was partly against the backdrop of the psychoanalytic method, which cast a new light on the consumer and contributed to the emergence of a new type of consumer, that Dichter operated as a 'midwife' in the unfolding of post-war European consumer culture. Secondly, I argue that it was Dichter's aim to influence and change the consumer in their buying behaviour and he therefore operated as an 'educator'.

In their seminal article on the construction of social agency, John W. Meyer and Ronald L. Jepperson (2000) argued that the phenomena we describe with terms such as act/action/agent are not of natural origin but that instead, social agency is constructed artificially. Thus, the specific meaning implied in these terms depends on the kind of understanding a particular society develops around the question of qualification: who is qualified, and qualified due to which criteria, to be in charge of and responsible for action. The cultural construction of social agency is therefore always connected to specific agents and is dependent on their ability to act; and it is important to note that this ability is something society assigns. In short, only those who are authorised by society are able to act. It is precisely this cultural construction of social agency within modern society that interests Meyer and Jepperson.

Both authors start out from the idea that the ability of responsible agency has been attributed to the individual as recently as in the course of modernity. The possibility and experience of being an individual is therefore a cultural construct losing its coherence as soon as one tries to hide this constructive character; it is thus a concept containing many presuppositions. From a sociological viewpoint, it is too unspecific to talk about the individual as such. In fact, from a strictly sociological perspective, it only makes sense to talk about persons acting within society via roles. It is unlikely that someone acts on exclusively individual terms. At most, one could state individual actions in the context of the deviation from prevailing norms, merely representing a variation of the usual. In other words, the individual ability to act displays itself in the way a person carries out special roles in special contexts, such as within the family, the public space, the office or the holiday setting. One must assume the interdependence between the individual, the person and the displayed role which is produced culturally and is therefore a historically variable outcome of social interaction. The whole range of roles that are at the individual's disposal are therefore the product of the social relations into which individuals are born.

Keeping the previous remarks in mind and turning towards the focus of this chapter, it follows that the idea of the consumer only concerns a specific role modern individuals have at their disposal. This role is a cultural construct and historically mutable. However, we still know relatively little about the antecedents of this role and the research related to this area is still in its infancy. Many questions remain open: how, for example, has the cultural construction of the modern consumer emerged? Who was responsible for its production? Since when does this role exist? And what about the key features of this role?

Among others, Frank Trentmann (2005a, 2006) dealt with this question by asking 'Who is the consumer?' As a historian, he is especially concerned with issues of origins and chronology. His research is concerned with the problem of when the term and concept of the consumer was first equipped with distinct socio-political characteristics. As far as the United Kingdom is concerned, his surprising answer is that the 1890s first saw London's citizens acting collectively as consumers in the 'water wars' (Trentmann and Taylor 2005). The activation of formerly passive users, rendering them visible and proactive, proved decisive for the first appearance of a specifically consumer-related semantics – 'a difference that makes a difference', as Gregory Bateson would have put it.

Likewise, Trentmann's findings remain historically contested as there are plausible alternatives for locating the emergence of the consumer movement (Breen 2004; Haese 1960; Hilton 2003; Zahn 1960). In this context, especially the 1940s and 1950s – a period referred to in Germany as the 'economic miracle' ('Wirtschaftswunder') – have to be taken into account. The post-war years in many ways represent a caesura in modern society which equals that of the 1890s – at least as far as the question of the emergence and significance of the consumer's role is concerned. This was a period marked by exceptionally rapid economical development accompanied by mass consumption and full employment. Markets were virtually flooded with products and the interiors of middle- and working-class homes were becoming more and more luxurious, including television sets, telephones and refrigerators. For the first time, a broad mass of consumers experienced affluence and a cornucopia of choice.

During these years, the structure of the market turned upside down as a sellers' market changed into a buyers' market where demand controlled the supply (Vershofen 1959). Kruse (1959: 246) pointed out that within a sellers' market producers are active, while consumers are imagined as passive followers of the market: 'The consumers are merely the backdrop of this scenery: abstract, dead beings, only standing out by their demand for produced goods; a demand that simply and unquestionably exists as something the producers can count on.' After the shift, the demanding party was suddenly displaying an astonishing life of its own, which in turn brought the motivational researchers on to the scene.

> The analysis of the structure of demand has been pressed ahead by the psychological and sociological approaches of the theory. And this brought forth a remarkable change by which the realm of demand and request was illuminated and the volatility and irrationality as well as the consumer's ability to adapt and to be influenced were discovered.
>
> (Kruse 1959: 246)

In the course of these developments, marketing and consumer research was expanding enormously. What had previously been accessible by means of calculation and prediction grew increasingly obscure and inexplicable. Consumers began to defy control of the producers. On account of this defect, the need for marketing and consumer research increased further. In fact, the alienation between the consumer and the producer had never been more significant (Collins and Montgomery 1969; Hellmann 2003; Kapferer 1994; Packard 1958; Reinhardt 1993). I argue that it is the very outlines of this development that helps clarify the issue of the emergence and significance of the consumer's role. The increasing usage of marketing and consumer research during the post-war years triggered a number of considerable efforts to understand the shifts and changes of both the markets and consumers. As a result of these efforts, new methods, ideas and concepts emerged, all aiming at consumer-related research. As a consequence of these procedures, the answers to the questions about the emergence of the consumer's role in a way contributed to the making of this question itself. One could even say that post-war market and consumer research first produced what later became the object of its assignment. Following Michel Callon's thesis about the performance of markets, the phenomenon of post-war consumer research can be seen in analogy to the 'new markets' that were talked into existence by economists and business researchers (Callon 1998). Or, as Donald MacKenzie and Yuval Millo commented: 'Economics performs the economy, creating the phenomena it describes' (2003: 108). Thus, the emergence of consumer research is partly responsible for the discovery of the consumer as such (Brose 1958).

Though there were many who participated in this movement, there were only few who were important. In the following sections of this chapter, one of these important participants, Ernest Dichter, shall be discussed. In some respect, the market researcher Ernest Dichter shared the same fate as the American sociologist Talcott Parsons: both attracted a lot of attention during the 1940s, 1950s and 1960s; they were almost forgotten during the 1970s and 1980s and slowly rediscovered during the 1990s (Obrec 1999). As the American marketing researcher Barbara Stern argued recently:

> Dichter's vision has profoundly affected the 'richness of theorizing' about hidden factors in consumer behaviour. His introduction of Motivation Research is so fully assimilated in the field that it has changed the very grammar of marketing – the common language that underlies disciplinary thought. [Motivation research] is now part of

the marketing community's specialized language or 'code', a system of verbal conventions mastered by all users as a common tongue for research communication.

(Stern 2002: 21)

Dichter has often been called the 'father of motivation research' and, without doubt, he contributed considerably to the rise to prominence of marketing and consumer research during the 1940s and 1950s (Bartos 1986a, 1986b, 1986c; Engel et al. 1995; Packard 1958; Stern 2004). Following Niklas Luhmann and Thomas Kuhn, one could argue that in Dichter's case the originality and effect of his work can be attributed to the two 'paradigm shifts' of consumer-orientation and qualitative marketing research. According to Barbara Stern, Dichter's main contributions included 'turning attention to the consumer, adapting psychoanalytic concepts to research, and using therapy techniques to analyze marketplace behaviour.' Dichter was instrumental in the seismic shift away from the marketer's viewpoint to the consumer's viewpoint as the basis of marketing activities (Stern 2002: 20–21). In the following paragraphs, I will study how Dichter himself reflected on the roles he played in the making of post-war consumer culture, and I will use the metaphors he applied as a lens to understand the way he publicly projected his work.

10.2   Methods and functions of motivational research

In Plato's dialog *Theaitetos*, Socrates confronts Theaitetos with the statement that not only had his mother been a midwife – a fact that was well known – but that he, Socrates, performed this art as well by bringing about new information. Socrates drew attention to this fact because he had the impression that Theaitetos was pregnant. Socrates therefore felt that his own skills as 'midwife' were needed. The art of Socrates thus consisted of assisting 'parturient' souls to develop new ideas. In the dialogue, there is a further idea: 'And the greatest thing in my art is this: to be able to test, by every means, whether it's an imitation and a falsehood that the young men's intellect is giving birth to, or something genuine and true' (Plato 1973: 13). Midwives, like Socrates, are thus also deciding on the viability of new ideas. This implies that, if necessary, they advise to abort ideas and even perform these abortions.

Provided that one experimentally engages with the mentioned analogy, it is possible to describe Ernest Dichter as such a midwife. For Dichter was operating at the borderline between the visible and the invisible where forms are neither present nor absent but only noticeable by external circumstances – a state of affairs which is, by the way, typical for the situation of giving birth. Sticking to this analogy, one could say that the European and American societies of the 1940s and 1950s were 'pregnant' and on the edge of producing a new kind of consumer. In fact, nothing was completely visible and no one grasped the whole process as such. But, as I indicated above, certain changes suggested that something fermented in the bosom of society, something was on the edge of becoming visible. Such was the situation Dichter faced during the 1940s. His special skills as a catalyser and midwife of new ideas had partly developed due to his contact with Sigmund Freud's thoughts, which had pushed forth a revolution regarding man's self-awareness. Freud's psychoanalysis, his exploration of psychic and social anomalies, was striking because his investigations exceeded the boundaries of consciousness. He not only assumed the subconscious but also the unconscious, whose essential design was said to remain inaccessible (Fuchs 1998). This difference between conscious and unconscious layers of man's psyche – psychoanalysis' guiding principle of differentiation – opened up a completely new realm to the humanities. Suddenly, the focus was widening up. Especially, the observation of transgressions and frontier crossings proved to be particularly instructive as conscious and unconscious realms interlocked here.

It is not necessary to further explore the implications of Freud's psychoanalysis since the impact of his methods can be easily traced when it comes to Dichter's motivational research. Dichter himself repeatedly referred to this nexus. In his autobiography, for example, he wrote: '[My] methods were insofar psychoanalytic as I didn't let myself be fooled by the superficial answers of the interviewees. Instead, I tried to find out about their real motivations that were concealed' (Dichter 1977: 15). When one looks at Dichter's writings and tries to identify the semantics echoing the psychoanalytical principle of differentiation, one does come across several differentiations that are, in a functional respect, constructed in an equal manner (Tadajewski 2006).

Dichter, for example, distinguishes between right and wrong ideas, between outer appearance and real meaning, between superficial answers and true motivations and even between conscious and unconscious motivations. In direct terms, Dichter declared that 'we have learned to distinguish between what a man says and what he really means' (Dichter 1947: 432). Elsewhere he elaborated:

> In functional psychological research we distinguish between symptoms expressing the superficial rational explanations of an action,

and the real, deeper reasons which form the emotional basis of such actions, and are connected with the functional role a product plays in the user's life.

(Dichter 1949: 64)

Using a metaphor he wrote: 'The chase after the motivation is like an underwater-chase' (Dichter 1981: 23). Dichter always wanted to 'look behind the scenes' (Dichter 1981: 18), to 'observe the consumer's behaviour in order to find out what he [the consumer] really desires and dreams about; and I subsequently want to offer him exactly this product or service' (Dichter 1991: 231). Dichter aimed at a 'thorough investigation of the perceivable and often enough very aberrant behavioural patterns of the human kind' (Dichter 1981: 170). He was constantly on a 'motivation-safari' (Dichter 1981: 17). What he had in mind was 'the discovery and rediscovery of the inner person' (Dichter 1981: 96) and even the liberation of man: 'What I am really doing is freeing people from false beliefs and hopes. I want to move them to realize their proper desires so they do what they really want to do' (Dichter 1977: 140).

The metaphorical descriptions of his profession are very illuminating as well. For instance, he frequently compared himself to a doctor; once called himself a criminologist; and even talk of being an 'engineer' of society is heard. He called himself a psychological detective, and a modern cultural anthropologist who sketched the outlines of modern man (Dichter 1964: 7). Elsewhere, he again took up the imagery of the chase and the metaphor of a safari of motivations and combined them with the work practices of an archaeologist: 'It is this stalking after the prey that the motivational researcher enjoys as much as the scientist who removes the archaeological hill stratum by stratum and thereupon brings to light treasures that have been hidden for decades' (Dichter 1981: 41). Dichter carried out the business of a midwife through the method of the depth interview (Packard 1958: 53; Schreier and Wood 1948; Woodward et al. 1950). As Thomas summarised: 'The heart and soul of motivational research is the depth interview, a largely (1 to 2 hours) one-to-one, personal interview, conducted directly by the motivational researcher' (1998: 54).

Dichter described this practice in the following way: 'In our depth interviews I often want to know what really makes people happy. I want to find out which of their dreams and desires may rank as true motivation that, subsequently, can be used for advertisement purposes' (Dichter 1977: 387). In the course of interviews that sometimes lasted for several hours, Dichter and his trained investigators asked consumers why they appreciated or rejected certain products and services. In consumers' elaborations, Dichter searched for emerging semantics of motivations which he supposed to be true and relevant. The interviewees delivered the raw material and the task of the motivational researchers was to adjust and refine this material (Miller and Rose 1997). In order to meet the clients' requests, the initially amorphous mass of information given by the interviewees had to be revised. The aim was to 'produce an acceptable profile and to present it; a profile that satisfies the clients and assures an optimal penetration of the market' (Gries 2005: 15).

In this sense, motivational research enabled consumers to talk – literally – for themselves. It helped them to find out what they really wanted, it helped them get in contact with themselves and uncover the inner sanctum of their soul. Therefore, motivational research allowed Dichter to perform the function of a midwife – a role that Socrates had been claiming for himself. Motivational research served as the consumer's mouthpiece, it gave them a voice and freed them from their previous state of voicelessness and passivity. One only has to look at Dichter's 1965 research study into the commercialisation of seat belts, for example (Führer and Stalzer 2005: 26). In the study, Dichter established a matrix of four types of seat-belt users, after having subdivided people into belt users and non-belt users. Each type possessed a profile that did not necessarily emerge directly from the answers given by the interviewees but rather emerged from the interpretation, concretising and reworking undertaken by Dichter and his researchers. Dichter's contribution to the emergence of the modern consumer thus consisted of differentiating an anonymous public into types of consumers and focusing on the interpretation of consumers' voices.

By transforming previously silent and passive consumers, who were formerly seen as equipped only with the two-dimensional identity of being either buyers or non-buyers, into communicative, active and psychologically highly complex individuals, motivational research took part in the cultural construction of social agency which transformed post-war societies. As Miller and Rose put it so succinctly in their study of the uses of motivational research at the Tavistock Institute of Human Relations in London in the 1950s:

> The 'consumer' emerged as a highly problematic entity, by no means a passive tool of the manipulations of the advertisers, but someone to be known in detail, whose passions and desires were to be charted,

for whom consumption was an activity bound into a whole form of life that must be anatomised and acted upon.

(Miller and Rose 1997: 6)

Motivational research therefore proved to be a highly creative practice – provided that it was exercised by well-trained experts (Dichter 1961). A survey on beer tasting undertaken by the Tavistock Institute, for example, stressed the vital role of the interviewer as creative interpreter:

> To cope with these conditions, an experimental situation was designed in which 'the group worked in almost complete isolation for 3-day stretches'. . . . Individual tasting was done as a member of a pair, with one person taking over the 'ego-functions of writing down and organising the verbal reports'. Tasting was done blind for the most part, and the drinks were handled three at a time. A poet provided the group 'access to the sort of memories of experience with which we were dealing', while an expert with experience of the brewers' and the consumers' concerns with flavour helped build up a useful vocabulary for describing tastes.

(Miller and Rose 1997: 23)

This act of building up a useful vocabulary for describing tastes can be understood as a crucial process in authorising the consumer's voice. But this could only be accomplished through the support of the motivational researcher, and his actions therefore have to be conceived of as an act of midwifery. Collins and Montgomery (1969: 110) argued in this respect that

> this stress on creativity and the search for fundamental insights is probably the most important contribution of Dichter as a practitioner of motivational research. Despite the (to the un-American ear) very off-putting strain of salesmanship in his writings it is clear that he is a distinguished virtuoso in the social and psychological diagnostic function, which is the essence of motivational research.

Provided that the Socratic analogy applies to our case, we would have to reconsider how humbly Socrates ranked his share:

> Because I have in common with midwifes the following characteristics: I am unproductive of wisdom, and there is truth in the criticism many people made of me before now, to the effect that I question

> others but don't make any pronouncements about anything myself,
> because I have no wisdom in me. The reason for it is this: God com-
> pels me to be a midwife, but has prevented me from giving birth.
>
> (Plato 1973: 13)

Naturally, after the birth comes the upbringing of children. For Ernest
Dichter, it was not enough to merely be a midwife who was putting
forth a new generation of consumers. In addition, Dichter was interested in the education of these consumers. One of Dichter's strongest
critics, Vance Packard, suspected that the entire marketing community
was driven by this belief in the 'education of eager future consumers'
(Packard 1958: 190). If the main function of education consists in altering a person, it is striking to note how often Dichter talked about
changing and altering the consumer: 'We want to alter people – not
because some do-gooder has said so but because we want to give more
pleasure to people and ameliorate their lives' (Dichter 1991: 20).

According to Dichter, the alteration of people amounted to the
improvement of their living conditions and was linked to the accumu-
lation of wealth, a heightening of contentedness, a rise in the standard
of living, and ultimately even implied a refinement of the human
kind (Gries 2005: 11). This view is confirmed by the Austrian Dichter-
biographer Christoph Steiner: 'Dichter [saw himself] as educationalist
and motivator guiding people towards social maturity and responsibility' (2005: 37), and a contemporary marketing researcher critically
summarised:

> Sure enough the intention to change exhibited by motivational
> research can be expressed in much more prosaic terms: the motiva-
> tional researcher is not trying to find out what people want but he
> is trying to get people to want what he wants them to want..... He
> is out to manipulate, to persuade, to make something happen, to get
> people to want what if left to their own devices they might not want
> at all.
>
> (Jameson 1971: 190)

Dichter himself of course idealised his own role as educator of the
masses and even recommended his motivational strategies as a solution
of international development problems:

> If we motivate an African to get up, cut down some trees, build a
> dwelling that is more solid than his old one, earn money – in order
> to buy some things for the household, clothes, a radio for him and

his family – we don't make him unhappy, no, for the first time we make him really happy.

(Dichter 1991: 20)

On the one hand, this quotation suggests another parallel with Plato, namely with his cave allegory. Plato introduced this famous allegory in the seventh chapter of his book *Politeia* which deals with the difference between illusions and true understanding. Dichter's suggestion to advise Africans to improve their lives has to be interpreted against the background of a specific idea of the civilisation process. While those Africans were seemingly convinced that their existing lives were good enough, for Dichter, their attitude resembled the illusion of the person trapped in the cave, who needed the enlightenment of true understanding by the motivational researcher. On the other hand, the ethnocentrism exhibited in the above quotation is directly related to Dichter's self-image of being a progressive educator of mankind: 'What I do is actually nothing but a deeper kind of education.... What is the purpose of education if it doesn't serve to give people a reality check, to make them think or to help them to find new ways of organizing their lives' (Dichter 1991: 151).

Surprisingly, in his role as an educator Dichter made the mistake to comprehend the consumer as a trivial machine, just as teachers often see their pupils as simple machines (Hellmann 2006; Luhmann 2002: 89). Dichter, for instance, once said that 'the average citizen is far from being adult' (1964: 555) and had thus to be ranked as a child in constant need of education. As the Austro-American architect of cybernetics Heinz von Foerster (1985) has shown, only trivial machines can be precisely governed via specific inputs that equal their outputs, an equation that becomes a symbol for effective controllability. Complex human beings of course elude this realm of controllability due to their self-referential drive. In humans, the effects of a specific input are not predictable and input as well as output often defies control.

Despite his doubtless insight into the complexity of human behaviour, Dichter at times used metaphors that gave away his underlying views: 'Essentially, human motivations are more similar to a machine with a multitude of driving wheels, gears and clutches' (Dichter 1981: 67). Elsewhere he said that 'motivation functions like a clockwork or machine' (Dichter 1977: 90). Referring to the achievements of motivational research, he finally announced: 'The attempt to change human behaviour without knowledge [of human motivations] resembles a driver whose engine strikes and who tries to fix the problem without opening the bonnet of his car' (Dichter 1991: 104). If one follows this description, the motivational researcher can be seen as a kind of mechanic oiling the wheels of the consumer's motivation machine until the requested effect becomes apparent. Accordingly, Dichter compared himself to a technician whose aim consists in empathising with the soul of a technical device (Dichter 1991: 72). In this respect, Dichter proves to be a 'real' educator, including all the faults that this profession needs in order to survive and succeed within the classroom. In order to function, both market and consumer research as well as the entire advertising industry have to hold up the illusion of their objects' controllability. They have to treat people who are clearly non-trivial machines as if they were trivial machines – only 'on a higher level' (Dichter 1991: 108).

10.3   Prolegomena to a sociology of the consumer

Metaphors are interpretative and communicate devices of immense importance in modern society since they allow individuals, groups and organisations to make sense of themselves. In the case of Ernest Dichter, his uses of metaphors helped him manipulate the public interpretation of Motivation Research. Yet at the same time, metaphors develop their own subconscious, they both reveal and conceal meanings. This chapter attempted to show that Dichter used metaphors in order to mobilise specific sources of authority and legitimacy which connected him to the idea(l) of the powerful, independent and proactive consumer. But at times, they also rather gave away what Dichter really thought about the capacity of consumers for informed decision making.

The preceding thoughts concerning Ernest Dichter and his role as midwife and educator merely deal with his life and works in extracts. Many aspects have been neglected here and some were only taken into consideration because of specific presumptions. This was intended since our dealings with Dichter shall be understood as a case study providing a basis for a different and rather explorative question. This question is connected to Meyer's and Jepperson's initial thoughts about the cultural construction of social agency – laying stress on the role of the consumer. The research into the sociology of the consumer is in its early stages. There have been numerous investigations concerning the history and the development of consumer society and referring to this, researchers have gained important and illuminating insights (Brettschneider 2000; Campbell 1987; König 2000; McKendrick et al. 1982; Siegrist et al. 1997). Nevertheless, the agents of the consumer society have attracted sparse attention (Campbell 1987; Haupt 2004; Hellmann 2005; Martineau 1955; Miles 1998; Nairn and Berthon 2003; Taeusch 1928; Trentmann 2005b, 2006).

The case of Ernest Dichter can serve as a kind of prolegomena to the sociology of the consumer insofar as the formation of consumer-related roles, types and structures are the outcome of reciprocal negotiations and depend on multilayered communication processes carried out within specific fields, spheres and systems. Role-specific attributes of 'the consumer' as a socio-cultural construct emerge by talking, writing and reading about consumers. With regard to the discovery of the consumer during the 1940s and 1950s, Dichter supported and contributed to this emergence by means of his market and consumer research. Surely, he was not the only protagonist of this movement but he nevertheless was one of the key figures of modern market and consumer research. He was both admired and heavily criticised, interpreted and misunderstood, hence deeper investigations of the role he played in the drama that became the century of the consumer suggests itself.

Translated from German by Christian Strauch

References

Bartos, R. 1986a. Qualitative research: what it is and where it came from. *Journal of Advertising Research* 26: RC3–RC6.

———— 1986b. Founding fathers of advertising research. *Journal of Advertising Research* 26: 13–14.

———— 1986c. Ernest Dichter: motive interpreter. *Journal of Advertising Research* 26: 15–20.

Breen, T. H. 2004. *The Marketplace of Revolution: How Consumer Politics Shaped American Independence.* New York: Oxford University Press.

Brettschneider, R. 2000. *Konsumgesellschaft. Entwicklungslinien und Perspektiven.* Wien: Picus.

Brose, H. W. 1958. *Die Entdeckung des Verbrauchers. Ein Leben für die Werbung.* Düsseldorf: Econ.

Callon, M. Ed. 1998. *The Laws of the Markets.* London: Blackwell.

Campbell, C. 1987. *The Romantic Ethic and the Spirit of Modern Consumerism.* London: Blackwell.

Collins, L., Montgomery, C. 1969. The origins of motivational research. *British Journal of Marketing* 3 (2): 103–113.

Dichter, E. 1947. Psychology in market research. *Harvard Business Review* 25: 432–443.

———— 1949. A psychological view of advertising effectiveness. *Journal of Marketing* 14 (1): 61–66.

———— 1961. Seven tenets of creative research. *Journal of Marketing* 25 (4): 1–4.

———— 1964. *Handbuch der Kaufmotive: Der Sellingappeal von Waren, Werkstoffen und Dienstleistungen* [*Handbook of Consumer Motivations*]. Düsseldorf: Econ.

———— 1977. *Motivforschung – mein Leben. Die Autobiographie eines kreativ Unzufriedenen*. Frankfurt am Main.: Lorch.

———— 1981. *Das Grosse Buch der Kaufmotive*. Düsseldorf: Econ.

———— 1991. *Gezielte Motivforschung. So machen Sie mehr aus Ihrem Produkt*. München: mvg-Verlag.

Engel, J. F., Blackwell, R. D., Miniard, P. W. 1995. *Consumer Behavior* (8th Edition). Forth Worth: Dryden Press.

Fuchs, P. 1998. *Das Unbewußte in Psychoanalyse und Systemtheorie. Die Herrschaft der Verlautbarung und die Erreichbarkeit des Bewußtseins*. Frankfurt am Main.: Suhrkamp.

Führer, C., Stalzer, L. 2005. Motivforschung als Basis der Marketingberatung. *medien & zeit* 20 (4): 24–35.

Gries, R. 2005. Die Geburt des Werbeexperten aus dem Geist der Psychologie. Ernest Dichter: Der 'Motivforscher' als Experte der Moderne. *medien & zeit* 20 (4): 4–17.

Haese, H. 1960. *Konsum-Revolution*. Stuttgart: Seewald.

Haupt, H.-G. 2004. Der Konsument. In: U. Frevert, H.-G. Haupt (Eds), *Der Mensch des 20. Jahrhunderts*. Frankfurt am Main.: Campus, 301–323.

Hellmann, K.-U. 2003. *Soziologie der Marke*. Frankfurt am Main.: Suhrkamp.

———— 2005. Der ideale Kunde: möglichst gebunden und immer treu. Vorläufiges zu einem aktuellen Thema. In: H. Jacobsen, S. Voswinkel (Eds), *Der Kunde in der Dienstleistungsbeziehung*. Opladen: VS Verlag, 101–126.

———— 2006. Erziehung in der Umwelt des Erziehungssystems. Funktionale Äquivalenzen zwischen Erziehung und Werbung. In: Y. Ehrenspeck, D. Lenzen (Eds), *Beobachtungen des Erziehungssystems: systemtheoretische Perspektiven*. Wiesbaden: VS Verlag, 132–151.

Hilton, M. 2003. *Consumerism in Twentieth-Century Britain: The Search for a Historical Movement*. Cambridge: Cambridge University Press.

Jameson, C. 1971. Theory and nonsense of motivation research. *European Journal of Marketing* 5 (4): 189–197.

Kapferer, C. 1994. *Zur Geschichte der deutschen Marktforschung. Aufzeichnungen eines Mannes, der dabei war*. Hamburg: Marketing Journal.

König, W. 2000. *Geschichte der Konsumgesellschaft*. Stuttgart: Steiner.

Kruse, A. 1959. Was wissen wir vom Konsumentenverhalten? Entwicklungstendenzen der theoretischen Forschung. *Der Markenartikel* 4: 246–253.

Luhmann, N. 2002. *Das Erziehungssystem der Gesellschaft*. Frankfurt am Main.: Suhrkamp.

MacKenzie, D., Millo, Y. 2003. Constructing a market, performing theory: the historical sociology of a financial derivates exchange. *American Journal of Sociology* 109 (1): 107–145.

Martineau, P. 1955. It's time to research the consumer. *Harvard Business Review* 33: 45–54.

McKendrick, N., Brewer, J., Plumb, J. 1982. *The Birth of a Consumer Society: The Commercialization of Eighteenth-Century England*. London: Europa.

Meyer, J. W., Jepperson, R. L. 2000. The 'actors' of modern society: the cultural construction of social agency. *Sociological Theory* 18: 100–120.

Miles, S. 1998. *Consumerism as a Way of Life*. London: Sage.

Miller, P., Rose, N. 1997. Mobilizing the consumer: assembling the subject of consumption. *Theory, Culture & Society* 14 (1): 1–36.

Nairn, A., Berthon, P. 2003. Creating the customer: the influence of advertising on consumer market segments – evidence and ethics. *Journal of Business Ethics* 42 (1): 83–99.

Obrec, L. 1999. Marketing, motives and Dr. Freud. *Detroiter Magazine* (December).

Packard, V. 1958. *Die geheimen Verführer. Der Griff nach dem Unbewußten in Jedermann*. Düsseldorf: Econ.

Plato. 1973. *Theaitetos*. Oxford: Oxford University Press.

Reinhardt, D. 1993. *Von der Reklame zum Marketing. Geschichte der Wirtschaftswerbung in Deutschland*. Berlin: Akademie Verlag.

Schreier, F. T., Wood, A. J. 1948. Motivation analysis in market research. *Journal of Marketing* 13 (2): 172–182.

Siegrist, H., Kaelble, H., Kocka, J. (Eds) 1997. *Europäische Konsumgeschichte. Zur Gesellschafts- und Kulturgeschichte des Konsums (18. bis 20. Jahrhundert)*. Frankfurt am Main.: Campus.

Steiner, C. 2005. Ernest Dichter – ein Projekt. *medien & zeit* 20 (4): 36–39.

Stern, B. 2002. The importance of being Ernest: a tribute to Dichter. *Journal of Advertising Research* 42 (4): 19–22.

—— 2004. The importance of being Ernest: commemorating Dichter's contribution to advertising. *Journal of Advertising Research* 44 (2): 165–169.

Tadajewski, M. 2006. Remembering motivation research: toward an alternative genealogy of interpretive consumer research. *Marketing Theory* 6 (4): 429–466.

Taeusch, C. F. 1928. Classification of customers. *Harvard Business Review* 6 (4): 401–409.

Thomas, J. 1998. Motivational research: explaining why consumers behave the way they do. *Direct Marketing* 60 (12): 54.

Trentmann, F. 2005a. Knowing consumers – histories, identities, practices: an introduction. In: idem. (Ed.) *The Making of the Consumer: Knowledge, Power and Identity in the Modern World*. Oxford: Berg, 1–27.

—— (Ed.) 2005b. *The Making of the Consumer: Knowledge, Power and Identity in the Modern World*. Oxford: Berg.

—— 2006. The modern genealogy of the consumer: meanings, identities and political synapses. In: J. Brewer, F. Trentmann (Eds), *Consuming Cultures: Global Perspectives, Historical Trajectories, Transnational Exchanges*. Oxford: Berg, 19–69.

Trentmann, F., Taylor, V. 2005. From users to consumers: water politics in nineteenth-century London. In: F. Trentmann (Ed.) *The Making of the Consumer: Knowledge, Power and Identity in the Modern World*. Oxford: Berg, 53–79.

Vershofen, W. 1959. *Die Marktentnahme als Kernstück der Wirtschaftsforschung. Neuausgabe des ersten Bandes des Handbuchs der Verbrauchsforschung*. Berlin: Heymann.

von Foerster, H. 1985. Zukunft der Wahrnehmung: Wahrnehmung der Zukunft, in: idem. *Sicht und Einsicht. Versuche zu einer operativen Erkenntnistheorie*. Braunschweig: Vieweg, 3–14.

Woodward, J. L., Hofler, D., Haviland, F., Hyman, H., Peterman, J., Rosten, H. 1950. Depth interviewing. *Journal of Marketing* 14 (5): 721–724.

Zahn, E. 1960. *Soziologie der Prosperität*. Köln: Kiepenheuer & Witsch.

11

A Backward Republic or 'Brave New Austria'? Market and Motivation Research in Dichter's Home Country after the Second World War

Andrea Morawetz

11.1   Ernest Dichter: the 'One-Man Psychological Marshall Plan'

When Ernest Dichter made his first steps into the world of consumer research at the Wirtschaftspsychologische Forschungsstelle (Institute for Economic Psychology) at the University of Vienna, his environment was influenced by personalities like Karl and Charlotte Bühler, Paul F. Lazarsfeld and Moritz Schlick. In the 1920s and early 1930s, Vienna still offered an intellectual climate which reflected the greatness and glory of the Habsburg Empire. Yet, after the Treaty of St Germain in 1919, Austria was a small state that was considered unable to survive both economically and politically. Both factors had a lasting influence on the young Dichter. His repeated stress on countering 'fatalist' thinking was a result of his encounters with Viennese intellectual and social culture (Dichter 1989).

The main focus of this article, however, is Dichter's work and influence in Austria after the Second World War. To gain a better understanding of the specific Austrian economic and social circumstances within which Dichter operated, we will look in more detail at the time span from the end of the 1940s to the first half of the 1970s. At the beginning of the period surveyed here, commercial market research was once again gaining ground and Austria was beginning to experience its own economic miracle. By the mid-1970s, economic growth had flattened out and the country entered a prolonged phase of stagnation. Within this period, Dichter attempted to re-enter Austria with his brand of motivational research and successfully advised Austrian companies on their marketing strategy. His take on consumer research and psychology was not left unopposed by 'home-grown' Austrian market researchers and, like elsewhere in Europe, he had to assert himself against critics.

In later years, Dichter regarded his re-emigration into post-war Europe as a 'one-man psychological Marshall Plan' (Dichter 1988: 294). He thus described his work in his former home country less as an economic move but more as an altruistic, charitable endeavour. He portrayed his experience as an import from across the Atlantic intending to bolster the Austrian economy. His 'homecoming' to Austria and his experiences as a returnee, however, were far from entirely positive, especially as Austrian officials after 1945 did not make much effort to invite intellectuals and scientists who had escaped from the Austro-Fascist regime back into the country. Those who did return – less than two out of ten Austrian emigrants actually did return – were often confronted with open rivalry, thinly veiled anti-Semitism and slick political opportunism (Stadler 1988: 28).

Dichter's relationship to Austria was therefore not without tension. He was, for example, only granted the right to receive the payment of his pension after the intervention of the then Chancellor Bruno Kreisky (1976). Nevertheless, he did not consider himself driven by anger and resentment but by the desire to bring new and unconventional thinking back into his old home country. Owing to his career in the United States, he had developed abilities and skills which were thought of as vital for a new, democratic Austrian state: rather then accepting 'fate', the new citizens of the new state should develop advantages and meet new challenges. To quote Dichter in his own words:

> The Austria that I am dreaming of would do a lot that the larger countries wouldn't dare doing. Austria could be the research laboratory for the others. And it would be accepted as a teacher, as it does not present a great threat and arouses less jealousy.
>
> (Dichter 1989)

In spite of this often trumpeted humanistic attitude, Dichter's research skills of course had their price, also for Austrian companies. In this article, I will therefore also look at whether or not Dichter managed to 'translate' his American research and marketing experiences into useful advice for his Austrian clients and to what extent he influenced the making of modern Austrian management practice.

11.2   From Beckert to Packard

During the military occupation of Austria in the 1940s, both market and opinion research were on the upswing. One example for this development is the foundation of Austria's first post-war market and opinion research institute by Siegfried Beckert in 1949. Beckert's institute closely cooperated with, and received initial support from, the international Gallup organisation (Kapferer 1994: 104). At the same time, the German tradition of consumer research in Austria was brought to life again with the Institute for Industrial Research (Institutes für Industrieforschung – IfI), being set up in 1948. This tradition reached back to the late 1930s, when the advertising expert and Dichter-critic Hanns F. J. Kropff led the Association for Consumer, Market and Sales Research, an Austrian branch of the Nuremberg-based Society for Consumption Research (GfK). This association was replaced by the Vienna Institute for Consumer and Sales Research in 1941, which was led by Rolf Grünwald (Grünwald 1963: 8). From 1948 onwards, Grünwald and Kropff found themselves in leading positions again – this time at the Institute for Industrial Research, the former as chief of the research department, the latter as its president (Liebherr 1978: 7–8).

Even through the predecessor of the IfI was founded during the era of National Socialism and in cooperation with the Nuremberg GfK, Grünwald was convinced that this was the beginning of an 'Austrian School' of market research (Grünwald 1955: 117). Where the continuation of a specifically Austrian tradition could have been assumed, however, the war left no ties: Lazarsfeld's Institute for Economic Psychology had been closed down as early as 1938 and was not reopened after the end of the Second World War (Neurath 1979: 16). Surprisingly, historians of Austrian market and consumer research have so far failed to concern themselves with the work and legacy of this research centre (Pompl 1974). The cultural historian Andrea Ellmeier identified two reasons for this. First of all, the emigration of numerous employees of Lazarsfeld's research centre led to its virtual disappearance from collective memory and, secondly, the socialist political activism of many of its employees led to a deliberate sidelining of the centre (Ellmeier 2005: 77).

The foundation of the first market research institutes in post-war Austria is inextricably linked to improvement of the economic situation after 1948 when the rationing of industrial goods and foodstuffs was slowly being phased out. In 1949, Austria's GDP once again reached its pre-war level, and in 1950 the same applied to the consumption standard. Austrian consumers' growing demand was met in consecutive 'waves' of consumption of food, clothing and later on of consumer goods like domestic appliances (Seidel 2005: 56). Market research institutes both spurned and benefited from the improvement of private consumption. The Institute for Market Research, for example, founded by Walter Fessel in 1950 and later merged with the Austrian GfK, first attracted clients from the textile industry, the food sector and later manufacturers of semi-luxury household goods (Wandl 1994: 158). The early 1950s marked the starting point of a mass consumer society in Austria. After the final discontinuation of rationing cards in 1953, the population could finally choose from a slowly increasing range of products. Furthermore, the range of goods available no longer only addressed the upper classes but increasingly aimed at middle- and lower-income groups, too. Moreover, the gradual implementation of new distribution systems, like self-service supermarkets, brought new opportunities of choice for consumers and challenges for producers of consumer brands (Eder 2005).

The institutes of Siegfried Beckert and Walter Fessel were the two largest and most important market research institutions at that time and began increasingly to follow 'American' trends in data gathering and interpretation methods (Meyer 1957: 222–223). Nevertheless, Rolf Grünwald vehemently insisted on a special position of his Institute for Industrial Research and also on the primacy of the qualitative 'German' – as opposed to the quantitative 'American' – market research method. In spite of his admiration for the pragmatic and quantitative research orientation developed in the United States, Grünwald argued that this modus operandi would be too mechanistic for European countries, which did not require the large-scale mass surveys that had been developed in the United States from the 1920s. For only seven million 'not too questionnaire-receptive inhabitants' in Austria, he did not regard American methods as adequate (Grünwald 1955: 120). As we will see, the return of motivational research to Austria in the 1950s rendered such argumentation less pervasive. During this decade, a battle between the 'German' and the 'American' market research philosophy was being fought, and although Motivation Research arguably followed the more qualitative, insightful 'Germanic' tradition, it now seemed to contribute to the 'Americanisation' of Austrian market research (Strotzka 1958: 121).

11.3 Facts and fiction: Cross-examining Motivation Research

The new fascination with 'hidden' desires and motives of consumers was often opposed by critical voices that doubted the academic soundness and adequacy of Motivation Research. In particular, the annual Konferenz für Werbewissenschaft ('Conference for Advertising Research') proved to be a platform for the exchange of views between national and international scientists and experts (Skowronnek 1973). In working groups on the subjects of advertising, market and Motivation Research, people like Otto Angehrn, Georg Bergler, Ernest Dichter and Elisabeth Noelle-Neumann contributed scientific papers and thus, different opinions and positions were given voice (*Die Industrie* 1961). The central figure of this conference was university professor Karl Skowronnek, who had been concerned with the uses of scientific methods in advertising and market research from the end of the 1940s. On the one hand, Skowronnek appreciated contacts to representatives of the Nuremberg School of market research (Gesellschaft für Konsumforschung – GfK), which is documented in his article 'Tomorrow's Buyer' for Georg Bergler's *Festschrift* (Skowronnek 1960). On the other hand, he approved of the fact that Motivation Research had 'led to a recent impulse for the research of the depth-psychological processes in advertising' (Skowronnek 1964: 169). Skowronnek in some way both supported the Nuremberg School and Dichter's Motivation Research, thus preserving a multifaceted and interdisciplinary advertising theory of the type Victor Mataja had proposed at the beginning of the twentieth century (Mataja 1910; Müller 1986: 63).

Furthermore, Motivation Research and the issue of consumer desires were also discussed in the Austrian media. The weekly magazine of the Association of Austrian Industrialists, *Die Industrie* (*The Industry*), deserves to be mentioned in this respect. This magazine concerned itself with Motivation Research more intensively between 1958 and 1961. Especially, articles and reviews by the journalist Roland Nitsche are extremely revealing. Although Nitsche welcomed Motivation Research in general, for example, when reviewing the publications of Hanns F. J. Kropff and Harry Henry (Nitsche 1960a, 1960b), he found less flattering words for Ernest Dichter's seminal work *The Strategy of Desire*: 'So many sentences, so few definite statements.' Dichter's 'culture-philosophical justification' of seduction, said Nitsche, was void of substance. Dichter is portrayed as a prosaic strategist who silenced his 'moral conscience' with the fact that he was not the first seducer, and his 'practical conscience' with the argument that a scientifically led increase of consumption was an economic necessity (Nitsche 1961).

Nitsche's attack on Dichter's ethical position is significant as it raises the question of the relationship between Motivation Research, manipulation and consumer sovereignty. This was a very prominent question especially in 1961, the year the Austrian consumer movement had formed the Association for Consumer Information (VKI). Although there had been predecessors of this organisation in the 1950s, now both employers and employees reacted to the increase of private consumption, greater product range and the increased need for information of consumers (Ellmeier 2005: 148–159). The market researcher Adolf Bauer, too, called for more consumer protection and the right of consumers to be informed in his 1961 publication entitled *Der freie und unberechenbare Mensch: Kritik der Markt-, Meinungs- und Motivforschung. (The Free and Unpredictable Human Being. A Criticism of Market-, Opinion- and Motivation Research)* (Bauer 1961).

In this work, Bauer painted the following picture of the market research sector: fierce competition between market research institutes for a small number of clients; financial and methodological dependence on English and/or American market research companies; rejection by 'old school' market and consumer researchers of the 'new' motivation researchers. However, Bauer showed a great deal of sympathy for Motivation Research as he thought of traditional market research as being far too concerned with representativeness and standardisation. He claimed that Motivation Research had developed because clients increasingly doubted the validity and usefulness of market research results: 'If you want to find out about a human being as a whole, you cannot disregard the human and instead use "holy" objective methods' (Bauer 1961: 262). In spite of that, he also saw the dangers in Motivation Research because of the interpretative leeway it gave to the researcher. In practice, motivation researchers were in danger of not being objective enough in their interpretation of human motives. Although a motivation researcher 'unmasks lies', she/he was only a human being who was at risk to unmask her/himself (Bauer 1961: 252). The presumption 'that you turn to a neutral [market research] Institute that concerns itself with the project completely unbiased and which you therefore can trust' was an illusion according to Bauer. Bauer regarded Motivation Research as only partly significant and strongly dependent on the respective interests of client and institute (Bauer 1961: 254).

11.4 The market for Motivation Research

The surveys, reports and research papers filed at the Ernest Dichter Archive in Vienna show that Dichter's first steps back into the Austrian market were taken ten years after he had entered other European markets, like Germany, France and Great Britain. Austria represented a significantly smaller market and only few large, financially strong companies were able to afford Motivation Research services. In 1961, when Dichter suggested a market and Motivation Research project to the Austrian Tobacco Association, several market research institutes already existed that offered Motivation Research and psychological tests in addition to their regular activities. The two then largest market research institutes were Siegfried Beckert's Austrian Opinion and Market Research Institute (the Austrian branch of the international Gallup organisation) and Werner Fessel's Institute for Market Research. Both companies had been using psychological methods since at least 1957 (Meyer 1957: 222–f). The fear of falling behind international trends due to the smallness of the Austrian market for market research may have been crucial for the extension of the methodical spectrum of both institutes. In this, the Austrian branch of Gallup's organisation even contradicted its founding father's dictum as George H. Gallup himself had rejected Motivation Research during a visit to Vienna in 1958 (*Die Industrie* 1958).

Apart from these two dominating institutes, there was the smaller AVB-Institute for Market and Opinion Research, founded in the north-Austrian industrial town of Linz in 1955. This institute specialised in target marketing and had itself tried to cover a market niche by finding a compromise between 'nose-counting' market research and depth-psychological Motivation Research. This institute's research practice consisted of finding out motives through informal group discussions and through one-on-one interviews. After that, if necessary, the representativeness of the results should be analysed by cross-section research analysis. The credo of the institute was to analyse the market from the point – of view of the consumer and not from the producer's perspective. This change of perspective slowly brought about the integration of marketing into Austrian companies' management practice (Gross 1958). Finally, the foundation of the Info-Institute in 1961 can be interpreted as a result of this increasing awareness of marketing among Austrian businesses. The Info-Institute had derived from the market research department of the Austrian subsidiary of Unilever and had specialised in target, motivation and advertising research (*Trend* 1971b). Thus, at the beginning of the 1960s, at least four market research companies existed that competed fiercely for clients and they intended to compete with what they saw as the 'newcomer' Dichter.

This situation became even worse during the mid-1960s, when the growth of demand for market research slowed down considerably (Fink 1964; Rüdiger 1989: 12). A 'downright rocketing advancement' of

Motivation Research, however, took place at the end of this decade (Nitsche 1967). This went hand in hand with an improvement in economic growth, which started to pick up in 1968 and lasted until the mid-1970s (Sieder et al. 1996: 13). Rolf Grünwald argued that the increasing need for Austrian companies to find out more about the 'motivation of demand' was the reason for the advancement of Motivation Research (Grünwald 1967: 12). Thus, the upswing of Motivation Research can also be regarded as a sign of a generational change within Austrian companies.

Apart from the now well-established large market research institutes of Fessel, Institute for Empirical Social Studies (ifes), Info and Nielsen, about twenty small institutes had been founded by the end of the 1960s. Surprisingly, most of them specialised in Motivation Research. The decision had in part operational and economic reasons, as motivational research surveys could be carried out with fewer personnel (*Trend* 1971b). The boom in these business start-ups, however, also had a downside as it brought about a myriad of far too small and thus economically unviable enterprises. This was a problem as the number of financially strong clients was still relatively small, with only around 40 to 50 manufacturers of branded products and large banks conducting regular market surveys (*Trend* 1972b). Thus, in spite of increasing awareness of the importance of market and Motivation Research only a few companies actually implemented a research-oriented marketing policy.

The business magazine *Trend* carried out a survey in 1972 which showed that nearly half of the responding companies (45 per cent) relied on their own instinct when it came to market observation. Furthermore, 38 per cent of the companies – more than half of those were small companies – had never carried out statistical surveys of their markets. The cost of market research posed a problem even for national companies. The price for motivation surveys, at the beginning of the 1970s – about 400 to 1,200 Austrian schillings (*c*. $20–50) per interview – was so high that even the majority of the food and semi-luxury goods producers refrained from using these surveys (*Trend* 1972a). An opinion poll carried out by the Info-Institute in 1973 showed that half of 236 surveyed companies had never ordered a Motivation Research to find out more about the needs of their customers. The rather sad conclusion of the institute's survey read: 'Austrian marketing managers spare themselves the dilemma between human satisfaction of needs and technically cold exploitation of consumers' needs because they often only explore their customers – the market – superficially' (*Trend* 1973b). The development of the market for Motivation Research in Austria was thus hampered by one main factor: the market was exceptionally small, with only a few financially strong companies coveted by an increasing number of market research businesses.

11.5 'Habemus Dichter' – Dichter's Austrian surveys

The environment in which Dichter became active at the beginning of the 1960s was thus characterised by a situation in which most Austrian companies still needed to be 'converted' to become users of market and Motivation Research (*Bestseller* 1983; Fink 1964). A poll by the Info-Institute in 1973 showed huge differences in the attitude towards market research in internationally interlinked and purely Austrian companies: 33 per cent of companies in international ownership used market research regularly, while only 8 per cent of Austrian companies did so (*Trend* 1973b). Nevertheless, Dichter managed to set up relations with a number of established Austrian companies. After the first contact at the beginning of the 1960s, Austria's then largest daily newspaper *Kurier* decided to engage Dichter in 1962 for advice on advertising policy. Other clients Dichter acquired in those years were the Austrian Tobacco Association, owned by the Austrian state, and Hager-Advertising, one of the largest national advertising agencies, part of the Austrian food giant Mautner Markhof. In the second half of the 1960s, further contacts to the City of Vienna were established, which was looking for new ways to improve its services for citizens. In addition, the Tivoli Chocolate & Confectionery factory, one of the largest confectionery manufacturers, became his client. Thus, Dichter worked on altogether five plans for motivation and market surveys in the 1960s. In the case of the City of Vienna and the Austrian Tobacco Association, however, the surveys never came to fruition. In both, the cost factor played a major role. Given that Dichter intended to carry out 150 depth-psychology interviews at a cost of 300,000 Austrian schillings (*c.*12,000 US dollars at that time) the City of Vienna abandoned the plan.

Dichter's remuneration and the quality of his services were especially criticised in the course of his survey for the confectionery manufacturer Tivoli in 1967 (Dichter 1967). This criticism went hand in hand with a growing dissatisfaction with the business policy of the company's new general director, Georg Mautner Markhof. Among other consultants, Georg Mautner Markhof had also engaged Dichter in order to relaunch the financially troubled company and re-engage with consumers' changing tastes. In the survey, Dichter advised the company to pay much more attention than before to market segmentation and to

Figure 11.1   Ernest Dichter Explains his Philosophy of Packaging, 1971.

improving the overall image of the Tivoli brand. In addition, he advised the company to re-create its advertising and packaging in a way that the chocolate products could be interpreted by consumers as a special treat, a reward and as a soothing form of energy in stressful circumstances (Dichter 1967; see also Figure 11.1).

Ironically, it was Dichter's involvement that led to Mautner Markhof's retirement from the company's board. As a result, Tivoli again lacked a succinct corporate strategy and a few years later the manufacturer's fate was sealed. As production ceased at the beginning of the 1970s, Dichter's concept for the reinvention of the company had become obsolete. Although Dichter cannot be held responsible for the decline of the Tivoli brand, the incident cast doubt on him and the entire sector of Motivation Research. The Tivoli survey was in fact the last piece of research that was coordinated by Dichter himself for an Austrian company. When asked about the point of engaging Dichter, Mautner Markhof tried to justify his choice but admitted that it would have been better to back up his results with those of other market research institutes. In other words: Dichter's findings had not been representative (*Trend* 1971a).

Nevertheless, his Tivoli survey was by far more differentiated and representative than the projects carried out at the beginning of the 1960s for the *Kurier* newspaper and the Hager advertising agency. All these surveys followed the established concept of in-depth interviews and projective tests. However, concerning the number of surveyed consumers, Dichter's sample showed large differences. While for the Tivoli survey 207 interviews in different stages and with different target groups had been carried out, the survey for the Hager advertising agency only featured 52 interviews and the *Kurier* survey only 29. The small number of interviews for the *Kurier* can be justified by the fact that after a status report, the survey was not continued (Dichter 1962a). Still, the number of interviewees for the Hager agency, managed by Manfred Mautner Markhof, was small – even by Dichter's standards. This becomes even more evident if one considers the subject of the research: 'A Motivational Research Study of the Marketing Possibilities for an Austrian Beer in the United States of America' (Dichter 1962b).

At the centre of this survey stood the beer brand 'Schwechater' produced by the Mautner Markhof food company. In this research, in-depth interviews were complemented by taste, label and bottle tests which were carried out in and around New York. Unlike Austrian beer, the methods that Dichter applied in this case leave behind a stale aftertaste as part of the interviews were completed with residents of Croton-on-Hudson, a white, middle-class village that was hardly representative of race, gender and income distribution of the American home market. Thus, Dichter carried out this survey in a rather hasty manner with respondents who were already experienced with in-depth interviews.

Nevertheless, the magic 'Dichter Factor' must have worked because a few years later he was again hired by a member of the Mautner Markhof family – now for the survey on Tivoli confectionery. During the survey for 'Schwechater' beer, Dichter seemed to have had the right intuition at the right time without abiding by the usual laws of statistical representativeness. Georg Mautner Markhof was also aware of Dichter's exceptional intuition and stated retrospectively: 'With two thirds of his personality, Dichter is all talk, but with one third he is a genius' (*Trend* 1971a). This shows that to a certain degree it was insignificant for entrepreneurs like Mautner Markhof as to whether they could expect representativeness of 'scientific' methodology from Dichter. What they wanted was the intuitive genius. Once a major new idea promised a marketing breakthrough a fully representative survey could also be carried out by another, presumably cheaper, research company. It was probably also helpful that Dichter appeared as an American with Austrian background exactly at a time when the 'Americanisation' of Austrian consumers' buying behaviour became an important social point of discussion (Eder 2005: 30).

Especially, the entrepreneurial family Mautner Markhof proved to be receptive to new methods of corporate management. This attitude was part of a tradition. Already Manfred Mautner Markhof senior supported the work of Lazarsfeld's Research Centre for Economic Psychology (Neurath 1988: 30). Thus, Ernest Dichter was surrounded by business partners who were not only of the same disposition but also enormously influential within Austrian economic circles:

> The big families of beer producers, the Mautner Markhofs [...], enjoy a reputation of wealth and power like only few in the Alpine Republic's economic life. The head of the Mautner Markhof family, engineer Manfred senior, has become a symbolic figure, who is on the one hand presented as a shining example of an art-supporting entrepreneur (receiver of the Badge of Honour of the City of Vienna) and on the other hand is exposed to the nation's rage as the truly capitalistic enemy.
>
> (*Trend* 1970)

Even if Dichter and Mautner Markhof senior may have never met each other, both of them were in their own way symbolic figures of their respective time, and their activities can by all means be described as ambivalent.

11.6   Following the footsteps of the 'Pope of Advertising'

In spite of all his critics, Dichter's methods were also adopted in Austria. After he had supervised the Hager advertising agency in 1962, the interest in Motivation Research increased enormously. Georg Herberstein, then chief executive of Austria's second-largest advertising agency, dreamed of provocative advertising strategies that should 'tear down taboos' and should influence 'the lowest motivation level in the human being'. The prominent Viennese psychoanalyst Wilfried Daim supported him in this undertaking: in 1964, the two men managed to increase the number of life insurance policies sold within a year by 60 per cent by implementing a psychologically planned advertising campaign. Herberstein set up his own agency in 1969 with the help of some of the clients of the Hager agency, while Daim remained his adviser and resided in a villa on the outskirts of Vienna where he received his pilgrimaging clients and where he developed his depth-psychological advertising strategies (*Trend* 1973a).

Here, first parallels to Dichter's 'liturgy' become apparent. Concerning their methodological approach, Georg Herberstein and especially Wilfried Daim openly referred to Dichter. Closely linked to this alleged claim for competence was also the claim for remuneration that brought in handy profits. For his advisory services, Daim cashed in between 20,000 and 100,000 Austrian schillings. Compared to Dichter's surveys that price seems humble. The costs for a project supervised by Dichter came to an average of about 300,000 Austrian schillings. Thus, compared to Dichter, Daim seemed to have played the role of the 'Discount Pope of Advertising', even though for many Austrian entrepreneurs he did not appear affordable (*Trend* 1973a).

However, neither Dichter, Daim nor Herberstein were infallible. The latter, for instance, failed to convince a west-Austrian textile company that did not approve of the progressive ideas of the two Viennese. Thus, Daim's 'motivations battery' featuring positive and negative motivation associations found just as little approval as the bedclothes he designed featuring depth-psychological symbols, called 'Laww' (*Trend* 1973a). Daim's ideas bear striking resemblance to a similar attempt made by the German advertising specialist Alfons Brugger during the interwar period. Following the results of psychological research, Brugger had created the fictional brand name 'Ker Olwano', which featured both 'male' and 'female' elements. Brugger's aim was to create a trademark that was liked by both men and women. However, instead of being accepted euphorically by advertising experts, a heated quarrel about the implementation of depth-psychological findings for commercial reasons was the result. In this dispute, Hanns F. J. Kropff was the main critic, claiming that with conservative entrepreneurs, excessive use of eroticism would lead to a bad reputation of advertising in general (Morawetz 2004: 96). Although the social environment had changed by the 1960s, the 'Laww' concept of Herberstein and Daim seemed just as untrustworthy to the textile company as 'Ker Olwano' did to many advertising experts during the interwar period.

A further trend in the late 1960s was that market research women increasingly appeared in top positions in a sector that had so far been dominated by men. For instance, Eva Braunegger founded her Institute for Market and Opinion Research in 1968 and stressed the significance of motivation and communication research (*Bestseller* 1983). Today, she is best known for her survey for the Austrian mineral water brand 'Römerquelle', which led the company to change the product's brand image by disassociating it from the idea of a beverage for those recovering from illness (Lehmann 1994: 33). In this respect, our co-author Helene Karmasin must be mentioned as well. When Ernest Dichter was on the lookout for a representative in Austria, Karmasin took over the management of the Austrian Institute of Motivational Research, which had also been founded in 1968 (*Bestseller* 1983; Karmasin 2004). From the 1970s onwards, when Dichter's gospel of motivation-oriented market surveys seemed to be in decline, he restricted his activities in Austria to lectures and publications.

11.7   The definition of success

Whether a business strategy is successful or not depends on the definition of its objectives. But what about Ernest Dichter's intention to bring 'new thinking' into his 'old home country'? In fact, Motivation Research itself was nothing entirely new in Austria at the beginning of the 1960s when Dichter first began to work for Austrian companies. Yet, at least indirectly, Dichter was responsible for the increasing interest in Motivation Research at the end of the 1950s. Vance Packard's *Hidden Persuaders*, for example, led to heated discussions among Austrian social scientists and communication experts about Motivation Research.

Another small success for Dichter was the fact that he managed to raise the awareness for Motivation Research by working for well-known companies like the *Kurier* newspaper, the Austrian Tobacco Association and the Mautner Markhof family. However, this must be put into perspective: only three surveys exceeded the planning stage (in 1962 and 1967). As shown before, these surveys only became possible due to the commitment of the Mautner Markhof family. Although not entirely successful, these surveys were part of a movement to integrate marketing-orientated thinking into Austrian management practice. Dichter's potential field of work was extremely limited, but his lectures and presentations, such as at the Conference for Advertising Research, managed to reach a far larger audience. If one were to measure Dichter's success in infusing Austrian entrepreneurship with marketing-orientated ideas, the result would be an uneven score. While a majority of companies were unimpressed with 'new' methods of corporate management, some larger Austrian companies showed a keen interest in adopting new, 'American' marketing and research methods. Although not wholly successful, Ernest Dichter definitely contributed to the acceleration of this development.

References

Bauer, A. 1961. *Der freie und unberechenbare Mensch: Kritik der Markt-, Meinungs- und Motivforschung*. Nuremberg: Glock und Lutz.

Bestseller 1983. Motivjagd mit Gefühl: Qualitative Marktforschung in Österreich (March 1983).

Dichter, E. 1962a. *Fortschrittsbericht zu einer Motivstudie über die Verkaufs- und Werbeprobleme des 'Kurier'*. Ernest Dichter Archive, University of Vienna, Report No. 2216.

——— 1962b. *A Motivational Research Study of the Marketing Possibilities for an Austrian Beer in the United States of America*. Ernest Dichter Archive, University of Vienna, Report No. 2250.

——— 1967. *Bericht zu einer Motiv- und Marketingstudie für Tivoli. Produktprogramm, Werbe- und Imagestrategie von Tivoli*. Ernest Dichter Archive, University of Vienna, Report No. 2804.

——— 1988. Zeitzeuge (Contemporary witness). In: F. Stadler (Ed.), *Vertriebene Vernunft II: Emigration und Exil österreichischer Wissenschaft*. Vol. 2. Vienna: Jugend und Volk, 293–296.

——— 1989. Das Österreich, von dem ich träume. *Trend* (April 1989).

Die Industrie. 1958. Dr. Gallup gegen die Motivforscher (21 June).

——— 1961. Weltbekannte Vortragende auf der Werbewirtschaftlichen Tagung. (20 October).

Eder, F. 2005. Vom Mangel zum Wohlstand: Konsumieren in Wien 1945–1980. In: S. Breuss (Ed.), *Die Sinalco-Epoche: Essen, Trinken, Konsumieren nach 1945*. Vienna: Czernin, 24–33.

Ellmeier, A. 2005. Konsum, Politik und Geschlecht: Österreich in den 1950er und 1960er Jahren. PhD thesis, University of Vienna.

Fink, M. 1964. Wie man den Absatz verbessern kann. *Die Industrie* (13 March).

Gross, W. 1958. Die Marktforschung im neuen Wirtschaftsdenken. *Die Industrie* (21 November).

Grünwald, R. 1955. Die Stellung der Markt- und Verbrauchsforschung in Österreich. *Jahrbuch der Absatz- und Verkaufsforschung* 1: 117–122.

——— 1963. *Was ich Vershofen verdanke: Ein Beitrag für eine Erinnerungsschrift an den Ehrenpräsidenten des Instituts für Industrieforschung.* Vienna: Institute for Industrial Research.

——— 1967. *Bedarfsforschung in regionaler Sicht: Ergebnisse und Erfahrungen aus der österreichischen Institutspraxis.* Vienna: Institute for Industrial Research.

Kapferer, C. 1994. *Zur Geschichte der deutschen Marktforschung: Aufzeichnungen eines Mannes, der dabei war.* Hamburg: Marketing Journal.

Karmasin, H. 2004. Produkte als Botschaften. Frankfurt am Main.: Ueberreuter.

Kreisky, B. 1976. Letter to Anton Vitzthum, Pension Insurance Institution of Employees and Workers (PVA). 13 September. Bruno Kreisky-Archive, Vienna.

Lehmann, W. 1994. *Die Marke – 'Römerquelle'.* Vienna: Brandstätter.

Liebherr, F. 1978. Drei Jahrzehnte Marktforschung in Österreich: Zum 30jährigen Bestand des Institutes für Industrieforschung. In: IfI (Ed.), *Festschrift zum 30jährigen Bestehen des Institutes für Industrieforschung.* Vienna: Institute for Industrial Research, 5–15.

Mataja, V. 1910. *Die Reklame: Eine Untersuchung über Ankündigungswesen und Werbetätigkeit im Geschäftsleben.* Leipzig: Duncker & Humblot.

Meyer, P. W. 1957. *Marktforschung: Ihre Möglichkeiten und Grenzen.* Duesseldorf: Econ-Verlag.

Morawetz, A. 2004. 'Kontakt' in der 'Österreichischen Reklame' – Reklamefachzeitschriften der 20er und 30er: Zwischen Wissensvermittlung und Selbstvergewisserung. MA thesis, University of Vienna.

Müller, R. 1986. Zum wissenschaftlichen Lebenswerk von Karl Skowronnek. In: *Werbeforschung und Praxis* 31 (2): 62–63.

Neurath, P. 1979. *Paul F. Lazarsfeld (1901–1976) und die Entwicklung der empirischen Sozialforschung.* Vienna: Institute for Sociology.

——— 1988. Paul Lazarsfeld und die Anfänge der modernen psychologischen Markt- und Konsumentenforschung in Wien. *Werbeforschung & Praxis* 33 (2): 29–31.

Nitsche, R. 1960a. Motivforschung: Dichtung und Wahrheit. *Die Industrie* (27 May).

——— 1960b. Motivforschung im Kreuzverhör. *Die Industrie* (7 October).

——— 1961. Motivforschung auf der Suche nach Selbstrechtfertigung. *Die Industrie* (21 April).

——— 1967. Der Verbraucher in der Industriewirtschaft (VII): Um die Konsummotive. *Die Industrie* (21 April).

Pompl, J. 1974. Der gegenwärtige Stand der Marktforschung in Österreich. In: F. Swoboda (Ed.), *Werbepolitik: Beiträge zur Werbelehre aus Theorie und Praxis.* Vienna: Böhlau, 104–114.

Rüdiger, W. 1989. Der Markt der Marktforschung in Österreich. In: Verband der Marktforscher Österreichs (Ed.), *Das Handbuch der Marktforschung.* Vienna: Signum, 11–14.

Seidel, H. 2005. *Österreichs Wirtschaft und Wirtschaftspolitik nach dem Zweiten Weltkrieg.* Vienna: Manz.

Sieder, R., Steinert, H., Tálos, E. 1996. Wirtschaft, Gesellschaft und Politik in der Zweiten Republik. In: idem. (Eds.), *Österreich 1945–1995: Gesellschaft – Politik – Kultur.* Vienna: Verlag für Gesellschaftskritik, 9–32.

Skowronnek, K. 1960. Der Käufer von morgen. In: W. Vershofen, P. W. Meyer (Eds), *Der Mensch im Markt: Eine Festschrift zum 60. Geburtstage von Georg Bergler*. Berlin: Duncker & Humblot, 223–236.

——— 1964. *Wesen und Wert der Werbung*. Vienna: Gewerbeverlag.

——— 1973. Zwanzig Jahre 'Werbewissenschaftliche Tagung'. *WWG-Informationen* 18 (56): 1–3.

Stadler, F. 1988. 'Vertriebene Vernunft': Rückblick und Zusammenschau. In: idem. (Ed.), *Vertriebene Vernunft II: Emigration und Exil österreichischer Wissenschaft*. Vol. 2. Vienna: Jugend und Volk, 27–40.

Strotzka, H. 1958. Meinungsuntersuchung und Meinungsbildung größerer Gruppen. In: Österreichische Werbewissenschaftliche Gesellschaft (Ed.), *Bericht der Fünften Werbewissenschaftlichen Tagung*. Vienna: Österreichische Werbewissenschaftliche Gesellschaft, 118–122.

Trend. 1970. Der Bier-Krieg (April).

——— 1971a. Schokoladen-Tivoli: Zerronnene Hoffnung (June).

——— 1971b. Die Spürhunde (June).

——— 1972a. Marketing: Die kreative Maschinerie (September).

——— 1972b. Im Gleichschritt (November).

——— 1973a. Die Traumdeuter (July).

——— 1973b. Marketing-Untersuchung (November).

Wandl, C. 1994. Die Einführung des Marketing in den Unternehmungen der österreichischen Wirtschaft. PhD thesis, University of Linz.

12
The Reception of Ernest Dichter and the Resistance to Motivation Research in Francophone Europe

Véronique Pouillard

12.1 Introduction

As noted in a recent paper bearing upon the history of Motivation Research in Europe, the impact of Dichter's theories and practice in French-speaking Europe remains understudied (Schwarzkopf 2005: 40–9). The most substantial research on the topic so far has been carried out by Marc Meuleau in his doctoral dissertation on the history of marketing in France, and I heavily rely upon his work, especially in the first part of this chapter (Meuleau 1992). The main primary sources used in this chapter are contemporary accounts, notably the writings of the French advertising man Marcel Bleustein-Blanchet, founder of the agency Publicis in 1926, today the world's fourth largest communications group, and of the writer Georges Pérec, whose novel *Les choses* – possibly the second most important among his works after *La vie mode d'emploi* – tells the story of two French motivation researchers in the 1960s. In addition, I selectively review the content of 87 research reports for French firms and French-speaking accounts filed at the Ernest Dichter Archive in Vienna. My point here is not to deliver a complete study of the topic, but rather to draw a first sketch and identify the main features of a topic that deserves further enquiry.

The introduction of Motivation Research in French-speaking Europe took place in the post-war years when market research techniques that were introduced between the wars, among others by American advertising agencies like J. Walter Thompson (Hultquist 2003: 471–501; Pouillard 2005b: 169–204), became reassessed by French and Belgian marketing practitioners. Prior to the introduction of market research by JWT, which conducted a first market survey on car owners in Belgium in 1927, France and Belgium were renowned for the empirical attitudes of its advertising agencies and media sellers (Hultquist 2003: 482–484). However, JWT, the largest American agency in Europe by then, showed far better results in Belgium than in France. This is the result of, at least in part, cultural differences as the market covered by the Belgian office in Antwerp was less resistant to American techniques, communication styles and products in comparison to the French market (Pouillard 2005a). Polls and panel techniques became considerably more efficient during the period between 1930 and 1960 (Meuleau 1992: 900–901).

Motivation Research is a form of qualitative market research and the first empirical attempts in this direction, aiming at understanding the unconscious motivations for buying, appeared in France before 1945 in, among others, the attempts of Robert Lengele to track the market for consumer products. However, as Meuleau noted, these remained highly quantitative and were driven to the conscious rather than to the unconscious motivations of buyers (Meuleau 1992: 905).

Motivation Research was officially launched in France by Paul Gremont, director of the advertising sales division at Renault and an alumnus of HEC, France's foremost management school, in a talk at a meeting of CEGOS – France's largest business and management training provider – in 1957 (Meuleau 1992: 940–941, 951). Gremont had spent some time in the United States and was eager to share his discovery of Motivation Research. Meuleau underlines the importance for young HEC graduates of travelling to the United States to discover the latest marketing techniques as an aid in promoting the development of market research back in France. Motivation Research became a part of the skills of young HEC graduates in the late 1950s, when the school began to teach marketing (Meuleau 1992: 943–944). Considered a technique complementary to market research, Motivation Research was occasionally used. The market research company DYNAMAR (Compagnie Internationale de Dynamique des Marchés), created in 1959 in France by British Petroleum, played an important role in developing the psychological aspects of consumer research. The beginnings of Motivation Research were slow and Meuleau therefore drew the conclusion that Motivation Research failed to become essential in the 1950s before it became the major innovation in commercial studies in France (Meuleau 1992: 903, 951–952).

The French Institute for Motivation Research (Institut Français pour l'Etude de Motivation) was created in 1958 under the aegis of CEGOS in the same year as the market research institute ETMAR, in direct association with the Dichter institute in Croton-on-Hudson (Martin 1992:

293–294), underlining the direct importation of American techniques (Meuleau 1992: 905, 931). This happened a year before the establishment of similar institutes in London and in Rome (Schwarzkopf 2005: 44–45). At the same time, Motivation Research theory arrived in French-speaking countries through Harry Henry's textbook on Motivation Research, published in 1959 and translated into various European languages (Henry 1959). Paris was not unknown to Ernest Dichter, who had studied at the Sorbonne before the Second World War, where he obtained a *Licence dès Lettres* (Dichter 1961b).

12.2 American influences – and the response

Before the Second World War, international advertising agencies used simply to translate their messages for international markets. After the war, the large international advertising and PR agencies developed skills that anticipated the concept of culturally diversified marketing. The global reach of agencies like JWT and the worldwide branding of groups like Unilever (organised by its in-house agency Lintas) necessitated the concept of adaptation in advertising campaigns. Therefore, the decades of the 1950s and 1960s ushered in a deeper understanding of local markets in global marketing. It was also after the Second World War that marketing became a central discipline in the French-speaking markets (Chessel 1998). Marketing, understood as a set of theories and practices that focused on consumer needs, was essentially an American concept imported into France after the 1940s (Meuleau 1992: 976–977). Yet transatlantic exchanges of concepts and practices of course progressed in both ways. In a speech in 1957 to assembled French sales managers, Ernest Dichter advised the businessmen to develop an extensive knowledge of the buying motivations of the American public:

> The psychological reaction of a man towards his car, of a woman towards her washing machine, or of a child towards toothpaste, seem to be based on the same human laws in Canada, in Belgium, in Australia, in Italy, in France, in the US, everywhere in the world. We seem to be the more universally human when we are facing an inanimate object.
>
> (Dichter 1957: 2)

This universality was the reason why French businessmen needed to familiarise themselves with the American market. The idea, explored in detail by Dichter, was that American consumers were the largest market for French products not only because they were buying for practical reasons but also because a new social philosophy (Dichter 1957: 3) made this a model society. In itself, the argument did not differ from the one developed in the early twentieth century in the first advertising manuals published in French-speaking countries (Mosselmans 1908).

Beyond its acknowledged links to the work of Sigmund Freud, Paul Lazarsfeld and more generally the 'Vienna School' of advertising psychological research (Zeisel 1968: 3–12), Dichter's work was also read by the French within the tradition of the pragmatic uses of psychology in advertising, beginning with the seminal work of Walter Dill Scott. Scott had influenced early twentieth-century French advertising practitioners, and most notably the work of the Belgian advertising man Paul Mosselmans, who wrote the first advertising handbook in French (1908), and that of Gérin and Espinadel (1911) who wrote *La publicité suggestive*, a book that would have a lasting influence on the first generation of French advertising men (Hennion and Méadel 1989: 196).

In his 1957 speech on the influence of Motivation Research on sales management, Dichter advocated the need to understand why American citizens were buying. He explained that his motivational studies showed that the products bought by the American consumer were symbols of desires and social ambition. He divided this product-cum-symbol into six categories (Dichter 1957: 4–7):

- the need for roots – especially in buying household appliances;
- the need for taste – taste being much more developed than before;
- the need for new experiences and new sensations – in food for example;
- the need to transgress limits – like in the sales of sports equipment;
- the desire to reach a higher cultural level (Dichter links this both to the desire to broaden one's universe and to become rooted in the past) and
- the pursuit of happiness ('joie de vivre' in his French text).

Dichter then developed the main principles of Motivation Research, ending his speech with a wish he expressed to the French as 'an American of European origin': 'I wholeheartedly wish that the economy of your big country will develop very quickly to the point where motivational research will become as needed for you as it already is for most of the advanced industries and advertising agencies in the United States' (Dichter 1957: 13).

In the French business world, it was the advertising profession that responded most positively to Dichter's outlook. A prominent figure in the popularisation of Dichter in French advertising thought and practice was Marcel Bleustein-Blanchet, founder of the agency Publicis. In his book *Mémoires d'un Lion* (Bleustein-Blanchet 1988: 239–241), he built up the mythic quality of his career in advertising, describing a French success story in advertising from the foundation of his first agency in 1926. Bleustein dedicated three pages to 'Ernst' Dichter – curiously, Bleustein kept the German original of Dichter's first name – whom he called 'the magician'. For the French adman, advertising broached a new dimension with Dichter. Introducing briefly the person of Dichter to his French readers, Bleustein claimed that he had been the first in his country to bring interest to bear upon Dichter's work. He invited Dichter to a two-day seminar in Villennes-sur-Seine, near Paris, during 1961, in order to 'not only explain his methods to my collaborators, but mostly the explosive charge of truth that they are holding' (Bleustein-Blanchet 1988: 239).

The reason for Bleustein's enthusiasm lay in the fact that Dichter was the first to show the true nature of the symbolism residing in objects: 'We believe that we are buying a car for the services it is going to give us. Actually, we buy speed and will power, or even sexual power.' This use of products as symbolic support of the most profound desires was exemplified by Bleustein in a contemporary study by Publicis for Gillette's razorblades, quoting the product's slogan 'Your Skin's Great Lover' – 'la grande amoureuse de votre peau' (Bleustein-Blanchet 1988: 240). Bleustein's praise was, however, nuanced. He confessed that he first worried that Dichter might be mocking him – and therefore the consumers. Bleustein's answer to this rhetorical question was that objects are the extension of human beings and that it was therefore logical that those objects should attract consumer fantasies. The French adman acknowledged this by using depth psychology in some of his campaigns, such as for Rosy lingerie, for Flodor potato crisps, and for Boursin cheese.

Bleustein formulated one caveat: messages based on depth psychology should not completely replace traditional advertising. Advertising, added Bleustein, could not solely be the discourse of our hidden desires, or it risked becoming manipulation. Bleustein thus echoed the strong criticisms that advertising faced in post-war France. In order to respond to that criticism, Bleustein reminded his readers that advertising should remain first a means of disseminating information, presenting the product, its composition, directions for use, retail outlets and price. The same argument had been used by French and Belgian advertising professionals to defend the self-regulation of their profession against state intervention (Pouillard 2005b). 'The truth', Bleustein suggested, 'is that it is high time to consider the consumer as a complete individual.' The consumer could no longer be treated as a backward child or as a gullible peasant.

Bleustein referred directly to the charlatanesque reputation of the first generations of advertising men before this profession forged for themselves a new identity. After the generation of the charlatans came that of the technicians, who, for Bleustein, saw in the consumer a purely rational being. The founder of Publicis dismissed this as a utopian fantasy. It was finally Dichter who 'reveals to us that this ambiguous character [the consumer] is truly a knot of desires – this is revolutionary'. Bleustein praised Dichter but also wanted to reconcile the two visions of a rational and an emotionally driven consumer, as if one were American and the other European: 'Why not admit that [the consumer] is all of that; prejudice and rationality, instincts and intelligence, desire and sublimation?' This view, according to Bleustein, was the last step towards global communication (Bleustein-Blanchet 1988: 241–242).

12.3   Sin, fun and the Cold War: Dichter's studies in French-speaking Europe

The 87 research reports compiled by Dichter's Motivational Research Institute in French-speaking Europe show an interest in a rather consistent corpus of recurring topics. Most of these studies were commissioned by advertising agencies, notably local ones like R. L. Dupuy (Dichter 1950), for which Dichter analysed the market for milk and milk-based products. The majority of Dichter's work in French-speaking Europe concerned France, but he also worked for companies in Belgium and Switzerland, and for firms in France's main export markets. They therefore can be seen as exemplifying the hot topics for the profession at that time.

Some of the archived documents are proposals for Motivation Research studies, others are the final reports of studies developed by Dichter's French office. From one enquiry to another, the methods were rather similar, based on qualitative research, with a series of results of tests being described, including the in-depth interviews that characterised Dichter's method. One type of Dichter's research surveys concerned media. Dichter's Paris office, for example, studied the magazines *Jours de France* and *France-Soir*. Other research surveys studied televisions and record players (Dichter 1965a). Dichter's surveys on household appliances are dedicated to ovens, other kitchen appliances and vacuum cleaners. Dichter's studies explored the morality behind consumers' motivations, especially around the culpability of the house-wives in using new time-saving appliances, an attitude understood by Dichter as the 'resistance of the puritan consumer' (Dichter 1957: 11; also Bowden and Offer 1996: 250–251).

The automobile sector formed a rather substantial portion in the activities of Dichter's French subsidiary, with general studies on the motivations of drivers. Substantial research was conducted, for instance, for Renault, including its performance in the Belgian market. Another study analysed the performance of Chrysler and Simca in Europe (Dichter 1970). This focus on the automobile sector appears to be a reflex of the 'classical' era of market research. When settling in continental Europe in 1927, the American advertising agency J. Walter Thompson had dedicated its first market research study to the market for cars and trucks. Dichter renewed this genre with an attention to the desires of the drivers. This new question was meant to become central in the advertising messages of the sector, replacing the old advertising discourse based on technical details, maintenance of the product and service to the client (Malaval 2001). The petrol industry was represented as well, with recurring motivation studies for the Total group (Dichter 1963, 1967).

Dichter's reports certainly verify the characteristics studied by Kristin Ross (1995) in her book *Fast Cars, Clean Bodies*. She studied the parallel development of the experience of French decolonisation and the development of hygiene and the growth of car ownership in the country. The reports of Dichter's institute were no exception to the clichés about the lack of hygiene in French society. In a proposal for a motivational study of dental hygiene in France submitted to the group Cadum-Palmolive in 1961, preliminary questions about the attitudes of the French consumers to the use of toothpaste dealt with the hypotheses that the perceived lack of hygiene might be the result of the high price of toothpaste, of a national resistance to authority and to advertising, and even that the taste of haute cuisine conflicted with dental hygiene products (Dichter 1961c: 3–4).

Specificities of the French and French-speaking markets appear in the list, but much more in the content of the studies and the questions asked than in the selection of the products themselves. For example, there is rather little to be found in the corpus of Dichter's work in France on the luxury sector, probably the most specific to France. The only study pertaining to this sector was conducted for the department store 'Le

Printemps', in addition to a speech given by Dichter in 1965 on 'Mode, Esthétique 1975' (Dichter 1965b). Fashion and design issues were also considered in relation to Nylor spectacles, the market for dyes and for knitting wools, and car design. The mass market was clearly at centre stage, which is even more clear when it comes to the food products studied by Dichter's institute. Most were industrial foods, like Liebig soups, Bel cheeses, a study for the development of the market for French industrial cheeses Le Tartare and Caprice des Dieux in Italy, several reports on the consumption of chocolate in France and one proposal for a study on Droste chocolate. These studies provided guidelines for the organisation of efficient advertising based on extensive qualitative studies, but also new and creative ways to see and sell products that seemed often very basic, innocuous or even contradictory to the advertising message, as in a speech given by Dichter at a symposium on 'Marketing Opportunities for Highly Viscous Products' in the early 1980s, in which he claimed that milk and milk products needed 'more sin and fun' (Dichter 1983).

The work of Dichter's French institute showed an interest in the future – whether in the design of record players for young consumers, the selling of the somewhat puzzling idea of dry cleaning, the promotion of the new tourism area of Roussillon or the projecting of the market for chewing gum. The future also became an end in itself, as some contemporary documents and articles were written about forecasting the future of consumers and of consumer culture in France. One of these articles asked what the consumer of the year 2000 would be like. Dichter's forecasting for everyday life in 2000 was sometimes off the mark, like his reference to the use of modular architecture, but at times also very accurate, for example when emphasising the take-up of ready-made meals, home-shopping (matching e-commerce today) and biodegradable packaging (Colin-Simard 1979).

Dichter's institute in Paris also became involved in studies that analysed the difficult and ever-changing political identities of the francophone peoples in a new Europe that was forged together by the threats of the Cold War and global economic competition. In order to address these issues, many governments resorted to the fascinating tool-box of public relations. In the United States, the practice of PR had emerged during the 1910s and 1920s in the activities of consultants like Ivy Lee and Edward Bernays (Ewen 1996). A similar movement and body of political PR expertise emerged in Europe in the context of the Cold War and – as regards France and Belgium – the conflicts over the decolonisation of Algeria and the Congo.

The Paris institute, for example, dealt openly with questions of national stereotypes, like the problems of hygiene and rural markets in France and identified national production with national identity: 'When we think of France, we think of perfumes, wine; Switzerland, precision watches; Belgium, lace; United States, cars, technical achievements, etc.' (Dichter 1959). However, Dichter's ideas went beyond dealing with the difficulties faced by most international advertising agencies at that time in selling global products on local markets. Dichter was convinced that a democratic consumer society offered near-perfect conditions to convey a humanist message. This appeared in his idea of the European Union as a possible homogeneous market after the Rome Treaty. His point was that all national products had become ambassadors of good will in a period of conflict – the Cold War (Dichter 1959: 2). In 1959, Dichter addressed the question of the national image of Belgium and strongly advocated the uses of governmental public relations for image campaigns that strengthened Belgian products' country-of-origin (COO) image: 'We judge countries by very much the same standards which we use to judge products and brands' (Dichter 1959: 12). Dichter's work reached French-speaking Europe exactly at the time when the first World Congress for Public Relations took place within the framework of the International Exhibition in Brussels in 1958.

12.4   Non, je ne regrette rien: France absorbs Dichter

The image of consumers being trapped in the multiple techniques criss-crossing their minds is still viable today. Today, 'depth' psychological techniques allow marketers to analyse consumers' implicit memory of advertising messages and unconscious memorisation. The techniques of cognitive sciences and the neurosciences have given birth to the notion of 'Neuromarketing'. The critique of these new techniques has found staunch advocates in France (Beigbeder 2000; Bénilde 2007). But, of course, criticism of manipulative advertising and marketing in France goes right back to the post-war era and was, in large parts, formed through intellectual engagement with the work of Ernest Dichter. Vance Packard's critique of Dichter's motivational theories was published in a French translation as *La persuasion clandestine* in 1958 and immediately read by a wide audience. Dichter's own major book was translated three years later into French under the title *La Stratégie du désir* (Dichter 1961a).

This interest in Dichter needs to be linked to the climate of criticism towards advertising that, until today, seems stronger in France than anywhere else in Europe. From the pamphlet of the writer and physician Georges Duhamel, who in the 1930s harshly criticised the American advertising industry in *Scènes de la vie future* (Duhamel 1930), the French critique of American advertising methods has never been completely relinquished. The idea of a specifically French conscience rebellious to advertising has been investigated by historian Marc Martin for the interwar period (Martin 1989: 27–48). French responses towards Fordism in the 1920s and 1930s and the European Recovery Program (Marshall Plan) in the 1950s show similar features. Although a mission of twelve French advertising executives visited the United States in 1953 and concluded that French industries should make more intensive use of market research, consumer studies and public relations, social visions of an Americanised future came usually in one form only: as a dystopia (Hultquist 2003: 492). The hostile campaigns in France against Coca-Cola are probably the most famous example of a typically French rejection of an American marketing campaign (Kuisel 1991: 96–116; Meuleau 1992: 976–977).

The accusations against Motivation Research in France bore upon two major points. On the one hand, motivation studies were seen as a precondition of mass manipulation, as these studies were an attempt to understand consumers' desires in order to act on them. On the other hand, Motivation Research was charged with leading to a homogenisation of advertising campaigns (Hennion and Méadel 1989: 197). Some ten years after Packard's book was published in France, the critical debate was taken up by the Situationists, a small group of international political and artistic agitators with roots in Marxism, Lettrism and the early twentieth-century European avant-garde. France's foremost representatives of this movement, Guy Debord, published his *Société du Spectacle* (Society of the Spectacle) in 1967 in which he chastised the increasing commoditisation and commercialisation of European societies. The students' movement of spring 1968 took up these arguments and turned them into practical activism against capitalist structures in France (Debord 1967; Rocard and Gutman 1968). From a broader point of view, the French intelligentsia's critique of Americanised consumer society, from Roland Barthes's *Mythologies* to Jean Baudrillard's *La Société de Consommation* can all be read as a critique of the model of society built and promoted by Dichter's reports. The centrality of the object as a vector of desire, for example, was at the heart of the short pieces written by Barthes (Barthes 1957; Baudrillard 1970).

Market research, media planning and motivation studies had by then transformed the advertising profession, leading to more extensive use of quantitative and sociologic methods, more complex mathematic models and a growing importance of the advertising agencies in crafting commercial messages. All of this required a more and more specialised and educated workforce within the marketing and media industry (Martin 1992: 293–294). This new workforce, inevitably, shared a new kind of outlook on society which was more likely to perceive social relationships and all human life as a sales opportunity. France's post-war literary elite vituperated these new professions – market researchers, advertising executives, sales men – as a dangerous and devious bunch (Vercors 1966). It was this newly skilled workforce that was at the core of *Les choses*, a novel published in 1965 by the French writer Georges Pérec. In this short book – some 120 pages – Pérec delivered a clever satire of consumption society through the contradictions of a young French couple, Jérôme and Sylvie. As Kristin Ross argued, Pérec wrote *Les choses* with a pile of *Madame Express* – the magazine directed by Francoise Giroud and Jean-Jacques Servan-Schreiber – at his side. When Jean-Paul Sartre and Simone de Beauvoir were still the symbol of French Marxist intellectuals, Giroud and Servan-Schreiber were their Americanised counterparts.

Pérec made the relationship between Jérôme and Sylvie disappear behind their very quest: the objects, or *Les choses*, which were the real heroes of this non-story. Pérec's critical look glided from the interior of a Parisian flat, to 'them [ils]', who progressively became 'this young couple' and, only at the beginning of chapter three, Jérôme and Sylvie. Their identity is of little importance. However, Pérec stressed that they were both motivational researchers. Through describing their lives, Pérec provided another critique, disqualifying all scientific pretensions of the motivational research: 'History, there again, had chosen for them' (Pérec 1965). They dropped their studies, discouraged by the prospect of teaching in high schools and because 'they were not devoured by the desire of knowing'. The apparently cold description of these impersonal lives was used by Pérec as a powerful means of describing the mental depression engendered by living with a longing for objects that become an end in itself. Jérôme and Sylvie were building their own alienation, without Pérec being more explicit about the morals of this story – there barely was any story. Through the experience of Jérôme and Sylvie, Pérec delivered a vision of the making of motivation studies in 1960s France, then a booming profession:

New agencies opened every month, from nothing, or close to nothing. Finding a job was easy. It consisted, most of the time, in running errands in parks, at schools at the end of classes, or to suburban social housing, to ask mothers if they had noticed a recent ad, and what they thought about it. Such express polls, called *testings* or minute-enquiries, were paid a hundred francs each. It was not much, but still better than baby-sitting, night watch, dishwashing, and all the derisive jobs – leaflet distribution, writings, timing of ad broadcasts, street peddling, sub-tutoring, which were traditionally reserved for students. Moreover, the youthfulness of the agencies, their quasi-craftsman stage, the novelty of the methods, and the quasi-complete lack of qualified workers could make some hope for fast promotions, vertiginous ascension. It was not a bad move. They spent a few months organizing questionnaires. Then the director of an agency, running out of time, trusted them: they went to the Province, a tape recorder under the arm [...].

(Pérec 1965)

Pérec's description shows how Jérôme and Sylvie were absorbed by a system of objects they contributed to build. Through the cold, descriptive lists of their objects of study as well as of the possessions desired and treasured by the young couple, Pérec drew a picture of the superficiality and the vacuity of their lives. He was most ironic about the kind of know-how needed in this new society: Jérôme and Sylvie eventually became the directors of a provincial communications agency, but all their science was limited to 'a certain way of quoting, at opportune moments, Wright Mills, William Whyte, or, even better, Lazarsfeld, Cantril or Herbert Hyman, of whom they had not read three pages' (Pérec 1965: 23). By the end of the novel, it becomes clear that the activities of Jérôme and Sylvie inadvertently contribute to the 'normality' that allowed France to wage its brutal and secretive war against the people of Algeria.

12.5   Conclusions

The rural markets for cars and stoves, the *yé-yé* generation and the selling of record players, chewing-gum, industrial cheeses and processed foods: the topics of Dichter's studies themselves reveal the social contradictions within an increasingly 'Americanised' French consumer culture. Trying to sell a product that symbolised maternity – milk – with 'more sin and fun' can only be seen as challenging. Despite his humanist vision, the reports of Dichter's institute could not always avoid to reproduce national clichés, as we have seen in the report on dental hygiene in France. However, the dissemination of Dichter's work on French-speaking European markets also reveals a strong ability to forecast future trends.

Resistance to Dichter's theories in France, and to a lesser extent in Belgium, are a part of a larger intellectual critique that addressed the alienation of society through consumption. When bearing specifically upon advertising, such critiques could be witnessed at regular intervals of time, from Duhamel to contemporary writings opposed to the use of neurosciences in advertising research. Psychology was used by the French-speaking advertising professionals from the 1900s, and similarly there were constant debates about the impact that such methods had on consumers. French advertising psychologists can be described in terms of generations, the first being the continental pioneers in advertising (Mosselmans, Gérin, Espinadel), the second being the psycho-technicians (Bleustein-Blanchet), the third being the motivational researchers (directly inspired by Dichter) and the fourth being the contemporary researchers who apply the neuroscientific practices developed since the 1990s.

Similarly, critiques responded to these practical and theoretical evolutions. They stemmed from heterogeneous backgrounds and they were not exclusively French. Some major intellectual critics of Dichter in France and Belgium can be linked to Marxism, but not all of them. Similar reactions to Dichter were witnessed in the United Kingdom (Schwarzkopf in this book). It would therefore be wrong to argue that anxieties surrounding Motivation Research were in some ways manifestations of French cultural 'exceptionalism'. It is, however, useful to note that the debate around Dichter's theses attracted major intellectual figures, like Georges Pérec, and that even the advertising practitioners who felt inspired by Dichter put some nuance in their praise. The reading of Dichter's theses by Bleustein-Blanchet was especially revealing in this respect. Bleustein-Blanchet, who embodied national French advertising, was both fascinated by the potential of Dichter's theses and cautious about their uses, especially in terms of the unconscious desires of consumers.

References

Barthes, R. 1957. *Mythologies*. Paris: Seuil.
Baudrillard, J. 1970. *La société de consommation. Ses mythes, ses structures.* Paris: Seuil.
Beigbeder, F. 2000. *99 Francs*. Paris: Grasset.

Bénilde, M. 2007. *On achète bien les cerveaux. La publicité et les médias.* Paris: Editions Raisons d'Agir.

Bleustein-Blanchet, M. 1988. *Mémoires d'un Lion.* Paris: Librairie Académique Perrin.

Bowden, S., Offer, A. 1996. The technological revolution that never was: gender, class, and the diffusion of household appliances in interwar England. In: V. de Grazia, E. Furlough (Eds), *The Sex of Things. Gender and Consumption in Historical Perspective.* Berkeley: University of California Press, 244–274.

Chessel, M. E. 1998. *La publicité, naissance d'une profession, 1900–1940.* Paris: CNRS.

Colin-Simard, A. 1979. Partons en voyage avec Ernest Dichter. Ce que sera notre vie en l'an 2000. *Le Journal du Dimanche* 28 October.

Debord, G. 1967. *La Société du Spectacle.* Paris: Gallimard.

Dichter, E. 1950. A creative problem analysis and proposal of motivational research for M. Poinsot, Agence Dupuy. Ernest Dichter Archive, University of Vienna, Report No. 1360.

———— 1957. L'influence du motivational research sur les ventes en 1957. Ernest Dichter Archive, University of Vienna, Report No. 4674.

———— 1959. Brand image and national image. Speech by Ernest Dichter before the Belgian Association of Advertising Agencies, Brussels, 19–21 October 1959. Ernest Dichter Archive, University of Vienna, Report No. 4710.

———— 1961a. *La stratégie du désir. Une philosophie de la vente.* Paris: Fayard.

———— 1961b. Seven tenets of creative research. *Journal of Marketing* 25 (4): 1–4.

———— 1961c. Proposition pour une étude des motivations sur l'hygiène dentaire en France, soumise à la Société Cadum-Palmolive. Ernest Dichter Archive, University of Vienna, Report No. 2072.

———— 1963. Gas and oil film and television advertising in the United States prepared for Total. Ernest Dichter Archive, University of Vienna, Report No. 1087.

———— 1965a. Rapport final d'une Etude de Motivation concernant la vente des Téléviseurs, des Electrophones et des Magnétophones. Ernest Dichter Archive, University of Vienna, Report Nos 2428–2429.

———— 1965b. Mode, Esthétique 1975. Ernest Dichter Archive, University of Vienna, Report No. 4987.

———— 1967. Letter-proposal for a motivational research study on the image of 'Total' + non-satisfied needs in the field of 'Total' gasoline, oil, and gas stations. Ernest Dichter Archive, University of Vienna, Report No. 2776.

———— 1970. Proposition pour une étude motivationelle concernant le problème du 'Couple Simca-Chrysler' dans le marché commun. Ernest Dichter Archive, University of Vienna, Report No. 3149.

———— 1983. Milk products and milk need more sin and fun. Symposium Brussels, 9 September 1983. Ernest Dichter Archive, University of Vienna, Report No. 5032.

Duhamel, G. 1930. *Scènes de la vie future.* Paris: Mercure de France.

Ewen, S. 1996. *PR! A Social History of Spin.* New York: Basic Books.

Gérin, O. J., Espinadel, C. 1911. *La publicité suggestive. Théorie et pratique.* Paris: Dunod.

Hennion, A., Méadel, C. 1989. The artisans of desire: the mediation of advertising between product and consumer. *Sociological Theory* 7 (2): 191–209.

Henry, H. 1959. *L'étude de motivation. Sa pratique et ses applications comme instrument de la politique de production, de ventes et de publicité.* Paris: Editions in octavo.

Hultquist, C. E. 2003. Americans in Paris: the J. Walter Thompson Company in France, 1927–1968. *Enterprise & Society* 4 (3): 471–501.

Kuisel, R. F. 1991. Coca-Cola and the Cold War: the French face of Americanization, 1948–1953. *French Historical Studies* 17 (1): 96–116.

——— 1993. *Seducing the French: the Dilemma of French Americanization.* Berkeley: University of California Press.

Malaval, C. 2001. *La presse d'entreprise française au XXe siècle. Histoire d'un pouvoir.* Paris: Belin.

Martin, M. 1989. Structures de société et consciences rebelles: les résistances à la publicité dans la France de l'entre-deux-guerres. *Le Mouvement Social* 146: 27–48.

——— 1992. *Trois siècles de publicité en France.* Paris: Odile Jacob.

Meuleau, M. 1992. *Les HEC et l'évolution du management en France (1881–années 1980), volume 3, Vers une nouvelle gestion de l'entreprise.* Thèse d'Etat: Paris X-Nanterre.

Mosselmans, P. M. 1908. *La publicité. Comment s'en servir.* Brussels: Imprimerie Verteneuil et Desmet.

Pérec, G. 1965. *Les choses.* Paris: Julliard.

Pouillard, V. 2005a. American agencies in Europe: J. Walter Thompson's Belgian business in the interwar years. *Business History* 47 (1): 44–58.

——— 2005b. *La publicité en Belgique (1850–1975). Des courtiers aux agences internationales.* Bruxelles: Académie Royale de Belgique.

Rocard, G., Gutman, C. 1968. *Sois belle et achète. La publicité et les femmes.* Paris: Gonthier.

Ross, K. 1995. *Fast Cars, Clean Bodies. Decolonization and the Reordering of French Culture.* Cambridge, MA: MIT Press.

Schwarzkopf, S. 2005. Ernest Dichter (1907–1991) and motivation research: an international perspective. *Medien & Zeit* 20 (4): 40–9.

Vercors (with Paul Silva-Coronel). 1966. *Quota, ou les Phléthoriens.* Paris: Stock.

Zeisel, H. 1968. L'école viennoise des recherches de motivation. *Revue Française de Sociologie* 9 (1): 3–12.

13
Ernest Dichter Motivates the British: Motivation Research and Contested Professional Legitimacies in Britain

Stefan Schwarzkopf

13.1 Ernest Dichter and the demise of English puritanism

Both friends and critics of Ernest Dichter often worked not only on the assumption that he was the 'father of motivation research', but also on the idea that his skilful manipulation of consumer desires allowed Dichter to enjoy global success. The expansion of Dichter's Institute for Motivational Research to Great Britain, Italy, France, Switzerland, Germany and Austria after the Second World War is often quoted as a proof for the success of his business strategy. Dichter managed to dominate parts of the market for Motivation Research in the United States and later in Europe. Behind this seemingly unstoppable rise of a self-made 'marketing guru', however, lay considerable critical objections and professional rivalries which Dichter had to overcome in order to enjoy economic success for his research company. In all of the countries into which he exported his peculiar brand of consumer analysis, his research theories and practices were appropriated, reworked and reinterpreted. Moreover, his theories had to compete with other theoretical schools in the area of psychological market research in the countries he expanded to. These 'local' schools were often far better adapted to the conditions of national consumer preferences. Dichter also fought a far more important, yet almost invisible, enemy: his reputation – or perhaps notoriety – not only followed him to the various European countries where he set up shop during the 1950s. He was already well known in those countries. His success in Britain, for instance, was severely hampered by the impact of Vance Packard's *Hidden Persuaders* (1957) and the general climate of the cultural Cold War, which left British public opinion in fear of brainwashing techniques and the 'technical' manipulation of human emotions by financial interests and governments (Bourke 2005: 167–192; Schwarzkopf 2005).

Ernest Dichter offered his services from a preliminary 'Motivational Research Centre' in London's West End before setting up shop in 1959 (*Advertiser's Weekly* 1959). The offices of Ernest Dichter Associates in Video House on Whitfield Street – right among TV production companies and advertising agencies – employed eight psychologists, one psychoanalyst, and an interviewing staff of 150 people, 50 of whom were trained by the New York Dichter organisation as qualified 'depth interviewers' (Pearson and Turner 1965: 138). What might have looked like a large subsidiary and a considerable attempt to make inroads into the British market was in fact not at all one of Dichter's success stories. Of the one million dollars international turnover that Dichter achieved annually in the early 1960s, only about 6–7 per cent was earned by the London office (£ 20,000–£ 30,000).

In its first five years in London, Dichter's office conducted some 100 surveys, among other things about attitudes of the English towards car polish, contraceptives, cosmetics and chocolate. In the interviews Dichter gave to newspapers and journalists, he admitted that the country exhausted him. Not only was Britain, in his words, 'the most puritanical country in the world', he was also appalled by how unmoved average British consumers were in the face of their new affluence. He found that certain cosmetics such as nail varnish were perceived by British women as a product good enough for the ladies of easy virtue in Soho. He was also amazed at the fact that many British consumers would not be sold on the idea of central heating, as this was seen to be a 'thing for softies' (Dichter 1960a).

What Dichter discovered in London in the late 1950s and early 1960s was that the core of British society was still in the grip of a 14-year system of food rationing and governmental savings campaigns. While war-torn Germany had left the era of rationing already in 1949, it was only ten years after the war in July 1954 that British housewives could finally burn their little grey rationing books. As late as summer 1951, when the world visited London for the 'Festival of Britain', puzzled American tourists had to obtain rationing vouchers at their hotel counters, which allowed them to purchase confectionery. Thus, when Ernest Dichter came to Britain only five years after the end of rationing, he found a country that largely lived after the tune of 'waste not – want not!'

Moreover, post-war Britain was a country which in many ways was still structured by the tight boundaries of class and class-based local communities. In this world, it was not necessarily the state's institutions but the pub, the football club or the trade union which offered social security and a sense of belonging. In order to avoid being talked about at the Working Men's Club or even being excluded from these social structures, new consumer products – a motorbike, a transistor radio – had to be communicated by their owners in a way that kept social resentment as low as possible. Consumers that were able to afford a little more were careful not to show their riches in fear of upsetting neighbours in that community. The greed-based, conspicuous consumption first noted by Veblen found its limitations in the working-class housewives who would easily see a new blouse drying on the council estate's courtyard as an attack on the social glue of the community (Benson 1994: 204–232; Black and Pemberton 2004; Johnson 1988; Langhamer 2005; Scott 2008; Zweiniger-Bargielowska 2000).

The self-seeking, pleasure-seeking young consumer that was of interest to Dichter only just started to emerge around London's West End, Soho, Carnaby Street and Chelsea's King's Road. Here, record stores, fashion outlets and coffee shops invited consumers of a younger generation to spend money on all things colourful and American. Even in the shabby working-class quarters of Notting Hill and Notting Dale teenagers began to openly emulate and sometimes violently compete with the lively sense of style and self-assertion brought by Caribbean immigrants from the West Indies (Breward 2000; Mort 1996). Dichter was quick to realise that these changing cultures of class and consumption in Britain could be tapped in order to gain a deeper understanding about what made people buy certain products. In a survey done for a British contraceptives manufacturer, for example, Dichter's London office found that the young working-class population was very much interested in sexuality, spending money and in enjoying the offerings of an affluent consumer society, like long-playing records, cigarettes, jeans, cosmetics, leather jackets, scooters, boots and mini-skirts (Abrams 1959; Dichter 1965; Pearson and Turner 1965: 138–141).

One of the relatively few success stories Ernest Dichter enjoyed in the United Kingdom was his invention of the 'New Kind of Woman'. When in the early 1960s British women's magazines kept declining in their circulation, George Newness Ltd., publisher of *Woman's Own*, commissioned Dichter to investigate the market for women's magazines. Dichter discovered that better education, television, affluence and women's employment had caused a movement towards greater independence among young, wealthy women. As a result, Dichter concluded in his report, 'a new kind of woman' had emerged 'who can combine, adjust and compromise femininity with independence, personal fulfilment and family responsibilities and modesty with basic human values as she perceives them' (Dichter 1964a: 33).

In the wake of Dichter's 1964 report on this 'new kind of woman', magazines such as *Woman's Own* were modernised (Robinson 1993) and the new journal *Nova* appeared, which embodied all the Dichterian theories about that 'new woman'. *Nova* revolutionised the British women's magazine market. Published from 1965 to 1975, *Nova* employed cutting-edge writers, designers and editors who mixed an enthusiasm for sex, fun and fashion with editorial issues such as gender equality, contraception and racism to challenge the idea of what a woman's magazine should be. Alongside its important editorial legacy, *Nova* became a style bible for a whole generation of British designers, stylists and musicians (Beard 2002).

An analysis of the research studies compiled by Dichter's London office shows that he was en vogue with clients for about ten years, when most companies employed Dichter for one-off studies in order to test whether his advice was worth the money. The first Motivation Research studies commissioned by British companies date back to 1950. Between 1950 and 1972, Dichter completed some 137 studies for British companies. Almost 40 per cent of these studies (53), however, were merely proposals for studies or small-scale pilot studies. The Dichter Archive in Vienna records more than 3,000 research studies which Dichter did for American companies, some 488 completed by Dichter in Germany and 318 in Switzerland. This suggests that Britain was a relatively small market for Dichter's services compared to Germany and the United States. French (87) and Italian (11) research studies are even less impressive in their numbers. However, this does not mean that Dichter was not influential in these countries or had no impact on the modernisation of marketing there. As Pouillard (in this book) and Arvidsson (2007) have shown, Dichter's research activities in France and Italy had a tremendous impact on the emergence of a new consumer society in both countries after the Second World War.

Dichter's largest British clients were Cadbury (chocolate), Imperial Tobacco (John Player cigarettes), W.D. & H.O. Wills (Strand cigarettes), Carrerras (cigarettes and the youth market), Unilever (dentifrice), General Electrics (telephones), Imperial Chemical Industries (paint), Smith Kline (analgesic), Esso (petrol advertising) and ABC Television (TV commercials). He also compiled a study for the BBC in 1950 on people's attitude towards the Anglican Church and for the British Institute of Management in 1960 on inventiveness and modern management tools (Dichter 1950, 1960b). Long-term, profitable relationships, however, only emerged with Cadbury and various cigarette manufacturers (John Player and Carreras). Demand for Dichter's expertise in the United Kingdom declined rapidly in the late 1960s; by the mid-1970s, Dichter had left and his company was taken over by a former associate, William Schlackman. Schlackman had been an employee of Ernest Dichter Associates; by 1964, he ran his own company, Schlackman Research Organisation, later the Schlackman Group. In the late 1960s and during the 1970s and 1980s, he became recognised as Britain's most imaginative practitioner of qualitative research, who carried out industrial research for Imperial Tobacco, research on sensitivity panels and sociological studies for environmental planning projects (Blythe 2005; Schlackman 1959, 1997).

The collection of research reports filed at the Dichter Archive also offers another remarkable find: the interest of advertising agencies in Dichter's research services. Well-established London advertising agencies, like Crawford's, Higham's, Foote, Cone & Belding, Saward Baker, Pritchard Wood, Osborne Peacock and even the London office of the world's largest advertising agency, J. Walter Thompson, commissioned research reports from Dichter Associates during the late 1950s and 1960s (Dichter 1964b). To some extent, this throws light at the hypocrisy of British advertising executives and market researchers with regard to Ernest Dichter. While he was rejected by the majority of his British colleagues, a lot of them seemed to have been keenly interested in how he conducted his research (Anon. 1957a).

13.2   Dichter and the market researchers in Tweed

Despite the relative failure of Ernest Dichter's organisation on the British market, references to Dichter and to motivational research as a bewildering and fascinating new research technique are to be found in every British publication on marketing and advertising research since the mid-1950s. The reasons for Dichter's short period in the United Kingdom, which lasted just over a decade, are manifold. On the one hand, large American advertising agencies began to dominate British advertising by the 1960s, and these agencies imported different varieties of motivational research (Advertising Age 1958: 5–20; Bogart 2003; Schwarzkopf 2007; West 1988). By the late 1960s, motivational research as the 'sexy' new thing to do in marketing had lost its appeal. This decline in interest was made worse by the fact that Dichter never really managed in the first place to gain that status of a 'must do' or 'must have' among British manufacturers. Responsible for this was an unlikely alliance between British market researchers and middle-class cultural criticism. Both forces surrounded Dichter with so much negative propaganda that he remained a bizarre novelty to be looked at but not touched.

From the first moment British psychologists and market researchers began to research the 'hidden' side of consumer behaviour, they also appropriated this technique to their own needs. When Dichter set up shop in London in 1959, numerous researchers in Britain had already worked on the subject and were able to offer this new method to their clients (Adler 1956: 93–98; Gloag 1959: 80; Henry 1958: 219; Tunstall 1964: 124–133). The situation in France was different, where the owner of the country's largest advertising agency, Publicis, Marcel Bleustein-Blanchet, introduced Dichter's Motivation Research as a new 'secret' and he also wrote the preface to the French edition of Dichter's *Strategy of Desire* in 1962 (Pouillard in this book).

Dichter met in Britain with an established and extremely self-conscious elite of market researchers, who had mostly been trained in the 1920s and 1930s in statistics and economics at Cambridge, Oxford and the London School of Economics (Abrams 1951: 44, 53–62; Bulmer 1985; Henry 1971: 347–362). For these statisticians and economists, consumer psychology was something perceived as an adjunct to the economic study of the consumer or something that could be derived from a properly conducted statistical survey of consumer decision making in a given market. These researchers had been educated in the interwar years in the idea that the very meaning of market research lay in mastering sampling techniques, the statistical theory of the sample and the interpretation of results from sample surveys. This background contributed to a self-perception of many people in that industry who imagined themselves as a scientific elite whose task it was to use the findings of market research in order to make society more efficient and democratic.

A Penguin paperback entitled *Science and the Nation*, edited by the Association of Scientific Workers, for example, introduced consumer research as 'part of national planning mechanisms' and made the case for *consumer* research to be carried out under state auspices, because *market* research 'does not necessarily distinguish between the irrational prejudices and tastes of the consumer and his real needs' (Association of Scientific Workers 1947: 132–143). This understanding of the researcher as the rational 'scientist-entrepreneur' left little, if any, space for Dichter, who had by now become accustomed to fit into the US system of 'hero-entrepreneurs', who characterised the US advertising and marketing scene. Across the Atlantic, men like Leo Burnett, David Ogilvy, William Bernbach, James Webb Young and Rosser Reeves became singular geniuses of advertising creation. Their celebrity style of presenting the 'adman' as the heart of entrepreneurial, corporate America was seen with suspicion in Britain. The idea of the British, quantitatively oriented market researcher as the engineer of a good consumer society clashed directly with Ernest Dichter's self-made image of a 'mad genius' (Mayer 1958: 243) or an intuitively working 'medium', who sensed consumer motivations without having to measure them. Thus, when Dichter arrived in Britain, he found himself in a situation where many people in market research already used motivational research techniques and could convince their clients that they conducted motivational research far better: more statistically, more technical and more 'scientific'.

Among many other critics of Dichter in Britain, the market and motivation researcher Harry Henry was probably the most vocal. He attacked Dichter's style as 'un-scientific', 'naïve' and consisting of sexualised 'gobbledegook' (Henry 2005). In 1958, one year before Dichter expanded to London, Henry published a textbook on this subject, through which he managed to establish himself as Britain's foremost motivation researcher. Moreover, most British market researchers who competed with Dichter in one way or another were very careful in mentioning in their publications that Ernest Dichter was the main culprit of Vance Packard's *Hidden Persuaders*. Moreover, while all American and English publications consistently referred to Dichter as 'Ernest' or 'Dr Ernest Dichter', Harry Henry, who had served as a gunner and field statistician under Field Marshal Montgomery, was the only one who denied Dichter this transatlantic citizenship by referring to him as 'Ernst' Dichter – by that re-Germanising the Austrian Jew who fled the Germanisation of his home country.

13.3 Ernest Dichter and the cultural barriers against 'America'

Ernest Dichter had to face the strongest objections from the front put up against him by post-war cultural criticism. As the journalists Pearson and Turner in their 1965 book on the *Persuasion Industry* observed, motivational research always 'had a sinister ring' in Britain and the 'image created by Vance Packard's *The Hidden Persuaders* put off a lot of British manufacturers' (Pearson and Turner 1965: 138). Packard's book itself was promoted by British newspapers as an 'alarming' account (*Sunday Times*), and the 'waking nightmare' of the 'depth-merchandisers' (Hyams 1957) was likened to 'George Orwell's Big Brother world' (*Daily Mail*). In the late 1950s and throughout the 1960s, British public opinion expressed a great deal of fear about the vulnerability of citizens and consumers and the ethical dilemmas involved in the rise of governmental and commercial propaganda. A plethora of books and movies in that era, for example James Brown's *Techniques of Persuasion*, and Cold War spy movies like *The Manchurian Candidate* and *The Ipcress Files*, convinced British readers and movie-goers that psychological manipulation (brainwashing) were techniques that were already widely used by governments and advertisers (Brown 1963: 179–189; Gundrey 1965). These new developments were perceived as very real threats to the autonomy of individuals. When *The Times* featured an article on Ernest Dichter's research methods on 14 April 1959, a letter to the editor written by the LSE sociologist Terence Morris appeared on the same pages three days later describing 'motivational research … together with "subliminal advertising" as one of the long shadows of the Admass society of 1984' (Anon. 1959; Morris 1959).

At the same time, popular suspicions of marketing were at their highest in Britain because the new medium of television allowed a much more intimate form of persuasion directly inside people's homes. The sense of power and fear that surrounded particular advertising research techniques was felt very strongly, even within the British marketing community. The Managing Director and Chairman of Foote, Cone & Belding, Brian MacCabe, for instance, told members of the Market Research Society in January 1956:

> You are potentially dangerous because you are so potentially powerful that your power spells danger to Britain. In fact, some of you are already powerful and, therefore, probably already dangerous. Just how dangerous you will become will depend almost entirely on what sense of responsibility you have.
>
> (MacCabe 1956)

Part and parcel of this claim to power was the assertion that advertising was essentially a form of psychological manipulation and that marketing research methods – like Dichter's depth interviews – were the driving force behind a new type of commercialisation based on the malleability of passive consumer masses.

Packard warned the readers of the British edition of his bestseller that Britain already had its home-grown manipulators and that both Americans and British consumers could not be sure that they were not 'worked upon by the depth persuaders' (1957: 9). The cultural barriers against Dichter's theories in Britain were extraordinarily high in a society that was deeply startled by anxieties about 'hidden' persuasion and 'subliminal advertising'. In particular, the revelation in summer 1957 of James Vicary's experiments in the United States on the subliminal persuasion of unsuspecting cinema-goers to buy popcorn and Coca-Cola caused havoc and prompted the British advertising industry to launch an investigation into the background of these new, 'American' psychological methods (Institute 1958). Between 1956 and 1957, *The Times* and the BBC – then the two foremost institutions of 'safeguarding' British culture – devoted considerable space and air time to the experiments conducted by Vicary and his Subliminal Projection Company.

A number of commentators in the press stressed the political implications of subliminal advertising, especially when it turned out that the Soviet Union had started its own research programme on this new persuasion technique (Anon. 1957b, 1958). These scares about the powers of psychologically dexterous advertisers and spin-doctors joined the uneasiness many British commentators felt about the increasing influence of American media, American music stars and American products on British society. Authors like the Labour peer Francis Williams echoed warning cries about the 'sexualisation' of Britain by American advertising and American cinema (Williams 1962).

Ernest Dichter and his London associates seemingly vindicated these impressions about an organisation that was out to manipulate people at all cost and that had no regards whatever for the cultural differences between Britain and the United States. When asked by journalists about the working practices applied in their market studies, one of Dichter's London associates openly admitted:

> In the USA we have been at it for over twenty years and the sort of problems we face are not specifically American problems but those common to all affluent societies. We have a tremendous library back at Croton-on-Hudson, with three or four million case studies stacked away. I can usually look at a problem and say 'this is just the thing the American market faced back in 1943'.
>
> (Turner and Pearson 1965: 139)

13.4 The cultural appropriation of motivational research

Thus, when Dichter first arrived in Britain, he found himself fenced in on the one hand by contemporary British cultural criticism, which already knew him before he expanded to London, and on the other hand by a powerful league of professional market researchers and consumer psychologists.

One of these institutions which competed directly with Ernest Dichter in London was the Tavistock Institute for Human Relations. The institute was founded in 1946 with the aid of a grant from the Rockefeller Foundation. It was set up for the specific purpose of actively relating the psychological and social sciences to the needs and concerns of post-war British society. The institute soon acquired a high level of expertise in using psychological and psychoanalytical models in the areas of industrial democracy, group relations training and marital and group therapy. This psychological and psychoanalytical expertise made the institute very attractive for advertising agencies and manufacturers which faced problems in marketing their products. When the institute began to experience financial difficulties due to the expiry of its grant from the Rockefeller Foundation, it began to open itself up to the requests from agencies and marketers.

As early as September 1950, the Tavistock Institute was asked to investigate problems related to the consumption of ice cream with a view on increasing the level of ice cream consumption during the winter period. According to its definition of the nature of human relations, a department within the institute began to investigate this problem by organising group discussions on ice cream in order to uncover the hidden psychodynamics of ice cream consumption as well as the unconscious 'meaning' of ice cream for consumers. In the course of its studies, the institute discovered that ice cream was a 'pleasure food' which could alleviate anxieties and depressions connected with the loss of the motherly breast. Accordingly, the ice cream manufacturer was advised to stress in his advertising the rewarding, pleasurable nature of his product. Moreover, since housewives were found to feel 'guilty' about offering ice cream as a desert at home – it did not require extra work on their side and thus could be seen as lazy – the advertiser was again advised to present ice cream as a 'motherly' gift by housewives to children and husband (Dicks 1970; Miller 1999; Miller and Rose 2000; Richards 2000; Trist and Murray 1990).

In a similar way, by applying group discussion techniques and the Freudian terminology of guilt, fear and suppressed desires, the Tavistock Institute helped hair-care producers to create a 'home perm culture' in Britain and devised a typology of drinkers for the Dublin producers of Guinness. Between 1950 and 1965, the institute conducted more than 30 studies into the issue of brand loyalty in the market for petrol, for Colman's mustard, Cadbury chocolate, studies into the attitudes of housewives towards frozen fish shapes (for Birds Eye), on vitamin C drinks, baby foods, toilet paper, gravy, on Bovril and Marmite, as well as the psychological attitudes of men towards shaving (for Gillette). What is remarkable about these research activities is that some of the largest advertisers and their advertising agencies in the post-war era like Unilever, Shell, British Petroleum, Colman's, Cadbury, Guinness and their agencies S. H. Benson and Lintas, already began to demand psychological and psychoanalytical expertise to solve their marketing problems by the early 1950s, years before Ernest Dichter set up shop in London. The largest advertising agency in London at that time, the American J. Walter Thompson (JWT) agency, and its market research subsidiary BMRB, engaged Dichter in talks as early as 1955. Because Dichter's ideas and approach did not suit JWT's clients, the agency decided to set up its own Motivation Research study group under Norman Philip, Ian Haldane and Pamela Vince (Downham 1993: 94–95; Himmelweit and Vince 1958).

The second example of cultural appropriation of Motivation Research in Britain is the large American advertising agency McCann-Erickson and its most prominent market researcher Harry Henry. As director of the British research subsidiary (MarPlan) of McCann-Erickson, Henry was ideally placed to channel some of the new American thought on Motivation Research into the United Kingdom without allowing Ernest Dichter to influence this process (Henry 1958, 1959; Morton-Williams 1959). Henry had strong theoretical and institutional back-up from the psychologist Herta Herzog, Creative Director of McCann-Erickson New York.

Henry's own take on motivational research from a 'British' perspective began in 1953, with a paper he gave to the Lausanne Conference of the European Society of Opinion and Market Research (ESOMAR) entitled 'We cannot ask "Why"' (Henry 1971: 293–311). In this paper, Henry positioned himself in the tradition of the Dichter-critical market researchers Paul Lazarsfeld, Herta Herzog and Alfred Politz (Politz 1956–1957). He argued that little credence could be attached to the answers given when informants were asked directly about the reasons for their behaviour. For Henry, it was a pointless waste of time and money to ask 'why' consumers preferred a certain brand, as most consumers simply did not know themselves or would not be willing to tell investigators. Most consumers, Henry argued, would try and rationalise their behaviour according to a certain impression they wanted to present to others. To get to the truth, market researchers needed to take cross-bearings from a set of indirect approaches in order to arrive at deductions which approximated to that truth.

Henry was clever enough not to mention Dichter personally in his paper, yet he nevertheless managed to build him up as a straw man in front of his listeners. Despite their deficiencies, Dichter's research methods were of course much more refined and avoided a simplistic approach to the question of why consumers purchased a product. Dichter worked his way around the psychological barriers of consumers by asking often seemingly unrelated questions and by allowing participants to report seemingly unrelated feelings. Henry's scepticism towards these methods reflected a typically British unease about the intrusion which market research inevitably meant for ordinary consumers. While American consumers had grown used to being measured, polled, analysed and investigated, British people often rejected market research investigators as unwelcome intruders into the sacred private sphere of family and home. Not only consumers, but also British manufacturers felt that enquiries into the deeper psychological strata of a human being were somehow inappropriate (Downham 1993: 95; McDonald and King 1996: 267–275). Market research of the type proposed by Harry Henry was thus a specific answer to a number of cultural and attitudinal barriers to consumer investigations in Britain before the 1970s.

Henry, who was about ten years younger than Dichter, used his Lausanne paper to position himself as a force to be reckoned with within the field of market research in Britain. In the coming years, Henry elaborated on his findings and eventually published his standard work, *Motivation Research*, which was reprinted twice and later translated into seven languages. The book began with accusing the 'charlatans' in Motivation Research for abusing this useful research tool by surrounding it with the fog of 'psychoanalytical jargon, usually concerned with sex'. Furthermore, he accused Freudian motivation researchers (that is, Dichter) for being too much concerned with themselves and not enough with their clients' needs:

The psychoanalyst – particularly the Freudian variety – is far better fitted for the role of benevolent witch-doctor, with his prattle of repressions, masturbation and phallic symbols, and the like, and a good deal of the early extravagances which were associated with Motivation Research arose from excessive concentration on these fascinating gimmicks.

(Henry 1958: 27)

While the first part of the book dealt with Henry's enemies in a more general tone, the last chapter attacked Dichter directly. Here, Dichter is called an 'indefatigable pamphleteer', who produced more promotional material relating to his own organisation than all the other research organisations together (Henry 1958: 216).

In line with his role model Alfred Politz, Henry concluded his book by calling for a more 'scientific' form of motivational research that abstained from inadequate sampling, the oversimplification of results and the largely intuitive interpretations of problems in marketing. Yet, even though Henry regarded depth interviews, ink-blot tests, projective techniques and association tests as 'dishonest nonsense' (Henry undated), Dichter's innovations nevertheless forced him and other grandees of British market research, such as Mark Abrams and J. Walter Thompson's John Treasure, into positioning themselves vis-à-vis the unstoppable rise of qualitative consumer research (Abrams 1960; Treasure 1959).

13.5 Conclusion

Ernest Dichter's impact on British marketing, market research and consumer culture was significant despite the strong resistance against his person. Dichter's global fame and the widely publicised stories of Dichter miraculously curing ailing brands, pushed British advertising service providers into adopting new, more holistic methods in understanding consumer behaviour. Dichter's major success in the British market, the invention of the 'New Kind of Woman', as well as his relative failure in the long term show that the acceptance of certain managerial and marketing techniques depends heavily on a wider cultural and societal setting. The readiness of British society for Motivation Research as a marketing innovation was strongly determined by factors outside the strategic control of Ernest Dichter and his associates. These factors related to the dominance of national professional traditions in conducting market research, fears of Americanisation, consumer anxieties about the undue influence of marketers and the cultural–political climate provided by the global Cold War.

Ernest Dichter's mixed business record in Britain shows that the transfer of marketing practices across cultures can meet considerable limitations and resistance not only from civil society and pressure groups but also from local professional elites who manage to brand innovations or newcomers as non-indigenous. In this case, the allegedly 'American' and 'sexual' character of this genuinely European social research technique was used by British market researchers in strategies of 'othering'. Similar strategies have subsequently been used by a number of civil society movements in Europe and most recently again by critical writers like Ziauddin Sardar and Wyn Davies (2003). The long-term, cross-cultural success of Motivation Research was highly dependent on its successful cultural embedding and the successful management of the symbolic language with which relevant stakeholder groups surrounded the social and cultural relevance of these techniques.

References

Abrams, M. 1951. *Social Survey and Social Action*. London: Heinemann.
—— 1959. *The Teenage Consumer*. London: London Press Exchange.
—— 1960. Market analysis: how consumers make their choice. In: Green Meadow Foundation (Ed.), *Motivation Research and Depth Communication*. Zurich: Green Meadow Foundation, 25–34.
Adler, M. 1956. *Modern Market Research*. London: Crosby Lockwood.
Advertiser's Weekly. 1959. Motivational research progress. 24 April: 4.
Advertising Age (Ed.) 1958. *The Pros and Cons of Motivation Research*. Chicago: Advertising Age.
Anon. 1957a. Dr Abrams' doubts about motivation technique. *Advertiser's Weekly* 20 September: 7.
Anon. 1957b. Case for press advertising: meeting the subliminal 'threat'. *The Times* 28 September: 3.
Anon. 1958. Subliminal 'not professional'. *The Times* 5 July: 5.
Anon. 1959. Pioneer of motivation research. *The Times* 14 April: 7.
Arvidsson, A. 2007. 'Liebe' und Konsum: Ernest Dichter's Soziologie im Werk Francesco Alberoni's. In: R. Gries, S. Schwarzkopf (Eds), *Ernest Dichter: Doyen der Verführer*. Vienna: Mucha, 203–217.
Association of Scientific Workers (Ed.) 1947. *Science and the Nation*. Harmondsworth: Penguin.
Beard, A. 2002. 'Put in just for pictures': fashion editorial and the composite image in 'Nova', 1965–1975. *Fashion Theory: the Journal of Dress, Body & Culture* 6 (1): 18–41.
Benson, J. 1994. *The Rise of Consumer Society in Britain, 1880–1980*. London: Longman.
Black, L., Pemberton, H. (Eds). 2004. *An Affluent Society? Britain's Post-war 'Golden Age' Revisited*. Aldershot: Asghate.
Blythe, I. 2005. *The Making of an Industry: The Market Research Society, 1946–1986. A History of Growing Achievement*. London: Market Research Society.
Bogart, L. 2003. *Finding Out: Personal Adventures in Social Research*. Chicago: Ivan R. Dee.
Bourke, J. 2005. *Fear: A Cultural History*. London: Virago.
Breward, C. 2000. In the eye of the storm: Oxford Circus and the fashioning of modernity. *Fashion Theory: the Journal of Dress, Body & Culture* 4 (1): 3–26.

Brown, J. 1963. *Techniques of Persuasion: From Propaganda to Brainwashing.* Penguin: Harmondsworth.

Bulmer, M. 1985. *The Development of Sociology and of Empirical Social Research in Britain.* In: M. Bulmer (Ed.), *Essays on the History of British Sociological Research.* Cambridge: Cambridge University Press, 3–36.

Dicks, H. 1970. *Fifty Years of the Tavistock Clinic.* London: Routledge.

Downham, J. 1993. *British Market Research Bureau: The First Sixty Years, 1933–1993.* London: BMRB International.

Dichter, E. 1950. Some preliminary findings based on a pilot investigation on people's attitude to the Anglican Church. Ernest Dichter Archive, University of Vienna, Report No. 2159.

——— 1960a. Practical recommendations on advertising: Esso Petroleum Company Ltd. Ernest Dichter Archive, University of Vienna, Report No. 1756.

——— 1960b. Inventiveness: the most important tool in management. Ernest Dichter Archive, University of Vienna, Report No. 4716.

——— 1964a. A motivational research study on the British woman in today's culture for 'Woman's Own'. Ernest Dichter Archive, University of Vienna, Report Nos 2432 and 2433.

——— 1964b. Test of TV commercials of 'Horlicks'. Ernest Dichter Archive, University of Vienna, Report No. 2436.

——— 1965. Sexual attitudes in the United Kingdom – today. Ernest Dichter Archive, University of Vienna, Report No. 2614.

Gloag, J. 1959. *Advertising in Modern Life.* London: Heinemann.

Gundrey, E. 1965. *A Foot in the Door: An Expose of High-Pressure Sales Methods.* London: Frederick Muller.

Himmelweit, H. T., Vince, P. 1958. *Television and the Child: An Empirical Study of the Effect of Television on the Young.* London: Oxford University Press.

Henry, H. undated. *Statistics, Bikinis, and Motivation Research.* Undated manuscript, Harry Henry papers at Esher, Surrey.

——— 1958. *Motivation Research: Its Practice and Uses for Advertising, Marketing and Other Business.* London: Crosby Lockwood.

——— 1959. *Motivation Research and the Television Commercial.* London: ATV Series of Technical Research Studies.

——— 1971. *Perspectives in Management, Marketing and Research.* London: Crosby Lockwood.

——— 2005. Interview with the author, Esher (Surrey), 22 October 2005.

Hyams, E. 1957. The hidden persuaders. *New Statesman* 26 October: 524–526.

Institute of Practitioners in Advertising. 1958. *Subliminal Communication.* London: IPA.

Johnson, P. 1988. Conspicuous consumption and working-class culture in late Victorian and Edwardian Britain. *Transactions of the Royal Historical Society* 38: 27–42.

Langhamer, C. 2005. The meanings of home in postwar Britain. *Journal of Contemporary History* 40 (2): 341–362.

MacCabe, B. 1956. Your power spells danger. *Advertiser's Weekly* 24 April: 4.

Mayer, M. 1958. *Madison Avenue USA.* New York: Harper.

McDonald, C., King, S. (Eds). 1996. *Sampling the Universe: The Growth, Development and Influence of Market Research in Britain since 1945.* Henley-on-Thames: NTC.

Miller, E. 1999. *The Tavistock Institute Contribution to Job and Organizational Design.* Aldershot: Ashgate.

Miller, P., Rose, N. 2000. Mobilizing the consumer: assembling the subject of consumption. *Theory, Culture and Society* 14 (1): 1–36.

Morris, T. 1959. Motive research. *The Times* 17 April: 15.

Mort, F. 1996. *Cultures of Consumption: Masculinities and Social Space in Late Twentieth-Century Britain.* London: Routledge.

Morton-Williams, J. 1959. Motivation research. *Marketing* 28 (4): 199, 219.

Packard, V. 1957. *The Hidden Persuaders.* London: Longmans.

Politz, A. 1956–1957. 'Motivation research' from a research viewpoint. *Public Opinion Quarterly* 20 (4): 663–673.

Richards, G. 2000. Britain on the couch: the popularization of psychoanalysis in Britain, 1918–1940. *Science in Context* 13 (2): 183–230.

Robinson, S. 1993. Woman's Own. In: S. G. Riley (Ed.), *Consumer Magazines of the British Isles.* London: Greenwood Press, 230–234.

Sardar, Z., Wyn Davies, M. 2003. *Why Do People Hate America?* Cambridge: Icon.

Schlackman, W. 1959. Motivation research in packaging. *Sales Appeal* (October): 57–58, 64.

―――― 1997. A discussion of the use of sensitivity panels in market research. *Journal of the Market Research Society* 39 (1): 145–162.

Schwarzkopf, S. 2005. They do it with mirrors: advertising and British Cold War consumer politics. *Contemporary British History* 19 (2): 133–150.

―――― 2007. Transatlantic invasions or common culture? Modes of cultural and economic exchange between the American and the British advertising industries, 1951–1989. In: M. Hampton, J. Wiener (Eds), *Anglo-American Media Interactions, 1850–2000.* London: Routledge, 254–274.

Scott, P. 2008. Marketing mass home ownership and the creation of the modern working-class consumer in inter-war Britain. *Business History* 50 (1): 4–25.

Treasure, J. 1959. Bridging the gap between motivation research and sales. In: *Seminar on Motivation.* Brussels: Chambre des Agences-Conseils en Publicité, 109–115.

Trist, E., Murray, H. (Eds). 1990. *The Social Engagement of Social Science: A Tavistock Anthology.* London: Free Association.

Tunstall, J. 1964. *The Advertising Man in London Advertising Agencies.* London: Chapman & Hall.

Pearson, J., Turner, G. 1965. *The Persuasion Industry.* London: Eyre & Spottiswoode.

West, D. C. 1988. Multinational competition in the British advertising agency business, 1936–87. *Business History Review* 62: 467–501.

Williams, F. 1962. *The American Invasion: On American Economic Penetration of Great Britain.* London: Anthony Blond.

Zweiniger-Bargielowska, I. 2000. *Austerity in Britain: Rationing, Controls and Consumption, 1939–1955.* Oxford: Oxford University Press.

14

The 'Depth Boy' – Ernest Dichter and the Post-war German Advertising Elite

Dirk Schindelbeck

14.1   A look back at the life of an advertising executive

At the beginning of the 1960s, when Ernest Dichter's star was at its zenith and he was still attracting attention around the world, Hans Wündrich-Meißen (1900–1986), proprietor and managing director of one of the most high-profile German advertising agencies, was preparing to say a final farewell to the advertising business. To celebrate this occasion appropriately, the old gentleman was planning to produce a little book of anecdotes, poems and stories on the topic of advertising. In it, he would look back from a position of detachment, draw up a balance sheet and incidentally get down on paper some of the things that had always needed saying. To that extent it is no surprise that this book sheds a great deal of light on the true feelings of the author, and consequently the experiences of the generation of German advertising practitioners born between 1895 and 1910. In one of these stories about the 'Depth Boy' (Der Tiefenheini), Wündrich-Meißen's resentment towards the younger generation of advertising men, who had fallen under the spell of motivational research, becomes concrete and tangible (Wündrich-Meißen 1965: 26–29). The story tells how in a train compartment an elderly gentleman (that is Wündrich-Meißen) is arrogantly 'enlightened' by a much younger advertising consultant about the fundamental principles of motivational research. At the end of the story the gentleman, having listened politely to his young colleague, leaves the compartment, but not before he has told him in no uncertain terms that his business was based on nothing but truisms and fictitious 'insights'.

This unambiguous viewpoint earned Wündrich-Meißen the plaudits of a whole generation of German advertising men. In common with many successful colleagues and agents, such as Hanns W. Brose (born 1899), Ludwig Freiherr von Holzschuher (born 1903), Wilhelm Hohnhausen (born 1903), Hubert Strauf (born 1904) and Hubert Troost (born 1910), his 'glory days' were not until after the Second World War, for it was only with the advent of the currency reform of 1948 that the free market conditions existed which enabled him and his fellow advertising practitioners to achieve economic success, their knowledge and expertise now being in demand and well remunerated. Wealth only came to these men when they were already well into their forties or even fifties, although when it did come it was a rapid process. Given that they had no more than about 15 years of professional life ahead of them, it is no surprise that the post-war West German advertising elite defended their positions with grim determination. Yet the departure from the scene between 1962 and 1965 of these 'grand old men of the German advertising fraternity' (*Der Spiegel*) was sudden and comprehensive.

It is no accident, then, that at about the same time that motivational research came to the fore as the standard approach for the advertising experts, the US agency system was sweeping all before it in Germany. After all, in the wake of the first major sales crises such as the bankruptcy of the Borgward brand in 1961, advertising now needed to prove itself and show that it was capable of bringing about real purchasing decisions in the face of competition which was becoming tougher all the time. One after another, the classical advertising executives' positions in the leading firms were being eliminated, as more and more work was delegated to outside advertising agencies. The generational change through which the advertising sector was passing was accompanied by a structural reorganisation on an unprecedented scale. The patriarchal style of management that the 'old-style bosses' had cultivated and maintained in their firms was now a thing of the past. The new advertising practitioners aspired to run their business with a small dedicated team of specialists working together, a methodology already practised by the Düsseldorf-based team advertising agency, the GGK (Gredinger, Gerstner & Kutter) and the German branch of Doyle, Dane & Bernbach. This new professional culture was also expressed in a markedly changed self-image of employees in this sector: among the new parameters there suddenly appeared – quite unexpectedly as far as the Germans were concerned – the figure of the 'creative worker'. From now on advertising was no longer to be merely the business of exercising influence but also had to be something resembling art. There were clear signs that this was happening in the year 1964, which saw both the establishment of the Art Directors Club and the launch of a new periodical, the *Jahrbuch der Werbung* (*Advertising Yearbook*), which covered a cross-section of advertising activity in Germany and continues to flourish to this day.

14.2 The German Advertising Club

Of course, the former bosses had their clubs, too, but what they discussed there was not so much the artistic merits of their own products as the purpose and effects of different methods of advertising. There was, for example, the Deutsche Werbe-Klub (DWK) (German Advertising Club), which had been formed as early as 1923 by a hundred or so of the leading advertising professionals. This club even published its own club newspaper, the *Werbe-Rundschau*, in which – in contrast to, for example, *Gebrauchsgraphik* (*Graphic Design*) or *Das Plakat* (*The Poster*) – mainly advertising strategic questions were addressed. To qualify to become a member, however, a proven track record in the field was required. It was three years, no less, before Wündrich-Meißen was accepted into this illustrious circle, and he only gained acceptance on the strength of an impressive piece of scholarship. For him – at this time he was concerned with the placing of small ads – inevitably every imaginable form of advertising was worthy of consideration. The systematic study and comparison of different forms of advertising soon led him to a hitherto neglected area: advertising leaflets and brochures. In 1927, he presented the result of his labours: the first German academic study of advertising to deal exclusively with this specialism. In the preface, he confidently announced:

> You and I, dear reader, are plunged into the depths of despair when we consider the thousands of clumsily expressed leaflets that for years have been regularly landing on our doormats, that sit around in magazines, or that some well-meaning person presses into our hands at fairs, exhibitions and the like. One quick glance and we never look at them again. It's no exaggeration to say that 80% of today's leaflets are a waste of money.

It hardly needs saying that Wündrich-Meißen used the 300 pages of his book to demonstrate to his readers what a leaflet should really look like (Wündrich-Meißen 1927). Even though this book was dealing with an almost completely unexplored subject, in its way it was steeped in the traditions of German advertising science, which since 1910 had been obsessively concerned – true to the great nineteenth-century scientific traditions – with clarifying and systematising the complex field of advertising. Hans Weidenmüller (1926), Rudolf Seyffert (1929), Johannes Schmiedchen (1927) and many others were keen to give the individual advertising executive practical assistance in a handy format (Schindelbeck 2003). But the writing they produced was advertising science almost in the manner of Hegel, in which concepts were elucidated, definitions given and order created. This desire for order is indeed understandable, as it was not even clear which field of academic investigation was primarily appropriate to the subject of 'advertising' – business management, aesthetics, psychology, communications strategy or even philosophy. There was no clearly defined career path for the advertising practitioner. Some came to advertising from journalism, others had been painters, while yet others had been exhibition organisers, business managers, or inventors.

Even if this diversity meant that publications on advertising that appeared in German-speaking countries in the 1920s were both varied and confusing, all authors were remarkably united on one point. They saw themselves as strategists of influence, as an elite, who reflected on the masses and how to lead them (or rather, how to entice them to make certain purchases). In almost no other country were the after-effects of the theory of mass psychology, which had been written about by Gustave LeBon as early as 1895, more strongly felt than in Germany. It is therefore not surprising that the old German science of advertising was fundamentally sender-oriented and thus almost automatically wedded to the AIDA formula. As early as the 1920s, the first beginnings of market research (known in German as *Absatzforschung*) made their appearance and there were experiments with advertising psychology. Among the few early studies, Hanns F. J. Kropff and Bruno Randolph's book *Marktanalyse* (1928) und Theodor König's *Reklame-Psychologie* (*The Psychology of Advertising*), published in König 1927, are both worthy of mention (Regnery 2003).

14.3 Controlled, bribed, streamlined: advertising careers in the Third Reich

On the day the National Socialists came to power the currently practised sender-orientation (*Führerprinzip* or 'leadership principle') became the state doctrine. Within the framework of *Gleichschaltung*, which was put in place without delay, not only the economy but also the entire advertising system was reordered. In the autumn of 1933, the 'Werberat der deutschen Wirtschaft' (Advertising Council of the German Industry) was instituted, a quasi-government authority under Goebbels that controlled every single advertisement in the German Reich through the *Allgemeine Anzeigengesellschaft* (General Advertisement Association) or ALA. Everything that was regarded as 'Jewish American' advertising – such as the agency system – now came under fire, and membership in the National Socialist *Reichsfachschaft Deutscher Werbefachleute* or NSRDW (Professional Association of German Advertising Practitioners) was made compulsory (Rücker 2000; Wündrich 1992).

The speed and willingness with which the great majority of advertising practitioners submitted to the new system without offering the slightest resistance still seems frightening today. Most gave an enthusiastic welcome to what the National Socialists called 'German advertising' (*Werbung*) as opposed to 'Jewish-American publicity' (*Reklame*). The Nazi political economy – which regulated every last detail of the advertising industry, like everything else, from the installation of an all-powerful 'Advertising Council' and fixed remuneration, to new 'German' concepts like 'Bogenanschlagwesen' for poster advertising – was felt by most of them to be a beneficial guideline, which both established their professional status and gave them confidence in their expertise (Berghoff 2003; Westphal 1989). What the advertising practitioners liked best about the new system was the greater degree of importance the state now attributed to them as specialists in persuasion. Never before in their history had they enjoyed such a strong position in relation to industry managers as they did in the Nazi state. The one-time doormats, who in the 1920s had been hired and fired at will, had suddenly become persons commanding respect and, indeed, exercising control. They even made seasoned employers tremble. Most of them were still unaware that they were destined to become compliant henchmen for Goebbels as part of his mighty propaganda apparatus in the not too distant future.

Wündrich-Meißen, too, lost no time in joining the NSRDW, which gave him automatic membership of the Reichskulturkammer, the state body that governed all creative industries in NS-Germany (radio, theatre, press, film, arts), and naturally he became a Nazi Party member. Even if he often felt a little uncomfortable that he had to 'run with the pack', nevertheless the fascination of being able to play a part in a great national enterprise still proved too strong. As far as its racial ideology was concerned, the Nazi approach to the advertising industry was relatively liberal in its early years, so any misgivings that might have arisen could be dismissed without much difficulty. Thus almost everyone who applied for membership in the Reichsfachschaft, the professional body for advertisers and commercial artists, was accepted – and that included quite a number of Jewish or 'Jewish-related' graphic artists. It was only after the *Reichskristallnacht* in November 1938 that the 76 special licences were revoked, on the basis of the 'decree for the exclusion of Jews from economic activity'.

This exclusion (*Ausschaltung*) from economic activity affected Jewish advertising people in Vienna much sooner and more strongly than their fellow Jews in the German Reich, as the Viennese advertising scene had always been more Jewish in character. According to a contemporary observer, of the 300 or so advertising agencies, prospectus dealers and advertisement offices (*Annoncenvermittlung*) that existed in Vienna in 1936, only about 10 were fully in the hands of non-Jewish owners (Glockemeier 1936: 78). After the unification of the German Reich with the Austrian state in 1938, Jewish advertising professionals were first marginalised, then dispossessed and later detained and killed. During 1938, Jewish advertising bureaus were plundered and/or sold to their German-Austrian rivals (*Arianisation*). Those market research and advertising professionals who had fled Austria since 1933, like Paul Lazarsfeld and Ernest Dichter, left behind a vacuum that the followers of the NS-ideology were only too happy to fill.

The most prominent representative of this section of opportunists was the advertising practitioner and marketing academic Hanns F. J. Kropff (see in detail Semrad 2004). Kropff, an Austrian citizen, had been an advertising manager for a large Cologne department store and various other German and Austrian businesses. From 1936, his star began to rise: he became Lecturer for advertising psychology and advertising strategy at Vienna Business School (Hochschule für Welthandel), and he represented Austria in the Werberat der Deutschen Wirtschaft, the central government council which regulated the German advertising industry. Like Wündrich-Meißen a member of the NSDAP, Kropff established his name with publications that attacked the 'Jewish-American' character of much contemporary advertising and which praised Goebbels's attempts at subjecting commercial advertising to total state control. In his 1934 classic on advertising psychology Kropff, for example, warned readers about the 'dangerous' and 'inconsistent' ideas of psychoanalytic advertising research and instead called for research that helped outline how and why the Germans had developed the deep wish to follow the 'Führer' and sacrifice themselves for the collective idea of nationhood (Kropff 1934: 4–5, 39–40). In his 1939 book, *Totality of Advertising*, Kropff projected an entirely new vision of advertising. Rather than promoting individual brands and products, advertising should be part of the total effort of the state to direct consumption; rather than helping 'private' industry interests, advertising should become an instrument of macro-economic policy (Kropff 1939: 5–12, 17–18). Naturally, the book was imbued with homages to the 'Führer' and 'Dr Goebbels'. In return for the ingratiation of the advertising elite, the NS-regime granted favours to those who toed the party line. In his 1965 book of anecdotes, Wündrich-Meißen gave a telling illustration of what a pampered elite the advertising practitioners, as specialists in persuasion, had become under the Nazi system:

> As 'NS-Reichsfachschaftswerber' (officially registered advertising professionals) we had a pennant on our car. It fluttered proudly on the right mudguard and, perhaps because it had been cleverly designed by experts, it made us look far more important than we actually were. It was the finest pennant that any Fachschaft [professional association] had ever had. A number of people stood to attention as we passed. Pub landlords in the smaller towns treated us like government ministers.
>
> (Wündrich-Meißen 1965: 109)

Unsurprisingly, in the closing phase of the Second World War there was a marked increase in the number of expressions of loyalty and devotion to the Nazi system emanating from advertising practitioners, together with crude vilification of enemy countries' propaganda. In 1943, Wündrich-Meißen himself had this to say:

> No matter how efficient American advertising men may be, if the political leadership cannot make the nation feel in its heart that war is a struggle for the existence of each individual, in other words, if the great flame of true national enthusiasm does not carry the broad masses with it, then the work of the advertising men – however technically good and valuable it may be in detail – will ultimately fail to deliver great national success. This is where the greatest problems for American wartime propaganda will lie. What they lack above all is a clear war aim. We have such an aim in the struggle against World Jewry, Bolshevism and the plutocracy – and it is decisive for the life and future of every one of us.
>
> (Wündrich-Meißen 1943)

14.4 A new age meets an old elite

With their particular experiences of the Nazi period, the old advertising specialists resumed work in the new Federal Republic of Germany. They had a free hand as there was no younger generation of qualified successors, and Jewish rivals of old like Ernest Dichter and Paul Lazarsfeld had emigrated or had been killed. When we look at their products, the verdict, especially with respect to the aesthetic quality of the work, can only be that in many cases the Nazi period lived on without a break. The didactic tone and advertising jingles reminiscent of children's books continued to dominate the columns of small ads and the advertising films during the 1950s. In view of the advanced age of this elite group of specialists, it is, of course, easy to understand their tendency to take up a position somewhere between the old and the new eras, and draw as much as possible on their accumulated store of professional experience. For the sake of appearances, however, at least with regard to organisational structures (the agency system), it seemed politic to align themselves with the United States as the victorious power.

Under the surface, though, they clung to the old ways with extraordinary tenacity. Never mind that the Nazi system as such had been politically discredited; from the point of view of the old advertising men with their Nazi mindset this had no relevance whatever for commercial advertising. In their heart of hearts, most of them were proud to have learned their trade in the spirit of the rich advertising tradition of Germany, rather than the 'new rich' American variety. Massive anti-American antipathies, like those that Johannes Schmiedchen expressed when he referred to the *Dollarikaner* (Dollar-Americans) in 1953, chimed with the mode of thought of this generation of advertising men:

> Today, American advertising specialists are spreading the idea that they lead the world in proficiency and success as advertising practitioners; and in Germany more than anywhere they have found a listening ear. Whether the Americans would have succeeded in coping so well with the difficulties that their fellow professionals in Germany have had to overcome 'with their hands tied behind their backs' is another matter. They have yet to demonstrate their ability to do this, and as good colleagues we would not wish it upon them to have to try.
>
> (Schmiedchen 1953: 19)

This privately cultivated feeling of superiority that resulted from belonging to an honourable, if misunderstood, German tradition could not, of course, be openly shared with the outside world. Yet from the mid-1950s, the mere mention of the name of Ernest Dichter was enough to arouse widespread condemnation of 'American' advertising methods.

Thus Hubert Strauf, who was responsible for the Coca-Cola advertising campaigns in West Germany, and had dealings with American clients on a daily basis, once said: 'Certainly I discussed many things with Ernest Dichter, but I always ended up doing things my own way' (Strauf 1989). Until well into the 1960s, the older generation of German advertising men determinedly held fast to the sender-oriented thinking based on the idea of the elite and the masses.

The words of Hans Domizlaff (1892–1971), a German advertising and brand consultant, are another clear proof of this. At the same time, they document a deeply felt fear of the person of Ernest Dichter. When asked in an interview whether or not the new motivational research was able to ascertain the motives for making a purchase and then document them for advertising clients, Domizlaff replied:

> From what I have so far seen and heard about motivational research – and this probably applies to Herr Dichter and others – it's just the same old platitudes, nothing that the professionals don't already know. It doesn't begin to explain what we in Germany have experienced. … Motivational research is such a complicated area that you cannot systematise it as the Americans try to do. It can't be done – thank God. Otherwise my job would be, well … 'under threat' is perhaps too strong; but there are certain things that have to be left to the judgement and instinct of the individual to a certain degree, the same as for the work of the artist. You can't systematise it.
>
> (Domizlaff 1959)

14.5 The dubious fame of the masters of influence

In Germany, it was not customary – and for many of those concerned it was far from desirable – to discuss the business of influencing the masses in public. To them, it seemed to make no sense to elevate those who were the object of the work of influencing to the level of equal partners in a discussion of the strategies designed to influence them. If ever there was a case for an elite to guard their privacy it was here, among the 'senders'. And even in the extremely rare cases where an ambitious advertising specialist looked out beyond his circle of fellow professionals and used technical considerations to underpin a complete theory of society or even the state itself, he usually failed to attract much attention. This, at least, was the bitter experience that befell Hans Domizlaff, author of no fewer than 18 books, after the Second World War. The titles of his books alone ought to have revealed to anyone that this author was concerned with more than just technical advertising knowhow. Here was someone who was aiming at nothing less than public trust, and who had created the universal instrument of the brand for this purpose. With such overriding goals it made no difference 'whether I am advising a business enterprise or the state itself'. This was a man who was thinking about the laws of style as the one and only force that could shape society, a man who had a concept of the philosophical and ethical foundations of an 'entrepreneurial state', and much else besides (Domizlaff 1931, 1939, 1950, 1952). Yet Domizlaff, who had hoped to make a name for himself as a veritable theoretician of society on the basis of his enormous productivity as a writer, failed lamentably in his endeavour. By the 1960s, he was as good as forgotten.

How different it was for Ernest Dichter, and yet he too had made efforts to achieve public recognition with scholarly works on social theory. It was, however, a work by another author that would make him famous and brand him a psycho-magician and master of mass persuasion. Vance Packard's 1957 book of popular science, *The Hidden Persuaders*, precipitated a social earthquake, the aftershocks of which could still be felt decades later (Packard 1957). It was an overnight bestseller, and it not only attracted an extraordinary amount of press coverage but, in Germany, also introduced a kind of Copernican revolution in the perception and evaluation of advertising in general (*Der Spiegel* 1957). Thanks to Packard, widespread public debate on the legitimacy and power of the strategies employed by advertisers became socially acceptable and the consequences were far-reaching. Hans Magnus Enzensberger's book on the 'Consciousness Industry', for example, would have been unthinkable without the debate surrounding Ernest Dichter and motivational research (Enzensberger 1960). In intellectual circles in particular, Packard's book was often quoted as evidence of the ethically reprehensible stratagems of capitalism and/or US imperialism. Much of the nomenclature of left-wing social criticism such as 'manipulation', 'late capitalism', 'false needs' and 'consumption terror' are the product of these ideas.

The fervour of the public debate gradually became a problem for the older German advertising men. On the one hand, they did not share Dichter's fame but, on the other hand, they were automatically damned by association. It is understandable that, given the unfortunate situation into which the whole sector had been precipitated through no fault of its own, Dichter was subject to a good deal of personal resentment. In order to enhance his own image and protect the entire advertising industry from harm, the Head of Advertising at the Hoechst company even felt obliged to give his autobiography the title 'I was not a Hidden Persuader' (Damrow 1981; Gries 1999).

This suited Ernest Dichter nicely. He was not responsible for Packard's book, but it brought him worldwide fame and in Germany it gave him the most effective springboard he could have wished for. It opened up new business prospects at a time when he had just reached the symbolically significant age of 50. Yet, the publicity created by Packard's book naturally played into the hands of those who since the 1930s had tried to 'clean up' German and Austrian advertising and rid it of its Jewish and American influences. Like Japanese knotweed, indestructible and slowly growing, the NS-advertising elite raised its head again and by the mid-1950s once more dominated much of German advertising research. Hanns F. J. Kropff, who had been ousted from his post in 1945, became Director of the Institute of Advertising Research in Munich in 1949, President of the Institute of Industrial Research in Vienna, and Professor in Advertising at the University of Frankfurt/Main in 1954, where he taught until 1961 (Semrad 2004). Old NS networks helped him and many others return to influence and power after 1945. Kropff's 1934 book, *Psychology in Advertising*, was republished in 1951 under the title *New Psychology in New Advertising* (Kropff 1951). In 1957, Kropff co-organised a workshop on Ernest Dichter and Motivation Research at which the participants mainly seemed to have been interested in character assassination. The later doyenne of German opinion polling, Elisabeth Noelle-Neumann, who herself had benefited from NS university scholarships and had written for Goebbels's house magazine *Das Reich*, used the workshop to rubbish Dichter's methods wholesale as being neither useful for clinical nor for statistical research (Becker 2007; Kropff 1960: 411; Noelle-Neumann 1963: 271). A few years later, Kropff once again attacked Dichter for not having familiarised himself sufficiently with the research literature on consumer motivations that had emerged in Germany since the mid-1930s (Kropff 1960: 410–411). The nasty cynicism hidden in this attack is truly astounding: Kropff, who played a major part in 'Arianising' Vienna's advertising and market research industry since 1936 criticised Dichter, the Jewish refugee, for having fled his perpetrators.

In terms of the market conditions in Europe and in particular in West Germany, the point in time of Dichter's arrival on the scene in the old continent could scarcely have been more propitious. It was almost as if Germany was just waiting for him. This was because unlike the United States, where modern consumer society had been developing continuously since the 1920s, in Germany the market had entered a period of rapid change in the mid-1950s. The catching-up phase was finally over as the basic consumer needs of even the poorer sections of the population had been met. In the early 1960s, new trend-setting aspirational consumer groups emerged, not from the working-class background of the reconstruction generation but from the white-collar milieu with its desire to impress and its ambitions of social advancement. This brought a fundamental change in general consumer attitudes, whereby catch-up consumption increasingly gave way to prestige consumption. As the supply of goods had significantly expanded by this time, in many areas the market was characterised by fierce competition. Increasingly, the problem was to achieve optimal positioning for products and services through quality of experience and communication ('added benefits'). The focus of attention was on the consumer's psyche. Dichter and his collaborators in subsidiary offices in Zurich, Munich and Frankfurt completed nearly 500 motivational research studies and proposals for German companies, mainly between 1960 and 1973. Among others, his German clients comprised the likes of Mercedes Benz, Siemens, Schwarzkopf, Braun, Salamander, WMF, Quelle, Ford, Dr Oetker, Columbus Line, Schott and many other large- and medium-sized German companies. Without Motivation Research, Western German advertising of the 1960s and early 1970s would not have been what it was.

14.6 Motivational research and the German Advertising Trade Press

Never before had a public discussion had such an effect on the debate within the industry as in the case of Ernest Dichter. It was a new and unfamiliar experience and led to great uncertainty. This is the impression that we gain from the debate about motivational research in the advertising press, for example, in the industry journal *Die Anzeige*. As late as 1954, the term was not even mentioned. Then, between 1956 and 1958, there was an explosion of reporting and argument, a development that resulted in the journal showing increasing respect for the trend and even introducing a new section headed 'Market, Motivation and Consumer Research'. The year 1959 marked the climax and turning point. This was the year when motivational research became hotly and intensively debated – so much so that the editors of *Anzeige* felt obliged to pay due reverence to the increased importance of the new miracle discipline by instituting a section headed 'Advertising Psychology/Motivational Research'. In the very next year, however, motivational research forfeited its stand-alone status, and between 1961 and 1967 the section in question was known as 'Market, Sales, Motivation and Consumer Research'; in other words, motivational research was accorded only the rank of a subdiscipline within the broader academic subject heading. Undoubtedly, Rosser Reeves's book, *Reality in Advertising* (1961), which delighted Dichter's critics in the United States and was also influential in Germany, had a decisive part to play in this turnaround. By 1968, the inclusion in *Die Anzeige* of 'Motivational Research' as a separate section was no longer on the agenda.

In terms of content, the articles dealing with 'motivational research' confirm that the emotional excitement it had aroused in the early 1960s was beginning to wane. At first, there was a perception characterised by admiration and reservation in roughly equal proportions, and this is reflected in the conduct of the debate. One article was entitled 'Opportunities and Limitations of Motivational Research' (*Die Anzeige* 1957a). Another was headed 'Motivational Research – New Approach or New Gimmick' (*Die Anzeige* 1957b). In 1958, critics returned with increasing frequency to the threat of mutual exclusion or annihilation between Motivation Research and market research, which was believed to have been forced on to the defensive by the former and was perceived as more 'German' than the modish Motivation Research. The topics covered included 'Motivational Research and Conventional Market Research' (*Die Anzeige* 1958a) and 'Motivational Research – an Important Sub-Division of Market Research' (*Die Anzeige* 1958b). From 1959 onwards, the polemical undertones of the debate can be more clearly heard, as in 'Motivational Research Under Fire' (*Die Anzeige* 1959) and in 'Masquerade and Shady Tricks' (*Die Anzeige* 1963).

In the industry journal *Der Markenartikel*, reception of motivational research was even more muted than in *Die Anzeige*: questions were asked like 'Where does Motivational Research Stand Today?' (*Der Markenartikel* 1958). The journal's critical stance is also made plain with a title like 'Motivational Research. Problematic Sciences' (*Der Markenartikel* 1960). An article headed 'Immoral Motivational Research' (*Der Markenartikel* 1959) reported on a conference in Rüschlikon in Switzerland, at which 'the American depth propagandists were already on the defensive'. According to the report, several participants had taken exception to the use of manipulation, expressing the view that 'trying to eliminate or drown out the consumer's conscious judgement raised ethical problems and could undermine personal responsibility'. Many had defiantly proclaimed: 'We should not allow ourselves to be intimidated by American fairy tales.' In the following years, too, opinion seemed to have been predominantly critical. In 1962, for example, there was a demand for 'Motivational Research with an Eye to Reality' (*Der Markenartikel* 1962) and time and again there were calls for it to be relativised or indeed subsumed.

In contrast to the sceptical and polemical attitude displayed in the specialist journals mentioned above, discussion of motivational research in the *Werbe-Rundschau*, edited by Wündrich-Meißen, was more open-minded and positive. Moreover, the sensitivity with which it was treated was significantly greater than in the rival journals. Number 52 of the *Werbe-Rundschau*, 1962, for example, dealt in detail with Ernest Dichter. The name of Ernest Dichter frequently cropped up as the author of lengthy articles in the *Werbe-Rundschau*. As early as the end of 1957 the *Werbe-Rundschau* called for a conference on motivational research, and in the following issue, under the heading 'Fashionable Doctor of the Economy or Charlatan? Motivational Researchers between Scylla and Charybdis' (*Werbe-Rundschau* 1958a), the journal reminded orthodox market researchers that they 'had yet to confront Dr Dichter with their arguments'. In December, Wündrich-Meißen stepped forward to tackle the question of motivational research personally with a contribution entitled 'Is the Effect of our Techniques of Persuasion Growing Stronger – or Weaker? A Dialogue between Advertising Practitioners'. But he only wanted to admit 'proper' motivational researchers as participants in the dialogue:

> It would be interesting to hear the views of motivational researchers on this (but only those that speak from a wealth of practical experience). As far as I am concerned, I believe that you can only awaken demand for the product for a short time in this way. The name of the product must be linked with a firmly based rational idea of the product – as well as the workings of the unconscious. Both emotional and rational reasons for making a purchase must work together if a healthy and long-lasting demand for a product is to be created.
>
> (*Werbe-Rundschau* 1958c)

This is the creed that Wündrich-Meißen subsequently repeated time after time, namely the importance of synthetising 'German' and 'American' advertising methods. In other words, motivational research needed to be complemented by other methods. In several large-scale books, which at the same time represented a cross-section of the work of his advertising agency, Wündrich-Meißen tried again and again to show what this meant in practice for professional advertising. In these books, which were lavishly illustrated with many examples of advertisements and which he gave to many of his clients, Wündrich-Meißen spoke about the scientific method of motivational research, while stressing that in order to achieve the maximum effect they would have to be combined with other methods (Wündrich-Meißen 1961, 1963).

German advertising experts attacked motivational research on the grounds that it was not exact, that it was too subjective, and that the number of test persons was too small to draw reliable conclusions. What better than to set up a debate between eminent experts on the merits of motivational research. In late February 1958, such a confrontation took place in the main hall of the Institute of Business Management in Frankfurt/Main. The doyen of classical German market research, Georg Bergler, and Ernest Dichter were pitched against each other to debate the question: 'Motivational Research or Market Research?' Once again it was the *Werbe-Rundschau* that published a detailed report on this gladiatorial contest. But what Ernest Dichter had to say about the birth, self-image and method of work of motivational research in front of the assembled experts had a disarming effect on those present and on his opponent, Bergler. Rather than interpreting current debates in terms of a confrontation between traditional, quantitatively oriented market research and newish Motivation Research, Dichter saw both research activities as complementary:

> We very often collaborate with market research and opinion polling institutes. I am not so arrogant as to claim or wish to give the impression that motivational research is the last word or that motivational research is the only way forward. The aim of market research is generally to establish the facts. In motivational research we ask: What can we learn from this for the future? How must we tackle the problem in order to find a solution? Our investigations are by no means purely academic. We are more concerned about combining the two approaches. Market research describes what is. Motivational research looks for the links between things and tries to draw conclusions about what measures need to be taken to solve a problem. Our main interest is diagnosis and therapy. The sort of questions we ask are 'What goes on in the heads of customers or potential customers? What is the attitude of these people towards certain views, activities or issues? What are the unconscious factors that guide them? How can we influence them more strongly?'

Why are the market researchers so jealous of motivational research? Why do they reject it? Why do they oppose it? We must always remember that if market research alone had been able to achieve the tasks it had been set we should never have needed to try motivational research! We always start with the word 'why' and always finish with 'how to'. Why do people act in this or that way? Why do they drink this coffee and not that other one? Why do they drive this car rather than that other one? When you ask the 'why' question you reveal the strangest puzzles. It is, of course, interesting that according to our research 72 per cent of car buyers choose the same car time and again. But it is more important and more revealing to know why they do this!…Our conclusion is that emotional factors are more important than rational factors.

(Werbe-Rundschau 1958b)

What his opponent, Georg Bergler, the grand old man of German market research, had to say in response merely confirmed that Ernest Dichter, with his shrewd psychological approach, had touched a raw nerve when he talked about jealousy. Like a rabbit in the headlights, Bergler could not help focusing on the 'American invention', instead of tackling the substance of the matter. If anyone thought, he announced, that motivational research was anything new then they were mistaken. Long before Dichter, researchers had investigated consumers' motives for buying, especially in connection with the Society for Consumption Research in Nuremberg (GfK), founded in 1936. These days, he said, it was constantly being put about that many methods of economic research had been first discovered in America. In the debate, Bergler quoted the typewriter and the sewing machine as examples for how European inventions took roots in the American market first and were then re-exported to Europe as allegedly 'American' products (*Werbe-Rundschau* 1958b).

14.7 Conclusion: Dichter's methods infiltrate the German market

Despite Bergler's, Noelle-Neumann's and Kropff's attempts at branding Ernest Dichter's theories as foreign, 'American' and 'un-German', there are a number of German star brands which carry the hallmark of Dichter's marketing methodology. Wündrich-Meißen's advertising agency in Stuttgart, for example, established a permanent research department as early as the mid-1950s. Undoubtedly, his close familiarity with Dichter's theories and methods gave Wündrich-Meißen a keener sensitivity for what is today known as brand personality or product personality. Take, for example, the idea that products have a gender, and that this gender should affect, even predetermine, the style in which it is presented through the advertising medium. The older German advertising practitioners were not familiar with this idea, at least not in such a radical form. Ernest Dichter had developed a consistent body of methodologies that allowed him to position a brand based on the emphasis on the gender of a product. He employed this marketing and positioning tool when he developed the motif-psychological concept behind probably the biggest success in the chocolate market in German post-war history, the Milka brand. In two comprehensive studies, he had worked out the basis for the brand communication of this chocolate, which was consciously designed to be feminine. The marketing of Milka chocolate, which since the early 1970s was systematically developed along feminine lines ('the sweetest temptation since the invention of chocolate') ensured the product a continuous expansion of its market share in particular vis-à-vis its rival, Ritter-Sport chocolate, with its strongly masculine image (Dichter 1972, 1973).

A few years previously, Hans Wündrich-Meißen had been faced with a problem the solution to which likewise depended on giving serious consideration to the question of the specific gender of the product and how best to exploit it to achieve the maximum market potential. For decades in Germany, there was general agreement that spirits like brandy, for instance, were drunk almost exclusively by men, and that – for a whole range of reasons based on social psychology and cultural history – it would never enter anyone's head to even consider targeting women as potential purchasers and consumers of a product like this. Accordingly, all the brands of this particular spirit in Germany were given a masculine positioning. In particular, the Asbach brand took pride in a veritably martial image in the product publicity, whether in the trenches of the First World War, a hunting party of landed gentry pursuing a wild boar or as an accessory to a managers' card game. For decades, all Asbach's competitors in Germany, dazzled by its success, blindly followed its lead. They never caught up with it; but neither did it ever occur to them that an unusual, feminine positioning might open up quite new consumer strata.

Hans Wündrich-Meißen was the first to offer the German consumer market a feminine brandy in the shape of the Chantré brand. Paradoxically, it was because its positioning was so diametrically opposed to that of Asbach that it was able to open up undreamt-of market potentials. In the 1960s and 1970s, Chantré became a hit, its slogan 'die weiche Welle' ('the smooth wave') fulfilled Dichter's basic aim to assuage any feelings of guilt for enjoying a luxury product, and represented a specifically feminine way of addressing the public, which had grown out of the personality of the product. The very name of Chantré hinted at a quite different world, that of the French gourmet culture, poles apart from the dour world of the Asbach fraternity. One could almost be forgiven for thinking that Chantré was only a liqueur and not a hard drink at all. The guilty conscience we all suffer whenever we partake of anything with a high percentage of alcohol was ritually soothed and anaesthetised by the continual background music of the 'smooth wave'. Even today, a good 20 years after his death, Hans Wündrich-Meißen is still believed by many to have turned tens of thousands of German housewives into alcoholics with his magic slogan. But that is another story (Schindelbeck 1995).

References

Becker, J. 2007. Zu den Memoiren von Elisabeth Noelle-Neumann. *Vorgänge* 180: 124–144.

Berghoff, H. 2003. 'Times change and we change with them.' The German advertising industry in the 'Third Reich': between professional self-interest and political repression. *Business History* 46 (1): 128–147.

Damrow, H. 1981. *Ich war kein geheimer Verführer: aus dem Leben eines Werbeleiters.* Rheinzabern: Gitzel.

Der Markenartikel 1958. No. 3: 153–156.

——— 1959. No. 10: 856–859.

——— 1960. No. 5: 394.

——— 1962. No. 1: 46–48.

Der Spiegel 1957. Die Einflüsterer. 7 August.

Dichter, E. 1972. *Bericht zu einer Motivstudie über Schokoladen im allgemeinen und die Marke Suchard bzw. Suchard/Milka im speziellen.* Ernest Dichter Archive, University of Vienna, Report No. 2413C.

——— 1973. *Bericht zu einer qualitativen Untersuchung der Milka-Werbekonzeption 1972 (in Kombination mit einer teilweisen Überprüfung unserer Grundlagenstudie 1971.* Ernest Dichter Archive, University of Vienna, Report No. 2699C.

Die Anzeige 1957a. No. 5: 362–364.

——— 1957b. No. 10: 796–801.

——— 1958a. No. 4: 286–288.

——— 1958b. No. 4: 288–290.

——— 1959. No. 2: 106–108.

——— 1963. No. 15: 14–17.

Domizlaff, H. 1931. *Die Propagandamittel der Staatsidee.* Hamburg: Altona-Bahrenfeld.

——— 1939. *Die Gewinnung des öffentlichen Vertrauens. Ein Lehrbuch der Markentechnik.* Hamburg: Hanseatische Verlags Anstalt.

——— 1950. *Brevier für Könige, Massenpsychologisches Praktikum.* Hamburg: Dulk.

———— 1952. *Es geht um Deutschland. Massenpsychologische Stichworte für eine sozialpolitische Reform.* Hamburg: Dulk.

———— 1959. Eine Marke soll dem Verbraucher eine klare und lebendige Vorstellung geben – warum Vertrieb und Werbung so oft verschiedener Meinung sind. Ein Interview mit Hans Domizlaff. *Werberundschau*, Nos 32 and 33.

Enzensberger, H. M. 1960. *Einzelheiten. Part 2: Bewusstseinsindustrie.* Frankfurt am Main: Suhrkamp.

Glockemeier, G. 1936. *Zur Wiener Judenfrage.* Wien: Günther Verlag.

Gries, R. 1999. Zum Selbstbild westdeutscher Werbeunternehmerin der Nachkriegszeit: eine ideologiegeschichtliche Bestandsaufnahme. In: G. Schulz (Ed.), *Geschäft mit Wort und Meinung: Medienunternehmer seit dem 18. Jahrhundert.* München: Oldenbourg, 251–274.

König, T. 1927. *Reklame-Psychologie: ihr gegenwärtiger Stand, ihre praktische Bedeutung.* München: Oldenbourg.

Kropff, H. F. J., Randolph, B. 1928. *Marktanalyse: Untersuchung des Marktes und Vorbereitung der Reklame.* München: Oldenburg.

———— 1934. *Psychologie in der Reklame als Hilfe zur Bestgestaltung des Entwurfs.* Stuttgart: Poeschel.

———— 1939. *Totalität der Werbung. Ein Beitrag zur Vorbereitung ihrer Rationalisierung und zum Einbau in die neue Absatzlehre,* Berlin: C. Heymann.

———— 1951. *Neue Psychologie in der neuen Werbung. Methodische Grundlagen für die praktische Anwendung.* Stuttgart: Poeschel.

———— 1960. *Motivforschung. Methoden und Grenzen.* Essen: Girardet.

Noelle-Neumann, E. 1963. *Umfragen in der Massengesellschaft.* Reinbek bei. Hamburg: Rowohlt.

Packard, V. 1957. *Die geheimen Verführer. Der Griff nach dem Unbewussten in jedermann.* Düsseldorf: Econ.

Reeves, R. 1961. *Reality in Advertising.* New York: Knopf.

Regnery, C. 2003. *Die deutsche Werbeforschung 1900–1945.* Münster: Monsenstein und Vannerdat.

Rücker, M. 2000. *Wirtschaftswerbung unter dem Nationalsozialismus: rechtliche Ausgestaltung der Werbung und Tätigkeit des Werberats der Deutschen Wirtschaft.* Frankfurt/Main: Lang.

Schindelbeck, D. 1995. 'Asbach Uralt' und 'Soziale Marktwirtschaft': Zur Kulturgeschichte der Werbeagentur in Deutschland am Beispiel von Hanns W. Brose (1899–1971). *Zeitschift für Unternehmensgeschichte* 40: 235–252.

———— 2003. Pionier der Werbewirtschaft. *Damals* 35 (4): 62–65.

Schmiedchen, J. 1927. *Neues Handbuch der Reklame.* Berlin: R. Wicher.

———— 1953. *Kurzer Beitrag zur Geschichte der deutschen Wirtschaftswerbung, ihrer Männer, ihrer Organisationen, ihrer Presse.* Tübingen: Werkring Verlag.

Semrad, B. 2004. Vertrieben, verdrängt oder vergessen? Die 'Wiener Schule' der Werbeforschung und ihre fachhistorsichen Implikationen. In: S. Averbeck, K. Beck, A. Kutsch, U. Nawratil (Eds), *Grossbothener Vorträge zur Kommunikationswissenschaft, V.* Bremen: edition lumiere, 135–164.

Seyfferts, R. 1929. *Allgemeine Werbelehre.* Stuttgart: C. E. Poeschel.

Strauf, H. 1989. Interview with the author, 4 January 1989 (transcript in possession of author).

Weidenmüller, H. 1926. *Vom Begriffbau der Anbietlehre*. Berlin: Industrieverlag Spaeth & Linde.

Werbe-Rundschau 1958a. No. 24: 5–12.

——— 1958b. No. 24: 107–110.

——— 1958c. No. 30: 210–216.

Westphal, U. 1989. *Werbung im Dritten Reich*. Berlin: Transit.

Wündrich, H. 1992. Wirtschaftswerbung während der NS-Zeit. *Geschichtswerkstatt* 25: 4–12.

Wündrich-Meißen, H. 1927. *Der Prospekt als geschäftliches Werbemittel*. Wien: C. Barth.

——— 1943. Die Einschaltung der amerikanischen Werbefachleute in die Kriegspropaganda. *Wirtschaftswerbung* 5: 85.

——— 1961. *Systematische Erarbeitung des Werbeerfolgs*. Gerlingen-Schillerhöhe: Wündrich-Meissen Agentur.

——— 1963. *Rationale Konsum-Neuigkeit und emotionaler Wunschtraum als Synthese künftiger Bedarfweckung*. Gerlingen-Schillerhöhe: Wündrich-Meissen Agentur.

——— 1965. *Werbers Anekdotenbuch*. Stuttgart: Conradi Verlag.

15

'Victim of a Technical Hitch…': Ernest Dichter as Proprietor of a Guesthouse with Bugging Installation

Dirk Schindelbeck

From the memoirs of the German advertising expert Hans Wündrich-Meißen – abridged and newly arranged by Dirk Schindelbeck

In his autobiographical novel 'Kerner becomes an adman', the German advertising practitioner Hans Wündrich-Meißen alleges to have met Ernest Dichter in the United States as early as 1932. In his function as senior manager of the Berlin-based (Jewish) advertising agency 'Rudolf Mosse', Wündrich-Meißen visited the New York subsidiary of the agency in order to inspect American advertising methods from close range. Although it is impossible to establish whether Wündrich-Meißen really visited New York at that time, it is clear that American advertising practices fascinated and influenced him. The novel appeared in a serialised form in Wündrich-Meißen's magazine, *Werbe-Rundschau*, during 1957 (Nos 19 to 29) and charted his career between 1924 and 1945, a time that saw his rise to become one of Germany's foremost advertising men. The central character of the novel, Erwin Kerner, is Wündrich-Meißen himself. But there are other familiar characters, too: we read about the antics of Dominikus von Mitzlaff' (Hans Domizlaff) and about an advertising researcher in New York, a Dr Potter (Ernest Dichter). Other characters kept their real names, like Heinrich van Bracht (Director of the Cologne office of the Mosse agency), Paul Faßnacht (Director of the New York office of the Mosse agency) and Alfred Politz (Director of the Mosse headquarters in Berlin).[1]

The reason why Wündrich-Meißen moves the timing of his first encounter with Dichter back to 1932 – when Dichter was still in Vienna – and, thus, before the rise to power of Adolf Hitler in Germany, are to be found in the author's desire to disconnect himself from his relationship to the NS regime. Like many other Germans, Wündrich-Meißen was an opportunist rather than a staunch supporter of the national socialists. His magazine *Werbe-Rundschau* welcomed the new regime, he became Lecturer at the Höhere Reichswerbeschule in Berlin (the central NS government training school for advertising professionals in Germany between 1935 and 1945) and he collaborated in NS progaganda activities, like the 'Kohlenklau' campaign (a NS government energy savings campaign). By bringing the date of his first visit to the American advertising world and his first meeting with Ernest Dichter forward to 1932, Wündrich-Meißen was able to present himself as an early, liberal transatlanticist. Notwithstanding, his account of American advertising practices is rife with references to sexual stereotypes which are, of course, meant to suggest a close relationship between 'American' Motivation Research and the more dubious aspects of Freudian psychoanalytic theories.

In the following extract from the novel (taken from: *Werbe-Rundschau*, Nos 23 and 24/1957), Wündrich-Meißen describes Ernest Dichter as a kind of mysterious 'magician at the controls', who, in order to optimise his method of motivational research, opens a guesthouse in New York's Central Park, where he uses his unwitting guests as guinea pigs for an experiment in his 'emotional theatre'. For the purposes of market research, Dichter listens in as his guests express their honest opinions, as opposed to what they might tell an interviewer, on products such as tea, soap or aftershave that apparently just happen to be lying around in the guesthouse rooms – and whose function in reality is to act as a stimulus. That way, the German advertising practitioner Wündrich-Meißen appears to draw a parallel between the entire American advertising world – motivational research in particular – and the organisation of Nazi propaganda, characterised by emotional stimulation and secret observation, with no respect for human dignity or even the most intimate human needs.

'We wanted to accommodate you in a typical American hotel,' said Faßnacht, 'but right now a reunion of war veterans from all over

America is taking place here. There's not a bed to be had in any of the hotels; the only room we could find that was definitely available was this little guesthouse run by our friend Dr Potter. It's a kind of hobby for him, which may be the reason why it's so extraordinarily well looked after. Don't you agree, James?'

The butler nodded, gave a slight bow and said: 'Very true, Mr Faßnacht.' Kerner thought he could detect a hint of a mocking smile on the crumpled face. 'Which are the rooms for the gentlemen from Germany?' 'Numbers four and six, if that's all right, with a view of the park.' Kerner noticed that the butler (who was speaking in German) had a slight Austrian accent.

'Fine – we'll wait here in the hall. Please inform Dr Potter that his guests have arrived.' Faßnacht led the new arrivals to a corner seat as the butler, with a quiet 'Very well, Mr Faßnacht', disappeared from view behind a half-closed curtain, moving with measured tread. Kerner turned round once again. The butler opened a door to a brightly lit room. Kerner caught a brief glimpse of a short man in a white coat wearing a pair of headphones. In the background, he noticed a large switchboard. Quickly the door was closed.

'Please take a seat, Herr Kerner!'

Faßnacht touched a bell push and a pretty chambermaid, wearing a short lacy skirt, came into the room. 'Would you bring the tea please, my child,' said Faßnacht, speaking in English and giving the girl a wink at the same time. She made an embarrassed curtsy and disappeared. 'A little surprise, you'll find out in a minute.' Kerner and Bracht were beginning to feel slightly uncomfortable. Faßnacht seemed to notice: 'There may be something about this house that seems a little strange to you. Please don't get the wrong idea. This is merely an unusual establishment, but you'll very soon feel perfectly at home here. As I said, a hobby for an extraordinary man. Ah, here he comes!'

The men stood up and were introduced to Dr Potter.

It was the man from the strange control room into which the butler had disappeared. He had changed out of his white coat and was now smartly dressed in a dark suit and an old-fashioned stiff collar with a dove-grey tie. The shape of his head was that of an intellectual. Piercing yet kindly dark eyes behind gold-rimmed spectacles fascinated the onlookers. A small, almost feminine hand was extended to Kerner and van Bracht.

Dr Potter took his seat beside them and the girl set out the tea things without a word. She poured the tea. 'Cold tea? And so weak?' thought Kerner. Van Bracht too seemed surprised. 'Your health!' said Faßnacht.

Kerner and van Bracht sipped cautiously and tasted whiskey. Faßnacht chuckled at the joke he had played on them and then immediately became the obliging businessman. 'Dr Potter is a friend of our firm and a colleague. He is a psychologist of the Vienna School. Over there at the Mosse agency they do a lot of work with psychologists. Perhaps you are not yet familiar with the motivational research that we practise. But we'll come back to that later. . . . '

The doorbell rang. The butler went to the door and welcomed more guests, a respectable older couple with their handsome and virtuous-looking daughter. Kerner was reassured by the sight of them. Dr Potter got to his feet to welcome the guests and instruct the butler to see to their every need. When he had returned to the table Faßnacht laid out the programme for the coming days. 'Well, gentlemen, after I've told you a little about our work – and there's unlikely to be much that you don't know already – you will probably be ready to retire to bed. You can only make comparisons, have a look at new methods and pick up a few tips. We meet again in my office in the morning.' Kerner, who had a notepad open in front of him, was jotting things down, while van Bracht was still enjoying his tea. Kerner asked: 'Is eight o'clock OK for you?'

'Not at eight, gentlemen!' shouted Faßnacht, 'only cleaners and company presidents have any right to be at work at that time of the morning. Let's say – after nine.' Dr Potter interjected: 'Paul, don't forget you've got the radio recording of Crooney's soap opera to do tomorrow. That would be interesting for our guests. I'm sure that would be new to them!' 'Many thanks, doctor. Yes – I've been racking my brains to think what I could show them. Thanks to Politz, the Crawford people and other foreign influences the agency service in Germany has come such a long way in the service area that there's very little they can learn from us.'

Van Brach spoke next.

'We've been doing some thinking too. You see, the rise of the agency system has caused an upheaval within the German advertising industry. We didn't realise that we in Europe had learned so much – we only need mention Mataja, and the posters – that we were already almost mature enough to have an agency system of our own. All it would take was one small step. The response we met with in Germany, however, was the usual one that all revolutionary innovations come up against: people took fright and decided to go on the defensive. Associations were founded to protect their interests against the progressively minded people who were promoting the agency system. Many advertising managers in large companies started to fear for their influence and their positions if the virtuoso agencies were able to offer employers more creative opportunities than they themselves could. We who work in the agencies are beginning to be maligned as Jewish lackeys' – he looked at Kerner – 'and being too pally with foreigners. Few advertising consultants recognise the inevitability of the development. Despite the need for cooperation only the individualist has a future.'

Dr Potter, who had been eyeing Kerner and van Bracht with studied casualness, suddenly asked: 'How old are you, Herr van Bracht?' Van Bracht reacted immediately and said in a matter-of-fact way: 'Forty – or twice twenty, if you like; two lives, Dr Potter – who knows if there'll be a third.' Kerner noticed that Potter and van Bracht both looked at each other as if they knew what he meant. Then van Bracht went on: 'Politz sees the political and economic development clearly and correctly. Prosperity will bring people together. Hitler and his people will give the Germans bread and circuses so their dream of a return of the good old days seems to be coming true. Hitler will be a surrogate Kaiser and everyone will be well off. The advertising business will not suffer too badly. But – if I may be a little dramatic – the outposts of the agency idea won't survive. They are Jewish and foreign. That alone is a death sentence. And they rely too strongly on the performance criterion. In their world, no feeble advertisement is allowed to slip through, as might otherwise happen, and no one turns a blind eye if someone slips up – because the competition is just waiting to pounce! They don't understand that in Germany yet, and that's why quite a few otherwise very dear colleagues are not sorry to see the brownshirts gaining ground.'

Embarrassed silence. Kerner noticed that no one had anything positive or comforting to say. Dr Potter was the first to speak: 'Would you gentlemen care for a little fresh air in the park? You can collect the house keys from James – and by the way, you can call him Johann if you like. We try to make it feel like a private house here. There's no night porter.' He stood up: 'I wish you good night. I hope I shall be able to tell you something about my work too. Depth psychology gives us some strange and wonderful insights for our advertising. Doesn't it, Paul?' Dr Potter smiled at Faßnacht, then with a bow he walked briskly across the fine Kirman carpet and disappeared behind the curtain. 'Strange chap but I quite like him', thought Kerner, whilst Faßnacht, who was just pouring another drink, murmured: 'He's a bit of an oddball. Disciple of Freud. But extremely important for us. He has a terrific motivational research method; I really must tell you about it; heavens above, I almost forgot! That really would have been something. …' At that moment, the telephone on the table in front of the curtain started ringing. Quick as a flash, James, or Johann, appeared and answered it. He put his hand over the receiver and said, in a dignified manner: 'It's for you, Mr Faßnacht.' Faßnacht went over, sat on the edge of the table and telephoned. The two friends looked at each other but said nothing. They both felt, without being able to put it into words, that there was something mysterious about the house.

'Perhaps it's just that it's new, and it's the first evening,' said Kerner quietly and glanced over at the butler, who was busying himself with the flowers in the hall window, 'tomorrow everything will look completely different. There's been such a lot to take in. Do you feel terribly tired too?' 'Well, it certainly isn't a house of ill repute. Whatever it might be, the main thing is, it's like a home from home. . . . Your very good health, my dear Kerner.' They drank each other's health from the highly alcoholic teacups.

Faßnacht moved over to join them. 'I have to be off now. There's something not quite right with the manuscript for the radio broadcast. Now I shall have to write it myself with my poor little hands. The two copywriters are at the end of their tether because the client keeps demanding more changes. – What else did I want to tell you? Oh I know, about Dr Potter and his house, yes, you absolutely must be told about that – if only I had time. . . . ' The butler had come close to Faßnacht and said obsequiously: 'If you don't mind, Mr Faßnacht, your taxi is here.' 'All right then – there'll be plenty of time tomorrow. Goodbye, gentlemen, and sleep well. Whatever you dream about in the first night will come true.' Faßnacht was led out by the butler. He quickly returned. He had keys in his hand.

'If I may, gentlemen, I should like to show you to your rooms.' It was like an order. They stood up and allowed themselves to be led up the stairs. On the walls of the staircases and halls hung beautiful old engravings of Vienna, London and Paris. The house breathed culture, as the saying goes. Everything was neat and clean, stylish and homely. Kerner was the first to be taken to his room. A comfortable-looking double bed waited invitingly. Under the benevolent gaze of the butler he bid goodnight to van Bracht. [. . .]

In the morning Dr Potter's guests met in the breakfast room. A table had been reserved for Kerner and van Bracht in the corner of the room, which was furnished in the sober American style of the early nineteenth century. Kerner was surprised that such upright seats could be so comfortable.

Van Bracht was arriving late. There was the older couple with the charming daughter. Proudly and quietly they waited for their breakfast to be served. In the middle of the room sat a group of what appeared to be college girls, whose chatter was just about bearable for the motionless family. The bundles of books secured with a strap identified them as students. Further to the left Kerner saw an old gentleman with the air of a professor, reading a large book. At the next table, a young couple were billing and cooing. Obviously honeymooners. Kerner waited for van Bracht. The breakfast trolley was wheeled in. Under the watchful eye of the butler two girls, who could have come straight from Hollywood, served the guests with orange juice, grapefruit, coffee, toast and ham.

The two German guests were just being served breakfast when van Bracht entered the room. He looked around shyly, caught sight of the butler and ran quickly over to Kerner; he sat down and leaned forward over the table. 'Morning, Kerner, don't ask me anything. We'll talk later.'

The butler seemed to be observing them constantly. It all made Kerner feel quite uneasy. Hastily the two of them gobbled down their breakfast and left the room. Once outside the door of the building van Bracht spoke: 'Kerner, I have a confession to make. Last night I had a visitor in my room. A lady. [...] She left around daybreak without anyone noticing. As soon as I was sure she was safely out I went back to my room. As I got undressed I accidentally dropped my collar stud. I looked for it and found a strange opening above the skirting board, hidden behind an inconspicuous grille. And I discovered several more. In the room, near the bed, in the bathroom and in the toilet. There were little microphones in there!' Kerner could scarcely believe his ears. As they walked along Fifth Avenue van Bracht carried on talking hurriedly and excitedly. 'This Dr Potter has installed bugging devices. I don't know what possessed him to put us there! I shall give him a piece of my mind. I shall telegraph Politz!' Kerner laid a hand on his shoulder to calm him down. 'Please don't upset yourself. You could be mistaken. It could all be a misunderstanding. Faßnacht will explain everything. He'll have to.'

'What if this Potter chap has got some ulterior motive? You know nothing about the *Deutsche Bund* here in New York, a thoroughly right-wing organisation that's been influenced by the National Socialists. And I'm a Jew!' 'Oh give it a rest!' snapped Kerner. 'Don't keep talking about it. It seems to me it's more than just your religion, you've got a complex about it!' [...]

Van Bracht seemed a little relieved: 'Fine, thank you – but now to Faßnacht!' At the corner of 58th Street the two admen hailed a taxi and gave the address of the agency. In silence, they allowed themselves to be driven through the maze of streets. In front of an austere building of stone and glass they got out. Compared to this the modern Mosse building in Jerusalemer Straße in Berlin, splendid though it was, seemed more like a suburban villa. Clearly, the Mosse office did not occupy the whole building. Lawyers, doctors, theatrical agencies and film studios were listed on the large noticeboard in the entrance hall. An elevator whisked them up to the 12th floor. They entered the reception hall of Mosse New York. A serious-looking, well-built girl with a certain muted sex appeal, wearing black horn-rimmed spectacles to emphasise her importance, took their cards and made a telephone call to announce their arrival.

The walls were adorned with magazine advertisements in heavy baroque picture-frames, testimony to the achievements and social prestige of the company. Illuminated by indirect light, a structure composed of glass tiles glowed like an altar, each tile bearing a different company logo: the basis of the 15 per cent.[2] 'You are awaited, Mr van Bracht and Mr Kerner.'

Miss Muted Sex Appeal pressed a button and like an 'Open Sesame' a door moved in front of them. They went into a more brightly lit room in which two young ladies with quite undeniable sex appeal were sitting. One of them stood up and, revealing a magnificent set of teeth, said teasingly: 'Follow me please…' and sashayed ahead of them down a long corridor decorated with glass cabinets in which packaging designs were displayed to admiring visitors like jewels. They were only too happy to follow, as they were eager to speak to Faßnacht. Another door was opened, a Chippendale room, and in the middle, in front of the massive desk – Dr Potter.

Seeing a mixture of indignation and astonishment on the faces of van Bracht and Kerner, the psychologist immediately raised his hands in a conciliatory gesture. He went towards the visitors and held out his hand, which Kerner shook but van Bracht declined with a curt bow. 'I have done you a great wrong, Herr van Bracht,' began Dr Potter, sounding remorseful yet still somehow self-assured, 'you have fallen victim to an unfortunate technical hitch for which no apology can make amends. There are only two things I can do – first, explain everything, and second, destroy the recording, which has caused me great embarrassment.'

He went to the desk, picked up a record and smashed it over his knee till all that remained were tiny pieces. These he threw into the waste paper basket. 'You have my word, Herr van Bracht, that this was the recording that was made by mistake last night in your room. I'm not deceiving you. I would not hold it against you if you had that suspicion.' Van Bracht looked past Potter at the window, behind which the Manhattan skyline towered over them like a range of mountains.

The two Germans had not spoken a word. Motioning to two armchairs, Dr Potter invited them to sit down. Then, placing his thin splayed-out fingers together, he began his lecture. 'If you wish to apportion blame then my butler bears some responsibility, but to a greater extent I myself am to blame, as I forgot to inform James that it was only by chance that you came to my house, not like the usual guests, who are actually experimental subjects for my research. Please understand: if through my observations I divest homo sapiens of the epithet "sapiens", this does not mean that I am failing to show respect for human dignity. It is all in the interests of science and everything is treated as confidential.…Unfortunately, not everyone is equally scrupulous. I happen to know that my method is utilised by scandal magazines, gossip columns and by certain divorce lawyers. I even know of a detective agency that specialises in such things.'

With a gesture of his hand he seemed to want to sweep these aspects aside. 'You may be thinking in terms of psychologism and violation of privacy. You are on the wrong track, gentlemen! Look at it this way. If we want to test certain articles, say soap or aftershave, using the old direct method, then prestige thinking leads to rationalisation; the experimental subjects tell lies when questioned, without realising it. We need the complete openness that you find between married couples or good friends, colleagues or lovers. So we have this homely guesthouse, and by way of a welcoming gesture from the management we offer a bar of bath soap with an exciting fragrance for the lady or a bottle of some interesting new aftershave for the gentleman. Or a jolly bunch of college girls are presented with a plate of snacks – tasty little titbits – that they have never tried before, or perhaps we might leave a delicate piece of lingerie for a young bride.…All we need is the audio.'

'Starting from the initial emotional reactions to our innovations, we return, so to speak, to the motivational stimulus. It's all an extremely interesting psychological experiment, which, together with other tried and tested methods, will help to enhance the quality of our motivational research.' He paused for a moment. Kerner could almost see the flag on his mast flying high again after remorse had lowered it. 'Copy writing – that is, putting words together after you have

learned how people are put together.' That was the flag. . . . Despite this thoughtful conclusion, Kerner could not resist making a sarcastic comment, especially as van Bracht was still standing there motionless:
'Well we certainly learned plenty on our first day . . . '

Notes

1. Hans Domizlaff (1892–1971) was a German graphic designer and advertising consultant who contributed to the development of German adverting thought between the 1920s and the 1950s. He defined advertising as a marketing technique of building public trust. He also pioneered the idea of advertising as part of brand building (Markentechnik). His largest clients were Siemens and the Hamburg cigarette makers Reemtsma. Alfred Politz was born in Berlin in 1902 and, after graduating with a doctoral degree in theoretical physics, worked for the German Mosse advertising agency. Like Dichter, he fled to the United States in 1937 where he initially worked for Elmo Roper. By the 1950s, Politz had become one of America's foremost market researchers who promoted the development of sampling techniques (random sampling) in American social and market research. In the text, Wündrich-Meißen also refers to 'Crawford' in Berlin; this is the English W. S. Crawford agency, which during the late 1920s opened dependencies in Berlin and Paris.
2. Unlike European advertising agencies, American agencies received a remuneration of 15 per cent of the value of advertising placed by the agency. Their European counterparts, often much smaller agencies, had to manage with a much smaller service fee.

Part V
Conclusion

16
Motivation Research – Episode or Paradigm Shift? From Ernest Dichter to Consumer Ethnography, Neuromarketing and Bio-power

Stefan Schwarzkopf and Rainer Gries

16.1 Dichter, America and the politics of desire

Reflecting upon the central tenets of his work and the greater meaning of his life, Ernest Dichter once admitted that material possessions, wealth and money would not lead to happiness. Instead, he recognised that happiness was a shifting idea that had its sources in hobbies and close family relations as much as in perceived economic success (Dichter 1979: 190). Did the great motivator, America's hidden persuader, the twentieth century's original guru of consumer marketing finally see the errors of his ways and become an advocate of alternatives to high-pressure capitalism? Well, hardly. To the very end, Dichter remained committed to his strategy of using motivational research to turn consumers' and citizens' 'misery of choice' into a set of activities invested with enjoyment and dreams of fulfilment (Dichter 1960a: 242). What he called the 'strategy of desire' indeed marked an epochal step in the development of Western societies in general and of modern consumer culture in particular. Given the salience of the issue of consumerism in current debates about American cultural dominance, globalisation and human autonomy, it is of importance to review the role of Ernest Dichter and of Motivation Research in the making of the way we live now.

As our contributors have argued, Dichter's research practices and publications helped usher in an era that put the consumer at the forefront of activities in commercial markets and in public affairs alike. While much consumer and advertising research before the 1930s saw consumers mostly as reactive and passively open to marketing stimuli, Dichter was

269

enthused by the idea of an active and libidinal consumer. In this vision, the consumer had the potential to get to know and thus manipulate for their own ends the libidinal economy that drove their decision making. Manufacturers and advertisers had to recognise that consumers were the main actors in the market place because they created meaning around products and this meaning was ultimately responsible for allocating a distinct position for a product on consumers' mental maps. Although consumer researchers like Burleigh Gardner and Sidney Levy (1955) quickly realised that this mechanism gave advertisers even more powers over consumers since advertising spent millions of dollars in strategically manipulating symbols in the marketplace, Dichter's indefatigable optimism saw an opportunity of liberation even in crowded and mature markets where intense brand competition was rife. Consumers' ability to reflect on their desires and selectively enjoy their urges gave them the ultimate weapon in the relentless struggle between rationality and the emotions.

Rather than trying to escape the market place with its ever-present danger of being manipulated by dexterous advertisers, Dichter wanted consumers to engage even more in market exchanges in order to rid themselves of rationalisations and inhibitions, which he saw as the real psychological enslavers of human kind. Only a person who was able to accept the inescapable reality of desires would be able to use them to their advantage. To achieve this state of enhanced self-knowledge, consumers had to adopt a more proactive and optimistic attitude towards the product choices they made: 'We are only gradually freeing ourselves from the tyranny of things. To do this more effectively we must understand the role these objects play in our human and consumer motivations' (Dichter 1964: viii). Or, in the words of David Bennett, Dichter sent the 'Id' instead of the 'Ego' to go shopping in the belief that the former would help consumers to breathe freely among the myopia of choice, while the latter would only strangle them in its attempts at cutting down the bill (Bennett 2005).

The chapters of this book presented reinterpretations of Ernest Dichter's life and the making of post-war consumer culture. While Dichter, a genius in self-marketing, presented himself often as a revolutionary, an outsider and nonconformist, it has become clear that his take on the consumer psyche was part of a whole movement to discover how consumers and citizens made decisions in situations characterised by imperfect information distribution regarding product benefits and perceived utility. It has also become clear that Dichter's seemingly unique interest in the emotional, subconscious and immeasurable side of consumer behaviour had a history running back to at least the 1930s, when the first outlines of a more holistic understanding of consumers emerged (Allen 1941; Dichter 1947b; Levy 2008). Despite his phenomenal media presence, it would be wrong to label Dichter as the 'Father of Motivation Research' as often done. Those searching for the origins of Motivation Research will have to seek the grail in the transatlantic research constellation that emerged in Vienna and New York around Paul Lazarsfeld, in Chicago around Pierre Martineau and Sidney Levy, and in Nuremberg at the Society for Consumption Research (GfK) around Paul Vershofen (Fullerton 2009; Levy 1999; Schwarzkopf 2006).

In parallel to Ernest Dichter's interpretation of consumer motivations, there emerged a whole host of schools and individuals whose influence is yet to be discovered and contextualised. Among them were the Tavistock Institute in London (Miller and Rose 1997), Paul Lazarsfeld's former wife Herta Herzog in the United States (working for McCann Erickson), Joseph Wallace Wulfeck of the Advertising Research Foundation (Wulfeck 1945; Wulfeck and Bennett 1954) and the group of motivation researchers in Chicago that included Lloyd Warner, Burleigh Gardner, Sidney Levy, Steuart Henderson Britt, Pierre Martineau, Dik Warren Twedt and Louis Cheskin (Fullerton in this publication; Packard 1957: 25–42). This group of researchers was an immensely influential contemporary alternative to Ernest Dichter's Freudian interpretations of consumer behaviour. Yet, were it not for Sidney Levy's attempts at keeping their legacy alive they would hardly be remembered today (Levy 2003, 2005). By focusing entirely on Ernest Dichter rather than acknowledging the full scale of competition among post-war consumer researchers, historians are of course in danger of granting posthumous PR victories to the most relentless self-marketer of them all. It was his outstanding dexterity at self-marketing and his ability to get embroiled in controversies which secured Dichter both his prominent place in post-war popular culture and denied him a seat at the high-table of academia – a fact he was well aware of.

Dichter is perhaps also better remembered than his competitors because he decided to take such an active stance in the cultural Cold War. Unlike all other motivation researchers, he used his research activities to popularise the idea that the American notion of consumer culture could bring the world's 'free' nations together in a peaceful pursuit of common happiness. Interestingly, though, we also saw how hard he worked at selling the 'American way of life' to American consumers in the first place. Before spreading his gospel in Europe, Africa and Asia, Dichter convinced the puritan American middle class that they were not simply purchasing a pack of cigarettes or a car but that the indulgence in new products alleviated the neuroses and anxieties caused by the suppression of their desires. American consumers had to be convinced that the eruption of their libidinal energies in the supermarket could bring political meaning, economic might and a sense of social purpose back to a superpower that was in danger of losing itself in the quagmire of self-doubt.

By helping white, middle-class Americans to throw off the moral baggage their ancestors had brought with them from Protestant Europe, Dichter helped America to return back to the centre of the world. His research and his popular writings reconnected America to the moral debates surrounding consumption and behaviour that preoccupied European social scientists at the time when Dichter and many other Jewish intellectuals left Europe. Historians have detected a distinct element in America's political and economic culture from the late nineteenth century, which led many political and corporate leaders to believe in America's civilising mission: a nation that could use commodity exports and commercial innovations in foreign diplomacy as a way of bringing about a commonwealth of freely trading democracies which in turn were guided not by military power but by America's moral leadership (de Grazia 2005; Mennell 2007). Unlike any other market and consumer researcher, Dichter set himself up right at the spearhead of this civilising mission, albeit a mission that first of all had to 'civilise' America by using 'liberated' consumerism to make this nation fit for global leadership.

While there were several schools of 'depth' or motivational research in Europe and the United States since at least the 1940s, Dichter's role in the making of post-war consumer society was significant. Unlike Paul Lazarsfeld, for example, Dichter was much more interested in constructing a holistic and complete picture of consumers and their behaviour in a given social setting. He was of course careful enough never to systematically spell out the tenets of his construct as, for instance, done by Abraham Maslow (1943). Well knowing that empiricists would have ripped his model apart after a few Ford- or Rockefeller-funded research projects, and well versed in the Freudian notion that the meaning of attitudes is negotiated between analyst and analysand, Dichter defined Motivation Research as a renaissance-style memory theatre, a kabbalistic museum and cabinet of curiosities filled with ad hoc methods and ideas. Like the seventeenth-century Jesuit polymath Athanasius Kircher, Dichter believed that brain and mind were analogous to a theatre in which a perennial drama gets played out (Breidbach and Ghiselin 2006;

Dichter 1944; Yates 1966: 320–331). Accordingly, Dichterian Motivation Research was at times a bizarre but always fascinating mix of Freudian psychoanalysis, Old Testament and post-war self-help 'ego' psychology, which allowed researchers to make (commercial) sense of the psychic drama of pleasure, guilt, repression, transubstantiation and redemption.

This rather colourful collection of theoretical and methodological approaches to the consuming subject made Dichter an unlikely yet influential pioneer of the transition of American corporate culture. His weighty and occasionally erratic presence in post-war popular culture symbolically moved the consumer towards the centre of the stage at a time when corporations desperately tried to find a holistic model of consumers that helped them cut through the seeming irrationality of their behaviour and thus minimised the risks involved in new product launches and new advertising campaigns. Dichter's Motivational Research therefore acted like a signpost at the crossroads of post-war commercial culture, when consumers became both more powerful and more elusive. By the 1950s, corporate marketers had woken up to the fact that it was not enough to simply sell what people needed and wanted, but new needs and wants had to be created all the time in order to stay ahead of the competition. In the costly battles between increasingly similar products and services, like washing powders, cigarettes, soft drinks, cars and retail outlets, brands had to be turned into symbols that promised much, much more than merely functional benefits (Cheskin and Ward 1948; Collins and Montgomery 1969; Levy 1959). Motivation Research à la Dichter offered solutions to both problems: it helped detect and overcome consumer resistance in the battle between pleasure and guilt and create new desires. It also promised to lay open the hidden realm of the consumer subconscious, thus allowing marketers to find out where and how consumers located their product offerings on their mental maps.

16.2   Motivation Research today – end of a story?

It is therefore not surprising that Dichterian Motivation Research today is, if not forgotten, a theoretically largely unreflected body of thought right at the core of the marketing discipline. When asked about the relevance of Ernest Dichter for today's marketing communication practitioners, Lois Pavlis of the Viennese market research company Joe & Co. answered that one could as well ask an electrician about the relevance of Thomas Edison for his profession (Lahm 2007: 100). The basis of the paradox is clear: without Edison, the electrician's job would not exist, and yet Edison's pioneering inventions have been usurped into the ubiquitous daily practices and infrastructures of the cords, cables and appliances we all take for granted. Ernest Dichter is therefore both everywhere and nowhere in the structures of today's theories and practices of marketing and consumer culture.

Nothing would be further removed from reality than to assume that Dichterian Motivation Research was dead and irrelevant for our times. A hard and searching look at some 'mainstream' marketing textbooks used in business schools today reveals that Dichter's consumer typology, for example, his typology of consumption motives (power, masculinity, security, individuality, status, femininity, reward, disalienation) and his holistic view of the interaction between brands and consumers did indeed survive the rise and rise since the 1960s of an empiricist and mainly strategy-oriented orthodoxy in the marketing faculty (Baines et al. 2007: 111–112; Solomon 2007: 196–200; Usunier and Lee 2005: 92–93, 548–549). This orthodoxy felt increasingly uneasy about the wide-ranging interpretative freedom that motivational researchers of the Freudian type allowed themselves in analysing consumption situations. Interpretative freedom necessarily resulted in a view of consumers as essentially complex, unmanageable and uncontrollable. Consumer researchers of the generation that followed Dichter were bedazzled by the opportunities that statistical modelling seemed to offer and created a view of the consumer as a measurable and thus controllable variable in strategic marketing management (Collins and Montgomery 1970; Kassarjian 1971; Kotler 1965).

Since the mid-1990s, however, marketing as a social science has undergone its own postmodern turn, which resulted in prominent consumer researchers questioning the management- and strategy-oriented microeconomic theories of consumer behaviour that often saw consumers as rational but passive information processors. With the arrival of postmodern marketing theory, Barbara Stern, Russell Belk, Elizabeth Hirschman, John O'Shaughnessy, Morris Holbrook and many others have hailed a reawakening interest in Motivation Research and in Ernest Dichter in particular (Belk et al. 2000; O'Shaughnessy and O'Shaughnessy 2003: 71–81, 2008: 37–41; Ratneshwar and Mick 2005; Ratneshwar et al. 2000; Stern 1990, 1998; Thompson 1993). Dichter himself realised that the tension between the statistically more rigid models of consumer behaviour and his own, somewhat 'looser', approach to the essentially elusive consumer clashed over the question of interpretation. Anticipating the intellectual quarrels following the cultural turn in marketing research and consumer studies by about three decades, he argued that the social sciences in general were 'prematurely concerned with techniques rather than with interpretation and understanding' (Dichter 1960a: 55). In many ways, this verdict chimes with the unease currently felt across many sections of the marketing faculty about the discipline's lack of conceptual clarity, which makes it prone to bogus empiricism and 'pure' measurement for measurement's sake (O'Shaughnessy 2009: 80).

Postmodern marketing research with its cultivated scepticism about notions of rationality and its sensitivity towards the socially and culturally constructed nature of models of consumer behaviour is therefore well placed to reappropriate Dichter and Motivation Research. The same faction in consumer research that sees consumer behaviour as holistic and irreducible has also given rise to a renewed interest in ethnographic consumer research methods. Interestingly, Dichter and his contemporaries already noted the remarkable similarity in method and outlook between Motivation Research and cultural anthropology. In his popular handbooks on consumer motivations and in his autobiography, Dichter put himself directly in the tradition of Mircea Eliade, Maurice Rheims and Margaret Mead (Eliade 1952; Rheims 1959). Dichter and Mead communicated with each other on various occasions and frequently discussed each other's research methods (Dichter 1964: 37–41, 1979: 159). The basis of this shared interest was that both researchers used long-term observation rather than laboratory-style experimentation to investigate the interaction between people and the objects that surrounded them.

Like Margaret Mead, Dichter saw that people – 'civilised' and 'native' – assigned agency to the objects that surrounded them: 'Anthropological literature, when it concerns itself with objects and their symbolic meaning in various cultures, often enters into the field of the soul, the meaning of objects' (Dichter 1964: 95). As early as 1947, he presented himself as a cultural anthropologist when he secretly filmed cigarette smokers in New York and tried to analyse the way they lit cigarettes and held them in their hands in terms of their membership of social classes and their unconscious need for security and self-rewards (Dichter 1947a: 86–99). In a letter that Mead sent to Dichter, the anthropologist assured him: 'I have been studying the natives in New Guinea and Samoa and you have become fascinated with the natives of New York' (Dichter 1979: 46). Letters and conversations such as these were of course a highly prized form of legitimisation for the embattled Motivation Researcher. Putting himself in the vicinity of the progressive queen of anthropological research in the United States, Dichter presented himself essentially as a cultural anthropologist who did for the 'American tribe' what the anthropologist did for the 'primitive Trobriand Islanders or far-off Samoans' (Dichter 1964: 39–42).

Following the resurging interest in, but also frustrations with, dominant models of lifestyle and psychographic segmentation of consumers, the late 1990s have once again seen a growing attention paid to ethnographic methods in consumer research. The ethnographic perspective on consumer behaviour, too, rejects an 'anatomistic, overly individualistic, information processor view of people as individuals who are to some extent sealed off and separated from their experiental worlds' (Cova et al. 2007: 5). Like Ernest Dichter, consumer ethnographers see all human life as essentially social and its confusing complexity as incomprehensible when seen purely through 'modern' structures like class, age, gender and income (Winnick 1961). Unlike the 'nose-counters' (Dichter) among consumer researchers, consumer ethnographers immerse themselves in specific, individual case studies of brand–consumer interaction and use a wide range of interpretative methods to unpick how products assume symbolic and social significance in consumers' lives (Arnould and Price 2006; Cova and Elliott 1998; Durgee 1991; Firat and Shultz II 1997; Hirschman 2007; Holbrook 2005; Mariampolski 2006, 2007; McCracken 2005).

Motivation Research has also seen a comeback in some sections of what is today called neuromarketing, an area devoted to the study of the neuropsychological foundations of consumer behaviour. Neuromarketing seeks to use non-invasive imaging techniques, for example functional MRI-scanning (fMRI) and electroencephalography (EEG), to find correlations between cognitive processes with regard to advertising and brand exposure (perception, attention, memory) and neuronal activity patterns in certain parts of the brain. Proponents of neuromarketing have measured how stimuli like advertising slogans, presentation of faces or price reductions in advertisements lead to increased activity in brain areas that are responsible for processing emotions (*n. amygdala*) and in areas that become involved in experiences of success and reward (*n. accumbens*). Neuromarketing, however, comes in a variety of forms and disguises and does not always involve a focus on the micro-level of neuronal activities. There also exists a remarkably innovative border area between micro-level neuromarketing and meso- and macro-level applications of cognitive psychology in marketing research. The latter have seen an astounding rise and led to research that investigated how music causes humans to bond and how this can be used by marketers in the retail environment to stimulate human bonding with products and brands. Readers will at this point, hopefully, activate their neocortices and remember how Ernest Dichter installed a gramophone-based sound system in his uncle's department store in the late 1920s (Egidi et al. 2008; Knutson 2007; Lee et al. 2007; Levitin 2006; Page and Raymond 2007; Penn 2007).

Some commentators have raised the point that neuromarketing is in danger of once again approaching consumer behaviour in a rather mechanistic fashion by focusing on neuronal activity only, by that confusing correlation and cause. Ernest Dichter would surely have been horrified by the reductionist epistemologies of some proponents of neuromarketing. And yet, much of the current neuromarketing and neuroeconomics research has brought the emotions and seemingly 'irrational' behaviour back on the agenda of consumer research (Figure 16.1). Our knowledge of how consumers are emotionally stimulated by their

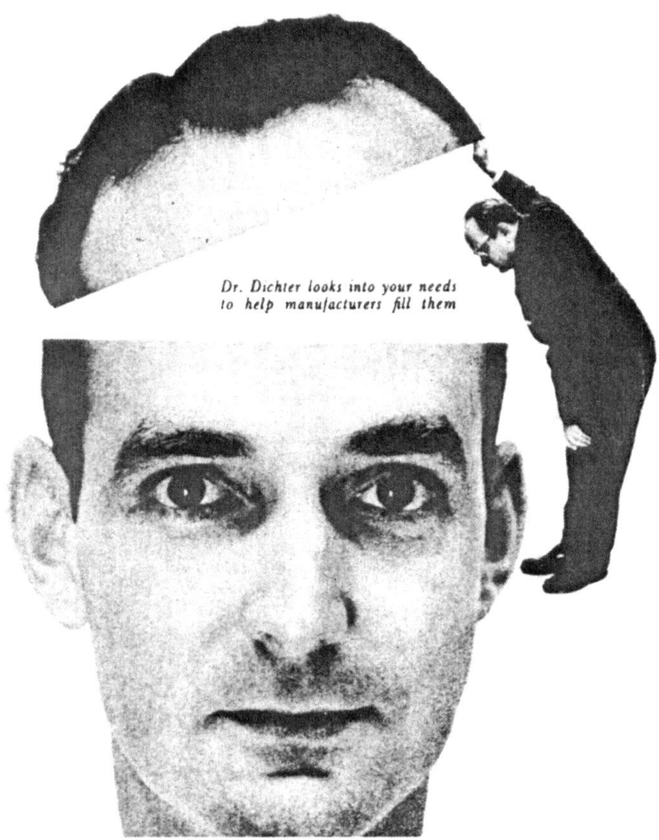

Figure 16.1 'Ernest Dichter looks into your needs', *c*.1960.

environment has led to the emergence of the field of multi-sensory marketing. Rather than bombarding consumers with visual messages and with information that is most likely to be processed by their neocortices, marketers today try to slip stimuli into consumers' subconsciouses through the ears and the nose: the smell of freshly baked bread from a supermarket in-store bakery has a measurable effect on a store's overall food sales and the sound of freshly laundered sheets being folded has already been used in some American supermarkets to promote the sales of detergent powders. A number of airlines, like Buzz (KLM) and Singapore Airlines have developed a corporate smell in addition to their corporate logo and corporate image. Increasingly, companies develop corporate sounds as well. It is indeed breathtaking to see how close popular marketing debates are once again to the holistic, subconscious and emotional gospel once preached by Dichter in the 1950s. The German marketing consultant group Nymphenburg, for example, recently found that men prefer straight and edged packaging whereas women prefer soft and rounded forms, and the London advertising consultant Mark Earls argues that product marketing is best done in such a way as to create group effects among people, that is, through word of mouth and shared experiences that give people a wider social goal to strive for. Plus ça change! (Dichter 1966a; Earls 2007; *The Economist* 2008; *Wirtschaftswoche* 2006).

In this new research environment, it is of little surprise that Freudian influences raise their heads again. A prime example for this is Gerald Zaltman's Metaphor Elicitation Technique (ZMET). Once described as the 'mutant methodological lovechild of Ernest Dichter and Walt Disney' (Brown 2005: 12), Zaltman's ZMET technique is built on the assumption that consumer behaviour models based on the idea of rational decision making are deeply flawed. Zaltman, a professor at Harvard Business School, claims that some 95 per cent of the thinking that drives consumer behaviour occurs unconsciously and that the unconscious is a hidden store of visual metaphors that influence our behaviour. In order to make that body of unconscious thought more accessible and decode the metaphorical thinking of consumers, Zaltman argues that metaphor research is the best means to uncover both conscious and unconscious goals and motives that drive consumer behaviour. Influenced by a mix of Jungian psychoanalysis and semiotics, Zaltman's research explores which metaphors (balance, transformation, social connection, container, resource, control) consumers use to make sense of their environment. Some beer brands, he argues, stand for social connection (exemplified in Budweiser's 'Whassup!' slogan), while others promise transformation for more individualistic consumers. Tuning in better to consumers' metaphors will connect a brand closer to its target market according to Zaltman (O'Shaughnessy and O'Shaughnessy 2004; Zaltman 1997, 2003; Zaltman and Coulter 1995; Zaltman and MacCaba 2007; Zaltman and Zaltman 2008).

After many decades of advertising and marketing research being dominated by the *homo oeconomicus*, the unconscious, the emotions and with them, in the words of Robert Heath, the 'hidden powers' of advertising are back in all their glory (Callebut 1994; Dijkesterhuis 2005; du Plessis 2005; Gladwell 2005; Gobé 2001; Gordon 2006; Hansen and Christensen 2009; Heath 2001, 2007; Heath and Hyder 2005; Holbrook 1988; O'Shaughnessy and O'Shaughnessy 2003, 2008; Shiv 2007; Pincus 2004; Rapaille 2006; Thomas 1998a, 1998b; Travis 2000; Wegner 2002; Wilson 2002; Woodside 2006). It is too early yet to make out precisely what place this new generation of market and consumer researchers will allocate to Ernest Dichter and whether Motivation Research will one day be acknowledged as a legitimate building stone in the long history of market research and of consumer psychology.

With the most heterogeneous European origins in Gestalt psychology, psychoanalysis and the philosophy of the Vienna Circle, Dichter became part of the rising tide of social science-oriented market research and consumer psychology during the 1940s and 1950s. After two decades of fame and success for Motivation Research, the 'integration of the richness of Motivation Research studies and the tough-mindedness and statistical sophistication of computer technology led to another type of research involving personality, variously called psychographic or lifestyle research' (Kassarjian 1971: 413; Lazer 1963; Plummer 1974; Wells and Tigert 1971). This, in turn, led to Dichter's Motivation Research being increasingly sidelined. This tendency was aggravated with the onset of the 'cognitive revolution' that led to the paradigmatic dominance of the cognitive sciences in the 1980s. The late 1990s finally witnessed the rise of what is now called 'affective sciences', which assume that many phenomena, ranging from individual cognitive processes to social behaviour, cannot be understood without taking into account motives, attitudes, moods and emotions (Davidson et al. 2003). While laboratory-based and statistically validated measurement techniques are today at the heart of virtually all research into consumer behaviour, the human sciences have come full circle by acknowledging the emotional and social basis of cognitive processes.

From the brief historical overview presented above, it is clear that we are once again at a turning point in our understanding of consumers and of markets. At such turning points, it is worthwhile looking back at earlier partings of the ways, at key drivers in the past and the way they oriented themselves. In his classic study on Motivation Research, Vance Packard, for instance, already predicted that by the year 2000 Motivation Research would look old-fashioned and outdated as a new generation of bio-technicians was more likely to use 'hard' bio-psychological methods to control people instead of the 'soft' investigative methods employed by Dichter and other motivation researchers: 'By then perhaps the biophysicists will take over with "biocontrol", which is depth persuasion carried to its ultimate' (Packard 1957: 195). In his dystopian vision, Packard predicted nothing less than the arrival of what Michel Foucault later termed the age of bio-power (Foucault 1981: 139–141). Foucault used the term to describe techniques that try to achieve the subjugation of bodies and of populations, that means disciplinary techniques that accustom the body and mind to surveillance, self-control, self-regulation and, above all, greater 'self-efficiency' in economic processes. On the macro-level, these techniques involve state intervention in economic production, but also in demography, public health and consumption.

Motivation Research and (state) capitalist bio-power were indeed never far apart. When visiting South Africa in the late 1950s, the South African government asked Ernest Dichter if his research techniques could help 'motivate' Bantu tribes to plant sweetcorn. Apparently, the colour yellow was a taboo for members of the tribe so they would not go anywhere near a sweetcorn field, not to mention plant, harvest and eat the yellow vegetable (Dichter 1964: 363–369). This request by the apartheid government came at the same time as a South African tobacco company employed Dichter's research institute to help them sell more cigarettes to the Bantu people. In 1959, the *New Yorker* magazine told its readers:

> Ernest Dichter...has practically cornered the motivational market. One of his assignments on his trip was making a motivational analysis of the smoking habits of the Bantus in South Africa, in order to coach a tobacco firm how to sell the Bantus more cigarettes. Dichter reported that more and more countries are switching to American psychological values which emphasize 'the good life' even though they reject the American label and philosophy on the products they buy. This indicates that our selling techniques abroad need to be revised. Dr Dichter's firm is now engaged in 'intermotivational' rather than 'intramotivational' research among 15 countries, weaving these

strands into meaningful patterns which their clients can understand and use to sell more merchandise, and bring the world closer to a psychological United Nations.

(McKelway 1959)

Although Dichter was always careful to describe his trade as part of the social sciences' wider attempts at understanding humanity and human behaviour, in reality he had nothing less in mind than a redefinition of the human self as such. For Dichter, this new self was to be based on acquisition, possession and consumption. As early as 1947, he declared that goods had to be seen as *the* modern way to express, expand and negotiate one's personality: 'It may soon be customary to describe an individual's personality not by referring to him as one who is timid or self-conscious or characterised by any other traits, but rather, for example, as one who wears an Adam hat, drives a Plymouth car, drinks PM whiskey, and wears Arrow ties and shirts' (Dichter 1947a: 212–213). In the global battles of the liberal political-economic system with its Fascist and Communist enemies, Dichter prescribed all democracies this cure of consumerism as the best way to create citizens with well-balanced character traits and a set of motivations that made them leer at their own prestige, status and ego-fulfilment rather than at the glorification of collective entities like nation state, race or class. For this reason, his work needs to be understood in much wider terms than as that of an eccentric or media-savvy 'consumer guru'. His life and work serve as a guidebook to the transformations in human self-knowledge in general during the twentieth century.

16.3   Dichter, anthropology and the disembedded consumer revisited

Ernest Dichter's research marks both an end and a beginning in the middle of the 'century of the consumer': the popularisation of his take on Motivation Research ended the dominance of traditional forms of market segmentation along demographic lines (class, sex, income and geography) and ushered in a focus on the symbolic exchanges that take place between consumer and brand (Cohen 2004: 292–331). It took the mainstream marketing community until the mid-1970s at least to fully appreciate the implications of this shift (Bagozzi 1975). Understanding the marketing and consumption process through the cultural anthropological lens as symbolic exchange elevated the consumer from merely being a passive 'buyer' and 'user' of a product to becoming an active creator, maker and investor in a symbolic relationship between human soul and what Dichter termed the soul of the product (Dichter 1960a: 145–147; Gabriel and Lang 2006: 44–63). As we have seen, marketing and motivation researchers like Dichter appropriated Mead's and Levi-Strauss's cultural anthropology in order to make sense of the symbolic relationship that emerged in the consumer markets they studied. The influx of cultural anthropology into the field of marketing research from the 1950s made it of course opportune to project essentially Western visions of consumption and consumer behaviour back onto non-Western societies and to imagine the world as one giant marketing opportunity for Western products.

As early as 1962 – that is, 20 years before Theodore Levitt's ground-breaking article on the globalisation of markets – Ernest Dichter described the outlines of a new being, the 'world customer', who would finally bring about this brave new world (Dichter 1962, 1963; Levitt 1983). Dichter predicted that national cultural differences between con-sumers worldwide were in terminal decline as the world's people came closer to each other and more consumer products moved across borders. At the heart of this assumption was Dichter's idea 'that an understand-ing of cultural anthropology will be an important tool of competitive marketing' (Dichter 1962: 113). Dichter's plan of proposing Motivation Research as a global solution to the question of what made citizens and consumers tick finally seemed to come together. Based on Freudian psychoanalysis and a curious mix of cultural anthropology and holistic Gestalt theory, Dichterian motivation analysis offered to lift all human beings out of their regressive embedding in cultural, religious, national, racial and political ties and declared them – as consumers – to be the rulers of a new world in which traditional boundaries and separations no longer mattered.

Behind the 1960s' parlance of optimism apparent in Dichter's sem-inal article on the world customer, a logic was at work which Roland Barthes had probed for its ideological content just a few years ear-lier. In his *Mythologies* (1957), the French philosopher argued that the bourgeoisie worked like an anonymous society of joint stock-holders: bourgeois values infiltrated society anonymously and secretly, without declaring itself as 'bourgeois' or as the product of a certain, histori-cally contingent, set of social relationships determined by power, class and exploitation. Bourgeois value became thus 'naturalised' as histori-cal contingency and accident were declared to be 'eternal' and 'human nature'. As an economic fact, the bourgeoisie was named and definable without difficulty: 'capitalism is openly professed' (Barthes 2000 [1957]:

126). But as a cultural ideology, the bourgeoisie obliterated its name. In that 'ex-nominating operation', the bourgeoisie became defined as 'the social class which does not want to be named' (ibid.). According to Barthes, the upper middle class spread its values across all areas of popular culture until all aspects of daily life, like films, readings, weddings, forms of cultural production and consumption, 'the cooking we dream of, the garments we wear' (Barthes 2000 [1957]: 128), came to be seen as the 'normal' and 'natural' expression of all human life and 'only one single human nature [was] left' (ibid.: 127). This single human nature ('eternal man') was based on social and cultural norms which were perceived as the evident laws of a seemingly natural order: 'It is as from the moment when a typist earning twenty pounds a month recognises herself in the big wedding of the bourgeoisie that bourgeois ex-nomination achieves its full effect. . . . A conjuring trick has taken place; it has turned reality inside out, it has emptied itself of history and filled it with Nature' (Barthes 2000 [1957]: 130, 131).

In order to perform this trick, the bourgeoisie needed conjurers and one of the smartest of them, Ernest Dichter, entered the stage by changing ideas of human nature before our eyes. While Packard and other critics were outraged by the way Dichter proposed to help General Motors sell more cars, they allowed their eyes to be distracted from the real magic performed in front of them. After Dichter was finished with them, large parts of the American public really believed that consumer desires and repressions as described by the great motivator were the natural and normal representation of what human nature per se was about. In order to perform this trick, Dichter needed an epistemological framework that allowed him to present Motivation Research as an activity that laid open a universal psychic structure that determined consumer behaviour. Both Freudian psychoanalysis and cultural anthropology provided him with such a framework. There are of course human universals, like shame, sexual attraction and certain forms of aggression. But Dichter's trick was to invent 'consumer desire' as such a human universal which could be unlocked for the benefit of economic growth, the spread of democracy, social development and peace. Ingeniously, he made people forget that the uninhibited, object-focused desire for products as redeemers of the repressed soul was a historically contingent outcome of a disembedded, competitive market economy as it emerged in Europe during the nineteenth century.

Making people believe this historically and socially formed concept of desire was an expression of universal human nature, was a feat requiring enormous chutzpah, and the fact that Dichter searched for sexual motives in order to sell chocolate or cars appears almost like a wilful act in order to distract the attention of the likes of Packard away from the real trick that was played out on the stage. While some people might take offence at the idea that products are invested by consumers with meaning of an affective and/or sexual nature, the real revolution brought about by Dichterian Motivation Research was the belief that consumer emotions and subconscious desires were an integral part of an unchangeable human nature. It is only before this backdrop that Dichter could describe himself essentially as a cultural anthropologist who studied the behaviour and mores of people 'regardless of whether they lived in Paris, Frankfurt, Chicago, New York or Samoa' (Dichter 1977: 135). Dichter defended his take on the consumer by arguing that it was a 'fact that we live in an era of consumerism' and that this consumerism existed 'within a psychological framework which is similar throughout the world' (Dichter 1960b: 63).

Naturally, the alleged 'fact' that all people all over the world are, under all circumstances, driven by the same consumer desire as exhibited by the American middle class meant that a new global social reality had emerged which needed 'a matching superstructure, an appropriate ideology' (Dichter 1960b: 65). Now that Motivation Research had discovered 'the way we really are: emotional, irrational, imperfect' and driven by 'ever-expanding needs' (Dichter 1960b: 66, 73), Dichter presented himself as the guru of a new age in which consumers were envisaged as fully mobile, emotionally agile and never at rest in the pursuit of their dreams; in other words, usefully disembedded.

> The basic motivations of the people in all countries are the same regardless of the economic or political system.... And consumer products are the new international language understood as thoroughly in the Soviet Union and Samoa as in Australia, South Africa, France or the United States.... Westerners berate themselves for their material goals and for leading a life of product acquisition. We feel that when we manufacture a new consumer product, it is somehow immoral. When the Russians do it, they consider it progress and morality. All over the world – in Russia with its sophisticated form of communism and in Samoa with its primitive form of communism – people are clamouring for more, not fewer consumer products.... Wherever I went, I found that it is the Western way of life which is held up as the desirable goal to be reached. Capitalist products are considered the desirable products to own and to use.
>
> (Dichter 1966b: 3, 12–13)

Dichter's once widely discussed ideas on consumer motivations have been granted a second life by the recent return to the subconscious and the emotions in marketing research. There can be no doubt that the future belongs to a more holistic understanding of the emotional and subconscious aspects of consumer behaviour. Those who hope to understand the past of this future are well advised to acknowledge forgotten research pioneers like Ernest Dichter, who attempted to position consumers in their social and cultural environment. At the same time, though, Dichter rejected the notion that this environment should be seen as a legitimate force to control consumer desires. It remains to be seen whether a future generation of consumer researchers will be able to refrain from this consumer guru's fallacy of denying the benevolent role of the 'super-ego' and of ignoring the social, economic and environmental damage caused by unrestrained consumer desires.

References

Allen, C. N. 1941. A psychology of motivation for advertisers. *Journal of Applied Psychology* 25: 378–390.

Arnould, E., Price, L. 2006. Market-oriented ethnography revisited. *Journal of Advertising Research* 46 (September): 251–262.

Bagozzi, R. 1975. Marketing as exchange. *Journal of Marketing* 39 (October): 32–39.

Baines, P., Fill, C., Page, K. 2007. *Marketing*. Oxford: Oxford University Press.

Barthes, R. 2000 [1957]. Myth today. In: S. Sontag (Ed.), *A Roland Barthes Reader*. London: Virago, 93–149.

Belk, R., Ger, G., Askegaard, S. 2000. The missing streetcar named desire. In: S. Ratneshwar, D. G. Mick, C. Huffman (Eds), *The Why of Consumption: Contemporary Perspectives on Consumer Motives, Goals and Desires*. London: Routledge, 98–119.

Bennett, D. 2005. Getting the Id to go shopping: psychoanalysis, advertising, Barbie dolls, and the invention of the consumer unconscious. *Public Culture* 17 (1): 1–25.

Breidbach, O., Ghiselin, M. T. 2006. Athanasius Kircher (1602–1680) on Noah's Ark: baroque 'intelligent design' theory. *Proceedings of the California Academy of Sciences* 57 (36): 991–1002.

Brown, S. 2005. *Writing Marketing: Literary Lessons from Academic Authorities*. London: Sage.

Callebut, J. 1994. *The Naked Consumer: The Secret of Motivational Research in Global Marketing*. Antwerp: Censydiam Institute.

Cheskin, L., Ward, L. B. 1948. An indirect approach to market reactions. *Harvard Business Review* 26 (5): 572–580.

Cohen, L. 2004. *A Consumers' Republic: The Politics of Mass Consumption in Postwar America*. New York: Vintage.

Collins, L., Montgomery, C. 1969. Origins of motivational research. *British Journal of Marketing* 3 (2): 103–113.

———— 1970. Whatever happened to motivation research? End of the messianic hope. *Journal of the Market Research Society* 12 (1): 1–11.

Cova, B., Elliott, R. 1998. Everything you always wanted to know about interpretative consumer research but were afraid to ask. *Qualitative Market Research: An International Journal* 11 (2): 121–129.

Cova, B., Kozinets, R., Shankar, A. Eds. 2007. *Consumer Tribes*. Oxford: Heinemann.

Davidson, R. J., Scherer, K. R., Goldsmith, H. H. Eds. 2003. *Handbook of Affective Sciences*. Oxford: Oxford University Press.

de Grazia, V. 2005. *Irresistible Empire: America's Advance Through Twentieth-Century Europe*. Cambridge, MA: Belknap Press.

Dichter, E. 1944. Psychodramatic research project on commodities as intersocial media. *Sociometry* 7 (4): 432.

———— 1947a. *The Psychology of Everyday Living*. New York: Barnes & Noble.

———— 1947b. Psychology in market research. *Harvard Business Review* 25 (Summer): 432–443.

———— 1960a. *The Strategy of Desire*. Garden City, NY: Doubleday.

———— 1960b. Motivation research and depth communication. In: Green Meadow Foundation (Ed.), *Motivation Research and Depth Communication*. Zurich: Green Meadow Foundation, 63–73.

———— 1962. The world customer. *Harvard Business Review* 40 (4): 113–122.

———— 1963. The world customer. Survey for *International Management*, Ernest Dichter Archive, University of Vienna, Report No. 4304.

———— 1964. *Handbook of Consumer Motivations: The Psychology of the World of Objects*. New York: McGraw-Hill.

———— 1966a. How word-of-mouth advertising works. *Harvard Business Review* (November–December): 147–166.

———— 1966b. Needed: a psychological bridge over the English Channel. Discussion paper, Ernest Dichter Archive, University of Vienna, Report No. 4742.

———— 1977. *Motivforschung – mein Leben: die Autobiographie eines kreativ Unzufriedenen*. Frankfurt am Main: Lorch.

———— 1979. *Getting Motivated by Ernest Dichter: The Secret Behind Individual Motivations by the Man Who Was Not Afraid to Ask 'Why'*. New York: Pergamon.

Dijkesterhuis, A. 2005. The unconscious consumer: effects of environment on consumer behaviour. *Journal of Consumer Psychology* 15 (3): 193–202.

du Plessis, E. 2005. *The Advertised Mind: Ground-breaking Insights into How Our Brains Respond to Advertising*. London: Kogan Page.

Durgee, J. F. 1991. Interpreting Dichter's interpretations: an analysis of consumption symbolism in *The Handbook of Consumer Motivations*. In: H. H. Larsen, D. G. Mick, G. Alsted (Eds), *Marketing and Semiotics: Selected Papers from the Copenhagen Symposium*. Copenhagen: Arnold Busk, 52–74.

Earls, M. 2007. *Herd: How to Change Mass Behaviour by Harnessing Our True Nature*. Oxford: Wiley.

Egidi, G., Nusbaum, H. C., Cacioppo, J. T. 2008. Neuroeconomics: foundational issues and consumer relevance. In: Haugtvedt, C., Schumann, D., Davidson, E. (Eds), *Handbook of Consumer Psychology*. Lawrence Erlbaum: New York, 1177–1214.

Eliade, M. 1952. *Images et symbols: essai sur le symbolisme magicoreligieux*. Paris: Gallimard.

Firat, A. F., Shultz II, C. J. 1997. From segmentation to fragmentation: markets and marketing strategy in the postmodern era. *European Journal of Marketing* 31 (3/4): 183–207.

Foucault, M. 1981. *The History of Sexuality. Vol. I: An Introduction*. Harmondsworth: Penguin.

Fullerton, R. 2009. When the owl of Minerva flew at dusk: marketing in Greater Germany, 1918–1939. *European Business Review* 21 (1): 92–104.

Gabriel, Y., Lang, T. 2006. *The Unmanageable Consumer*. 2nd Edition. London: Sage.

Gardner, B., Levy, S. 1955. The product and the brand. *Harvard Business Review* 33 (March–April): 33–39.

Gladwell, M. 2005. *Blink: The Power of Thinking without Thinking*. New York: Little, Brown.

Gobé, M. 2001. *Emotional Branding: the New Paradigm for Connecting Brands to People*. New York: Allworth Press.

Gordon, W. 2006. What do consumers do emotionally with advertising. *Journal of Advertising Research* 46 (1): 2–10.

Hansen, F., Christensen, S. R. 2009. *Emotions, Advertising and Consumer Choice*. Copenhagen: CBS Press.

Heath, R. 2001. *The Hidden Power of Advertising*. Henley-on-Thames: WARC.

—— 2007. Reinforcement and low attention processing. In: G. J. Tellis, T. Ambler (Eds), *The SAGE Handbook of Advertising*. London: Sage, 89–104.

Heath, R., Hyder, P. 2005. Measuring the hidden power of emotive advertising. *Journal of the Market Research Society* 47 (5): 467–486.

Hirschman, E. C. 2007. Metaphor in the marketplace. *Marketing Theory* 7 (3): 227–248.

Holbrook, M. B. 1988. The psychoanalytic interpretation of consumer behavior: I am an animal. *Research in Consumer Behavior* 3: 149–178.

—— 2005. Customer value and autoethnography: subjective personal introspection and the meanings of a photograph collection. *Journal of Business Research* 58: 45–61.

Kassarjian, H. 1971. Personality and consumer behaviour: a review. *Journal of Marketing Research* 8 (November): 409–418.

Knutson, B. 2007. Neural predictors of purchase. *Neuron* 53: 147–156.

Kotler, P. 1965. Behavioral models for analyzing buyers. *Journal of Marketing* 29 (October): 37–45.

Lahm, S. 2007. Motivation ist alles. *Extradienst* 9: 86–114.

Lazer, W. 1963. Lifestyle concepts and marketing. In: S. Greyser (Ed.), *Toward Scientific Marketing*. Chicago: American Marketing Association, 140–151.

Lee, N., Broderick, A. J., Chamberlain, L. 2007. What is 'neuromarketing'? A discussion and agenda for future research. *International Journal of Psychophysiology* 63 (2): 199–204.

Levitin, D. 2006. *This Is Your Brain on Music: The Science of a Human Obsession*. New York: Dutton.

Levitt, T. 1983. The globalization of markets. *Harvard Business Review* (May–June): 2–11.

Levy, S. 1959. Symbols for sale. *Harvard Business Review* 37 (July–August): 117–124.

———— 1999. Qualitative research. In: D. Rook (Ed.), *Consumers, Symbols and Research: Sidney J. Levy on Marketing*. London: Sage, 449–461.

———— 2003. Roots of marketing and consumer research at the University of Chicago, *Consumption, Markets and Culture* 6 (June): 99–110.

———— 2005. The evolution of qualitative research in marketing. *Journal of Business Research* 58 (March): 341–347.

———— 2008. History of qualitative research methods in marketing. In: R. Belk (Ed.), *Handbook of Qualitative Research Methods in Marketing*. Cheltenham: Edward Elgar, 3–16.

Mariampolski, H. 2006. *Ethnography for Marketers: A Guide to Consumer Immersion*. London: Sage.

———— 2007. Ethnography and observational research. In: M. van Hamersveld, C. de Bout (Eds), *Market Research Handbook*. Chichester: John Wiley, 435–445.

Maslow, A. 1943. A theory of motivation. *Psychological Review* 50: 370–396.

McCracken, G. 2005. *Culture and Consumption II: Markets, Meaning and Brand Management*. Bloomington, IN: Indiana University Press.

McKelway, St Clair. 1959. Meaningful patterns. *The New Yorker* (3 January): 17.

Mennell, S. 2007. *The American Civilizing Process*. Cambridge: Polity.

Miller, P., Rose, N. 1997. Mobilising the consumer: assembling the subject of consumption. *Theory, Culture and Society* 14 (1): 1–36.

O'Shaughnessy, J. 2009. *Interpretation in Social Life, Social Science and Marketing*. London: Routledge.

O'Shaughnessy, J., O'Shaughnessy, N. 2003. *The Marketing Power of Emotion*. Oxford: Oxford University Press.

———— 2004. *Persuasion in Advertising*. London: Routledge.

———— 2008. *The Undermining of Beliefs in the Autonomy and Rationality of Consumers*. London: Routledge.

Packard, V. 1957. *The Hidden Persuaders*. New York: MacKay.

Page, G., Raymond, J. 2007. Neuroscience and marketing: it's what it means that counts, not how it's done. *International Journal of Advertising* 26 (1): 132–134.

Penn, D. 2007. Brain science: in search of the emotional unconscious. In: M. van Hamersveld, C. de Bout (Eds), *Market Research Handbook*. Chichester: John Wiley, 481–498.

Pincus, J. 2004. The consequence of unmet needs: the evolving role of motivation in consumer research. *Journal of Consumer Behaviour* 3 (4): 375–387.

Plummer, J. T. 1974. The concept and application of life style segmentation. *Journal of Marketing* 38 (January): 33–37.

Rapaille C. 2006. *The Culture Code: An Ingenious Way to Understand Why People Around the World Live and Buy as They Do*. New York: Broadway.

Ratneshwar, S., Mick, D. G. Eds. 2005. *Inside Consumption: Consumer Motives, Goals, and Desires*. London: Routledge.

Ratneshwar, S., Mick, D. G., Huffman, C. 2000. Introduction: the 'why' of consumption. In: S. Ratneshwar, D. G. Mick, C. Huffman (Eds), *The Why of Consumption: Contemporary Perspectives on Consumer Motives, Goals and Desires*. London: Routledge, 1–18.

———— Eds. 2000. *The Why of Consumption: Contemporary Perspectives on Consumer Motives, Goals and Desires*. London: Routledge.

Rheims, M. 1959. *La vie étrange des objects: histoire de la curiosité.* Paris: Plon.

Schwarzkopf, S. 2006. Kontrolle statt Rausch? Marktforschung, Produktwerbung und Verbraucherlenkung im Nationalsozialismus zwischen Phantasien von Masse, Angst und Macht. In: A. von Klimo, M. Rolf (Eds), *Rausch und Diktatur: Inszenierung, Mobilisierung und Kontrolle in totalitären Systemen.* Frankfurt/Main: Campus, 193–216.

Shiv, B. 2007. Emotions, decisions and the brain. *Journal of Consumer Psychology* 17 (3): 174–178.

Solomon, M. 2007. *Consumer Behavior: Buying, Having, and Being.* Upper Saddle River, NJ: Pearson.

Stern, B. 1990. Literary criticism and the history of marketing thought: a new perspective on 'reading' marketing theory. *Journal of the Academy of Marketing Science* 18 (4): 327–334.

——— Ed. 1998. *Representing Consumers: Voices, Views, and Visions.* London: Routledge.

The Economist 2008. The way the brain buys. 20 December: 109–111.

Thomas, J. W. 1998a. Motivational research: explaining why consumers behave the way that they do. *Direct Marketing* (April): 54–57.

——— 1998b. Finding unspoken reasons for consumers' choices. *Marketing Research* (8 June): 10–11.

Thompson, C. J. 1993. Modern truth and postmodern incredulity: a hermeneutic deconstruction of the metanarrative of 'scientific truth' in marketing research. *International Journal of Research in Marketing* 10 (3): 325–338.

Travis, D. 2000. *Emotional Branding: How Successful Brands Gain the Irrational Edge.* New York: Prima Venture.

Usunier, J.-C., Lee, J. A. 2005. *Marketing Across Cultures.* Harlow: Pearson, Prentice Hall.

Wegner, D. M. 2002. *The Illusion of Conscious Will.* Cambridge, MA: Bradford Books, MIT Press.

Wells, W., Tigert, D. 1971. Activities, interests and opinions. *Journal of Advertising Research* 11 (August): 27–35.

Wilson, T. D. 2002. *Strangers to Ourselves: Discovering the Adaptive Unconscious.* Cambridge, MA: Belknap Press.

Winnick, C. 1961. Anthropology's contribution to marketing. *Journal of Marketing* 25 (July): 53–60.

Wirtschaftswoche 2006. Der neue Kaufrausch. 18 December (51): 74–82.

Woodside, A. G. 2006. Overcoming the illusion of will and self-fabrication: going beyond naïve subjective introspection to an unconscious/conscious theory of behavior explanation. *Psychology and Marketing* 23 (3): 1–16.

Wulfeck, J. W. 1945. The role of the psychologist in marketing and advertising research. *Journal of Applied Psychology* 29 (2): 95–102.

Wulfeck, J. W., Bennett, E. M. 1954. *The Language of Dynamic Psychology as Related to Motivation Research.* New York: McGraw-Hill.

Yates, F. A. 1966. *The Art of Memory.* London: Routledge and Kegan Paul.

Zaltman, G. 1997. Rethinking market research: putting people back in. *Journal of Marketing Research* 34: 424–437.

——— 2003. *How Customers Think.* Cambridge, MA: Harvard Business School Press.

Zaltman, G., Coulter, R. A. 1995. Seeing the voice of the customer: metaphor-based advertising research. *Journal of Advertising Research* 35 (July/August): 35–51.
Zaltman, G., MacCaba, Dara. 2007. Metaphor in advertising. In: G. J. Tellis, T. Ambler (Eds), *The SAGE Handbook of Advertising*. London: Sage, 135–154.
Zaltman, G., Zaltman, L. 2008. *Marketing Metaphoria: What Deep Metaphors Reveal about the Minds of Consumers*. Cambridge, MA: Harvard Business School Press.

Index